1984

Fame and Obscurity

Books by Gay Talese

FAME AND

OBSCURITY

Portraits by GAY TALESE

THE WORLD PUBLISHING COMPANY
New York and Cleveland

Published by The World Publishing Company
2231 West 110th Street, Cleveland, Ohio 44102

Published simultaneously in Canada by
Nelson, Foster & Scott Ltd.

FIRST PRINTING—*1970*

Library of Congress Catalog Card Number: 72–112433

Printed in the United States of America

WORLD PUBLISHING
TIMES MIRROR

Contents

Part Three: New York—
A Serendipiter's Journey

Author's Note

My thanks to my editor, Robert A. Gutwillig, for assembling this collection. Most of the selections are representative of a form of reporting being referred to these days as the "new journalism," the "new nonfiction," or "parajournalism," the latter a derogatory description coined by the critic Dwight MacDonald, who is somewhat suspicious of the form, feeling, as a few other critics do, that its practitioners compromise the facts in the interest of more dramatic reporting. I do not agree.

The new journalism, though often reading like fiction, is not fiction. It is, or should be, as reliable as the most reliable reportage although it seeks a larger truth than is possible through the mere compilation of verifiable facts, the use of direct quotations, and adherence to the rigid organizational style of the older form. The new journalism allows, demands in fact, a more imaginative approach to reporting, and it permits the writer to inject himself into the narrative if he wishes, as many writers do, or to assume the role of a detached observer, as other writers do, including myself.

I try to follow my subjects unobtrusively while observing them in revealing situations, noting their reactions and the reactions of others to them. I attempt to absorb the whole scene, the dialogue and mood, the tension, drama, conflict, and then I try to write it all from the point of view of the persons I am writing about, even revealing whenever possible what these individuals are *thinking* during those moments that I am describing. This latter insight is not obtainable, of course, without the full cooperation of the subject, but if the writer enjoys the confidence and trust of his subjects it is possible, through interviews, by asking the right question at the right time, to learn and to report what goes on within other people's minds.

I did this extensively in my book of last year, *The Kingdom and the Power,* and I hope to experiment still further with it in a book that I am involved with now, a study of tradition and change within three successive generations of an Italo-American family between 1900 and 1970. However, in this collection, *Fame and Obscurity,* I do not achieve all of what I suggest is possible in nonfiction because most of the selections included here were written originally as magazine articles, each having been produced within a period of between four and eight weeks. One exception is the DiMaggio profile, which took about ten weeks; another is the Sinatra profile, which took closer to three months (neither man was very cooperative, although I believe that this was ultimately more a help than a hindrance); and a third exception is the portrait of the bridge-builders, which was originally published as a short book entitled *The Bridge* and was researched, sporadically, over a period of several months—less research time than I think I would settle for today, particularly since one of my ambitions is to remain with my subjects long enough to see their lives change in some way. By way of comparison, I spent three years researching and writing *The Kingdom and the Power,* a human history of *The New York Times,* where I had once worked; and I have been researching the book about the Italian-American family, on and off, for about six years to date.

Still, *Fame and Obscurity* does include some of the best reporting and writing that I have done during the nineteen-sixties, representing a shift from the "old" journalism that I had practiced at *The Times* to the freer, more challenging approach that *Esquire* magazine permitted and encouraged under the editorship of Harold Hayes. My first contribution to *Esquire,* in 1960, was an essay on obscurity in New York City, a series of vignettes on the unnoticed people, the odd facts and bizarre events that had caught my fancy during my travels around town as a newspaperman. This was a beginning of what later became a book that Harper & Row published in 1961 entitled, *New York—A Serendipiter's Journey.* Rereading that book now, in the closing section of *Fame and Obscurity,* I recognize it as a young man's view of New York, envisioned with a mixture of wonderment and awe, and yet with a realization, too, of how destructive the city is, how it promises so much more than it fulfills, and how right E. B. White was when he wrote many years ago:

"No one should come to New York to live unless he is willing to be lucky." There is also in *Serendipiter's Journey* some early signs of my interest in using the techniques of fiction, an aspiration on my part to somehow bring to reportage the tone that Irwin Shaw and John O'Hara had brought to the short story. But I did not get very far with this in *Serendipiter's Journey,* finally relying more on the selection of my material than on style to reflect the glamour and gloom that I have always felt so strongly in New York.

After this tentative beginning, my first attempt at what would be called the "new journalism" began with some of the profiles on famous people that I did for *Esquire.* In the Joe Louis piece, for example, the article opens with Louis, fatigued after three frolicsome days and nights in New York City, arriving at the Los Angeles airport and being met by his wife, the lawyer—a scene that could have led into a short story situation; later in the article, the writing style falls back on straighter reportage, indicating my own uncertainty with the form at that point, but still later the approach is again scene-setting and dialogue and away from rigid reporting.

A more successful attempt at using fictional techniques for factual situations is in the profile of Joshua Logan, the theatrical director. I happened to be in the theater one afternoon watching Logan rehearse his play when, suddenly, he and his star, Claudia McNeil, got into an argument that not only was more dramatic than the play itself, but revealed something of the character of Logan and Miss McNeil in ways that I could never have done had I approached the subject from the more conventional form of reporting.

While researching the Frank Sinatra piece I also happened to be at the right place at the right time: on the night that Sinatra objected to the attire of the young man playing pool in the game room of the Daisy Discotheque, in Beverly Hills, I had been standing near the bar in the other room. While I missed the opening exchange between Sinatra and the young man, I did arrive in time to hear most of what transpired; later, with the cooperation of witnesses who had heard it all, I was able to reconstruct the scene.

As I noted earlier, Sinatra was not very cooperative during my stay in Beverly Hills. I had arrived at a bad time for him, he being upset by a head cold among other irritants, and I was unable to get the interview that I had expected. Nevertheless I did observe him periodically during the six weeks that I spent on research, watching him at recording sessions, on a movie set, at the gambling tables in Las Vegas, and I was able to perceive his changing moods, his irritation and suspicion when he thought that I was getting too close, his pleasure and courtesy and charm when he was able to relax among those whom he trusted. I gained more by watching him, overhearing him, and watching the reaction of those around him than if I had actually been able to sit down and talk to him.

Joe DiMaggio was an even more reluctant subject when I began the research on him in San Francisco. I had met DiMaggio six months before in New York, at which time he indicated that he would cooperate on the article; but his attitude was radically different after I had appeared outside his restaurant on Fisherman's Wharf. And yet the tense and chilly reception that I received, initially, provided me with an interesting opening scene in which I was not only a witness but a participant being ejected from the premises by DiMaggio himself. The fact that I was able to become reacquainted with DiMaggio a few days later was the result of a request that I had made through one of DiMaggio's friends and golfing partners that I be allowed to follow their foursome through one eighteen-hole round. During the golfing session, DiMaggio, who hates to lose golf balls, lost three of them. I found them. After that, DiMaggio's attitude toward me improved noticeably; I was invited to other golf matches and to join him in the evening with his other friends at Reno's bar, where much of my work was done.

Except for some minor word changes, such as restoring the colorful profanity of Peter O'Toole that *Esquire*'s editors had toned down, I have not updated any of these profiles in *Fame and Obscurity*. They appear in this volume as I wrote them years ago, and they stand simply as a collection of my earlier work. It is always gratifying to an author to have his work remain in print; and for his suggestion to do so, and for his arrangement of the pieces, I am again grateful to Mr. Gutwillig as well as to *Esquire*'s editor, Harold Hayes, who published most of them originally, and to the editors of Harper & Row, who permitted the reprinting of *New York—A Serendipiter's Journey, The Bridge,* and some of the profiles that had been included in an obscure earlier collection of mine entitled *The Overreachers.*

G.T.

November, 1969

Part One

Frank Sinatra
Has a Cold

Frank Sinatra, holding a glass of bourbon in one hand and a cigarette in the other, stood in a dark corner of the bar between two attractive but fading blondes who sat waiting for him to say something. But he said nothing; he had been silent during much of the evening, except now in this private club in Beverly Hills he seemed even more distant, staring out through the smoke and semidarkness into a large room beyond the bar where dozens of young couples sat huddled around small tables or twisted in the center of the floor to the clamorous clang of folk-rock music blaring from the stereo. The two blondes knew, as did Sinatra's four male friends who stood nearby, that it was a bad idea to force conversation upon him when he was in this mood of sullen silence, a mood that had hardly been uncommon during this first week of November, a month before his fiftieth birthday.

Sinatra had been working in a film that he now disliked, could not wait to finish; he was tired of all the publicity attached to his dating the twenty-year-old Mia Farrow, who was not in sight tonight; he was angry that a CBS television documentary of his life, to be shown in two

3

weeks, was reportedly prying into his privacy, even speculating on his possible friendship with Mafia leaders; he was worried about his starring role in an hour-long NBC show entitled *Sinatra—A Man And His Music,* which would require that he sing eighteen songs with a voice that at this particular moment, just a few nights before the taping was to begin, was weak and sore and uncertain. Sinatra was ill. He was the victim of an ailment so common that most people would consider it trivial. But when it gets to Sinatra it can plunge him into a state of anguish, deep depression, panic, even rage. Frank Sinatra had a cold.

Sinatra with a cold is Picasso without paint, Ferrari without fuel—only worse. For the common cold robs Sinatra of that uninsurable jewel, his voice, cutting into the core of his confidence, and it affects not only his own psyche but also seems to cause a kind of psychosomatic nasal drip within dozens of people who work for him, drink with him, love him, depend on him for their own welfare and stability. A Sinatra with a cold can, in a small way, send vibrations through the entertainment industry and beyond as surely as a President of the United States, suddenly sick, can shake the national economy.

For Frank Sinatra was now involved with many things involving many people—his own film company, his record company, his private airline, his missile-parts firm, his real-estate holdings across the nation, his personal staff of seventy-five—which are only a portion of the power he is and has come to represent. He seemed now to be also the embodiment of the fully emancipated male, perhaps the only one in America, the man who can do anything he wants, *anything,* can do it because he has the money, the energy, and no apparent guilt. In an age when the very young seem to be taking over, protesting and picketing and demanding change, Frank Sinatra survives as a national phenomenon, one of the few prewar products to withstand the test of time. He is the champ who made the big comeback, the man who had everything, lost it, then got it back, letting nothing stand in his way, doing what few men can do: he uprooted his life, left his family, broke with everything that was familiar, learning in the process that one way to hold a woman is not to hold her. Now he has the affection of Nancy and Ava and Mia, the fine female produce of three generations, and still has the adoration of his children, the freedom of a bachelor, he does not feel old, he makes old men feel young, makes them think that if Frank Sinatra can do it, it can be done; not that *they* could do it, but it is still nice for other men to know, at fifty, that it can be done.

But now, standing at this bar in Beverly Hills, Sinatra had a cold, and he continued to drink quietly and he seemed miles away in his private world, not even reacting when suddenly the stereo in the other room switched to a Sinatra song, *In the Wee Small Hours of the Morning.*

It is a lovely ballad that he first recorded ten years ago, and it now inspired many young couples who had been sitting, tired of twisting, to get up and move slowly around the dance floor, holding one another very close. Sinatra's intonation, precisely clipped, yet full and flowing, gave a deeper meaning to the simple lyrics—"In the wee small hours of the morning/while the whole wide world is fast asleep/you lie awake, and think about the girl . . ." *—it was, like so many of his classics, a song that evoked loneliness and sensuality, and when blended with the dim light and the alcohol and nicotine and late-night needs, it became a kind of airy aphrodisiac. Undoubtedly the words from this song, and others like it, had put millions in the mood, it was music to make love by, and doubtless much love had been made by it all over America at night in cars, while the batteries burned down, in cottages by the lake, on beaches during balmy summer evenings, in secluded parks and exclusive penthouses and furnished rooms; in cabin cruisers and cabs and cabanas—in all places where Sinatra's songs could be heard were these words that warmed women, wooed and won them, snipped the final thread of inhibition and gratified the male egos of ungrateful lovers; two generations of men had been the beneficiaries of such ballads, for which they were eternally in his debt, for which they may eternally hate him. Nevertheless here he was, the man himself, in the early hours of the morning in Beverly Hills, out of range.

The two blondes, who seemed to be in their middle thirties, were preened and polished, their matured bodies softly molded within tight dark suits. They sat, legs crossed, perched on the high bar stools. They listened to the music. Then one of them pulled out a Kent and Sinatra quickly placed his gold lighter under it and she held his hand, looked at his fingers: they were nubby and raw, and the pinkies protruded, being so stiff from arthritis that he could barely bend them. He was, as usual, immaculately dressed. He wore an oxford-grey suit with a vest,

* © *Redd Evans Music Corp.*

a suit conservatively cut on the outside but trimmed with flamboyant silk within; his shoes, British, seemed to be shined even on the bottom of the soles. He also wore, as everybody seemed to know, a remarkably convincing black hairpiece, one of sixty that he owns, most of them under the care of an inconspicuous little grey-haired lady who, holding his hair in a tiny satchel, follows him around whenever he performs. She earns $400 a week. The most distinguishing thing about Sinatra's face are his eyes, clear blue and alert, eyes that within seconds can go cold with anger, or glow with affection, or, as now, reflect a vague detachment that keeps his friends silent and distant.

Leo Durocher, one of Sinatra's closest friends, was now shooting pool in the small room behind the bar. Standing near the door was Jim Mahoney, Sinatra's press agent, a somewhat chunky young man with a square jaw and narrow eyes who would resemble a tough Irish plainclothesman if it were not for the expensive continental suits he wears and his exquisite shoes often adorned with polished buckles. Also nearby was a big, broad-shouldered two-hundred-pound actor named Brad Dexter who seemed always to be thrusting out his chest so that his gut would not show.

Brad Dexter has appeared in several films and television shows, displaying fine talent as a character actor, but in Beverly Hills he is equally known for the role he played in Hawaii two years ago when he swam a few hundred yards and risked his life to save Sinatra from drowning in a riptide. Since then Dexter has been one of Sinatra's constant companions and has been made a producer in Sinatra's film company. He occupies a plush office near Sinatra's executive suite. He is endlessly searching for literary properties that might be converted into new starring roles for Sinatra. Whenever he is among strangers with Sinatra he worries because he knows that Sinatra brings out the best and worst in people—some men will become aggressive, some women will become seductive, others will stand around skeptically appraising him, the scene will be somehow intoxicated by his mere presence, and maybe Sinatra himself, if feeling as badly as he was tonight, might become intolerant or tense, and then: headlines. So Brad Dexter tries to anticipate danger and warn Sinatra in advance. He confesses to feeling very protective of Sinatra, admitting in a recent moment of self-revelation: "I'd kill for him."

While this statement may seem outlandishly dramatic, particularly when taken out of context, it nonetheless expresses a fierce fidelity that is quite common within Sinatra's special circle. It is a characteristic that Sinatra, without admission, seems to prefer: *All the Way; All or Nothing at All.* This is the Sicilian in Sinatra; he permits his friends, if they wish to remain that, none of the easy Anglo-Saxon outs. But if they remain loyal, then there is nothing Sinatra will not do in turn—fabulous gifts, personal kindnesses, encouragement when they're down, adulation when they're up. They are wise to remember, however, one thing. He is Sinatra. The boss. *Il Padrone.*

I had seen something of this Sicilian side of Sinatra last summer at Jilly's saloon in New York, which was the only other time I'd gotten a close view of him prior to this night in this California club. Jilly's, which is on West Fifty-second Street in Manhattan, is where Sinatra drinks whenever he is in New York, and there is a special chair reserved for him in the back room against the wall that nobody else may use. When he is occupying it, seated behind a long table flanked by his closest New York friends—who include the saloonkeeper Jilly Rizzo, and Jilly's azure-haired wife, Honey, who is known as the "Blue Jew"—a rather strange ritualistic scene develops. That night dozens of people, some of them casual friends of Sinatra's, some mere acquaintances, some neither, appeared outside of Jilly's saloon. They approached it like a shrine. They had come to pay respect. They were from New York, Brooklyn, Atlantic City, Hoboken. They were old actors, young actors, former prizefighters, tired trumpet players, politicians, a boy with a cane. There was a fat lady who said she remembered Sinatra when he used to throw the *Jersey Observer* onto her front porch in 1933. There were middle-aged couples who said they had heard Sinatra sing at the Rustic Cabin in 1938 and "We knew then that he really had it!" Or they had heard him when he was with Harry James's band in 1939, or with Tommy Dorsey in 1941 ("Yeah, that's the song, *I'll Never Smile Again*—he sang it one night in this dump near Newark and we danced . . ."); or they remembered that time at the Paramount with the swooners, and him with those bow ties, The Voice; and one woman remembered that awful boy she knew then—Alexander Dorogokupetz, an eighteen-year-old heckler who had thrown a tomato at Sinatra and the bobby-soxers in the balcony had tried to flail him to death. Whatever became of Alexander Dorogokupetz? The lady did not know.

And they remembered when Sinatra was a failure and sang trash like *Mairzy Doats,* and they remembered his comeback and on this night they were all standing outside Jilly's saloon, dozens of them, but they could not get in. So some of them left. But most of them stayed, hoping that soon they might be able to push or wedge their way into Jilly's between the elbows and backsides of the men drinking three-deep at the bar, and they might be able to peek through and *see* him sitting back there. This is all they really wanted; they wanted to see him. And for a few moments they gazed in silence through the smoke and they stared. Then they turned, fought their way out of the bar, went home.

Some of Sinatra's close friends, all of whom are known to the men guarding Jilly's door, do manage to get an escort into the back room. But once they are there, they too must fend for themselves. On the particular evening, Frank Gifford, the former football player, got only seven yards in three tries. Others who had somehow been close enough to shake Sinatra's hand did *not* shake it; instead they just touched him on the shoulder or sleeve, or they merely stood close enough for him to see them and, after he'd given them a wink of recognition or a wave or a nod or called out their names (he has a fantastic memory for first names), they would then turn and leave. They had checked in. They had paid their respects. And as I watched this ritualistic scene, I got the impression that Frank Sinatra was dwelling simultaneously in two worlds that were not contemporary.

On the one hand he is the swinger—as he is when talking and joking with Sammy Davis, Jr., Richard Conte, Liza Minelli, Bernice Massi, or any of the other show-business people who get to sit at *the* table; on the other, as when he is nodding or waving to his *paisanos* who are close to him (Al Silvani, a boxing manager who works with Sinatra's film company; Dominic Di Bona, his wardrobe man; Ed Pucci, a 300-pound former football lineman who is his aide-de-camp), Frank Sinatra is *Il Padrone.* Or better still, he is what in traditional Sicily have long been called *uomini rispettati*—men of respect: men who are both majestic and humble, men who are loved by all and are very generous by nature, men whose hands are kissed as they walk from village to village, men who would *personally* go out of their way to redress a wrong.

Frank Sinatra does things *personally*. At Christmas time, he will personally pick dozens of presents for his close friends and family, remembering the type of jewelry they like, their favorite colors, the sizes of their shirts and dresses. When a musician friend's house was destroyed and his wife was killed in a Los Angeles mud slide a little more than a year ago, Sinatra personally came to his aid, finding the musician a new home, paying whatever hospital bills were left unpaid by the insurance, then personally supervising the furnishing of the new home down to the replacing of the silverware, the linen, the purchase of new clothing.

The same Sinatra who did this can, within the same hour, explode in a towering rage of intolerance should a small thing be incorrectly done for him by one of his *paisanos*. For example, when one of his men brought him a frankfurter with catsup on it, which Sinatra apparently abhors, he angrily threw the bottle at the man, splattering catsup all over him. Most of the men who work around Sinatra are big. But this never seems to intimidate Sinatra nor curb his impetuous behavior with them when he is mad. They will never take a swing back at him. He is *Il Padrone*.

At other times, aiming to please, his men will overreact to his desires: when he casually observed that his big orange desert jeep in Palm Springs seemed in need of a new painting, the word was swiftly passed down through channels, becoming ever more urgent as it went, until finally it was a *command* that the jeep be painted *now,* immediately, yesterday. To accomplish this would require the hiring of a special crew of painters to work all night, at overtime rates; which, in turn, meant that the order had to be bucked back up the line for further approval. When it finally got back to Sinatra's desk, he did not know what it was all about; after he had figured it out he confessed, with a tired look on his face, that he did not care when the hell they painted his jeep.

Yet it would have been unwise for anyone to anticipate his reaction, for he is a wholly unpredictable man of many moods and great dimension, a man who responds instantaneously to instinct—suddenly, dramatically, wildly he responds, and nobody can predict what will follow. A young lady named Jane Hoag, a reporter at *Life*'s Los Angeles bureau who had attended the same school as Sinatra's daughter, Nancy, had once been invited to a party at Mrs. Sinatra's California home at which Frank Sinatra, who maintains very cordial relations with his former wife, acted as host. Early in the party Miss Hoag, while leaning against a table, accidentally with her elbow knocked over one of a pair of alabaster birds to the floor, smashing it to pieces. Suddenly, Miss Hoag recalled, Sinatra's daughter cried, "Oh, that was one of mother's favorite . . ."—but before she could complete the sentence, Sinatra glared at her, cutting her off, and while forty other guests in the room all stared in silence, Sinatra walked over, quickly with his finger flicked the *other* alabaster bird off the table, smashing it to pieces, and then put an arm gently around Jane Hoag and said, in a way that put her completely at ease, "That's okay, kid."

Now Sinatra said a few words to the blondes. Then he turned from the bar and began to walk toward the poolroom. One of Sinatra's other men friends moved in to keep the girls company. Brad Dexter, who had been standing in the corner talking to some other people, now followed Sinatra.

The room cracked with the clack of billiard balls. There were about a dozen spectators in the room, most of them young men who were watching Leo Durocher shoot against two other aspiring hustlers who were not very good. This private drinking club has among its membership many actors, directors, writers, models, nearly all of them a good deal younger than Sinatra or Durocher and much more casual in the way they dress for the evening. Many of the young women, their long hair flowing loosely below their shoulders, wore tight, fanny-fitting Jax pants and very expensive sweaters; and a few of the young men wore blue or green velour shirts with high collars, and narrow tight pants and Italian loafers.

It was obvious from the way Sinatra looked at these people in the poolroom that they were not his style, but he leaned back against a high stool that was against the wall, holding his drink in his right hand, and said nothing, just watched Durocher slam the billiard balls back and forth. The younger men in the room, accustomed to seeing Sinatra at this club, treated him without deference, although they said nothing offensive. They were a cool young group, very California-cool and casual, and one of the coolest seemed to be a little guy, very quick of movement, who had a sharp profile, pale blue eyes, light brown hair, and squared eyeglasses. He wore a pair of brown corduroy slacks, a green shaggy-dog Shetland sweater, a tan suede jacket, and Game Warden boots, for which he had recently paid $60.

Frank Sinatra, leaning against the stool, sniffling a bit from his cold, could not take his eyes off the Game Warden boots. Once, after gazing at them for a few moments, he turned away; but now he was focused on them again. The owner of the boots, who was just standing in them watching the pool game, was named Harlan Ellison, a writer who had just completed work on a screenplay, *The Oscar*.

Finally Sinatra could not contain himself.

"Hey," he yelled in his slightly harsh voice that still had a soft, sharp edge. "Those Italian boots?"

"No," Ellison said.

"Spanish?"

"No."

"Are they *English* boots?"

"Look, I donno, man," Ellison shot back, frowning at Sinatra, then turning away again.

Now the poolroom was suddenly silent. Leo Durocher who had been poised behind his cue stick and was bent low just froze in that position for a second. Nobody moved. Then Sinatra moved away from the stool and walked with that slow, arrogant swagger of his toward Ellison, the hard tap of Sinatra's shoes the only sound in the room. Then, looking down at Ellison with a slightly raised eyebrow and a tricky little smile, Sinatra asked: "You expecting a *storm?*"

Harlan Ellison moved a step to the side. "Look, is there any reason why you're talking to me?"

"I don't like the way you're dressed," Sinatra said.

"Hate to shake you up," Ellison said, "but I dress to suit myself."

Now there was some rumbling in the room, and somebody said, "Com'on, Harlan, let's get out of here," and Leo Durocher made his pool shot and said, "Yeah, com'on."

But Ellison stood his ground.

Sinatra said, "What do you do?"

"I'm a plumber," Ellison said.

"No, no, he's not," another young man quickly yelled from across the table. "He wrote *The Oscar*."

"Oh, yeah," Sinatra said, "well I've seen it, and it's a piece of crap."

"That's strange," Ellison said, "because they haven't even released it yet."

"Well, I've seen it," Sinatra repeated, "and it's a piece of crap."

Now Brad Dexter, very anxious, very big opposite the small figure of Ellison, said, "Com'on, kid, I don't want you in this room."

"Hey," Sinatra interrupted Dexter, "can't you see I'm talking to this guy?"

Dexter was confused. Then his whole attitude changed, and Dexter's voice went soft and he said to Ellison, almost with a plea, *"Why do you persist in tormenting me?"*

The whole scene was becoming ridiculous, and it seemed that Sinatra was only half-serious, perhaps just reacting out of sheer boredom or inner despair; at any rate, after a few more exchanges Harlan Ellison left the room. By this time the word had gotten out to those on the dance floor about the Sinatra-Ellison exchange, and somebody went to look for the manager of the club. But somebody else said that the manager had already heard about it—and had quickly gone out the door, hopped in his car and drove home. So the assistant manager went into the pool-room.

"I don't want anybody in here without coats and ties," Sinatra snapped.

The assistant manager nodded, and walked back to his office.

It was the morning after. It was the beginning of another nervous day for Sinatra's press agent, Jim Mahoney. Mahoney had a headache, and he was worried but not over the Sinatra-Ellison incident of the night before. At the time Mahoney had been with his wife at a table in the other room, and possibly he had not even been aware of the little drama. The whole thing had lasted only about three minutes. And three minutes after it was over, Frank Sinatra had probably forgotten about it for the rest of his life—as Ellison will probably remember it for the rest of *his* life: he had had, as hundreds of others before him, at an unexpected moment between darkness and dawn, a scene with Sinatra.

It was just as well that Mahoney had not been in the poolroom; he had enough on his mind today. He was worried about Sinatra's cold and worried about the controversial CBS documentary that, despite Sinatra's protests and withdrawal of permission, would be shown on television in less than two weeks. The newspapers this morning were full of hints that Sinatra might sue the network, and Mahoney's phones were ringing without pause, and now he was plugged into New York talking to the *Daily News*'s Kay Gardella, saying: ". . . that's right, Kay . . . they made a gentleman's agreement to not ask certain questions about Frank's private life, and then Cronkite went right ahead: 'Frank, tell me about those associations.' *That* question, Kay—*out!* That question should never have been asked. . . ."

As he spoke, Mahoney leaned back in his leather chair, his head shaking slowly. He is a powerfully built man of thirty-seven; he has a round, ruddy face, a heavy jaw, and narrow pale eyes, and he might appear pugnacious if he did not speak with such clear, soft sincerity and if he were not so meticulous about his clothes. His suits and shoes are superbly tailored, which was one of the first things Sinatra noticed about him, and in his spacious office opposite the bar is a red-muff electrical shoe polisher and a pair of brown wooden shoulders on a stand over which Mahoney can drape his jackets. Near the bar is an autographed photograph of President Kennedy and a few pictures of Frank Sinatra, but there are none of Sinatra in any other rooms in Mahoney's public-relations agency; there once was a large photograph of him hanging in the reception room but this apparently bruised the egos of some of Mahoney's other movie-star clients and, since Sinatra never shows up at the agency anyway, the photograph was removed.

Still, Sinatra seems ever present, and if Mahoney did not have legitimate worries about Sinatra, as he did today, he could invent them— and, as worry aids, he surrounds himself with little mementos of moments in the past when he did worry. In his shaving kit there is a two-year-old box of sleeping tablets dispensed by a Reno druggist—the date on the bottle marks the kidnapping of Frank Sinatra, Jr. There is on a table in Mahoney's office a mounted wood reproduction of Frank Sinatra's ransom note written on the aforementioned occasion. One of Mahoney's mannerisms, when he is sitting at his desk worrying, is to tinker with the tiny toy train he keeps in front of him—the train is a souvenir from the Sinatra film, *Von Ryan's Express;* it is to men who are close to Sinatra what the PT-109 tie clasps are to men who were close to Kennedy—and Mahoney then proceeds to roll the little train back and forth on the six inches of track; back and forth, back and forth, click-*clack* click-*clack*. It is his Queeg-thing.

Now Mahoney quickly put aside the little train. His secretary told him there was a *very* important call on the line. Mahoney picked it up, and his voice was even softer and more sincere than before. "Yes, Frank," he said. "Right . . . right . . . yes, Frank. . . ."

When Mahoney put down the phone, quietly, he announced that Frank Sinatra had left in his private jet to spend the weekend at his home in Palm Springs, which is a sixteen-minute flight from his home in Los Angeles. Mahoney was now worried again. The Lear jet that Sinatra's pilot would be flying was identical, Mahoney said, to the one that had just crashed in another part of California.

On the following Monday, a cloudy and unseasonably cool California day, more than one hundred people gathered inside a white television studio, an enormous room dominated by a white stage, white walls, and with dozens of lights and lamps dangling: it rather resembled a gigantic operating room. In this room, within an hour or so, NBC was scheduled to begin taping a one-hour show that would be televised in color on the night of November 24 and would highlight, as much as it could in the limited time, the twenty-five-year career of Frank Sinatra as a public entertainer. It would not attempt to probe, as the forthcoming CBS *Sinatra* documentary allegedly would, that area of Sinatra's life that he regards as private. The NBC show would be mainly an hour of Sinatra singing some of the hits that carried him from Hoboken to Hollywood, a show that would be interrupted only now and then by a few film clips and commercials for Budweiser beer. Prior to his cold, Sinatra had been very excited about this show; he saw here an opportunity to appeal not only to those nostalgic, but also to communicate his talent to some rock-and-rollers—in a sense, he was battling The Beatles. The press releases being prepared by Mahoney's agency stressed this, reading: "If you happen to be tired of kid singers wearing mops of hair thick enough to hide a crate of melons . . . it should be refreshing to consider the entertainment value of a video special titled *Sinatra—A Man And His Music*. . . ."

But now in this NBC studio in Los Angeles, there was an atmosphere of anticipation and tension because of the uncertainty of the Sinatra voice. The forty-three musicians in Nelson Riddle's orchestra had already arrived and some were up on the white platform warming up. Dwight Hemion, a youthful sandy-haired director who had won praise for his television special on Barbra Streisand, was seated in the glass-enclosed control booth that overlooked the orchestra and stage. The camera crews, technical teams, security guards, Budweiser ad men were also standing between the floor lamps and cameras, waiting, as were a dozen or so ladies who worked as secretaries in other parts of the building but had sneaked away so they could watch this.

A few minutes before eleven o'clock, word spread quickly through the long corridor into the big studio that Sinatra was spotted walking through the parking lot and was on his way, and was looking fine. There seemed great relief among the group that was gathered; but when the lean, sharply dressed figure of the man got closer, and closer, they saw to their dismay that it was not Frank Sinatra. It was his double. Johnny Delgado.

Delgado walks like Sinatra, has Sinatra's build, and from certain facial angles does resemble Sinatra. But he seems a rather shy individual. Fifteen years ago, early in his acting career, Delgado applied for a role in *From Here To Eternity*. He was hired, finding out later that he was to be Sinatra's double. In Sinatra's latest film, *Assault on a Queen,* a story in which Sinatra and some fellow conspirators attempt to hijack the *Queen Mary,* Johnny Delgado doubles for Sinatra in some water scenes; and now, in this NBC studio, his job was to stand under the hot television lights marking Sinatra's spots on the stage for the camera crews.

Five minutes later, the real Frank Sinatra walked in. His face was pale, his blue eyes seemed a bit watery. He had been unable to rid himself of the cold, but he was going to try to sing anyway because the schedule was tight and thousands of dollars were involved at this moment in the assembling of the orchestra and crews and the rental of the studio. But when Sinatra, on his way to his small rehearsal room to warm up his voice, looked into the studio and saw that the stage and orchestra's platform were not close together, as he had specifically requested, his lips tightened and he was obviously very upset. A few moments later, from his rehearsal room, could be heard the pounding of his fist against the top of the piano and the voice of his accompanist, Bill Miller, saying, softly, "Try not to upset yourself, Frank."

Later Jim Mahoney and another man walked in, and there was talk of Dorothy Kilgallen's death in New York earlier that morning. She had been an ardent foe of Sinatra for years, and he became equally uncomplimentary about her in his nightclub act, and now, though she was dead, he did not compromise his feelings. "Dorothy Kilgallen's dead," he repeated, walking out of the room toward the studio. "Well, guess I got to change my whole act."

When he strolled into the studio the musicians all picked up their instruments and stiffened in their seats. Sinatra cleared his throat a few times and then, after rehearsing a few ballads with the orchestra, he sang *Don't Worry About Me* to his satisfaction and, being uncertain of how long his voice could last, suddenly became impatient.

"Why don't we tape this mother?" he called out, looking up toward the glass booth where the director, Dwight Hemion, and his staff were sitting. Their heads seemed to be down, focusing on the control board.

"Why don't we tape this mother?" Sinatra repeated.

The production stage manager, who stands near the camera wearing a headset, repeated Sinatra's words exactly into his line to the control room: "Why don't we tape this mother?"

Hemion did not answer. Possibly his switch was off. It was hard to know because of the obscuring reflections the lights made against the glass booth.

"Why don't we put on a coat and tie," said Sinatra, then wearing a high-necked yellow pullover, "and tape this. . . ."

Suddenly Hemion's voice came over the sound amplifer, very calmly: "Okay, Frank, would you mind going back over. . . ."

"Yes I *would* mind going back," Sinatra snapped.

The silence from Hemion's end, which lasted a second or two, was then again interrupted by Sinatra saying, "When we stop doing things around here the way we did them in 1950, maybe we . . ." and Sinatra continued to tear into Hemion, condemning as well the lack of modern techniques in putting such shows together; then, possibly not wanting to use his voice unnecessarily, he stopped. And Dwight Hemion, very patient, so patient and calm that one would assume he had not heard anything that Sinatra had just said, outlined the opening part of the show. And Sinatra a few minutes later was reading his opening remarks, words that would follow *Without a Song,* off the large idiot-cards being held near the camera. Then, this done, he prepared to do the same thing on camera.

"Frank Sinatra Show, Act I, Page 10, Take 1," called a man with a clapboard, jumping in front of the camera—*clap*—then jumping away again.

"Did you ever stop to think," Sinatra began, "what the world would be like without a song? . . . It would be a pretty dreary place. . . . Gives you something to think about, doesn't it? . . ."

Sinatra stopped.

"Excuse me," he said, adding, *"Boy,* I need a drink."

They tried it again.

"Frank Sinatra Show, Act I, Page 10, Take 2," yelled the jumping guy with the clapboard.

"Did you ever stop to think what the world would be like without a song? . . ." Frank Sinatra read it through this time without stopping. Then he rehearsed a few more songs, once or twice interrupting the orchestra when a certain instrumental sound was not quite what he wanted. It was hard to tell how well his voice was going to hold up, for this was early in the show; up to this point, however, everybody in the room seemed pleased, particularly when he sang an old sentimental favorite written more than twenty years ago by Jimmy Van Heusen and Phil Silvers—*Nancy,* inspired by the first of Sinatra's three children when she was just a few years old.

> *"If I don't see her each day*
> *I miss her. . . .*
> *Gee what a thrill*
> *Each time I kiss her. . . ."*

As Sinatra sang these words, though he has sung them hundreds and hundreds of times in the past, it was suddenly obvious to everybody in the studio that something quite special must be going on inside the man, because something quite special was coming out. He was singing now, cold or no cold, with power and warmth, he was letting himself go, the public arrogance was gone, the private side was in this song about the girl who, it is said, understands him better than anybody else, and is the only person in front of whom he can be unashamedly himself.

Nancy is twenty-five. She lives alone, her marriage to singer Tommy Sands having ended in divorce. Her home is in a Los Angeles suburb and she is now making her third film and is recording for her father's record company. She sees him every day; or, if not, he telephones, no matter if it be from Europe or Asia. When Sinatra's singing first became popular on radio, stimulating the swooners, Nancy would listen at home and cry. When Sinatra's first marriage broke up in 1951 and he left home, Nancy was the only child old enough to remember him as a father. She also saw him with Ava Gardner, Juliet Prowse, Mia Farrow, many others, has gone on double dates with him. . . .

> *"She takes the winter*
> *And makes it summer. . . .*
> *Summer could take*
> *Some lessons from her. . . ."*

Nancy now also sees him visiting at home with his first wife, the former Nancy Barbato, a plasterer's daughter from Jersey City whom he married in 1939 when he was earning $25 a week singing at the Rustic Cabin near Hoboken.

The first Mrs. Sinatra, a striking woman who has never remarried ("When you've been married to Frank Sinatra . . ." she once explained to a friend), lives in a magnificent home in Los Angeles with her younger daughter, Tina, who is seventeen. There is no bitterness, only great respect and affection between Sinatra and his first wife, and he has long been welcome in her home and has even been known to wander in at odd hours, stoke the fire, lie on the sofa and fall asleep. Frank Sinatra can fall asleep anywhere, something he learned when he used to ride bumpy roads with band buses; he also learned at that time, when sitting in a tuxedo, how to pinch the trouser creases in the back and tuck the jacket under and out, and fall asleep perfectly pressed. But he does not ride buses anymore, and his daughter Nancy, who in her younger days felt rejected when he slept on the sofa instead of giving attention to her, later realized that the sofa was one of the few places left in the world where Frank Sinatra could get any privacy, where his famous face would neither be stared at nor cause an abnormal reaction in others. She realized, too, that things normal have always eluded her father: his childhood was one of loneliness and a drive toward attention, and since attaining it he has never again been certain of solitude. Upon looking out the window of a home he once owned in Hasbrouck Heights, New Jersey, he would occasionally see the faces of teen-agers peeking in; and in 1944, after moving to California and buying a home behind a ten-foot fence on Lake Toluca, he discovered that the only way to escape the telephone and other intrusions was to board his paddle boat with a few friends, a card table and a case of beer, and stay afloat all afternoon. But he has tried, insofar as it has been possible, to be like everyone else, Nancy says. He wept on her wedding day, he is very sentimental and sensitive. . . .

What the hell are you doing up there, Dwight?"

Silence from the control booth.

"Got a party or something going on up there, *Dwight?*"

Sinatra stood on the stage, arms folded, glaring up across the cameras toward Hemion. Sinatra had sung *Nancy* with probably all he had in his voice on this day. The next few numbers contained raspy notes, and twice his voice completely cracked. But now Hemion was in the control booth out of communication; then he was down in the studio walking over to where Sinatra stood. A few minutes later they both left the studio and were on the way up to the control booth. The tape was replayed for Sinatra. He watched only about five minutes of it before he started to shake his head. Then he said to Hemion: "Forget it, just forget it. You're wasting your time. What you got there," Sinatra said, nodding to the singing image of himself on the television screen, "is a man with a cold." Then he left the control booth, ordering that the whole day's performance be scrubbed and future taping postponed until he had recovered.

Soon the word spread like an emotional epidemic down through Sinatra's staff, then fanned out through Hollywood, then was heard across the nation in Jilly's saloon, and also on the other side of the Hudson River in the homes of Frank Sinatra's parents and his other relatives and friends in New Jersey.

When Frank Sinatra spoke with his father on the telephone and said he was feeling awful, the elder Sinatra reported that *he* was also feeling awful: that his left arm and fist were so stiff with a circulatory condition he could barely use them, adding that the ailment might be the result of having thrown too many left hooks during his days as a bantamweight almost fifty years ago.

Martin Sinatra, a ruddy and tattoed little blue-eyed Sicilian born in Catania, boxed under the name of "Marty O'Brien." In those days, in those places, with the Irish running the lower reaches of city life, it was not uncommon for Italians to wind up with such names. Most of the Italians and Sicilians who migrated to America just prior to the 1900's were poor and uneducated, were excluded from the building-trades unions dominated by the Irish, and were somewhat intimidated by the Irish police, Irish priests, Irish politicians.

One notable exception was Frank Sinatra's mother, Dolly, a large and very ambitious woman who was brought to this country at two months of age by her mother and father, a lithographer from Genoa. In later years Dolly Sinatra, possessing a round red face and blue eyes, was often mistaken for being Irish, and surprised many at the speed with which she swung her heavy handbag at anyone uttering "Wop."

By playing skillful politics with North Jersey's Democratic machine, Dolly Sinatra was to become, in her heyday, a kind of Catherine de Medici of Hoboken's third ward. She could always be counted upon to deliver six hundred votes at election time from her Italian neighborhood, and this was her base of power. When she told one of the politicians that she wanted her husband to be appointed to the Hoboken Fire Department, and was told, "But, Dolly, we don't have an opening," she snapped, *"Make* an opening."

They did. Years later she requested that her husband be made a captain, and one day she got a call from one of the political bosses that began, "Dolly, congratulations!"

"For what?"

"Captain Sinatra."

"Oh, you finally made him one—thank you very much."

Then she called the Hoboken Fire Department.

"Let me speak to *Captain* Sinatra," she said. The fireman called Martin Sinatra to the phone, saying, "Marty, I think your wife has gone nuts." When he got on the line, Dolly greeted him:

"Congratulations, *Captain* Sinatra!"

Dolly's only child, christened Francis Albert Sinatra, was born and nearly died on December 12, 1915. It was a difficult birth, and during his first moment on earth he received marks he will carry till death—the scars on the left side of his neck being the result of a doctor's clumsy forceps, and Sinatra has chosen not to obscure them with surgery.

After he was six months old, he was reared mainly by his grandmother. His mother had a full-time job as a chocolate dipper with a large firm and was so proficient at it that the firm once offered to send her to the Paris office to train others. While some people in Hoboken remember Frank Sinatra as a lonely child, one who spent many hours on the porch gazing into space, Sinatra was never a slum kid, never in jail, always well-dressed. He had so many pants that some people in Hoboken called him "Slacksey O'Brien."

Dolly Sinatra was not the sort of Italian Mother who could be appeased merely by a child's obedience and good appetite. She made many demands on her son, was always very strict. She dreamed of his becoming an aviation engineer. When she discovered Bing Crosby pictures hanging on his bedroom walls one evening, and learned that her son wished to become a singer too, she became infuriated and threw a shoe at him. Later, finding she could not talk him out of it—"he takes after me"—she encouraged his singing.

Many Italo-American boys of his generation were then shooting for the same star—they were strong with song, weak with words, not a big novelist among them: no O'Hara, no Bellow, no Cheever, nor Shaw; yet they could communicate *bel canto*. This was more in their tradition, no need for a diploma; they could, with a song, someday see their names in lights . . . *Perry Como . . . Frankie Laine . . . Tony Bennett . . . Vic Damone . . .* but none could see it better than *Frank Sinatra.*

Though he sang through much of the night at the Rustic Cabin, he was up the next day singing without a fee on New York radio to get more attention. Later he got a job singing with Harry James's band, and it was there in August of 1939 that Sinatra had his first recording hit—*All or Nothing at All.* He became very fond of Harry James and the men in the band, but when he received an offer from Tommy Dorsey, who in those days had probably the best band in the country, Sinatra took it; the job paid $125 a week, and Dorsey knew how to feature a vocalist. Yet Sinatra was very depressed at leaving James's band, and the final night with them was so memorable that, twenty years later, Sinatra could recall the details to a friend: ". . . the bus pulled out with the rest of the boys at about half-past midnight. I'd said good-bye to them all, and it was snowing, I remember. There was nobody around and I stood alone with my suitcase in the snow and watched the taillights disappear. Then the tears started and I tried to run after the bus. There was such spirit and enthusiasm in that band, I hated leaving it. . . ."

But he did—as he would leave other warm places, too, in search of something more, never wasting time, trying to do it all in one generation, fighting under his *own* name, defending underdogs, terrorizing top dogs. He threw a punch at a musician who said something anti-Semitic, espoused the Negro cause two decades before it became fashionable. He also threw a tray of glasses at Buddy Rich when he played the drums too loud.

Sinatra gave away $50,000 worth of gold cigarette lighters before he was thirty, was living an immigrant's wildest dream of America. He arrived suddenly on the scene when DiMaggio was silent, when *paisanos* were mournful, were quietly defensive about Hitler in their homeland. Sinatra became, in time, a kind of one-man Anti-Defamation League for Italians in America, the sort of organization that would be unlikely for them because, as the theory goes, they rarely agreed on anything, being extreme individualists: fine as soloists, but not so good in a choir; fine as heroes, but not so good in a parade.

When many Italian names were used in describing gangsters on a television show, *The Untouchables,* Sinatra was loud in his disapproval. Sinatra and many thousands of other Italo-Americans were resentful as well when a small-time hoodlum, Joseph Valachi, was brought by Bobby Kennedy into prominence as a Mafia expert, when indeed, from Valachi's testimony on television, he seemed to know less than most waiters on Mulberry Street. Many Italians in Sinatra's circle also regard Bobby Kennedy as something of an Irish cop, more dignified than those in Dolly's day, but no less intimidating. Together with Peter Lawford, Bobby Kennedy is said to have suddenly gotten "cocky" with Sinatra after John Kennedy's election, forgetting the contribution Sinatra had made in both fund-raising and in influencing many anti-Irish Italian votes. Lawford and Bobby Kennedy are both suspected of having influenced the late President's decision to stay as a house guest with Bing Crosby instead of Sinatra, as originally planned, a social setback Sinatra may never forget. Peter Lawford has since been drummed out of Sinatra's "summit" in Las Vegas.

"Yes, my son is like me," Dolly Sinatra says, proudly. "You cross him, he never forgets." And while she concedes his power, she quickly points out, "He can't make his mother do anything she doesn't want to do," adding, "Even today, he wears the same brand of underwear I used to buy him."

Today Dolly Sinatra is seventy-one years old, a year or two younger than Martin, and all day long people are knocking on the back door of her large home asking her advice, seeking her influence. When she is not seeing people and not cooking in the kitchen, she is looking after her husband, a silent but stubborn man, and telling him to keep his sore left arm resting on the sponge she has placed on the armrest of a soft chair. "Oh, he went to some terrific fires, this guy did," Dolly said to a visitor, nodding with admiration toward her husband in the chair.

Though Dolly Sinatra has eighty-seven godchildren in Hoboken, and still goes to that city during political campaigns, she now lives with her husband in a beautiful sixteen-room house in Fort Lee, New Jersey. This home was a gift from their son on their fiftieth wedding anniversary three years ago. The home is tastefully furnished and is filled with a remarkable juxtaposition of the pious and the worldly—photographs of Pope John and Ava Gardner, of Pope Paul and Dean Martin; several statues of saints and holy water, a chair autographed by Sammy Davis, Jr. and bottles of bourbon. In Mrs. Sinatra's jewelry box is a magnificent strand of pearls she had just received from Ava Gardner, whom she liked tremendously as a daughter-in-law and still keeps in touch with and talks about; and hung on the wall is a letter addressed to Dolly and Martin: "The sands of time have turned to gold, yet love continues to unfold like the petals of a rose, in God's garden of life . . . may God love you thru all eternity. I thank Him, I thank you for the being of one. Your loving son, Francis. . . ."

Mrs. Sinatra talks to her son on the telephone about once a week, and recently he suggested that, when visiting Manhattan, she make use of his apartment on East Seventy-second Street on the East River. This is an expensive neighborhood of New York even though there is a small factory on the block, but this latter fact was seized upon by Dolly Sinatra as a means of getting back at her son for some unflattering descriptions of his childhood in Hoboken.

"What—you want me to stay in *your* apartment, in *that* dump?" she asked. "You think I'm going to spend the night in *that* awful neighborhood?"

Frank Sinatra got the point, and said, "Excuse *me*, Mrs. Fort Lee."

After spending the week in Palm Springs, his cold much better, Frank Sinatra returned to Los Angeles, a lovely city of sun and sex, a Spanish discovery of Mexican misery, a star land of little men and lithe women sliding in and out of convertibles in tense tight pants.

Sinatra returned in time to see the long-awaited CBS documentary with his family. At about nine p.m. he drove to the home of his former wife, Nancy, and had dinner with her and their two daughters. Their son, whom they rarely see these days, was out of town.

Frank, Jr., who is twenty-two, was touring with a band and moving cross country toward a New York engagement at Basin Street East with The Pied Pipers, with whom Frank Sinatra sang when he was with Dorsey's band in the 1940's. Today Frank Sinatra, Jr., whom his father says he named after Franklin D. Roosevelt, lives mostly in hotels, dines each evening in his nightclub dressing room, and sings until two a.m., accepting graciously, because he has no choice, the inevitable comparisons. His voice is smooth and pleasant, and improving with work, and while he is very respectful of his father, he discusses him with objectivity and in an occasional tone of subdued cockiness.

Concurrent with his father's early fame, Frank, Jr. said, was the creation of a "press-release Sinatra" designed to "set him apart from the common man, separate him from the realities: it was suddenly Sinatra, the electric magnate, Sinatra who is supernormal, not super*human,* but super*normal.* And here," Frank, Jr. continued, "is the great fallacy, the great bullshit, for Frank Sinatra *is* normal, *is* the guy whom you'd meet on a street corner. But this other thing, the supernormal guise, has affected Frank Sinatra as much as anybody who watches one of his television shows, or reads a magazine article about him. . . .

"Frank Sinatra's life in the beginning was so normal," he said, "that nobody would have guessed in 1934 that this little Italian kid with the curly hair would become the giant, the monster, the great living legend. . . . He met my mother one summer on the beach. She was Nancy Barbato, daughter of Mike Barbato, a Jersey City plasterer. And she meets the fireman's son, Frank, one summer day on the beach at Long Branch, New Jersey. Both are Italian, both Roman Catholic, both lower-middle-class summer sweethearts—it is like a million bad movies starring Frankie Avalon. . . .

"They have three children. The first child, Nancy, was the most normal of Frank Sinatra's children. Nancy was a cheerleader, went to summer camp, drove a Chevrolet, had the easiest kind of development centered around the home and family. Next is me. My life with the family is very, very normal up until September of 1958 when, in complete contrast to the rearing of both girls, I am put into a college-preparatory school. I am now away from the inner family circle, and my position within has never been remade to this day. . . . The third child, Tina. And to be dead honest, I really couldn't say what her life is like. . . ."

The CBS show, narrated by Walter Cronkite, began at ten p.m. A minute before that, the Sinatra family, having finished dinner, turned their chairs around and faced the camera, united for whatever disaster might follow. Sinatra's men in other parts of town, in other parts of the nation, were doing the same thing. Sinatra's lawyer, Milton A. Rudin, smoking a cigar, was watching with a keen eye, an alert legal mind. Other sets were watched by Brad Dexter, Jim Mahoney, Ed Pucci; Sinatra's makeup man, "Shotgun" Britton; his New York representative, Henri Giné; his haberdasher, Richard Carroll; his insurance broker, John Lillie; his valet, George Jacobs, a handsome Negro who, when entertaining girls in *his* apartment, plays records by Ray Charles.

And like so much of Hollywood's fear, the apprehension about the CBS show all proved to be without foundation. It was a highly flattering hour that did not deeply probe, as rumors suggested it would, into Sinatra's love life, or the Mafia, or other areas of his private province. While the documentary was not authorized, wrote Jack Gould in the next day's New York *Times,* "it could have been."

Immediately after the show, the telephones began to ring throughout the Sinatra system conveying words of joy and relief—and from New York came Jilly's telegram: "WE RULE THE WORLD!"

The next day, standing in the corridor of the NBC building where he was about to resume taping his show, Sinatra was discussing the CBS show with several of his friends, and he said, "Oh, it was a gas."

"Yeah, Frank, a helluva show."

"But I think Jack Gould was right in the *Times* today," Sinatra said. "There should have been more on the *man,* not so much on the music. . . ."

They nodded, nobody mentioning the past hysteria in the Sinatra world when it seemed CBS was zeroing in on the *man;* they just nodded and two of them laughed about Sinatra's apparently having gotten the word "bird" on the show—this being a favorite Sinatra word. He often inquires of his cronies, "How's your bird?"; and when he nearly drowned in Hawaii, he later explained, "Just got a little water on my bird"; and under a large photograph of him holding a whisky bottle, a photo that hangs in the home of an actor friend named Dick Bakalyan, the inscription reads: "Drink, Dickie! It's good for your bird." In the song, *Come Fly With Me,* Sinatra sometimes alters the lyrics—". . . just say the words and we'll take our birds down to Acapulco Bay. . . ."

Ten minutes later Sinatra, following the orchestra, walked into the NBC studio which did not resemble in the slightest the scene here of eight days ago. On this occasion Sinatra was in fine voice, he cracked jokes between numbers, nothing could upset him. Once, while he was singing *How Can I Ignore the Girl Next Door,* standing on the stage next to a tree, a television camera mounted on a vehicle came rolling in too close and plowed against the tree.

"Kee-rist!" yelled one of the technical assistants.

But Sinatra seemed hardly to notice it.

"We've had a slight accident," he said, calmly. Then he began the song all over from the beginning.

When the show was over, Sinatra watched the rerun on the monitor in the control room. He was very pleased, shaking hands with Dwight Hemion and his assistants. Then the whisky bottles were opened in Sinatra's dressing room. Pat Lawford was there, and so were Andy Williams and a dozen others. The telegrams and telephone calls continued to be received from all over the country with praise for the CBS show. There was even a call, Mahoney said, from the CBS producer, Don Hewitt, with whom Sinatra had been so angry a few days before. And Sinatra was *still* angry, feeling that CBS had betrayed him, though the show itself was not objectionable.

"Shall I drop a line to Hewitt?" Mahoney asked.

"Can you send a fist through the mail?" Sinatra asked.

He has everything, he cannot sleep, he gives nice gifts, he is not happy, but he would not trade, even for happiness, what he is. . . .

He is a piece of our past—but only we have aged, he hasn't . . . we are dogged by domesticity, he isn't . . . we have compunctions, he doesn't . . . it is our fault, not his. . . .

He controls the menus of every Italian restaurant in Los Angeles; if you want North Italian cooking, fly to Milan. . . .

Men follow him, imitate him, fight to be near him . . . there is something of the locker room, the barracks about him . . . bird . . . bird. . . .

He believes you must play it big, wide, expansively—the more open you are, the more you take in, your dimensions deepen, you grow, you become more what you are—bigger, richer. . . .

"He is better than anybody else, or at least they think he is, and he has to live up to it."   —Nancy Sinatra, Jr.

"He is calm on the outside—inwardly a million things are happening to him."   —Dick Bakalyan

"He has an insatiable desire to live every moment to its fullest because, I guess, he feels that right around the corner is extinction."
                                                           —Brad Dexter

"All I ever got out of any of my marriages was the two years Artie Shaw financed on an analyst's couch."   —Ava Gardner

"We weren't mother and son—we were buddies."   —Dolly Sinatra

"I'm for anything that gets you through the night, be it prayer, tranquilizers or a bottle of Jack Daniel."   —Frank Sinatra

Frank Sinatra was tired of all the talk, the gossip, the theory—tired of reading quotes about himself, of hearing what people were saying about him all over town. It had been a tedious three weeks, he said, and now he just wanted to get away, go to Las Vegas, let off some steam.

So he hopped in his jet, soared over the California hills across the Nevada flats, then over miles and miles of desert to The Sands and the Clay-Patterson fight.

On the eve of the fight he stayed up all night and slept through most of the afternoon, though his recorded voice could be heard singing in the lobby of The Sands, in the gambling casino, even in the toilets, being interrupted every few bars however by the paging public address: ". . . Telephone call for Mr. Ron Fish, Mr. Ron Fish . . . *with a ribbon of gold in her hair.* . . . Telephone call for Mr. Herbert Rothstein, Mr. Herbert Rothstein . . . *memories of a time so bright, keep me sleepless through dark endless nights.* . . ."

Standing around in the lobby of The Sands and other hotels up and down the strip on this afternoon before the fight were the usual prefight prophets: the gamblers, the old champs, the little cigar butts from Eighth Avenue, the sportswriters who knock the big fights all year but would never miss one, the novelists who seem always to be identifying with one boxer or another, the local prostitutes assisted by some talent in from Los Angeles, and also a young brunette in a wrinkled black cocktail dress who was at the bell captain's desk crying, "But I want to speak to Mr. Sinatra."

"He's not here," the bell captain said.

"Won't you put me through to his room?"

"There are *no* messages going through, Miss," he said, and then she turned, unsteadily, seeming close to tears, and walked through the lobby into the big noisy casino crowded with men interested only in money.

Shortly before seven p.m., Jack Entratter, a big grey-haired man who operates The Sands, walked into the gambling room to tell some men around the blackjack table that Sinatra was getting dressed. He also said that he'd been unable to get front-row seats for everybody, and so some of the men—including Leo Durocher, who had a date, and Joey Bishop, who was accompanied by his wife—would not be able to fit in Frank Sinatra's row but would have to take seats in the third row. When Entratter walked over to tell this to Joey Bishop, Bishop's face fell. He did not seem angry; he merely looked at Entratter with an empty silence, seeming somewhat stunned.

"Joey, I'm *sorry,*" Entratter said when the silence persisted, "but we couldn't get more than six together in the front row."

Bishop still said nothing. But when they all appeared at the fight, Joey Bishop was in the front row, his wife in the third.

The fight, called a holy war between Muslims and Christians, was preceded by the introduction of three balding ex-champions, Rocky Marciano, Joe Louis, Sonny Liston—and then there was *The Star-Spangled Banner* sung by another man from out of the past, Eddie Fisher. It had been more than fourteen years ago, but Sinatra could still remember every detail: Eddie Fisher was then the new king of the baritones, with Billy Eckstine and Guy Mitchell right with him, and Sinatra had been long counted out. One day he remembered walking into a broadcasting studio past dozens of Eddie Fisher fans waiting outside the hall, and when they saw Sinatra they began to jeer, "Frankie, Frankie, I'm *swooning, I'm swooning.*" This was also the time when he was selling only about 30,000 records a year, when he was dreadfully miscast as a funny man on his television show, and when he recorded such disasters as *Mama Will Bark,* with Dagmar.

"I growled and barked on the record," Sinatra said, still horrified by the thought. "The only good it did me was with the dogs."

His voice and his artistic judgment were incredibly bad in 1952, but even more responsible for his decline, say his friends, was his pursuit of Ava Gardner. She was the big movie queen then, one of the most beautiful women in the world. Sinatra's daughter Nancy recalls seeing Ava swimming one day in her father's pool, then climbing out of the water with that fabulous body, walking slowly to the fire, leaning over it for a few moments, and then it suddenly seemed that her long dark hair was all dry, miraculously and effortlessly back in place.

With most women Sinatra dates, his friends say, he never knows whether they want him for what he can do for them now—or will do for them later. With Ava Gardner, it was different. He could do nothing for her later. She was on top. If Sinatra learned anything from his experience with her, he possibly learned that when a proud man is down a woman cannot help. Particularly a woman on top.

Nevertheless, despite a tired voice, some deep emotion seeped into his singing during this time. One particular song that is well remembered even now is *I'm A Fool to Want You,* and a friend who was in the studio when Sinatra recorded it recalled: "Frank was really worked up that night. He did the song in one take, then turned around and walked out of the studio and that was that. . . ."

Sinatra's manager at that time, a former song plugger named Hank Sanicola, said, "Ava loved Frank, but not the way he loved her. He needs a great deal of love. He wants it twenty-four hours a day, he must have people around—Frank is that kind of guy." Ava Gardner, Sanicola said, "was very insecure. She feared she could not really hold a man . . . twice he went chasing her to Africa, wasting his own career. . . ."

"Ava didn't want Frank's men hanging around all the time," another friend said, "and this got him mad. With Nancy he used to be able to bring the whole band home with him, and Nancy, the good Italian wife, would never complain—she'd just make everybody a plate of spaghetti."

In 1953, after almost two years of marriage, Sinatra and Ava Gardner were divorced. Sinatra's mother reportedly arranged a reconciliation, but if Ava was willing, Frank Sinatra was not. He was seen with other women. The balance had shifted. Somewhere during this period Sinatra seemed to change from the kid singer, the boy actor in the sailor suit, to a man. Even before he had won the Oscar in 1953 for his role in *From Here to Eternity,* some flashes of his old talent were coming through— in his recording of *The Birth of the Blues,* in his Riviera-nightclub appearance that jazz critics enthusiastically praised; and there was also a trend now toward L.P.'s and away from the quick three-minute deal, and Sinatra's concert style would have capitalized on this with or without an Oscar.

In 1954, totally committed to his talent once more, Frank Sinatra was selected Metronome's "Singer of the Year," and later he won the U.P.I. disc-jockey poll, unseating Eddie Fisher—who now, in Las Vegas, having sung *The Star-Spangled Banner,* climbed out of the ring, and the fight began.

Floyd Patterson chased Clay around the ring in the first round, but was unable to reach him, and from then on he was Clay's toy, the bout ending in a technical knockout in the twelfth round. A half hour later, nearly everybody had forgotten about the fight and was back at the gambling tables or lining up to buy tickets for the Dean Martin-Sinatra-Bishop nightclub routine on the stage of The Sands. This routine, which includes Sammy Davis, Jr. when he is in town, consists of a few songs and much cutting up, all of it very informal, very special, and rather ethnic—Martin, a drink in hand, asking Bishop: "Did you ever see a Jew jitsu?"; and Bishop, playing a Jewish waiter, warning the two Italians to watch out "because I got my own group—the *Matzia*."

Then after the last show at The Sands, the Sinatra crowd, which now numbered about twenty—and included Jilly, who had flown in from New York; Jimmy Cannon, Sinatra's favorite sports columnist; Harold Gibbons, a Teamster official expected to take over if Hoffa goes to jail—all got into a line of cars and headed for another club. It was three o'clock. The night was young.

They stopped at The Sahara, taking a long table near the back, and listened to a baldheaded little comedian named Don Rickles, who is probably more caustic than any comic in the country. His humor is so rude, in *such* bad taste, that it offends no one—it is *too* offensive to be offensive. Spotting Eddie Fisher among the audience, Rickles proceeded to ridicule him as a lover, saying it was no wonder that he could not handle Elizabeth Taylor; and when two businessmen in the audience acknowledged that they were Egyptians, Rickles cut into them for their country's policy toward Israel; and he strongly suggested that the woman seated at one table with her husband was actually a hooker.

When the Sinatra crowd walked in, Don Rickles could not be more delighted. Pointing to Jilly, Rickles yelled: "How's it feel to be Frank's tractor? . . . Yeah, Jilly keeps walking in front of Frank clearing the way." Then, nodding to Durocher, Rickles said, "Stand up, Leo, show Frank how you slide." Then he focused on Sinatra, not failing to mention Mia Farrow, nor that he was wearing a toupee, nor to say that Sinatra was washed up as a singer, and when Sinatra laughed, everybody laughed, and Rickles pointed toward Bishop: "Joey Bishop keeps checking with Frank to see what's funny."

Then, after Rickles told some Jewish jokes, Dean Martin stood up and yelled, "Hey, you're always talking about the Jews, never about the Italians," and Rickles cut him off with, "What do we need the Italians for—all they do is keep the flies off our fish."

Sinatra laughed, they all laughed, and Rickles went on this way for nearly an hour until Sinatra, standing up, said, "All right, com'on, get this thing over with. I gotta go."

"Shaddup and sit down!" Rickles snapped. "I've had to listen to you sing. . . ."

"Who do you think you're talking to?" Sinatra yelled back.

"Dick Haymes," Rickles replied, and Sinatra laughed again, and then Dean Martin, pouring a bottle of whisky over his head, entirely drenching his tuxedo, pounded the table.

"Who would ever believe that staggering would make a star?" Rickles said, but Martin called out, "Hey, I wanna make a speech."

"Shaddup."

"No, Don, I wanna tell ya," Dean Martin persisted, "that I think you're a great performer."

"Well, thank you, Dean," Rickles said, seeming pleased.

"But don't go by me," Martin said, plopping down into his seat, "I'm drunk."

"I'll buy that," Rickles said.

By four a.m. Frank Sinatra led the group out of The Sahara, some of them carrying their glasses of whisky with them, sipping it along the sidewalk and in the cars; then, returning to The Sands, they walked into the gambling casino. It was still packed with people, the roulette wheels spinning, the crapshooters screaming in the far corner.

Frank Sinatra, holding a shot glass of bourbon in his left hand, walked through the crowd. He, unlike some of his friends, was perfectly pressed, his tuxedo tie precisely pointed, his shoes unsmudged. He never seems to lose his dignity, never lets his guard completely down no matter how much he has drunk, nor how long he has been up. He never sways when he walks, like Dean Martin, nor does he ever dance in the aisles or jump up on tables, like Sammy Davis.

A part of Sinatra, no matter where he is, is never there. There is always a part of him, though sometimes a small part, that remains *Il Padrone*. Even now, resting his shot glass on the blackjack table, facing the dealer, Sinatra stood a bit back from the table, not leaning against it. He reached under his tuxedo jacket into his trouser pocket and came up with a thick but *clean* wad of bills. Gently he peeled off a one-hundred-dollar bill and placed it on the green-felt table. The dealer dealt him two cards. Sinatra called for a third card, overbid, lost the hundred.

Without a change of expression, Sinatra put down a second hundred-dollar bill. He lost that. Then he put down a third, and lost that. Then he placed two one-hundred-dollar bills on the table and lost those. Finally, putting his sixth hundred-dollar bill on the table, and losing it, Sinatra moved away from the table, nodding to the man, and announcing, "Good dealer."

The crowd that had gathered around him now opened up to let him through. But a woman stepped in front of him, handing him a piece of paper to autograph. He signed it and then *he* said, "Thank you."

In the rear of The Sands' large dining room was a long table reserved for Sinatra. The dining room was fairly empty at this hour, with perhaps two dozen other people in the room, including a table of four unescorted young ladies sitting near Sinatra. On the other side of the room, at another long table, sat seven men shoulder-to-shoulder against the wall, two of them wearing dark glasses, all of them eating quietly, speaking hardly a word, just sitting and eating and missing nothing.

The Sinatra party, after getting settled and having a few more drinks, ordered something to eat. The table was about the same size as the one reserved for Sinatra whenever he is at Jilly's in New York; and the people seated around this table in Las Vegas were many of the same people who are often seen with Sinatra at Jilly's or at a restaurant in California, or in Italy, or in New Jersey, or wherever Sinatra happens to be. When Sinatra sits to dine, his trusted friends are close; and no matter where he is, no matter how elegant the place may be, there is something of the neighborhood showing because Sinatra, no matter how far he has come, is still something of the boy from the neighborhood—only now he can take his neighborhood with him.

In some ways, this quasi-family affair at a reserved table in a public place is the closest thing Sinatra now has to home life. Perhaps, having had a home and left it, this approximation is as close as he cares to come; although this does not seem precisely so because he speaks with such warmth about his family, keeps in close touch with his first wife, and insists that she make no decision without first consulting him. He is always eager to place his furniture or other mementos of himself in her home or his daughter Nancy's, and he also is on amiable terms with Ava Gardner. When he was in Italy making *Von Ryan's Express,* they spent some time together, being pursued wherever they went by the *paparazzi.* It was reported then that the *paparazzi* had made Sinatra a collective offer of $16,000 if he would pose with Ava Gardner; Sinatra was said to have made a counter offer of $32,000 if he could break one *paparazzi* arm and leg.

While Sinatra is often delighted that he can be in his home completely without people, enabling him to read and think without interruption, there are occasions when he finds himself alone at night, and *not* by choice. He may have dialed a half-dozen women, and for one reason or another they are all unavailable. So he will call his valet, George Jacobs.

"I'll be coming home for dinner tonight, George."

"How many will there be?"

"Just myself," Sinatra will say. "I want something light, I'm not very hungry."

George Jacobs is a twice-divorced man of thirty-six who resembles Billy Eckstine. He has traveled all over the world with Sinatra and is devoted to him. Jacobs lives in a comfortable bachelor's apartment off Sunset Boulevard around the corner from Whiskey à Go Go, and he is known around town for the assortment of frisky California girls he has as friends—a few of whom, he concedes, were possibly drawn to him initially because of his closeness to Frank Sinatra.

When Sinatra arrives, Jacobs will serve him dinner in the dining room. Then Sinatra will tell Jacobs that he is free to go home. If Sinatra, on such evenings, should ask Jacobs to stay longer, or to play a few hands of poker, he would be happy to do so. But Sinatra never does.

This was his second night in Las Vegas, and Frank Sinatra sat with friends in The Sands' dining room until nearly eight a.m. He slept through much of the day, then flew back to Los Angeles, and on the following morning he was driving his little golf cart through the Paramount Pictures movie lot. He was scheduled to complete two final scenes with the sultry blonde actress, Virna Lisi, in the film, *Assault on a Queen.* As he maneuvered the little vehicle up the road between the big studio buildings, he spotted Steve Rossi who, with his comedy partner Marty Allen, was making a film in an adjoining studio with Nancy Sinatra.

"Hey, Dag," he yelled to Rossi, "stop kissing Nancy."

"It's part of the film, Frank," Rossi said, turning as he walked.

"In the garage?"

"It's my Dago blood, Frank."

"Well, cool it," Sinatra said, winking, then cutting his golf cart around a corner and parking it outside a big drab building within which the scenes for *Assault* would be filmed.

"Where's the fat director?" Sinatra called out, striding into the studio that was crowded with dozens of technical assistants and actors all gathered around cameras. The director, Jack Donohue, a large man who has worked with Sinatra through twenty-two years on one production or other, has had headaches with this film. The script had been chopped, the actors seemed restless, and Sinatra had become bored. But now there were only two scenes left—a short one to be filmed in the pool, and a longer and passionate one featuring Sinatra and Virna Lisi to be shot on a simulated beach.

The pool scene, which dramatizes a situation where Sinatra and his hijackers fail in their attempt to sack the *Queen Mary,* went quickly and well. After Sinatra had been kept in the water shoulder-high for a few minutes, he said, "Let's move it, fellows—it's cold in this water, and I've just gotten over one cold."

So the camera crews moved in closer, Virna Lisi splashed next to Sinatra in the water, and Jack Donohue yelled to his assistants operating the fans, "Get the waves going," and another man gave the command, *"Agitate!"* and Sinatra broke out in song. "Agitate in rhythm," then quieted down just before the cameras started to roll.

Frank Sinatra was on the beach in the next situation, supposedly gazing up at the stars, and Virna Lisi was to approach him, toss one of her shoes near him to announce her presence, then sit near him and prepare for a passionate session. Just before beginning, Miss Lisi made a practice toss of her shoe toward the prone figure of Sinatra sprawled on the beach. As she tossed her shoe, Sinatra called out, "Hit me in my bird and I'm going home."

Virna Lisi, who understands little English and certainly none of Sinatra's special vocabulary, looked confused, but everybody behind the camera laughed. She threw the shoe toward him. It twirled in the air, landed on his stomach.

"Well, that's about three inches too high," he announced. She again was puzzled by the laughter behind the camera.

Then Jack Donohue had them rehearse their lines, and Sinatra, still very charged from the Las Vegas trip, and anxious to get the cameras rolling, said, "Let's try one." Donohue, not certain that Sinatra and Lisi knew their lines well enough, nevertheless said okay, and an assistant with a clapboard called, "419, Take 1," and Virna Lisi approached with the shoe, tossed it at Frank lying on the beach. It fell short of his thigh, and Sinatra's right eye raised almost imperceptibly, but the crew got the message, smiled.

"What do the stars tell you tonight?" Miss Lisi said, delivering her first line, and sitting next to Sinatra on the beach.

"The stars tell me tonight I'm an idiot," Sinatra said, "a gold-plated idiot to get mixed up in this thing. . . ."

"Cut," Donohue said. There were some microphone shadows on the sand, and Virna Lisi was not sitting in the proper place near Sinatra.

"419, Take 2," the clapboard man called.

Miss Lisi again approached, threw the shoe at him, this time falling short—Sinatra exhaling only slightly—and she said, "What do the stars tell you tonight?"

"The stars tell me I'm an idiot, a gold-plated idiot to get mixed up in this thing. . . ." Then, according to the script, Sinatra was to continue, ". . . do you know what we're getting into? The minute we step on the deck of the *Queen Mary*, we've just tattooed ourselves," but Sinatra, who often improvises on lines, recited them: ". . . do you know what we're getting into? The minute we step on the deck of that mother's-ass ship. . . ."

"*No*, no," Donohue interrupted, shaking his head, "I don't think that's right."

The cameras stopped, some people laughed, and Sinatra looked up from his position in the sand as if he had been unfairly interrupted.

"I don't see why that can't work . . ." he began, but Richard Conte, standing behind the camera, yelled, "It won't play in London."

Donohue pushed his hand through his thinning grey hair and said, but not really in anger, "You know, that scene was pretty good until somebody blew the line. . . ."

"Yeah," agreed the cameraman, Billy Daniels, his head popping out from around the camera, "it was a pretty good piece. . . ."

"Watch your language," Sinatra cut in. Then Sinatra, who has a genius for figuring out ways of not reshooting scenes, suggested a way in which the film could be used and the "mother" line could be rerecorded later. This met with approval. Then the cameras were rolling again, Virna Lisi was leaning toward Sinatra in the sand, and then he pulled her down close to him. The camera now moved in for a close-up of their faces, ticking away for a few long seconds, but Sinatra and Lisi did not stop kissing, they just lay together in the sand wrapped in one another's arms, and then Virna Lisi's left leg just slightly began to rise a bit, and everybody in the studio now watched in silence, not saying anything until Donohue finally called out:

"If you ever get through, let me know. I'm running out of film."

Then Miss Lisi got up, straightened out her white dress, brushed back her blonde hair and touched her lipstick, which was smeared. Sinatra got up, a little smile on his lips, and headed for his dressing room.

Passing an older man who stood near a camera, Sinatra asked, "How's your Bell & Howell?"

The older man smiled.

"It's fine, Frank."

"Good."

In his dressing room Sinatra was met by an automobile designer who had the plans for Sinatra's new custom-built model to replace the $25,000 Ghia he has been driving for the last few years. He also was awaited by his secretary, Tom Conroy, who had a bag full of fan mail, including a letter from New York's Mayor John Lindsay; and by Bill Miller, Sinatra's pianist, who would rehearse some of the songs that would be recorded later in the evening for Sinatra's newest album, *Moonlight Sinatra*.

While Sinatra does not mind hamming it up a bit on a movie set, he is extremely serious about his recording sessions; as he explained to a British writer, Robin Douglas-Home: "Once you're on that record singing, it's you and you alone. If it's bad and gets you criticized, it's you who's to blame—no one else. If it's good, it's also you. With a film it's never like that; there are producers and scriptwriters, and hundreds of men in offices and the thing is taken right out of your hands. With a record, you're *it*. . . ."

> *But now the days are short*
> *I'm in the autumn of the year*
> *And now I think of my life*
> *As vintage wine*
> *From fine old kegs. . . .*

It no longer matters what song he is singing, or who wrote the words
—they are all *his* words, *his* sentiments, they are chapters from the
lyrical novel of his life.

> *Life is a beautiful thing*
> *As long as I hold the string. . . .*

When Frank Sinatra drives to the studio, he seems to dance out of
the car across the sidewalk into the front door; then, snapping his fingers,
he is standing in front of the orchestra in an intimate, airtight room, and
soon he is dominating every man, every instrument, every sound wave.
Some of the musicians have accompanied him for twenty-five years,
have gotten old hearing him sing *You Make Me Feel So Young*.

When his voice is on, as it was tonight, Sinatra is in ecstasy, the room
becomes electric, there is an excitement that spreads through the orchestra and is felt in the control booth where a dozen men, Sinatra's
friends, wave at him from behind the glass. One of the men is the
Dodgers' pitcher, Don Drysdale ("Hey, Big D," Sinatra calls out, *"hey,
baby!"*); another is the professional golfer, Bo Wininger; there are also
numbers of pretty women standing in the booth behind the engineers,
women who smile at Sinatra and softly move their bodies to the mellow
mood of his music:

> *"Will this be moon love*
> *Nothing but moon love*
> *Will you be gone when the dawn*
> *Comes stealing through. . . ."*

After he is finished, the record is played back on tape, and Nancy
Sinatra, who has just walked in, joins her father near the front of the
orchestra to hear the playback. They listen silently, all eyes on them,
the king, the princess; and when the music ends there is applause from
the control booth, Nancy smiles, and her father snaps his fingers and
says, kicking a foot, *"Ooba-deeba-boobe-do!"*

Then Sinatra calls to one of his men. "Hey, Sarge, think I can have a
half-a-cup of coffee?"

Sarge Weiss, who had been listening to the music, slowly gets up.

"Didn't mean to wake ya, Sarge," Sinatra says, smiling.

Then Weiss brings the coffee, and Sinatra looks at it, smells it, then
announces, "I thought he'd be nice to me, but it's *really* coffee. . . ."

There are more smiles, and then the orchestra prepares for the next number. And one hour later, it is over.

The musicians put their instruments into their cases, grab their coats, and begin to file out, saying good-night to Sinatra. He knows them all by name, knows much about them personally, from their bachelor days, through their divorces, through their ups and downs, as they know him. When a French-horn player, a short Italian named Vincent DeRosa, who has played with Sinatra since The Lucky Strike "Hit Parade" days on radio, strolled by, Sinatra reached out to hold him for a second.

"Vicenzo," Sinatra said, "how's your little girl?"

"She's fine, Frank."

"Oh, she's not a *little* girl anymore," Sinatra corrected himself, "she's a big girl now."

"Yes, she goes to college now. U.S.C."

"That's great."

"She's also got a little talent, I think, Frank, as a singer."

Sinatra was silent for a moment, then said, "Yes, but it's very good for her to get her education first, Vicenzo."

Vincent DeRosa nodded.

"Yes, Frank," he said, and then he said, "Well, good-night, Frank."

"Good-night, Vicenzo."

After the musicians had all gone, Sinatra left the recording room and joined his friends in the corridor. He was going to go out and do some drinking with Drysdale, Wininger, and a few other friends, but first he walked to the other end of the corridor to say good-night to Nancy, who was getting her coat and was planning to drive home in her own car.

After Sinatra had kissed her on the cheek, he hurried to join his friends at the door. But before Nancy could leave the studio, one of Sinatra's men, Al Silvani, a former prizefight manager, joined her.

"Are you ready to leave yet, Nancy?"

"Oh, thanks, Al," she said, "but I'll be all right."

"Pope's orders," Silvani said, holding his hands up, palms out.

Only after Nancy had pointed to two of her friends who would escort her home, and only after Silvani recognized them as friends, would he leave.

The rest of the month was bright and balmy. The record session had gone magnificently, the film was finished, the television shows were out of the way, and now Sinatra was in his Ghia driving out to his office to begin coordinating his latest projects. He had an engagement at The Sands, a new spy film called *The Naked Runner* to be shot in England, and a couple more albums to do in the immediate months ahead. And within a week he would be fifty years old. . . .

> *Life is a beautiful thing*
> *As long as I hold the string*
> *I'd be a silly so-and-so*
> *If I should ever let go.* . . .

Frank Sinatra stopped his car. The light was red. Pedestrians passed quickly across his windshield but, as usual, one did not. It was a girl in her twenties. She remained at the curb staring at him. Through the corner of his left eye he could see her, and he knew, because it happens almost every day, that she was thinking, *It looks like him, but is it?*

Just before the light turned green, Sinatra turned toward her, looked directly into her eyes waiting for the reaction he knew would come. It came and he smiled. She smiled and he was gone.

The Loser

At the foot of a mountain in upstate New York, about sixty miles from Manhattan, there is an abandoned country clubhouse with a dusty dance floor, upturned barstools, and an untuned piano; and the only sounds heard around the place at night come from the big white house behind it—the clanging sounds of garbage cans being toppled by raccoons, skunks, and stray cats making their nocturnal raids down from the mountain.

The white house seems deserted, too; but occasionally, when the animals become too clamorous, a light will flash on, a window will open, and a Coke bottle will come flying through the darkness and smash against the cans. But mostly the animals are undisturbed until daybreak, when the rear door of the white house swings open and a broad-shouldered Negro appears in grey sweat clothes with a white towel around his neck.

He runs down the steps, quickly passes the garbage cans and proceeds at a trot down the dirt road beyond the country club toward the highway. Sometimes he stops along the road and throws a flurry of punches at imaginary foes, each jab punctuated by hard gasps of his breathing—

41

"hegh-hegh-hegh"—and then, reaching the highway, he turns and soon disappears up the mountain.

At this time of morning farm trucks are on the road, and the drivers wave at the runner. And later in the morning other motorists see him, and a few stop suddenly at the curb and ask:

"Say, aren't *you* Floyd Patterson?"

"No," says Floyd Patterson. "I'm his brother, Raymond."

The motorists move on, but recently a man on foot, a disheveled man who seemed to have spent the night outdoors, staggered behind the runner along the road and yelled, "Hey, Floyd Patterson!"

"No, I'm his brother, Raymond."

"Don't tell *me* you're not Floyd Patterson. I know what Floyd Patterson looks like."

"Okay," Patterson said, shrugging, "if you want me to be Floyd Patterson, I'll be Floyd Patterson."

"So let me have your autograph," said the man, handing him a rumpled piece of paper and a pencil.

He signed it—"Raymond Patterson."

One hour later Floyd Patterson was jogging his way back down the dirt path toward the white house, the towel over his head absorbing the sweat from his brow. He lives alone in a two-room apartment in the rear of the house, and has remained there in almost complete seclusion since getting knocked out a second time by Sonny Liston.

In the smaller room is a large bed he makes up himself, several record albums he rarely plays, a telephone that seldom rings. The larger room has a kitchen on one side and, on the other, adjacent to a sofa, is a fireplace from which are hung boxing trunks and T-shirts to dry, and a photograph of him when he was the champion, and also a television set. The set is usually on except when Patterson is sleeping, or when he is sparring across the road inside the clubhouse (the ring is rigged over what was once the dance floor), or when, in a rare moment of painful honesty, he reveals to a visitor what it is like to be the loser.

"Oh, I would give up anything to just be able to work with Liston, to box with him somewhere where nobody would see us, and to see if I could get past three minutes with him," Patterson was saying, wiping his face with the towel, pacing slowly around the room near the sofa. "I *know* I can do better. . . . Oh, I'm not talking about a rematch. Who would pay a nickel for another Patterson-Liston fight? I know *I* wouldn't. . . . But all I want to do is get past the first round."

Then he said, "You have no idea how it is in the first round. You're out there with all those people around you, and those cameras, and the whole world looking in, and all that movement, that excitement, and *The Star-Spangled Banner,* and the whole nation hoping you'll win, including the President. And do you know what all this does? It blinds you, just blinds you. And then the bell rings, and you go at Liston and he's coming at you, and you're not even aware that there's a referee in the ring with you.

". . . Then you can't remember much of the rest, because you don't want to. . . . All you recall is, all of a sudden you're getting up, and the referee is saying, 'You all right?' and you say, 'Of *course* I'm all right,' and he says, 'What's your name?' and you say, 'Patterson.'

"And then, suddenly, with all this screaming around you, you're down again, and you know you have to get up, but you're extremely groggy, and the referee is pushing you back, and your trainer is in there with a towel, and people are all standing up, and your eyes focus directly at no one person—you're sort of floating.

"It is not a *bad* feeling when you're knocked out," he said. "It's a *good* feeling, actually. It's not painful, just a sharp grogginess. You don't see angels or stars; you're on a pleasant cloud. After Liston hit me in Nevada, I felt, for about four or five seconds, that everybody in the arena was actually in the ring with me, circled around me like a family, and you feel warmth toward all the people in the arena after you're knocked out. You feel lovable to all the people. And you want to reach out and kiss everybody—men and women—and after the Liston fight somebody told me I actually blew a kiss to the crowd from the ring. I don't remember that. But I guess it's true because that's the way you feel during the four or five seconds after a knockout. . . .

"But then," Patterson went on, still pacing, "this good feeling leaves you. You realize where you are, and what you're doing there, and what has just happened to you. And what follows is a hurt, a confused hurt—not a physical hurt—it's a hurt combined with anger; it's a what-will-people-think hurt; it's an ashamed-of-my-own-ability hurt . . . and all you want then is a hatch door in the middle of the ring—a hatch door that will open and let you fall through and land in your dressing room instead of having to get out of the ring and face those people. The worst thing about losing is having to walk out of the ring and face those people. . . ."

Then Patterson walked over to the stove and put on the kettle for tea. He remained silent for a few moments. Through the walls could be heard the footsteps and voices of the sparring partners and the trainer who live in the front of the house. Soon they would be in the clubhouse getting things ready should Patterson wish to spar. In two days he was scheduled to fly to Stockholm and fight an Italian named Amonti, Patterson's first appearance in the ring since the last Liston fight.

Next he hoped to get a fight in London against Henry Cooper. Then, if his confidence was restored, his reflexes reacting, Patterson hoped to start back up the ladder in this country, fighting all the leading contenders, fighting often, and not waiting so long between each fight as he had done when he was a champion in the ninety-percent tax bracket.

His wife, whom he finds little time to see, and most of his friends think he should quit. They point out that he does not need the money. Even he admits that, from investments alone on his $8,000,000 gross earnings, he should have an annual income of about $35,000 for the next twenty-five years. But Patterson, who is only twenty-nine years old and barely scratched, cannot believe that he is finished. He cannot help but think that it was something more than Liston that destroyed him—a strange, psychological force was also involved, and unless he can fully understand what it was, and learn to deal with it in the boxing ring, he may never be able to live peacefully anywhere but under this mountain. Nor will he ever be able to discard the false whiskers and moustache that, ever since Johansson beat him in 1959, he has carried with him in a small attaché case into each fight so he can slip out of the stadium unrecognized should he lose.

"I often wonder what other fighters feel, and what goes through their minds when they lose," Patterson said, placing the cups of tea on the table. "I've wanted so much to talk to another fighter about all this, to compare thoughts, to see if he feels some of the same things I've felt. But who can you talk to? Most fighters don't talk much anyway. And I can't even look another fighter in the eye at a weigh-in, for some reason.

"At the Liston weigh-in, the sportswriters noticed this, and said it showed I was afraid. But that's not it. I can never look *any* fighter in the eye because . . . well, because we're going to fight, which isn't a nice thing, and because . . . well, once I actually did look a fighter in the eye. It was a long, long time ago. I must have been in the amateurs then. And when I looked at this fighter, I saw he had such a nice face . . . and then he looked at *me* . . . and *smiled* at me . . . and *I* smiled back! It was strange, very strange. When a guy can look at another guy and smile like that, I don't think they have any business fighting.

"I don't remember what happened in that fight, and I don't remember what the guy's name was. I only remember that, ever since, I have never looked another fighter in the eye."

The telephone rang in the bedroom. Patterson got up to answer it. It was his wife, Sandra. So he excused himself, shutting the bedroom door behind him.

Sandra Patterson and their four children live in a $100,000 home in an upper-middle-class white neighborhood in Scarsdale, New York. Floyd Patterson feels uncomfortable in this home surrounded by a manicured lawn and stuffed with furniture, and, since losing his title to Liston, he has preferred living full time at his camp, which his children have come to know as "daddy's house." The children, the eldest of whom is a daughter named Jeannie now seven years old, do not know exactly what their father does for a living. But Jeannie, who watched the last Liston-Patterson fight on closed-circuit television, accepted the explanation that her father performs in a kind of game where the men take turns pushing one another down; he had his turn pushing them down, and now it is their turn.

The bedroom door opened again, and Floyd Patterson, shaking his head, was very angry and nervous.

"I'm not going to work out today," he said. "I'm going to fly down to Scarsdale. Those boys are picking on Jeannie again. She's the only Negro in this school, and the older kids give her a rough time, and some of the older boys tease her and lift up her dress all the time. Yesterday she went home crying, and so today I'm going down there and plan to wait outside the school for those boys to come out, and. . . ."

"How old are they?" he was asked.

"Teen-agers," he said. "Old enough for a left hook."

Patterson telephoned his pilot friend, Ted Hanson, who stays at the camp and does public-relations work for him, and has helped teach Patterson to fly. Five minutes later Hanson, a lean white man with a crew cut and glasses, was knocking on the door; and ten minutes later both were in the car that Patterson was driving almost recklessly over the narrow, winding country roads toward the airport, about six miles from the camp.

"Sandra is afraid I'll cause trouble; she's worried about what I'll do to those boys; she doesn't want trouble!" Patterson snapped, swerving around a hill and giving his car more gas. "She's just not firm enough! She's afraid . . . she was afraid to tell me about that groceryman who's been making passes at her. It took her a long time before she told me about that dishwasher repairman who comes over and calls her 'baby.' They all know I'm away so much. And that dishwasher repairman's been to my home about four, five times this month already. That machine breaks down every week. I guess he fixes it so it breaks down every week. Last time, I laid a trap. I waited forty-five minutes for him to come, but then he didn't show up. I was going to grab him and say, 'How would you like it if I called *your* wife *baby*? You'd feel like punching me in the nose, wouldn't you? Well, that's what I'm going to do—if you ever call her *baby* again. You call her Mrs. Patterson; or Sandra, if you know her. But you don't know her, so call her Mrs. Patterson.' And then I told Sandra that these men, this type of white man, he just wants to have some fun with colored women. He'll never marry a colored woman, just wants to have some fun. . . ."

Now he was driving into the airport's parking lot. Directly ahead, roped to the grass airstrip, was the single-engine green Cessna that Patterson bought and learned to fly before the second Liston fight. Flying was a thing Patterson had always feared—a fear shared by, maybe inherited from, his manager, Cus D'Amato, who still will not fly.

D'Amato, who took over training Patterson when the fighter was seventeen or eighteen years old and exerted a tremendous influence over his psyche, is a strange but fascinating man of fifty-six who is addicted to Spartanism and self-denial and is possessed by suspicion and fear: he avoids subways because he fears someone might push him onto the tracks; never has married; never reveals his home address.

"I must keep my enemies confused," D'Amato once explained. "When they are confused, then I can do a job for my fighters. What I do not want in life, however, is a sense of security; the moment a person knows security, his senses are dulled—and he begins to die. I also do not want many pleasures in life; I believe the more pleasures you get out of living, the more fear you have of dying."

Until a few years ago, D'Amato did most of Patterson's talking, and ran things like an Italian *padrone*. But later Patterson, the maturing son, rebelled against the Father Image. After losing to Sonny Liston the first time—a fight D'Amato had urged Patterson to resist—Patterson took flying lessons. And before the second Liston fight, Patterson had conquered his fear of height, was master at the controls, was filled with renewed confidence—and knew, too, that even if he lost, he at least possessed a vehicle that could get him out of town, fast.

But it didn't. After the fight, the little Cessna, weighed down by too much luggage, became overheated ninety miles outside of Las Vegas. Patterson and his pilot companion, having no choice but to turn back, radioed the airfield and arranged for the rental of a larger plane. When they landed, the Vegas air terminal was filled with people leaving town after the fight. Patterson hid in the shadows behind a hangar. His beard was packed in the trunk. But nobody saw him.

Later the pilot flew Patterson's Cessna back to New York alone. And Patterson flew in the larger, rented plane. He was accompanied on this flight by Hanson, a friendly, forty-two-year-old, thrice-divorced Nevadan who once was a crop duster, a bartender, and a cabaret hoofer; later he became a pilot instructor in Las Vegas, and it was there that he met Patterson. The two became good friends. And when Patterson asked Hanson to help fly the rented plane back to New York, Hanson did not hesitate, even though he had a slight hangover that night—partly due to being depressed by Liston's victory, partly due to being slugged in a bar by a drunk after objecting to some unflattering things the drunk had said about the fight.

Once in the airplane, however, Ted Hanson became very alert. He had to, because, after the plane had cruised a while at 10,000 feet, Floyd Patterson's mind seemed to wander back to the ring, and the plane would drift off course, and Hanson would say, "Floyd, Floyd, how's about getting back on course?", and then Patterson's head would snap up and his eyes would flash toward the dials. And everything would be all right for a while. But then he was back in the arena, reliving the fight, hardly believing that it had really happened. . . .

". . . And I kept thinking, as I flew out of Vegas that night, of all those months of training before the fight, all the roadwork, all the sparring, all the months away from Sandra . . . thinking of the time in camp when I wanted to stay up until eleven-fifteen p.m. to watch a certain movie on The Late Show. But I didn't because I had roadwork the next morning. . . .

". . . And I was thinking about how good I'd felt before the fight, as I lay on the table in the dressing room. I remember thinking, 'You're in excellent physical condition, you're in good mental condition—but are you vicious?' But you tell yourself, 'Viciousness is not important now, don't think about it now; a championship fight's at stake, and that's important enough and, who knows? maybe you'll get vicious once the bell rings.'

". . . And so you lay there trying to get a little sleep . . . but you're only in a twilight zone, half asleep, and you're interrupted every once in a while by voices out in the hall, some guy's yelling 'Hey, Jack,' or 'Hey, Al,' or 'Hey, get those four-rounders into the ring.' And when you hear that, you think, 'They're not ready for you yet.' So you lay there . . . and wonder, 'Where will I be tomorrow? Where will I be three hours from now?' Oh, you think all kinds of thoughts, some thoughts completely unrelated to the fight . . . you wonder whether you ever paid your mother-in-law back for all those stamps she bought a year ago . . . and you remember that time at two a.m. when Sandra tripped on the steps while bringing a bottle up to the baby . . . and then you get mad and ask: 'What am I thinking about these things for?' . . . and you try to sleep . . . but then the door opens and somebody says to somebody else, 'Hey, is somebody gonna go to Liston's dressing room to watch 'em bandage up?'

". . . And so then you know it's about time to get ready. . . . You open your eyes. You get off the table. You glove up, you loosen up. Then Liston's trainer walks in. He looks at you, he smiles. He feels the bandages and later he says, 'Good luck, Floyd,' and you think, 'He didn't have to say that; he must be a nice guy.'

". . . And then you go out, and it's the long walk, always a long walk,

*and you think, 'What am I gonna be when I come back this way?' Then
you climb into the ring. You notice Billy Eckstine at ringside leaning
over to talk to somebody, and you see the reporters—some you like,
some you don't like—and then it's* The Star-Spangled Banner, *and the
cameras are rolling, and the bell rings. . . .*

*". . . How could the same thing happen twice? How? That's all I
kept thinking after the knockout. . . . Was I fooling these people all these
years? . . . Was I ever the champion? . . . And then they lead you out
of the ring . . . and up the aisle you go, past those people, and all you
want is to get to your dressing room, fast . . . but the trouble was in Las
Vegas they made a wrong turn along the aisle, and when we got to the
end, there was no dressing room there . . . and we had to walk all the
way back down the aisle, past the same people, and they must have been
thinking, 'Patterson's not only knocked out, but he can't even find his
dressing room. . . .'*

*". . . In the dressing room I had a headache. Liston didn't hurt me
physically—a few days later I only felt a twitching nerve in my teeth—
it was nothing like some fights I've had: like that Dick Wagner fight in
'53 when he beat my body so bad I was urinating blood for days. After
the Liston fight, I just went into the bathroom, shut the door behind me,
and looked at myself in the mirror. I just looked at myself, and asked,
'What happened?' and then they started pounding on the door, and saying, 'Com'on out, Floyd, com'on out; the press is here, Cus is here,
com'on out, Floyd. . . .'*

*". . . And so I went out, and they asked questions, but what can you
say? What you're thinking about is all those months of training, all the
conditioning, all the depriving; and you think, 'I didn't have to run that
extra mile, didn't have to spar that day, I could have stayed up that
night in camp and watched* The Late Show. *. . . I could have fought this
fight tonight in no condition. . . .'"*

"Floyd, Floyd," Hanson had said, "let's get back on course. . . ."

Again Patterson would snap out of his reverie, and refocus on the
omniscope, and get his flying under control. After landing in New Mexico, and then in Ohio, Floyd Patterson and Ted Hanson brought the little
plane into the New York airstrip near the fight camp. The green Cessna
that had been flown back by the other pilot was already there, roped
to the grass at precisely the same spot it was on this day five months later

when Floyd Patterson was planning to fly it toward perhaps another fight—this time a fight with some schoolboys in Scarsdale who had been lifting up his little daughter's dress.

Patterson and Ted Hanson untied the plane, and Patterson got a rag and wiped from the windshield the splotches of insects. Then he walked around behind the plane, inspected the tail, checked under the fuselage, then peered down between the wing and the flaps to make sure all the screws were tight. He seemed suspicious of something. D'Amato would have been pleased.

"If a guy wants to get rid of you," Patterson explained, "all he has to do is remove these little screws here. Then, when you try to come in for a landing, the flaps fall off, and you crash."

Then Patterson got into the cockpit and started the engine. A few moments later, with Hanson beside him, Patterson was racing the little plane over the grassy field, then soaring over the weeds, then flying high above the gentle hills and trees. It was a nice takeoff.

Since it was only a forty-minute flight to the Westchester airport, where Sandra Patterson would be waiting with a car, Floyd Patterson did all the flying. The trip was uneventful until, suddenly behind a cloud, he flew into heavy smoke that hovered above a forest fire. His visibility gone, he was forced to the instruments. And at this precise moment, a fly that had been buzzing in the back of the cockpit flew up front and landed on the instrument panel in front of Patterson. He glared at the fly, watched it crawl slowly up the windshield, then shot a quick smash with his palm against the glass. He missed. The fly buzzed safely past Patterson's ear, bounced off the back of the cockpit, circled around.

"This smoke won't keep up," Hanson assured. "You can level off."

Patterson leveled off.

He flew easily for a few moments. Then the fly buzzed to the front again, zigzagging before Patterson's face, landed on the panel and proceeded to crawl across it. Patterson watched it, squinted. Then he slammed down at it with a quick right hand. Missed.

Ten minutes later, his nerves still on edge, Patterson began the descent. He picked up the radio microphone—"Westchester tower . . . Cessna 2729 uniform . . . three miles northwest . . . land in one-six on final . . ."—and then, after an easy landing, he climbed quickly out of the cockpit and strode toward his wife's station wagon outside the terminal.

But along the way a small man smoking a cigar turned toward Patterson, waved at him, and said, "Say, excuse me, but aren't you . . . aren't you . . . Sonny Liston?"

Patterson stopped. He glared at the man, bewildered. He wasn't sure whether it was a joke or an insult, and he really did not know what to do.

"Aren't you Sonny Liston?" the man repeated, quite serious.

"No," Patterson said, quickly passing by the man, "I'm his brother."

When he reached Mrs. Patterson's car, he asked. "How much time till school lets out?"

"About fifteen minutes," she said, starting up the engine. Then she said, "Oh, Floyd, I just should have told Sister, I shouldn't have. . . ."

"*You* tell Sister; *I'll* tell the boys. . . ."

Mrs. Patterson drove as quickly as she could into Scarsdale, with Patterson shaking his head and telling Ted Hanson in the back, "Really can't understand these school kids. This is a religious school, and they want $20,000 for a glass window—and yet, some of them carry these racial prejudices, and it's mostly the Jews who are shoulder-to-shoulder with us, and. . . ."

"Oh, Floyd," cried his wife, "Floyd I have to get along here . . . you're not here, you don't live here, I . . . ."

She arrived at the school just as the bell began to ring. It was a modern building at the top of a hill, and on the lawn was the statue of a saint, and behind it a large white cross. "There's Jeannie," said Mrs. Patterson.

"Hurry, call her over here," Patterson said.

"Jeannie! Come over here, honey."

The little girl, wearing a blue school uniform and cap, and clasping books in front of her, came running down the path toward the station wagon.

"Jeannie," Floyd Patterson said, rolling down his window, "point out the boys who lifted your dress."

Jeannie turned and watched as several students came down the path; then she pointed to a tall, thin curly-haired boy walking with four other boys, all about twelve to fourteen years of age.

"Hey," Patterson called to him, "can I see you for a minute?"

All five boys came to the side of the car. They looked Patterson directly in the eye. They seemed not at all intimidated by him.

"You the one that's been lifting up my daughter's dress?" Patterson asked the boy who had been singled out.

"Nope," the boy said, casually.

"Nope?" Patterson said, caught off guard by the reply.

"Wasn't him, Mister," said another boy. "Probably was his little brother."

Patterson looked at Jeannie. But she was speechless, uncertain. The five boys remained there, waiting for Patterson to do something.

"Well, er, where's your little brother?" Patterson asked.

"Hey, kid!" one of the boys yelled. "Come over here."

A boy walked toward them. He resembled his older brother; he had freckles on his small, upturned nose, had blue eyes, dark curly hair and, as he approached the station wagon, he seemed equally unintimidated by Patterson.

"You been lifting up my daughter's dress?"

"Nope," the boy said.

"Nope!" Patterson repeated, frustrated.

"Nope, I wasn't lifting it. I was just touching it a little. . . ."

The other boys stood around the car looking down at Patterson, and other students crowded behind them, and nearby Patterson saw several white parents standing next to their parked cars; he became self-conscious, began to tap nervously with his fingers against the dashboard. He could not raise his voice without creating an unpleasant scene, yet could not retreat gracefully; so his voice went soft, and he said, finally:

"Look, boy, I want you to stop it. I won't tell your mother—that might get you in trouble—but don't do it again, okay?"

"Okay."

The boys calmly turned and walked, in a group, up the street.

Sandra Patterson said nothing. Jeannie opened the door, sat in the front seat next to her father, and took out a small blue piece of paper that a nun had given her and handed it across to Mrs. Patterson. But Floyd Patterson snatched it. He read it. Then he paused, put the paper down, and quietly announced, dragging out the words, *"She didn't do her religion. . . ."*

Patterson now wanted to get out of Scarsdale. He wanted to return to camp. After stopping at the Patterson home in Scarsdale and picking up Floyd Patterson, Jr., who is three, Mrs. Patterson drove them all back to the airport. Jeannie and Floyd, Jr., were seated in the back of the plane, and then Mrs. Patterson drove the station wagon alone up to camp, planning to return to Scarsdale that evening with the children.

It was four p.m. when Floyd Patterson got back to the camp, and the shadows were falling on the clubhouse, and on the tennis court routed by weeds, and on the big white house in front of which not a single automobile was parked. All was deserted and quiet; it was a loser's camp.

The children ran to play inside the clubhouse; Patterson walked slowly toward his apartment to dress for the workout.

"What could I do with those schoolboys?" he asked. "What can you do to kids of that age?"

It still seemed to bother him—the effrontery of the boys, the realization that he had somehow failed, the probability that, had those same boys heckled someone in Liston's family, the school yard would have been littered with limbs.

While Patterson and Liston both are products of the slum, and while both began as thieves, Patterson had been tamed in a special school with help from a gentle Negro spinster; later he became a Catholic convert, and learned not to hate. Still later he bought a dictionary, adding to his vocabulary such words as "vicissitude" and "enigma." And when he regained his championship from Johansson, he became the Great Black Hope of the Urban League.

He proved that it is not only possible to rise out of a Negro slum and succeed as a sportsman, but also to develop into an intelligent, sensitive, law-abiding citizen. In proving this, however, and in taking pride in it, Patterson seemed to lose part of himself. He lost part of his hunger, his anger—and as he walked up the steps into his apartment, he was saying, "I became the good guy. . . . After Liston won the title, I kept hoping that he would change into a good guy, too. That would have relieved me of the responsibility, and maybe I could have been more of the bad guy. But he didn't. . . . It's okay to be the good guy when you're winning. But when you're losing, it is no good being the good guy."

Patterson took off his shirt and trousers and, moving some books on the bureau to one side, put down his watch, his cuff links and a clip of bills.

"Do you do much reading?" he was asked.

"No," he said. "In fact, you know I've never finished reading a book in my whole life? I don't know why. I just feel that no writer today has anything for me; I mean, none of them has felt any more deeply than I have, and I have nothing to learn from them. Although Baldwin to me seems different from the rest. What's Baldwin doing these days?"

"He's writing a play. Anthony Quinn is supposed to have a part in it."

"Quinn?" Patterson asked.

"Yes."

"Quinn doesn't like me."

"Why?"

"I read or heard it somewhere; Quinn had been quoted as saying that my fight was disgraceful against Liston, and Quinn said something to the effect that he could have done better. People often say that—*they* could have done better! Well I think that if *they* had to fight, *they* couldn't even go through the experience of waiting for the fight to begin. They'd be up the whole night before, and would be drinking, or taking drugs. They'd probably get a heart attack. I'm sure that, if I was in the ring with Anthony Quinn, I could wear him out without even touching him. I would do nothing but pressure him, I'd stalk him, I'd stand close to him. I wouldn't touch him, but I'd wear him out and he'd collapse. But Anthony Quinn's an old man, isn't he?"

"In his forties."

"Well, anyway," Patterson said, "getting back to Baldwin, he seems like a wonderful guy. I've seen him on television and, before the Liston fight in Chicago, he came by my camp. You meet Baldwin on the street and you say, 'Who's this poor slob?'—he seems just like another guy; and this is the same impression *I* give people when they don't know me. But I think Baldwin and me, we have much in common, and some-day I'd just like to sit somewhere for a long time and talk to him. . . ."

Patterson, his trunks and sweat pants on, bent over to tie his shoelaces, and then, from a bureau drawer, took out a T-shirt across which was printed *Deauville*. He has several T-shirts bearing the same name. He takes good care of them. They are souvenirs from the high point of his life. They are from the Deauville Hotel in Miami Beach, which is where he trained for the third Ingemar Johansson match in March of 1961.

Never was Floyd Patterson more popular, more admired than during that winter. He had visited President Kennedy; he had been given a $35,000 jeweled crown by his manager; his greatness was conceded by sportswriters—and nobody had any idea that Patterson, secretly, was in possession of a false moustache and dark glasses that he intended to wear out of Miami Beach should he lose the third fight to Johansson.

It was after being knocked out by Johansson in their first fight that Patterson, deep in depression, hiding in humiliation for months in a remote Connecticut lodge, decided he could not face the public again if he lost. So he bought false whiskers and a moustache, and planned to wear them out of his dressing room after a defeat. He had also planned, in leaving his dressing room, to linger momentarily within the crowd and perhaps complain out loud about the fight. Then he would slip undiscovered through the night and into a waiting automobile.

Although there proved to be no need for bringing disguise into the second or third Johansson fights, or into a subsequent bout in Toronto against an obscure heavyweight named Tom McNeeley, Patterson brought it anyway; and, after the first Liston fight, he not only wore it during his thirty-hour automobile ride from Chicago to New York, but he also wore it while in an airliner bound for Spain.

"As I got onto this plane, you'd never have recognized me," he said. "I had on this beard, moustache, glasses and hat—and I also limped, to make myself look older. I was alone. I didn't care what plane I boarded; I just looked up and saw this sign at the terminal reading 'Madrid,' and so I got on that flight after buying a ticket.

"When I got to Madrid I registered at a hotel under the name 'Aaron Watson.' I stayed in Madrid about four or five days. In the daytime I wandered around to the poorer sections of the city, limping, looking at the people, and the people stared back at me and must have thought I was crazy because I was moving so slow and looked the way I did. I ate food in my hotel room. Although once I went to a restaurant and ordered soup. I hate soup. But I thought it was what old people would order. So I ate it. And after a week of this, I began to actually think I was somebody else. I began to believe it. And it is nice, every once in a while, being somebody else."

Patterson would not elaborate on how he managed to register under a name that did not correspond to his passport; he merely explained, "With money, you can do anything."

Now, walking slowly around the room, his black silk robe over his sweat clothes, Patterson said, "You must wonder what makes a man do things like this. Well, I wonder too. And the answer is, I don't know . . . but I think that within me, within every human being, there is a certain weakness. It is a weakness that exposes itself more when you're alone. And I have figured out that part of the reason I do the things I do, and cannot seem to conquer that one word—*myself*—is because . . . is because . . . I am a coward. . . ."

He stopped. He stood very still in the middle of the room, thinking about what he had just said, probably wondering whether he should have said it.

"I am a coward," he then repeated, softly. "My fighting has little to do with that fact, though. I mean you can be a fighter—and a *winning* fighter—and still be a coward. I was probably a coward on the night I won the championship back from Ingemar. And I remember another night, long ago, back when I was in the amateurs, fighting this big, tremendous man named Julius Griffin. I was only a hundred fifty-three pounds. I was petrified. It was all I could do to cross the ring. And then he came at me, and moved close to me . . . and from then on I don't know anything. I have no idea what happened. Only thing I know is, I saw him on the floor. And later somebody said, 'Man, I never saw anything like it. You just jumped up in the air, and threw thirty different punches. . . .' "

"When did you first think you were a coward?" he was asked.

"It was after the first Ingemar fight."

"How does one see this cowardice you speak of?"

"You see it when a fighter loses. Ingemar, for instance, is not a coward. When he lost the third fight in Miami, he was at a party later at the Fountainebleau. Had I lost, I couldn't have gone to that party. And I don't see how he did. . . ."

"Could Liston be a coward?"

"That remains to be seen," Patterson said. "We'll find out what he's like after somebody beats him, how he takes it. It's easy to do anything in victory. It's in defeat that a man reveals himself. In defeat I can't face people. I haven't the strength to say to people, 'I did my best, I'm sorry, and whatnot.' "

"Have you no hate left?"

"I have hated only one fighter," Patterson said. "And that was Ingemar in the second fight. I had been hating him for a whole year before that—not because he beat me in the first fight, but because of what he did after. It was all that boasting in public, and his showing off his right-hand punch on television, his thundering right, his 'toonder and lightning.' And I'd be home watching him on television, and *hating* him. It is a miserable feeling, hate. When a man hates, he can't have any peace of mind. And for one solid year I hated him because, after he took everything away from me, deprived me of everything I was, he *rubbed it in*. On the night of the second fight, in the dressing room, I couldn't wait until I got into the ring. When he was a little late getting into the ring, I thought, 'He's holding me up; he's trying to unsettle me—well, I'll get him!' "

"Why couldn't you hate Liston in the second match?"

Patterson thought for a moment, then said, "Look, if Sonny Liston walked into this room now and slapped me in the face, then you'd see a fight. You'd see the fight of your life because, then, a principle would be involved. I'd forget he was a human being. I'd forget I was a human being. And I'd fight accordingly."

"Could it be, Floyd, that you made a mistake in becoming a prize-fighter?"

"What do you mean?"

"Well, you say you're a coward; you say you have little capacity for hate; and you seemed to lose your nerve against those schoolboys in Scarsdale this afternoon. Don't you think you might have been better suited for some other kind of work? Perhaps a social worker, or. . . ."

"Are you asking why I continue to fight?"

"Yes."

"Well," he said, not irritated by the question, "first of all, I love boxing. Boxing has been good to me. And I might just as well ask you the question: 'Why do you write?' Or, 'Do you retire from writing every-time you write a bad story?' And as to whether I should have become a fighter in the first place, well, let's see how I can explain it. . . . Look, let's say you're a man who has been in an empty room for days and days without food . . . and then they take you out of that room and put you into another room where there's food hanging all over the place . . . and the first thing you reach for, you eat. When you're hungry, you're not choosy, and so I chose the thing that was closest to me. That was boxing. One day I just wandered into a gymnasium and boxed a boy. And I beat him. Then I boxed another boy. I beat him, too. Then I kept boxing. And winning. And I said, 'Here, finally, is something I can do!'

"Now I wasn't a sadist," he quickly added. "But I liked beating people because it was the only thing I could do. And whether boxing was a sport or not, I wanted to make it a sport because it was a thing I could succeed at. And what were the requirements? Sacrifice. That's all. To anybody who comes from the Bedford-Stuyvesant section of Brooklyn, sacrifice comes easy. And so I kept fighting, and one day I became heavyweight champion, and I got to know people like you. And you wonder how I can sacrifice, how I can deprive myself so much. You just don't realize where I've come from. You don't understand where I was when it began for me.

"In those days, when I was about eight years old, everything I got—I stole. I stole to survive, and I did survive, but I seemed to hate myself. My mother told me I used to point to a photograph of myself hanging in the bedroom and say, 'I don't like that boy!' One day my mother found three large X's scratched with a nail or something over that photograph of me. I don't remember doing it. But I do remember feeling like a parasite at home. I remember how awful I used to feel at night when my father, a longshoreman, would come home so tired that, as my mother fixed food before him, he would fall asleep at the table because he was that tired. I would always take his shoes off and clean his feet. That was my job. And I felt so bad because here I was, not going to school, doing nothing, just watching my father come home; and on Friday nights it was even worse. He would come home with his pay, and he'd put every nickel of it on the table so my mother could buy food for all the children. I never wanted to be around to see that. I'd run and hide. And then I decided to leave home and start stealing—and I did. And I would never come home unless I brought something that I had stolen. Once I remember I broke into a dress store and stole a whole mound of dresses, at two a.m., and here I was, this little kid, carrying all those dresses over the wall, thinking they were all the same size, my mother's size, and thinking the cops would never notice me walking down the street with all those dresses piled over my head. They did, of course. . . . I went to the Youth House. . . ."

Floyd Patterson's children, who had been playing outside all this time around the country club, now became restless and began to call him, and Jeannie started to pound on his door. So Patterson picked up his leather bag, which contained his gloves, his mouthpiece and adhesive tape, and walked with the children across the path toward the clubhouse.

He flicked on the light switches behind the stage near the piano. Beams of amber streaked through the dimly lit room and flashed onto the ring. Then he walked to one side of the room, outside the ring. He took off his robe, shuffled his feet in the rosin, skipped rope, and then began to shadowbox in front of the spit-stained mirror, throwing out quick combinations of lefts, rights, lefts, rights, each jab followed by a *"hegh-hegh-hegh-hegh."* Then, his gloves on, he moved to the punching bag in the far corner, and soon the room reverberated to his rhythmic beat against the bobbling bag—rat-tat-tat-*tetteta,* rat-tat-tat-*tetteta,* rat-tat-tat-*tetteta,* rat-tat-tat-*tetteta!*

The children, sitting on pink leather chairs moved from the bar to the fringe of the ring, watched him in awe, sometimes flinching at the force of his pounding against the leather bag.

And this is how they would probably remember him years from now: a dark, solitary, glistening figure punching in the corner of a forlorn spot at the bottom of a mountain where people once came to have fun—until the clubhouse became unfashionable, the paint began to peel, and Negroes were allowed in.

As Floyd Patterson continued to bang away with lefts and rights, his gloves a brown blur against the bag, his daughter slipped quietly off her chair and wandered past the ring into the other room. There, on the other side of the bar and beyond a dozen round tables, was the stage. She climbed onto the stage and stood behind a microphone, long dead, and cried out, imitating a ring announcer, "Ladieeees and gentlemen . . . tonight we present. . . ."

She looked around, puzzled. Then, seeing that her little brother had followed her, she waved him up to the stage and began again: "Ladiees and gentlemen . . . tonight we present . . . *Floydie Patterson.* . . ."

Suddenly, the pounding against the bag in the other room stopped.

There was silence for a moment. Then Jeannie, still behind the microphone and looking down at her brother, said, "Floydie, come up here!"

"No," he said.

"Oh, come up here!"

"*No,*" he cried.

Then Floyd Patterson's voice, from the other room, called: "Cut it out. . . . I'll take you both for a walk in a minute."

He resumed punching—rat-tat-tat-*tetteta*—and they returned to his side. But Jeannie interrupted, asking, "Daddy, how come you sweating?"

"Water fell on me," he said, still pounding.

"Daddy," asked Floyd, Jr., "how come you spit water on the floor before?"

"To get it out of my mouth."

He was about to move over to the heavier punching bag when the sound of Mrs. Patterson's station wagon could be heard moving up the road.

Soon she was in Patterson's apartment cleaning up a bit, patting the pillows, washing the teacups that had been left in the sink. One hour later the family was having dinner together. They were together for two more hours; then, at ten p.m., Mrs. Patterson washed and dried all of the dishes, and put the garbage out in the can—where it would remain until the raccoons and skunks got to it.

And then, after helping the children with their coats and walking out to the station wagon and kissing her husband good-bye, Mrs. Patterson began the drive down the dirt road toward the highway. Patterson waved once, and stood for a moment watching the taillights go. and then he turned and walked slowly back toward the house.

The Soft Psyche
of Joshua Logan

The theatre lights dimmed, and the jewels in the audience sparkled like a city seen at night from an airplane; then the music began, the curtain went up, and row upon row of bow ties settled, like a flutter of black butterflies, into their seats. It was the premier performance of *Mr. President* and, though the road reviews were disastrous and the show was unimproved at this Broadway opening, the audience rushed backstage at the final curtain with their furs and first-night faces to greet the director, Joshua Logan, with *"Dah*-ling, it was *mah*velous!" . . . "Joshua, congratulations!" . . . "Wonderful, Josh, wonderful!"

He knew they did not mean it, and *they* knew they did not mean it, but very little truth is exchanged backstage on opening nights; the newspaper critics panned the show, with one, John McClain of the *Journal-American,* asking: "Whatever became of the unerring hand of Mr. Logan?"

The unerring hand, Mr. Logan would have liked to have replied, had been tied behind his back by his associates during rehearsals, but such a disclosure would be to no avail and hardly gracious; and so here he was, in the Fall of 1962, stung successively by three critical flops (the two others being *All American* and *There Was a Little Girl*), knowing that his next Broadway play, opening in eight weeks, had better be good. Already there was talk around Sardi's that his directorial taste was lost in vulgarity, and some of his friends noticed with concern the increasing pressure he was subjecting himself to with *Tiger Tiger Burning Bright*. In 1941 and 1953, he had spent time in mental institutions.

From the very first week of *Tiger's* rehearsals, at the Booth Theatre on Forty-fifth Street, there was tension, strange reactions and uncertainty, and the actors—all but one of them Negroes—seemed suspicious of Logan and envious of each other's roles. Claudia McNeil, the star of *Tiger,* an enormous woman, very dark, glared silently each day at Logan, measuring him, seeming to possess in her attitude the secret of his weakness and the power to destroy him; and Joshua Logan, at fifty-four, white-haired, white-mustached, big and broadshouldered but somehow soft and very pale, stood in front of the Negro cast of this play about a mother who dominates her children in a dream world she has created in Louisiana—a play that gradually, as rehearsals progressed, churned up more and more memories for Logan, haunting memories of his days in Mansfield, Louisiana, on his grandfather's cotton plantation, where, in his boyhood dreams, he often saw himself as a strong man riding through the streets of Mansfield standing on a horse, arms folded high across his chest. In real life, young Joshua Logan had recognized in himself not the slightest resemblance to his imaginary masculine hero.

He saw himself as a flabby and effete boy who, since his father's early death, was reared on his maternal grandfather's plantation under the almost claustrophobic attention of females. There was his sister, Mary Lee, endlessly worrying about him; his Negro nurse, Amy Lane, often mad at him but always watching him through the kitchen window and saying, "Mah, he walkin' jes like ole Judge Logan!"; and there was his mother, Susan, who dressed him prettily, read him poetry, and tried to divert him from all that was crude or vulgar. One afternoon in the middle of a Biblical movie, just before Judith of Bethulia sliced off the head of Holofernes, Susan Logan, not wanting Joshua to see it, blocked his view by pushing him under the seat; then she whispered, sharply, "Think of a field of yellow daisies . . . think of a field of yellow daisies!"

Susan Logan was an elegant, genteel lady of the Old South whose family, like that of her late first husband's (he was also named Joshua Lockwood Logan), had originally settled in South Carolina. The first Joshua Lockwood had come to America from County Kent, England, and died sixteen miles outside of Charleston in the middle 1700's. While carrying his remains for burial to Charleston, the cortege was attacked by a pack of wolves and was compelled to bury his bones by the roadside nine miles from Charleston, and the widow was so shocked that she quickly returned to England. But some years later one of her sons, also named Joshua, returned to Charleston, and here his family later enjoyed a congeniality with two other Charleston families, the Logans and the Lees, and subsequently there was intermarriage; so today, Susan, descendant from the Lees, is not only the mother of the Broadway director, she is also his cousin.

By the 1830's some branches of the Lockwoods, Lees and Logans had moved from South Carolina down into Alabama, and a generation later others moved into northwest Louisiana, where Susan's father settled on a cotton plantation, into which she moved upon the death of her husband with her three-year-old son, Joshua, her infant daughter, Mary Lee, and that ruler of the rear of the house, Amy Lane.

Susan despised Mansfield; it was an uncultured, wide-open pioneer town of feuds and barroom brawls, having none of the tradition of the Old South, the Charleston of her dreams, but reeking instead of the Wild West, with its heavy accent on bad manners and maleness. Susan tried, as best she could, to see that none of the crudity of this town infected Joshua, and she succeeded even though one day, perhaps when a circus was moving into town, there suddenly registered in Joshua the image of the man riding through Mansfield standing up on a horse—a marvelous man, perfectly balanced; a free man, ignoring the reins.

As Joshua Lockwood Logan approached his teens, his grandfather began to complain that Susan was making the boy into a sissy. Joshua adored his grandfather ("I put Tabasco in my milk to please him") and soon became a superb swimmer, a subscriber to the Charles Atlas body-building course, and, at Culver Military Academy in Indiana—which Joshua attended because of his mother's remarriage in 1917 to Colonel Howard F. Noble, an administrator there—he also became trained as a boxer. Encouraged by Colonel Noble, to whom Joshua later dedicated his play, *The Wisteria Trees,* he trained hard in the ring, eventually winning the boxing title of the platoon, the company, the battalion, and finally the regiment. But every time he won, and had his hand held high in victory, Joshua would moan to himself, "Oh, God!"—the triumph meaning he had to fight somebody else, and he hated it.

After Culver there was Princeton, a school selected by Joshua's mother because it was "nice" and "there would be less drinking there"; and after Princeton, where he became president of the Triangle Club, and after a trip to Moscow where he studied for six months under Stanislavski, Joshua Logan settled in New York and embarked on a career as a theatrical director. When Colonel Noble died, Joshua's mother drove up to New York and moved in with him; and later, when he was directing two shows at once—one in New Jersey by night, the other in New York by day—his mother would greet him at Pennsylvania Station each morning with a pint of fruit juice. "The only way Josh could get away from his mother," said a friend who knew him very well, "was through the door of an insane asylum—a door that locked."

After his first mental breakdown in 1941, from sheer exhaustion and dejection over his work, he recovered in a Philadelphia sanitarium and, by 1942, was back on Broadway directing a successful show, *By Jupiter.* In 1953, while rehearsing *Kind Sir* and battling simultaneously with agents and lawyers over the film rights to Michener's novel, *Sayonara,* Logan had another breakdown; a year later, he had recovered and had another hit, *Fanny.*

Now, almost nine years later, in these daily rehearsals of *Tiger Tiger Burning Bright,* adapted for the stage by Peter S. Feibleman from his novel, *A Place Without Twilight,* Joshua Logan discovered that he was becoming so emotionally involved with the script, and identifying so strongly with its characters—and at the same time becoming intimidated by the actors, especially by Claudia McNeil, who he felt was acting like Amy Lane—that it seemed he might be involved once again with Mansfield, the source of his old wounds and boyhood complexities; a trip, one might assume, that he could ill afford to make. He needed the success of this play, and he had many obligations, both mundane and financial; he and his wife, Nedda, had two adopted children in private school; there was the upkeep on his fabulous apartment on the East River, and his directorial staff, and his film company, his chauffeur, his cook, his psychiatrist that he visits five mornings a week, his big Connecticut home with its sprawling grounds and magnificently manicured gardens. Though Logan earns in the neighborhood of $500,000 a year, it somehow seems barely enough and one evening after a hard day's rehearsal of *Tiger,* Logan left the theatre and said, wearily, "I work for gardens and psychiatrists."

He went easy on the actors. When they fumbled their lines, he remained patient. He gave them the benefit of his knowledge of "Southwestern" diction—"down there they pronounce it '*LOU*-iz-iana,' not 'Lou-e-*ZEE*-ana' "—and he would relieve the tension (or, at least, try) by telling anecdotes about past Broadway shows he directed, about Mary Martin in *South Pacific,* and about *Mister Roberts,* all the while speaking with warmth, and admitting that he did not yet know all the answers about how to stage *Tiger,* and welcoming any actor's suggestions at any time. "I'm not a puppeteer," he would tell them. "I am simply an editor, a sort of audience, and a friend, a sort of encourager that nobody should be scared of—or *angry* at."

Then, in the second week of rehearsals, things got worse. Parts of the first act were rewritten, the actors had to learn new lines and forget old ones, and they were disappointed that the role of the male lead, the prowling son who is to symbolize the tiger cat, went to Alvin Ailey, a dancer. Even some of Logan's associates, who sat in the dark theatre each day watching, were becoming uneasy.

"Goddamit, Josh, that Alvin just doesn't move like a tiger!"

"No," Logan admitted, "he's Nijinsky."

"For that part you need a black Brando."

"Yes," said Logan.

"We open in three weeks."

"Christ!" said Feibleman.

"Oh, don't worry," said Oliver Smith, the co-producer.

"I *am* worried," said Logan.

The next day, after Ailey had played a sultry scene with the curvaceous, hip-swinging Diana Sands, he suddenly flew across the stage and buried his face in a corner behind the curtain. There was silence for a second. Then, slowly, the theatre began to echo with what sounded like high, howling laughter; then, more quickly, the laughter dissolved into uncontrollable, almost hysterical sobbings. Everybody was stunned; nobody moved—neither on the stage nor in the orchestra.

Finally, Peter Feibleman, who had been sitting near the back of the theatre, came rushing down the aisle to Logan, sitting in the seventh row.

"Josh," Feibleman whispered, "you better do something."

"What can *I* do?" Logan said, running his hand through his long white hair. "He'll just have to get it out of him."

"I want the Miltown concession on this play," said Joe Curtis, one of Logan's assistants, sitting across the aisle.

"Trouble is," Logan said, "I'll take it all." Then, shaking his head as Ailey's sobbing continued, with Claudia McNeil now comforting him, Logan said to Curtis, "You know, I'm getting a real vicarious pleasure out of this. Alvin's doing just what I want to do—just lie down and cry!"

Still Logan, Feibleman and Oliver Smith all thought Ailey could do the part; he certainly *looked* the part, they agreed, possessing a muscular body that seemed more powerful than Sonny Liston's; and besides, it was a little late to be shopping around for a new tiger. Logan felt that, if the book were stronger, the actors would feel more secure; so for the next three days Logan disappeared with Feibleman in a little room off-stage and reworked the book—removing some of Feibleman's literary flavor in the spots where Logan felt the audience would want action.

"Where the hell *is* Logan?" Claudia McNeil grumbled, on the third morning of rehearsing lines under the production stage manager, David Gray, Jr. Claudia was still furious at Logan for having left the theatre at midafternoon earlier in the week without having "the courtesy, the respect" to let her know he'd not return that day; now, with Logan working elsewhere on the script and ignoring the acting completely, Claudia was smoldering. With the other actors gathered around her offstage, as in a family scene in the play itself, she roared: "Logan should be here! We ain't gettin' no direction."

"And our reputations are at stake," Diana Sands said.

"His is, too!" Claudia snapped. "He doesn't realize it, but if he thinks he's going blame this one on me if it's a flop, well, he ain't; I'll just get on that phone and call Sally Hammond over at the *Post,* or that guy at the *Tribune*—what'shisname? one that married that actress? Morgenstern, that's it—and I'll tell 'em the whole story, about how we have to come here and listen to nine of his jokes, and all about *LOU*-iz-iana, and then he don't show up for three days!"

The others nodded, and she went on, "All this rewriting should be done at night! What the hell does he do at night? *Sheet!* People gonna look at me and think I shot my bolt in *Raisin in the Sun* and have nothing new to offer; well, that ain't fair. . . . I got enough trouble, working with a lot of kids in this show, and carrying the responsibility for my whole race, being in the theatre thirty years, and this man Logan don't even show up! *Sheet!*"

A few minutes later, the door swung open, and in walked Logan, followed by Peter Feibleman, who was carrying fresh, revised pages of Act I. As Logan waved and walked down the side steps off the stage toward the orchestra, Claudia watched him go up the aisle toward the back of the theatre, and she waited; within ten minutes, she saw her chance.

In the middle of one of her monologues, Claudia caught a glimpse of Logan whispering to Feibleman. It was as if she were Amy Lane catching Joshua's little hand in the cookie jar. Flaring up, Claudia bellowed to Oliver Smith, the co-producer, sitting alone about nine rows back, *"Mr. Logan is talking! And I can't go on!"*

"I am *not* talking," Logan yelled from the back, his voice tense and angry.

"You *were* talking," Claudia said. "I could hear what you were saying!"

"I was *not* talking," he insisted. "Somebody else was talking. It was *not* me!"

"YOU were talking!" she shouted, hunching her big shoulders and blazing her big eyes at him. "And you spoiled the meter of my speech!"

"Look," Logan said, stomping down the aisle toward where Oliver Smith sat, "I do not want any more rages from *you!*"

"You're in a rage, not me!" she said.

"Well, I'm not going to stand for this!"

"You want me to leave?" she asked, challengingly.

"Look," he said, more softly, "everybody here is trying to get this play. I cannot s-t-a-n-d these outrages. What do you want us to do, close the show?"

Claudia now turned, hunched her shoulders again, and paced back and forth.

"Now," Logan said, trying to get things moving again, noticing that the rest of the cast was standing in almost fixed, dumb-struck poses on the stage. "Now, why don't you go back further and begin again?"

"I *can't* begin," she said, casually. "You spoiled my meter."

"O-h-h-h, Oliver," Logan groaned, his hand on his forehead, "I can't stand these rages!"

"Well," she shot in, "that's *your* problem."

"You're my problem!" Logan screamed.

Now, everybody in the theatre was squirming. Fortunately, Claudia did not answer him; she just shuffled around a bit, like a sumo wrestler waiting for the decision; in the prolonged silence, things calmed a bit, and Claudia did her monologue and David Gray yelled "Curtain," and everybody sighed. There was a break.

Standing outside the Booth Theatre, his hands in his pockets and the cold breezes of autumn whistling through his long white hair, Joshua Logan said, "Right now I'm allowing Claudia McNeil to do a lot of things just because I trust her, and admire her creative talent, and do not want to freeze that talent, and yet I know I have a block with her.

"You see," he said, "Amy Lane, every once in a while, would get mad and her face would turn grey. When Amy Lane was happy her face was brown, sometimes purple; but she used to scare me when she was mad; and when she was happy she used to help me, dress me, tie up my shoelaces and do my buttonholes; and now I've got this show, and a sort of Amy Lane that every once in a while turns grey. And I want to help her—I've *got* to help her—figure out the creative shoelaces and buttonholes. And sometimes I wonder if I'm strong enough to do that."

He walked around a bit more, inhaling deeply along Shubert Alley next to the theatre. "It's funny," he finally said, "but somehow I'm actually happy doing this play. Maybe it's the Negroes. Somehow, in a small way, I'm making up for . . . for how they have been made to feel. I don't know. But *something* must be making me happy. I remember, as a child, wanting to *be* a Negro; I remember their sweetness, their gentle voices, and mostly their freedom—they were free to run and run without shoes, without clothes, they didn't have to be clean, didn't have to go to church three times a week. They did not have, in the modern term, to conform. In a sense," he said, slowly, "they ruled *us*—kind of kept us in our place; they were more powerful, the power of the weak; only they weren't weak, they had the power of servility."

Now he was back in the dark theatre, the lights of the stage beaming on the actors going through a scene in the garden of their Louisiana shack; Claudia McNeil's voice was now softer because she had had a touch of laryngitis a few days before. But at the end of the scene, she raised her voice to its full power, and Logan, in a pleasant tone, said, "Don't strain your voice, Claudia."

She did not respond, only whispered to another actor on stage.

"Don't raise your voice, Claudia," Logan repeated.

She again ignored him.

"C L A U D I A!" Logan yelled, "don't you give me that actor's vengeance, Claudia!"

"Yes, Mr. Logan," she said with a soft, sarcastic edge.

"I've had enough of this today, Claudia."

"Yes, Mr. Logan."

"And stop Yes-Mr.-Logan-ing me."

"Yes, Mr. Logan."

"You're a shockingly rude woman!"

"Yes, Mr. Logan."

"You're being a beast."

"Yes, Mr. Logan."

"Yes, Miss Beast."

"Yes, Mr. Logan."

"Yes, Miss Beast!"

Suddenly, Claudia McNeil stopped. It dawned on her that he was calling her a beast; now her face was grey and her eyes were cold, and her voice almost solemn as she said, "You . . . called . . . me . . . out . . . of . . . my . . . name!"

"Oh, God!" Logan smacked his forehead with his hand.

"You . . . called . . . me . . . out . . . of . . . my . . . name."

She stood there, rocklike, big and angry, waiting for him to do something.

"Oliver!" Logan said, turning toward the co-producer, who had lowered his wiry, long body into his chair as if he were in a foxhole. He did not want to be cornered into saying something that might offend Logan, his old friend, but neither did he want Claudia McNeil to come barreling down the aisle and possibly snap his thin frame in half.

"Oliver," Logan went on, "I just don't know what to do with her. She's like some empress up there, or something. . . ."

"You're the empress!" she bolted back.

"All right, all right, I'm the empress," Logan said, too weary to argue about it. "What do we do now?"

"Get yourself another actress," she said.

"All right, fine," Logan said. "Fine," he repeated. "We can close the show, and, we can. . . ." Now he was walking up the aisle, and it seemed that he might be leaving the theatre.

"Look," Claudia quickly said. He stopped.

"Look," she began again, realizing that if this show closed *she* would be the reason for all the other actors' unemployment, "I . . . I gotta man at home I can get mad at . . . and I been in the theatre thirty years . . . and nobody is ever going to point a finger at me that I walked off a show . . . and. . . ."

She went on like this, and Logan knew he had her; he could have played with her a while, letting her sweat it out, but he didn't. Instead he walked toward the stage, climbed it, and then, faster now, he moved toward Claudia and, arms outstretched, moved into her, his white mustache pressing against her cheek—and then, dramatically, her big, black arms lashed around the back of his white shirt and pulled him close.

They were almost tearful in their reunion, these two big, soft figures under the lights; they suddenly were spent, and the cast gathered around and whistled, hollered and clapped.

Then, cheerfully, Claudia pulled back and, grinning as she shook her fist, said, "But when this show is over, I'm gonna hit you in the mouth *so-o-o hard!*"

"When this show is over," he laughed back, "you won't be able to catch me!"

"I'll catch you," she promised.

"You'll need a long reach," he said, "because I'll be *gone!*"

After this scene, the show improved tremendously in the final two weeks. Nobody was saying it was going to be a hit; but they *were* saying it would at least open. Claudia was not sure if Logan would condone another shooting match, so she calmed down. Logan, of course, did not look for trouble. If, while Claudia was rehearsing on stage, he wished to get some fresh air, he did not leave by way of the stage door (where she might see him) but would often slip through the darkness near the back of the theatre—an operation that meant he had to unhinge four latches and a lock and move quietly, in the manner he might have sneaked out of the house in Mansfield, hoping Amy Lane would not hear. On returning, he would be just as quiet; Claudia would be onstage but would not hear him: he was safe.

In addition to the improved relations between Logan and Claudia, the script was much better and Alvin Ailey had mastered the difficult tiger role, because he got control of himself, partly through Logan's help. Al Freeman, Jr.'s portrayal of Ailey's weak brother produced some fine comic acting, and the play was also strengthened by two late additions—Roscoe Lee Browne, who played the sinister clergyman who blackmails Ailey, and Paul Barry, the only white actor in the show, who won the part of a seedy Louisiana redneck over five other actors, one of them an old acquaintance of Joshua Logan's from *Mister Roberts*. Logan greeted his *Roberts* friend warmly, but soon realized that the actor was portraying a redneck as if he were a Naval officer, and so Logan shook his hand—"Thanks, Bob, but I think, chemically, and from the point of view of age, you're not right for the part"—and then said to Feibleman, "You can't go back, can you, Peter?"

"You sure can't, Josh," Feibleman said, quietly.

But if Logan were able to go back, there is no doubt it would be to the days of *Mister Roberts,* which he described as those "high, happy times" with that tragic young novelist, Thomas Heggen. They got along famously as co-authors of the play, Logan said, because "I was a corpulent manic depressive and Heggen was a thin manic depressive." Sprawled out one night on a red, yellow and blue rug that Nedda had bought at a Bridgeport junk shop, Logan and Heggen dashed off the whole second act in one hilarious session. The show ran on Broadway for 1,157 performances.

These were the days when Howard Lindsay declared that Logan was a "genius" and when the late Oscar Hammerstein II said Logan was blessed with everything a great director should have—a good eye for pictorial composition and movement, an ear for dialogue and diction, a charm that keeps a big company working happily together, a talent for analyzing a script and improving it by criticism and revision. Playwright Paul Osborn then said that Logan could not "walk along a street and watch a kid pick a cigarette butt up out of the gutter without wanting to grab the kid and tell him to pick it up better."

Then, in May, 1949, Heggen, who was unable to get his own writing going again, drowned in his bathtub. He was twenty-nine years old. But Logan has still tried to hold onto the memory of the glorious days of *Mister Roberts*. He named his son Thomas Heggen Logan, and he still keeps the old red, yellow and blue rug from the junk shop in an honored place within his Connecticut home.

Logan has had many triumphs since then—*South Pacific, The Wisteria Trees, Picnic*—but he still looks back on *Mister Roberts* as the high point, and still says, slowly and rather sadly, "That was the happiest time of my life."

In 1953 Logan was back in Louisiana to open *Kind Sir* in New Orleans, and was battling at the same time to get the screen rights to *Sayonara,* and then, almost too suddenly to know how it all happened, he found himself one day back in Mansfield. He wandered about the old plantation. He looked at the wisteria tree that his grandfather had been unable to chop down. Then, not quite realizing what he was doing, Joshua Logan crawled back into "Jolly Den," the playhouse that his grandfather had built long ago for Joshua and Mary Lee. Then Logan drove back to New Orleans. He committed himself to De Paul Hospital.

"You ask if I shall finally be able to stop going to the psychiatrist," he said, walking across Third Avenue toward his apartment one evening a week before the opening of *Tiger Tiger Burning Bright*. "Well, I don't really know. You ask what's the matter with me, what it is that keeps me from being satisfied or completely happy, or smug, or completely serene about my life, and I think it is something that happened to me when I was a young boy and set a standard for myself that I could never live up to. I could never be as good as I wanted to be—would never ride through Mansfield standing on a horse with my arms folded high in front of me."

This does not mean that Logan has failed to make *some* peace with himself in his later years; for one thing, he said, almost proudly, "I have finally stopped being a shit-kicker. Know what a shit-kicker is, don't you? That's one of those modest bastards, those falsely modest, aw-shucks guys"—and he demonstrated by walking, hands in pockets, head down, with feet dragging. No, he is by no means modest, he said, even though his mother is a bit disappointed in him, and once, after he had reminded her that he was a Pulitzer Prize winner (for *South Pacific*) she reminded him that *that* was for a collaboration—letting him know she knew the difference between a man who could win such a prize, and a man who could ride the horse *alone*.

"Anyway," Logan went on, "I know what I can do. I know I have the ability to organize accident. I know I can pump people full of confidence. I can reassure a person who is in doubt. I know that every artist is in despair, and to allow them more despair would kill hope, and so I try to bring hope and banish despair. When I feel it coming on, I will it away, when I can—I not always can—but I know if I should panic in the midst of a big production, then the production would fall apart. I have directed people who, they say, couldn't be directed, such as Marilyn Monroe, and I knew she needed affection, respect, love and care, and so that's what I did, and no matter how her panic showed, I never let it make me angry or impatient.

"But," he continued, now more slowly, thinking more deeply, "I think if I were free of whatever it is—if I were free-r—I think I could write . . . and write more than Marcel Proust . . . couldn't *stop* writing. But it is as though it were all dammed up to here," he said, gripping his throat with his left hand, "and I have a theory—*just* a theory—that if I wrote, it would please my mother *too much*. It would be what she wanted. And maybe . . . maybe *then* I'd become like my father. And I would die."

Now Logan was silent the rest of the way home. Then, on the fourteenth floor, the locale of his grand apartment overlooking the East River, he was greeted at the door by the butler and, in the next room, by Nedda, an erect, smiling, lovely woman who was his leading lady in one of his first big Broadway hits, *Charley's Aunt,* and who has remained constant through all his good and bad days. While Logan went into the other room for a moment, Nedda talked about their seventeen years of marriage that began, on December 8, 1945, with a civil ceremony in Greenwich, Connecticut; then they drove back to New York to inform Susan, who said, according to Nedda, "Well, isn't that lovely. Let us have a little glass of sherry."

In those days Nedda had been living at the Hotel Lombardy, on 111 East 56th Street, while Joshua's mother was at 102 East 56th Street; now, Nedda said, with her address being 435 East 52nd, Joshua's mother was at 424 East 52nd. "I am exactly the same distance from Mrs. Noble now as I was then," Nedda said, smiling as only a good actress can.

When Joshua returned to the room, and realized the conversation had gotten back to his mother, he joined Nedda in telling their favorite Susan Noble stories. Joshua recalled that once he received a letter from her telling him that one of his relatives had just been drafted, and was being sent to Fort Bragg, North Carolina, and how nice it was for the drafted relation to be in North Carolina "at rhododendron time."

And Nedda recalled a family trip they all made a few years ago to Charleston, during which a visit was made to the cemeteries where the earlier Lockwoods, Lees and Logans were buried. Upon seeing these familiar names on the gravestones, these names she had so long worshiped, Susan suddenly was as graceful as a young ballerina, picking her way delicately and joyously and whirling around; finally, seeing Nedda with a camera, Susan pulled Josh toward her and asked Nedda to shoot a picture of the two of them standing next to the tomb of a very special ancestor. "Stand *here, Josh . . .* over *here,"* Susan snapped, because Josh was too far from the gravestone, *"here* next to Dorothea . . . she's the important one; *she's* the one that makes us cousins!"

They told other stories about Susan, too, and Josh concluded, "Oh, she'll fascinate you!"

"She's seventy-six," said Nedda, "and she'll outlive us all."

"You *should* meet her," Logan said.

A few days later, on one of New York's most unseasonably warm autumn days, Susan Noble opened the door of her apartment. Behind her, under the mantel, a big fire was blazing. "Good moan-nin." She smiled. "I hope you don't mind the fa'ar."

She was a remarkable-looking woman, not seeming much older than fifty, with grey-blue eyes, a trim figure, and hair that was still black streaked with grey, and pulled back from her face, which was soft, gentle and vivacious. In the vestibule hung a portrait of Colonel Noble, straight-spined in military splendor; on another wall, a print by William Blake, and, in the living room, there was furniture from the South—from the plantation, some of it in the family for several generations. After pouring coffee and serving cookies, she displayed, on request, that which she treasures, the family album, and in no time at all her alert eyes were sparkling, her hand was moving softly over the pages, and her voice was dramatically rich.

"Look," she said, smiling at the little figure of Joshua in a colonial outfit, "pink satin. See! I did the coat. . . . And *here* is little May-rey. . . . And this was my mother's voice teacher. Wasn't she pretty? . . . And this, now *this* was my great-aunt. . . . And look at that dapper! Oh, I just adore that man, one of my cousins, Henry Lee! . . . And now this, this is Grandfather Lee, John Bachman Lee, named after old Dr. John Bachman, you know, a friend of Audubon, with many birds named Bachman. . . . And this, sitting next to John McHenry Nabors, is Nimrod, the dog named for that great hunter in the Bible . . ."—and then, at the mention of her father, she paused. "He thought I was pulling Josh too hard, but Josh grew up loving beauty. My father felt I was making Josh into a sissy, but that was not true. He was a *man*—a *man* from the time he was a child. And I did all I could to make him a man. That's all I *could* do! I couldn't play baseball. But," she said, "I also felt that a man has a right to that which is beautiful in life."

Then she glanced down at the book again. "Look," she said, her eyes once more sparkling, "there's Caroline Dorothy Logan, Josh's great-great-grandmother. . . . And here, here's Josh again! . . . And here, I believe, is Nedda. . . ."

On Saturday night, December 22, outside the Booth Theatre, all dressed up—as in a picture album—they came to see *Tiger Tiger Burning Bright*. There was Susan Noble arriving early . . . and next Nedda, in a fur cape and red satin dress . . . and Logan's assistant, Joe Curtis . . . and Oliver Smith . . . and Peter Feibleman, a white carnation in his trimly tailored tuxedo . . . and there was Richard Rodgers and Carson McCullers and Geoffrey Holder and Santha Rama Rau. . . .

"Where's Josh?" Roger Stevens, the co-producer, asked Nedda.

"102 degrees," she said.

He was in bed in his apartment, alone except for the children; he was, for the first time he could remember, sick on opening night. He was very pale and very quiet, and he spoke about a trip to Acapulco that he,

Nedda and the two children would take after Christmas. After that, he was not sure what he wanted to do. There were movies. There were other shows. But he did not know. It had been a tough year. He went on like this, talking softly, until eleven, when the telephone rang.

"Darling," said Nedda, her voice coming through over the clinking of glasses from Sardi's, "darling, Dick Rodgers wants to speak with you."

"Hello, Josh?"

"Hello, Dick!"

"Now, listen, Josh, this thing you got here tonight, no crap, Josh, it was marvelous!"

Logan seemed unable to speak.

"Really!" Rodgers went on, "I think it's the best job you've done in many years, Josh. It was brilliant! Can't tell you how much I enjoyed it!"

"Oh, Dick." Logan seemed almost happy enough for tears. "Thank you, Dick . . . thank you. . . ."

Then Nedda was back on the phone, then Feibleman, then Oliver Smith, and then others—all saying that the premiere of *Tiger* was a thing of beauty which the audience loved.

Since there was a New York newspaper strike then, Logan got the reviews over television while sitting in bed: Walter Kerr of the *Herald-Tribune* liked some parts, not others; Howard Taubman of the *Times* was ecstatic, giving it possibly his warmest review of the year; the other reviews varied, but one television announcer summed them up as "respectful."

This is all Logan had hoped for. Something respectful. He did not need the big, box-office smash; he'd had plenty of those. And what he *did* want, he suspected he might never get.

Well, at least he had stopped being a shit-kicker; and—who knows? Soon some new young genius might come up with another *Mister Roberts*. So Logan settled back in the big bed waiting for Nedda. Three days later he, Nedda and the children left for Acapulco.

And after thirty-three performances, the play closed.

The Silent Season
of a Hero

"I would like to take the great DiMaggio fishing," the old man said. "They say his father was a fisherman. Maybe he was as poor as we are and would understand."

—Ernest Hemingway, *The Old Man and the Sea*

It was not quite spring, the silent season before the search for salmon, and the old fishermen of San Francisco were either painting their boats or repairing their nets along the pier or sitting in the sun talking quietly among themselves, watching the tourists come and go, and smiling, now, as a pretty girl paused to take their picture. She was about twenty-five, healthy and blue-eyed and wearing a red turtle-neck sweater, and she had long, flowing blonde hair that she brushed back a few times before clicking her camera. The fishermen, looking at her, made admiring comments but she did not understand because they spoke a Sicilian dialect; nor did she notice the tall grey-haired man in a dark suit who stood watching her from behind a big bay window on the second floor of Di-Maggio's Restaurant that overlooks the pier.

He watched until she left, lost in the crowd of newly arrived tourists that had just come down the hill by cable car. Then he sat down again at the table in the restaurant, finishing his tea and lighting another cigarette, his fifth in the last half hour. It was eleven-thirty in the morning. None of the other tables was occupied, and the only sounds came from the bar where a liquor salesman was laughing at something the headwaiter had said. But then the salesman, his briefcase under his arm, headed for the door, stopping briefly to peek into the dining room and call out, "See you later, Joe." Joe DiMaggio turned and waved at the salesman. Then the room was quiet again.

At fifty-one, DiMaggio was a most distinguished-looking man, aging as gracefully as he had played on the ball field, impeccable in his tailoring, his nails manicured, his six-foot two-inch body seeming as lean and capable as when he posed for the portrait that hangs in the restaurant and shows him in Yankee Stadium swinging from the heels at a pitch thrown twenty years ago. His grey hair was thinning at the crown, but just barely, and his face was lined in the right places, and his expression, once as sad and haunted as a matador's, was more in repose these days, though, as now, tension had returned and he chain-smoked and occasionally paced the floor and looked out the window at the people below. In the crowd was a man he did not wish to see.

The man had met DiMaggio in New York. This week he had come to San Francisco and had telephoned several times but none of the calls had been returned because DiMaggio suspected that the man, who had said he was doing research on some vague sociological project, really wanted to delve into DiMaggio's private life and that of DiMaggio's former wife, Marilyn Monroe. DiMaggio would never tolerate this. The memory of her death is still very painful to him, and yet, because he keeps it to himself, some people are not sensitive to it. One night in a supper club a woman who had been drinking approached his table, and when he did not ask her to join him, she snapped:

"All right, I guess I'm *not* Marilyn Monroe."

He ignored her remark, but when she repeated it, he replied, barely controlling his anger, "No—I wish you were, but you're not."

The tone of his voice softened her, and she asked, "Am I saying something wrong?"

"You already have," he said. "Now will you please leave me alone?"

His friends on the wharf, understanding him as they do, are very careful when discussing him with strangers, knowing that should they inadvertently betray a confidence he will not denounce them but rather will never speak to them again; this comes from a sense of propriety not inconsistent in the man who also, after Marilyn Monroe's death, directed that fresh flowers be placed on her grave "forever."

Some of the older fishermen who have known DiMaggio all his life remember him as a small boy who helped clean his father's boat, and as a young man who sneaked away and used a broken oar as a bat on the sandlots nearby. His father, a small mustachioed man known as Zio Pepe, would become infuriated and call him *lagnuso,* lazy, *meschino,* good-for-nothing, but in 1936 Zio Pepe was among those who cheered when Joe DiMaggio returned to San Francisco after his first season with the New York Yankees and was carried along the wharf on the shoulders of the fishermen.

The fishermen also remember how, after his retirement in 1951, DiMaggio brought his second wife, Marilyn, to live near the wharf, and sometimes they would be seen early in the morning fishing off DiMaggio's boat, the *Yankee Clipper,* now docked quietly in the marina, and in the evening they would be sitting and talking on the pier. They had arguments, too, the fishermen knew, and one night Marilyn was seen running hysterically, crying as she ran, along the road away from the pier, with Joe following. But the fishermen pretended they did not see this; it was none of their affair. They knew that Joe wanted her to stay in San Francisco and avoid the sharks in Hollywood, but she was confused and torn then—"She was a child," they said—and even today DiMaggio loathes Los Angeles and many of the people in it. He no longer speaks to his onetime friend, Frank Sinatra, who had befriended Marilyn in her final years, and he also is cool to Dean Martin and Peter Lawford and Lawford's former wife, Pat, who once gave a party at which she introduced Marilyn Monroe to Robert Kennedy, and the two of them danced often that night, Joe heard, and he did not take it well. He was very possessive of her that year, his close friends say, because Marilyn and he had planned to remarry; but before they could she was dead, and

DiMaggio banned the Lawfords and Sinatra and many Hollywood people from her funeral. When Marilyn Monroe's attorney complained that DiMaggio was keeping her friends away, DiMaggio answered coldly, "If it weren't for those friends persuading her to stay in Hollywood she would still be alive."

Joe DiMaggio now spends most of the year in San Francisco, and each day tourists, noticing the name on the restaurant, ask the men on the wharf if they ever see him. Oh yes, the men say, they see him nearly every day; they have not seen him yet this morning, they add, but he should be arriving shortly. So the tourists continue to walk along the piers past the crab vendors, under the circling sea gulls, past the fish 'n' chip stands, sometimes stopping to watch a large vessel steaming toward the Golden Gate Bridge which, to their dismay, is painted red. Then they visit the Wax Museum, where there is a life-size figure of DiMaggio in uniform, and walk across the street and spend a quarter to peer through the silver telescopes focused on the island of Alcatraz, which is no longer a Federal prison. Then they return to ask the men if DiMaggio has been seen. Not yet, the men say, although they notice his blue Impala parked in the lot next to the restaurant. Sometimes tourists will walk into the restaurant and have lunch and will see him sitting calmly in a corner signing autographs and being extremely gracious with everyone. At other times, as on this particular morning when the man from New York chose to visit, DiMaggio was tense and suspicious.

When the man entered the restaurant from the side steps leading to the dining room he saw DiMaggio standing near the window talking with an elderly maître d' named Charles Friscia. Not wanting to walk in and risk intrusion, the man asked one of DiMaggio's nephews to inform Joe of his presence. When DiMaggio got the message he quickly turned and left Friscia and disappeared through an exit leading down to the kitchen.

Astonished and confused, the visitor stood in the hall. A moment later Friscia appeared and the man asked, "Did Joe leave?"

"Joe who?" Friscia replied.

"Joe DiMaggio!"

"Haven't seen him," Friscia said.

"You haven't *seen* him! He was standing right next to you a second ago!"

"It wasn't me," Friscia said.

"You were standing next to him. I saw you. In the dining room."

"You must be mistaken," Friscia said, softly, seriously. "It wasn't me."

"You *must* be kidding," the man said, angrily, turning and leaving the restaurant. Before he could get to his car, however, DiMaggio's nephew came running after him and said, "Joe wants to see you."

He returned expecting to see DiMaggio waiting for him. Instead he was handed a telephone. The voice was powerful and deep and so tense that the quick sentences ran together.

"You are invading my rights, I did not ask you to come, I assume you have a lawyer, you must have a lawyer, get your lawyer!"

"I came as a friend," the man interrupted.

"That's beside the point," DiMaggio said. "I have my privacy, I do not want it violated, you'd better get a lawyer. . . ." Then, pausing, Di-Maggio asked, "Is my nephew there?"

He was not.

"Then wait where you are."

A moment later DiMaggio appeared, tall and red-faced, erect and beautifully dressed in his dark suit and white shirt with the grey silk tie and the gleaming silver cuff links. He moved with big steps toward the man and handed him an airmail envelope, unopened, that the man had written from New York.

"Here," DiMaggio said. "This is yours."

Then DiMaggio sat down at a small table. He said nothing, just lit a cigarette and waited, legs crossed, his head held high and back so as to reveal the intricate construction of his nose, a fine sharp tip above the big nostrils and tiny bones built out from the bridge, a great nose.

"Look," DiMaggio said, more calmly. "I do not interfere with other people's lives. And I do not expect them to interfere with mine. There are things about my life, personal things, that I refuse to talk about. And even if you asked my brothers they would be unable to tell you about them because they do not know. There are things about me, so many things, that they simply do not know. . . ."

"I don't want to cause trouble," the man said. "I think you're a great man, and. . . ."

"I'm not great," DiMaggio cut in. "I'm not great," he repeated, softly. "I'm just a man trying to get along."

Then DiMaggio, as if realizing that he was intruding upon his own privacy, abruptly stood up. He looked at his watch.

"I'm late," he said, very formal again. "I'm ten minutes late. *You're* making me late."

The man left the restaurant. He crossed the street and wandered over to the pier, briefly watching the fishermen hauling their nets and talking in the sun, seeming very calm and contented. Then, after he had turned and was headed back toward the parking lot, a blue Impala stopped in front of him and Joe DiMaggio leaned out the window and asked, "Do you have a car?" His voice was very gentle.

"Yes," the man said.

"Oh," DiMaggio said. "I would have given you a ride."

Joe DiMaggio was not born in San Francisco but in Martinez, a small fishing village twenty-five miles northeast of the Golden Gate. Zio Pepe had settled there after leaving Isola delle Femmine, an islet off Palermo where the DiMaggios had been fishermen for generations. But in 1915, hearing of the luckier waters off San Francisco's wharf, Zio Pepe left Martinez, packing his boat with furniture and family, including Joe who was one year old.

San Francisco was placid and picturesque when the DiMaggios arrived, but there was a competitive undercurrent and struggle for power along the pier. At dawn the boats would sail out to where the bay meets the ocean and the sea is rough, and later the men would race back with their hauls, hoping to beat their fellow fishermen to shore and sell it while they could. Twenty or thirty boats would sometimes be trying to gain the channel shoreward at the same time, and a fisherman had to know ever rock in the water, and later know every bargaining trick along the shore, because the dealers and restaurateurs would play one fisherman off against the other, keeping the prices down. Later the fishermen became wiser and organized, predetermining the maximum amount each fisherman would catch, but there were always some men who, like the fish, never learned, and so heads would sometimes be broken, nets slashed, gasoline poured onto their fish, flowers of warning placed outside their doors.

But these days were ending when Zio Pepe arrived, and he expected his five sons to succeed him as fishermen, and the first two, Tom and

Michael, did; but a third, Vincent, wanted to sing. He sang with such magnificent power as a young man that he came to the attention of the great banker, A. P. Giannini, and there were plans to send him to Italy for tutoring and the opera. But there was hesitation around the DiMaggio household and Vince never went; instead he played ball with the San Francisco Seals and sportswriters misspelled his name.

It was DeMaggio until Joe, at Vince's recommendation, joined the team and became a sensation, being followed later by the youngest brother, Dominic, who was also outstanding. All three later played in the big leagues and some writers like to say that Joe was the best hitter, Dom the best fielder, Vince the best singer, and Casey Stengel once said: "Vince is the only player I ever saw who could strike out three times in one game and not be embarrassed. He'd walk into the clubhouse whistling. Everybody would be feeling sorry for him, but Vince always thought he was doing good."

After he retired from baseball Vince became a bartender, then a milkman, now a carpenter. He lives forty miles north of San Francisco in a house he partly built, has been happily married for thirty-four years, has four grandchildren, has in the closet one of Joe's tailor-made suits that he has never had altered to fit, and when people ask if he envies Joe he always says, "No, maybe Joe would like to have what I have. He won't admit it, but he just might like to have what I have." The brother Vince most admired was Michael, "a big earthy man, a dreamer, a fisherman who wanted things but didn't want to take from Joe, or to work in the restaurant. He wanted a bigger boat, but wanted to earn it on his own. He never got it." In 1953, at the age of forty-four, Michael fell from his boat and drowned.

Since Zio Pepe's death at seventy-seven in 1949, Tom, at sixty-two the oldest brother—two of his four sisters are older—has become nominal head of the family and manages the restaurant that was opened in 1937 as Joe DiMaggio's Grotto. Later Joe sold out his share and now Tom is the co-owner of it with Dominic. Of all the brothers, Dominic, who was known as the "Little Professor" when he played with the Boston Red Sox, is the most successful in business. He lives in a fashionable Boston suburb with his wife and three children and is president of a firm that manufactures fiber-cushion materials and grossed more than $3,500,000 last year.

Joe DiMaggio lives with his widowed sister, Marie, in a tan stone house on a quiet residential street not far from Fisherman's Wharf. He bought the house almost thirty years ago for his parents, and after their death he lived there with Marilyn Monroe; now it is cared for by Marie, a slim and handsome dark-eyed woman who has an apartment on the second floor, Joe on the third. There are some baseball trophies and plaques in the small room off DiMaggio's bedroom, and on his dresser are photographs of Marilyn Monroe, and in the living room downstairs is a small painting of her that DiMaggio likes very much: it reveals only her face and shoulders and she is wearing a very wide-brimmed sun hat, and there is a soft sweet smile on her lips, an innocent curiosity about her that is the way he saw her and the way he wanted her to be seen by others—a simple girl, "a warm bighearted girl," he once described her, "that everybody took advantage of."

The publicity photographs emphasizing her sex appeal often offended him, and a memorable moment for Billy Wilder, who directed her in *The Seven Year Itch,* occurred when he spotted DiMaggio in a large crowd of people gathered on Lexington Avenue in New York to watch a scene in which Marilyn, standing over a subway grating to cool herself, had her skirts blown high by a sudden wind below. "What the hell is going on here?" DiMaggio was overheard to have said in the crowd, and Wilder recalled, "I shall never forget the look of death on Joe's face."

He was then thirty-nine, she was twenty-seven. They had been married in January of that year, 1954, despite disharmony in temperament and time: he was tired of publicity, she was thriving on it; he was intolerant of tardiness, she was always late. During their honeymoon in Tokyo an American general had introduced himself and asked if, as a patriotic gesture, she would visit the troops in Korea. She looked at Joe. "It's your honeymoon," he said, shrugging, "go ahead if you want to."

She appeared on ten occasions before 100,000 servicemen, and when she returned she said, "It was so wonderful, Joe. You never heard such cheering."

"Yes I have," he said.

Across from her portrait in the living room, on a coffee table in front of a sofa, is a sterling-silver humidor that was presented to him by his

Yankee teammates at a time when he was the most talked-about man in America, and when Les Brown's band had recorded a hit that was heard day and night on the radio:

> . . . *From Coast to Coast, that's all you hear*
> *Of Joe the One-Man Show*
> *He's glorified the horsehide sphere,*
> *Jolting Joe DiMaggio . . .*
> *Joe . . . Joe . . . DiMaggio . . . we*
> *want you on our side. . . .*

The year was 1941, and it began for DiMaggio in the middle of May after the Yankees had lost four games in a row, seven of their last nine, and were in fourth place, five-and-a-half games behind the leading Cleveland Indians. On May 15th, DiMaggio hit only a first-inning single in a game that New York lost to Chicago, 13-1; he was barely hitting .300, and had greatly disappointed the crowds that had seen him finish with a .352 average the year before and .381 in 1939.

He got a hit in the next game, and the next, and the next. On May 24th, with the Yankees losing 6-5 to Boston, DiMaggio came up with runners on second and third and singled them home, winning the game, extending his streak to ten games. But it went largely unnoticed. Even DiMaggio was not conscious of it until it had reached twenty-nine games in mid-June. Then the newspapers began to dramatize it, the public became aroused, they sent him good-luck charms of every description, and DiMaggio kept hitting, and radio announcers would interrupt programs to announce the news, and then the song again: *"Joe . . . Joe . . . Di-Maggio . . . we want you on our side . . ."*

Sometimes DiMaggio would be hitless his first three times up, the tension would build, it would appear that the game would end without his getting another chance—but he always would, and then he would hit the ball against the left-field wall, or through the pitcher's legs, or between two leaping infielders. In the forty-first game, the first of a double-header in Washington, DiMaggio tied an American League record that George Sisler had set in 1922. But before the second game began a spectator sneaked onto the field and into the Yankees' dugout and stole DiMaggio's favorite bat. In the second game, using another of his bats, DiMaggio lined out twice and flied out. But in the seventh inning, borrowing one of his old bats that a teammate was using, he singled and broke Sisler's record, and he was only three games away from surpassing the major-league record of forty-four set in 1897 by Willie Keeler while playing for Baltimore when it was a National League franchise.

An appeal for the missing bat was made through the newspapers. A man from Newark admitted the crime and returned it with regrets. And on July 2, at Yankee Stadium, DiMaggio hit a home run into the left-field stands. The record was broken.

He also got hits in the next eleven games, but on July 17th in Cleveland, at a night game attended by 67,468, he failed against two pitchers, Al Smith and Jim Bagby, Jr., although Cleveland's hero was really its third baseman, Ken Keltner, who in the first inning lunged to his right to make a spectacular backhanded stop of a drive and, from the foul line behind third base, he threw DiMaggio out. DiMaggio received a walk in the fourth inning. But in the seventh he again hit a hard shot at Keltner, who again stopped it and threw him out. DiMaggio hit sharply toward the shortstop in the eighth inning, the ball taking a bad hop, but Lou Boudreau speared it off his shoulder and threw to the second baseman to start a double play and DiMaggio's streak was stopped at fifty-six games. But the New York Yankees were on their way to winning the pennant by seventeen games, and the World Series too, and so in August, in a hotel suite in Washington, the players threw a surprise party for DiMaggio and toasted him with champagne and presented him with this Tiffany silver humidor that is now in San Francisco in his living room. . . .

Marie was in the kitchen making toast and tea when DiMaggio came down for breakfast; his grey hair was uncombed but, since he wears it short, it was not untidy. He said good-morning to Marie, sat down and yawned. He lit a cigarette. He wore a blue wool bathrobe over his pajamas. It was eight a.m. He had many things to do today and he seemed cheerful. He had a conference with the president of Continental Television, Inc., a large retail chain in California of which he is a partner and vice-president; later he had a golf date, and then a big banquet to attend, and, if that did not go on too long and he were not too tired afterward, he might have a date.

Picking up the morning paper, not rushing to the sports page, Di-

Maggio read the front-page news, the people-problems of '66: Kwame Nkrumah was overthrown in Ghana, students were burning their draft cards (DiMaggio shook his head), the flu epidemic was spreading through the whole state of California. Then he flipped inside through the gossip columns, thankful they did not have him in there today—they had printed an item about his dating "an electrifying airline hostess" not long ago, and they also spotted him at dinner with Dori Lane, "the frantic frugger" in Whiskey à Go Go's glass cage—and then he turned to the sports page and read a story about how the injured Mickey Mantle may never regain his form.

It had all happened so quickly, the passing of Mantle, or so it seemed; he had succeeded DiMaggio as DiMaggio had succeeded Ruth, but now there was no great young power hitter coming up and the Yankee management, almost desperate, had talked Mantle out of retirement; and on September 18, 1965, they gave him a "day" in New York during which he received several thousand dollars' worth of gifts—an automobile, two quarter horses, free vacation trips to Rome, Nassau, Puerto Rico—and DiMaggio had flown to New York to make the introduction before 50,000: it had been a dramatic day, an almost holy day for the believers who had jammed the grandstands early to witness the canonization of a new stadium saint. Cardinal Spellman was on the committee, President Johnson sent a telegram, the day was officially proclaimed by the Mayor of New York, an orchestra assembled in center field in front of the trinity of monuments to Ruth, Gehrig, Huggins; and high in the grandstands, billowing in the breeze of early autumn, were white banners that read: "Don't Quit Mick," "We Love the Mick."

The banners had been held by hundreds of young boys whose dreams had been fulfilled so often by Mantle, but also seated in the grandstands were older men, paunchy and balding, in whose middle-aged minds DiMaggio was still vivid and invincible, and some of them remembered how one month before, during a pre-game exhibition at Old-timers' Day in Yankee Stadium, DiMaggio had hit a pitch into the left-field seats, and suddenly thousands of people had jumped wildly to their feet, joyously screaming—the great DiMaggio had returned, they were young again, it was yesterday.

But on this sunny September day at the Stadium, the feast day of Mickey Mantle, DiMaggio was not wearing No. 5 on his back nor a black cap to cover his greying hair; he was wearing a black suit and white shirt and blue tie, and he stood in one corner of the Yankees' dugout waiting to be introduced by Red Barber, who was standing near home plate behind a silver microphone. In the outfield Guy Lombardo's Royal Canadians were playing soothing soft music; and moving slowly back and forth over the sprawling green grass between the left-field bullpen and the infield were two carts driven by groundskeepers and containing dozens and dozens of large gifts for Mantle—a six-foot, one-hundred-pound Hebrew National salami, a Winchester rifle, a mink coat for Mrs. Mantle, a set of Wilson golf clubs, a Mercury 95-horsepower outboard motor, a Necchi portable, a year's supply of Chunky Candy. DiMaggio smoked a cigarette, but cupped it in his hands as if not wanting to be caught in the act by teen-aged boys near enough to peek down into the dugout. Then, edging forward a step, DiMaggio poked his head out and looked up. He could see nothing above except the packed towering green grandstands that seemed a mile high and moving, and he could see no clouds or blue sky, only a sky of faces. Then the announcer called out his name—*"Joe DiMaggio!"*—and suddenly there was a blast of cheering that grew louder and louder, echoing and reechoing within the big steel canyon, and DiMaggio stomped out his cigarette and climbed up the dugout steps and onto the soft green grass, the noise resounding in his ears, he could almost feel the breeze, the breath of 50,000 lungs upon him, 100,000 eyes watching his every move and for the briefest instant as he walked he closed his eyes.

Then in his path he saw Mickey Mantle's mother, a smiling elderly woman wearing an orchid, and he gently reached out for her elbow, holding it as he led her toward the microphone next to the other dignitaries lined up on the infield. Then he stood, very erect and without expression, as the cheers softened and the Stadium settled down.

Mantle was still in the dugout, in uniform, standing with one leg on the top step, and lined on both sides of him were the other Yankees who, when the ceremony was over, would play the Detroit Tigers. Then into the dugout, smiling, came Senator Robert Kennedy, accompanied by two tall curly-haired young assistants with blue eyes, Fordham freckles. Jim Farley was the first on the field to notice the Senator, and Farley muttered, loud enough for others to hear, "Who the hell invited *him?*"

Toots Shor and some of the other committeemen standing near Farley looked into the dugout, and so did DiMaggio, his glance seeming cold, but he remaining silent. Kennedy walked up and down within the dugout shaking hands with the Yankees, but he did not walk onto the field.

"Senator," said the Yankees' manager, Johnny Keane, "why don't you sit down?" Kennedy quickly shook his head, smiled. He remained standing, and then one Yankee came over and asked about getting relatives out of Cuba, and Kennedy called over one of his aides to take down the details in a notebook.

On the infield the ceremony went on, Mantle's gifts continued to pile up—a Mobilette motor bike, a Sooner Schooner wagon barbecue, a year's supply of Chock Full O'Nuts coffee, a year's supply of Topps Chewing Gum—and the Yankee players watched, and Maris seemed glum.

"Hey, Rog," yelled a man with a tape recorder, Murray Olderman, "I want to do a thirty-second tape with you."

Maris swore angrily, shook his head.

"It'll only take a second," Olderman said.

"Why don't you ask Richardson? He's a better talker than me."

"Yes, but the fact that it comes from you. . . ."

Maris swore again. But finally he went over and said in an interview that Mantle was the finest player of his era, a great competitor, a great hitter.

Fifteen minutes later, standing behind the microphone at home plate, DiMaggio was telling the crowd, "I'm proud to introduce the man who succeeded me in center field in 1951," and from every corner of the Stadium the cheering, whistling, clapping came down. Mantle stepped forward. He stood with his wife and children, posed for the photographers kneeling in front. Then he thanked the crowd in a short speech, and, turning, shook hands with the dignitaries standing nearby. Among them now was Senator Kennedy, who had been spotted in the dugout five minutes before by Red Barber, and been called out and introduced. Kennedy posed with Mantle for a photographer, then shook hands with the Mantle children, and with Toots Shor and James Farley and others. DiMaggio saw him coming down the line and at the last second he backed away, casually, hardly anybody noticing it, and Kennedy seemed not to notice it either, just swept past shaking more hands. . . .

Finishing his tea, putting aside the newspaper, DiMaggio went upstairs to dress, and soon he was waving good-bye to Marie and driving toward his business appointment in downtown San Francisco with his partners in the retail television business. DiMaggio, while not a millionaire, has invested wisely and has always had, since his retirement from baseball, executive positions with big companies that have paid him well. He also was among the organizers of the Fisherman's National Bank of San Francisco last year, and, though it never came about, he demonstrated an acuteness that impressed those businessmen who had thought of him only in terms of baseball. He has had offers to manage big-league baseball teams but always has rejected them, saying, "I have enough trouble taking care of my own problems without taking on the responsibilities of twenty-five ballplayers."

So his only contact with baseball these days, excluding public appearances, is his unsalaried job as a batting coach each spring in Florida with the New York Yankees, a trip he would make once again on the following Sunday, three days away, if he could accomplish what for him is always the dreaded responsibility of packing, a task made no easier by the fact that he lately has fallen into the habit of keeping his clothes in two places—some hang in his closet at home, some hang in the back room of a saloon called Reno's.

Reno's is a dimly-lit bar in the center of San Francisco. A portrait of DiMaggio swinging a bat hangs on the wall, in addition to portraits of other star athletes, and the clientele consists mainly of the sporting crowd and newspapermen, people who know DiMaggio quite well and around whom he speaks freely on a number of subjects and relaxes as he can in few other places. The owner of the bar is Reno Barsocchini, a broad-shouldered and handsome man of fifty-one with greying wavy hair who began as a fiddler in Dago Mary's tavern thirty-five years ago. He later became a bartender there and elsewhere, including DiMaggio's Restaurant, and now he is probably DiMaggio's closest friend. He was the best man at the DiMaggio-Monroe wedding in 1954, and when they separated nine months later in Los Angeles, Reno rushed down to help Di-

Maggio with the packing and drive him back to San Francisco. Reno will never forget the day.

Hundreds of people were gathered around the Beverly Hills home that DiMaggio and Marilyn had rented, and photographers were perched in the trees watching the windows, and others stood on the lawn and behind the rose bushes waiting to snap pictures of anybody who walked out of the house. The newspapers that day played all the puns—"Joe Fanned on Jealousy"; "Marilyn and Joe—Out at Home"—and the Hollywood columnists, to whom DiMaggio was never an idol, never a gracious host, recounted instances of incompatibility, and Oscar Levant said it all proved that no man could be a success in two national pastimes. When Reno Barsocchini arrived he had to push his way through the mob, then bang on the door for several minutes before being admitted. Marilyn Monroe was upstairs in bed, Joe DiMaggio was downstairs with his suitcases, tense and pale, his eyes bloodshot.

Reno took the suitcases and golf clubs out to DiMaggio's car, and then DiMaggio came out of the house, the reporters moving toward him, the lights flashing.

"Where are you going?" they yelled. "I'm driving to San Francisco," he said, walking quickly.

"Is that going to be your home?"

"That *is* my home and always has been."

"Are you coming back?"

DiMaggio turned for a moment, looking up at the house.

"No," he said, "I'll never be back."

Reno Barsocchini, except for a brief falling out over something he will not discuss, has been DiMaggio's trusted companion ever since, joining him whenever he can on the golf course or on the town, otherwise waiting for him in the bar with other middle-aged men. They may wait for hours sometimes, waiting and knowing that when he arrives he may wish to be alone; but it does not seem to matter, they are endlessly awed by him, moved by the mystique, he is a kind of male Garbo. They know that he can be warm and loyal if they are sensitive to his wishes, but they must never be late for an appointment to meet him. One man, unable to find a parking place, arrived a half-hour late once and DiMaggio did not talk to him again for three months. They know, too, when dining at night with DiMaggio, that he generally prefers male companions and occasionally one or two young women, but never wives; wives gossip, wives complain, wives are trouble, and men wishing to remain close to DiMaggio must keep their wives at home.

When DiMaggio strolls into Reno's bar the men wave and call out his name, and Reno Barsocchini smiles and announces, "Here's the Clipper!", the "Yankee Clipper" being a nickname from his baseball days.

"Hey, Clipper, Clipper," Reno had said two nights before, "where you been, Clipper? . . . Clipper, how 'bout a belt?"

DiMaggio refused the offer of a drink, ordering instead a pot of tea, which he prefers to all other beverages except before a date, when he will switch to vodka.

"Hey, Joe," a sportswriter asked, a man researching a magazine piece on golf, "why is it that a golfer, when he starts getting older, loses his putting touch first? Like Snead and Hogan, they can still hit a ball well off the tee, but on the greens they lose the strokes. . . ."

"It's the pressure of age," DiMaggio said, turning around on his bar stool. "With age you get jittery. It's true of golfers, it's true of any man when he gets into his fifties. He doesn't take chances like he used to. The younger golfer, on the greens, he'll stroke his putts better. The older man, he becomes hesitant. A little uncertain. Shaky. When it comes to taking chances the younger man, even when driving a car, will take chances that the older man won't."

"Speaking of chances," another man said, one of the group that had gathered around DiMaggio, "did you see that guy on crutches in here last night?"

"Yeah, had his leg in a cast," a third said. "Skiing."

"I would never ski," DiMaggio said. "Men who ski must be doing it to impress a broad. You see these men, some of them forty, fifty, getting onto skis. And later you see them all bandaged up, broken legs. . . ."

"But skiing's a very sexy sport, Joe. All the clothes, the tight pants, the fireplace in the ski lodge, the bear rug—Christ, nobody goes to ski. They just go out there to get it cold so they can warm it up. . . ."

"Maybe you're right," DiMaggio said. "I might be persuaded."

"Want a belt, Clipper?" Reno asked.

DiMaggio thought for a second, then said, "All right—first belt tonight."

* * *

Now it was noon, a warm sunny day. DiMaggio's business meeting with the television retailers had gone well; he had made a strong appeal to George Shahood, president of Continental Television, Inc., which has eight retail outlets in Northern California, to cut prices on color television sets and increase the sales volume, and Shahood had conceded it was worth a try. Then DiMaggio called Reno's bar to see if there were any messages, and now he was in Lefty O'Doul's car being driven along Fisherman's Wharf toward the Golden Gate Bridge en route to a golf course thirty miles upstate. Lefty O'Doul was one of the great hitters in the National League in the early Thirties, and later he managed the San Francisco Seals when DiMaggio was the shining star. Though O'Doul is now sixty-nine, eighteen years older than DiMaggio, he nevertheless possesses great energy and spirit, is a hard-drinking, boisterous man with a big belly and roving eye; and when DiMaggio, as they drove along the highway toward the golf club, noticed a lovely blonde at the wheel of a car nearby and exclaimed, "Look at *that* tomato!" O'Doul's head suddenly spun around, he took his eyes off the road, and yelled, "Where, *where?*" O'Doul's golf game is less than what it was—he used to have a two-handicap—but he still shoots in the 80's, as does DiMaggio.

DiMaggio's drives range between 250 and 280 yards when he doesn't sky them, and his putting is good, but he is distracted by a bad back that both pains him and hinders the fullness of his swing. On the first hole, waiting to tee off, DiMaggio sat back watching a foursome of college boys ahead swinging with such freedom. "Oh," he said with a sigh, "to have *their* backs."

DiMaggio and O'Doul were accompanied around the golf course by Ernie Nevers, the former football star, and two brothers who are in the hotel and movie-distribution business. They moved quickly up and down the green hills in electric golf carts, and DiMaggio's game was exceptionally good for the first nine holes. But then he seemed distracted, perhaps tired, perhaps even reacting to a conversation of a few minutes before. One of the movie men was praising the film *Boeing, Boeing,* starring Tony Curtis and Jerry Lewis, and the man asked DiMaggio if he had seen it.

"No," DiMaggio said. Then he added, swiftly, "I haven't seen a film in eight years."

DiMaggio hooked a few shots, was in the woods. He took a No. 9 iron and tried to chip out. But O'Doul interrupted DiMaggio's concentration to remind him to keep the face of the club closed. DiMaggio hit the ball. It caromed off the side of his club, went skipping like a rabbit through the high grass down toward a pond. DiMaggio rarely displays any emotion on a golf course, but now, without saying a word, he took his No. 9 iron and flung it into the air. The club landed in a tree and stayed up there.

"Well," O'Doul said, casually, "there goes *that* set of clubs."

DiMaggio walked to the tree. Fortunately the club had slipped to the lower branch and DiMaggio could stretch up on the cart and get it back.

"Every time I get advice," DiMaggio muttered to himself, shaking his head slowly and walking toward the pond, "I shank it."

Later, showered and dressed, DiMaggio and the others drove to a banquet about ten miles from the golf course. Somebody had said it was going to be an elegant dinner, but when they arrived they could see it was more like a county fair; farmers were gathered outside a big barn-like building, a candidate for sheriff was distributing leaflets at the front door, and a chorus of homely ladies were inside singing *You Are My Sunshine.*

"How did we get sucked into this?" DiMaggio asked, talking out of the side of his mouth, as they approached the building.

"O'Doul," one of the men said. "It's his fault. Damned O'Doul can't turn *anything* down."

"Go to hell," O'Doul said.

Soon DiMaggio and O'Doul and Ernie Nevers were surrounded by the crowd, and the woman who had been leading the chorus came rushing over and said, "Oh, Mr. DiMaggio, it certainly is a pleasure having you."

"It's a pleasure being here, ma'am," he said, forcing a smile.

"It's too bad you didn't arrive a moment sooner, you'd have heard our singing."

"Oh, I heard it," he said, "and I enjoyed it very much."

"Good, good," she said. "And how are your brothers Dom and Vic?"

"Fine. Dom lives near Boston. Vince is in Pittsburgh."

"Why, *hello* there, Joe," interrupted a man with wine on his breath, patting DiMaggio on the back, feeling his arm. "Who's gonna take it this year, Joe?"

"Well, I have no idea," DiMaggio said.

"What about the Giants?"

"Your guess is as good as mine."

"Well, you can't count the Dodgers out," the man said.

"You sure can't," DiMaggio said.

"Not with all that pitching."

"Pitching is certainly important," DiMaggio said.

Everywhere he goes the questions seem the same, as if he has some special vision into the future of new heroes, and everywhere he goes, too, older men grab his hand and feel his arm and predict that he could still go out there and hit one, and the smile on DiMaggio's face is genuine. He tries hard to remain as he was—he diets, he takes steam baths, he is careful; and flabby men in the locker rooms of golf clubs sometimes steal peeks at him when he steps out of the shower, observing the tight muscles across his chest, the flat stomach, the long sinewy legs. He has a young man's body, very pale and little hair; his face is dark and lined, however, parched by the sun of several seasons. Still he is always an impressive figure at banquets such as this—an *immortal,* sportswriters called him, and that is how they have written about him and others like him, rarely suggesting that such heroes might ever be prone to the ills of mortal men, carousing, drinking, scheming; to suggest this would destroy the myth, would disillusion small boys, would infuriate rich men who own ball clubs and to whom baseball is a business dedicated to profit and in pursuit of which they trade mediocre players' flesh as casually as boys trade players' pictures on bubble-gum cards. And so the baseball hero must always act the part, must preserve the myth, and none does it better than DiMaggio, none is more patient when drunken old men grab an arm and ask, "Who's gonna take it this year, Joe?"

Two hours later, dinner and the speeches over, DiMaggio is slumped in O'Doul's car headed back to San Francisco. He edged himself up, however, when O'Doul pulled into a gas station in which a pretty red-haired girl sat on a stool, legs crossed, filing her fingernails. She was about twenty-two, wore a tight black skirt and tighter white blouse.

"Look at *that,*" DiMaggio said.

"Yeah," O'Doul said.

O'Doul turned away when a young man approached, opened the gas tank, began wiping the windshield. The young man wore a greasy white uniform on the front of which was printed the name "Burt." DiMaggio kept looking at the girl, but she was not distracted from her fingernails. Then he looked at Burt, who did not recognize him. When the tank was full, O'Doul paid and drove off. Burt returned to his girl; DiMaggio slumped down in the front seat and did not open his eyes again until they'd arrived in San Francisco.

"Let's go see Reno," DiMaggio said.

"No, I gotta go see my old lady," O'Doul said. So he dropped DiMaggio off in front of the bar, and a moment later Reno's voice was announcing in the smoky room, "Hey, here's the Clipper!" The men waved and offered to buy him a drink. DiMaggio ordered a vodka and sat for an hour at the bar talking to a half dozen men around him. Then a blonde girl who had been with friends at the other end of the bar came over, and somebody introduced her to DiMaggio. He bought her a drink, offered her a cigarette. Then he struck a match and held it. His hand was unsteady.

"Is that me that's shaking?" he asked.

"It must be," said the blonde. "I'm calm."

Two nights later, having collected his clothes out of Reno's back room, DiMaggio boarded a jet; he slept crossways on three seats, then came down the steps as the sun began to rise in Miami. He claimed his luggage and golf clubs, put them into the trunk of a waiting automobile, and less than an hour later he was being driven into Fort Lauderdale, past palm-lined streets, toward the Yankee Clipper Hotel.

"All my life it seems I've been on the road traveling," he said, squinting through the windshield into the sun. "I never get a sense of being in any one place."

Arriving at the Yankee Clipper Hotel, DiMaggio checked into the largest suite. People rushed through the lobby to shake hands with him, to ask for his autograph, to say, "Joe, you look great." And early the next morning, and for the next thirty mornings, DiMaggio arrived punctually at the baseball park and wore his uniform with the famous No. 5, and the tourists seated in the sunny grandstands clapped when he first appeared on the field each time, and then they watched with nostalgia as he picked up a bat and played "pepper" with the younger Yankees, some of whom were not even born when, twenty-five years ago this summer, he hit in fifty-six straight games and became the most celebrated man in America.

But the younger spectators in the Fort Lauderdale park, and the sportswriters, too, were more interested in Mantle and Maris, and nearly every day there were news dispatches reporting how Mantle and Maris felt, what they did, what they said, even though they said and did very little except walk around the field frowning when photographers asked for another picture and when sportswriters asked how they felt.

After seven days of this, the big day arrived—Mantle and Maris would swing a bat—and a dozen sportswriters were gathered around the big batting cage that was situated beyond the left-field fence; it was completely enclosed in wire, meaning that no baseball could travel more than thirty or forty feet before being trapped in rope; still Mantle and Maris would be swinging, and this, in spring, makes news.

Mantle stepped in first. He wore black gloves to help prevent blisters. He hit right-handed against the pitching of a coach named Vern Benson, and soon Mantle was swinging hard, smashing line drives against the nets, going *ahhh ahhh* as he followed through with his mouth open.

Then Mantle, not wanting to overdo it on his first day, dropped his bat in the dirt and walked out of the batting cage. Roger Maris stepped in. He picked up Mantle's bat.

"This damn thing must be thirty-eight ounces," Maris said. He threw the bat down into the dirt, left the cage and walked toward the dugout on the other side of the field to get a lighter bat.

DiMaggio stood among the sportswriters behind the cage, then turned when Vern Benson, inside the cage, yelled, "Joe, wanna hit some?"

"No chance," DiMaggio said.

"Com'on, Joe," Benson said.

The reporters waited silently. Then DiMaggio walked slowly into the cage and picked up Mantle's bat. He took his position at the plate but obviously it was not the classic DiMaggio stance; he was holding the bat about two inches from the knob, his feet were not so far apart, and, when DiMaggio took a cut at Benson's first pitch, fouling it, there was none of that ferocious follow through, the blurred bat did not come whipping all the way around, the No. 5 was not stretched full across his broad back.

DiMaggio fouled Benson's second pitch, then he connected solidly with the third, the fourth, the fifth. He was just meeting the ball easily, however, not smashing it, and Benson called out, "I didn't know you were a choke hitter, Joe."

"I am now," DiMaggio said, getting ready for another pitch.

He hit three more squarely enough, and then he swung again and there was a hollow sound.

"Ohhh," DiMaggio yelled, dropping his bat, his fingers stung, "I was waiting for that one." He left the batting cage rubbing his hands together. The reporters watched him. Nobody said anything. Then DiMaggio said to one of them, not in anger nor in sadness, but merely as a simply stated fact, "There was a time when you couldn't get me out of there."

Peter O'Toole
on the Ould Sod

All the children in the classroom had their pencils out and were drawing horses, as the nun had instructed—all, that is, except one little boy who, having finished, was sitting idly behind his desk.

"Well," the nun said, looking down at his horse, "why not draw something else—a saddle, or something?"

A few minutes later she returned to see what he had drawn. Suddenly her face was scarlet. The horse now had a penis and was urinating in the pasture.

Wildly, with both hands, the nun began to flail the boy. Then other nuns rushed in and they, too, flailed him, knocking him to the floor, and not listening as he sobbed, bewilderedly, "But, but . . . I was only drawing what I saw . . . only drawing what I saw!"

"Oh, those bitches!" said Peter O'Toole, now thirty-one, still feeling the sting after all these years. "Those destitute, old unmarried birds with those withered, sexless hands! God, how I hated those nuns!"

He threw his head back, finished his Scotch, then asked the stewardess for another. Peter O'Toole was sitting in an airplane that one hour before had left London, where he has long lived in exile, and was flying to Ireland, his birthplace. The plane was filled with businessmen and rosy-cheeked Irishwomen, and also a scattering of priests, one of whom held a cigarette in what seemed to be a long, thin pair of wire tweezers —presumably so he would not touch tobacco with fingers that would later hold the Sacrament.

O'Toole, unaware of the priest, smiled as the stewardess brought his drink. She was a floridly robust little blonde in a tight green tweed uniform.

"Oh, look at that ass," O'Toole said softly, shaking his head, raising his eyes with approval. "That ass is covered with tweed made in Connemara, where I was born. . . . Nicest asses in the world, Ireland. Irishwomen still are carrying water on their heads and carrying their husbands home from pubs, and such things are the greatest posture builders in the world."

He sipped his Scotch and looked out the window. The plane was now descending, and through the clouds he could see the soft, verdant fields, the white farmhouses, the gentle hills of outer Dublin, and he said he felt, as returning Irishmen often do, both some sadness and some joy. They are sad at seeing again what it was that forced them to leave, and feel some guilt, too, for having left though they know they could never have fulfilled their dreams amid all this poverty and strangling strictness; yet they are happy because Ireland's beauty seems imperishable, unchanged from the time of their childhood, and thus each trip back home to Ireland is a blissful reunion with youth.

Though Peter O'Toole remains an uprooted Irishman by choice, he leaves London and returns to Ireland every now and then to do some drinking, to play the horses at the Punchestown racetrack outside Dublin, and to spend some solitary hours thinking. He had had very little time for private thinking recently; there had been those grueling two years in the desert with *Lawrence of Arabia,* and then starring on the London stage in Bertold Brecht's *Baal,* and then costarring with Richard Burton in the film, *Becket,* and then he would star in *Lord Jim,* with other films to follow.

Big money was rolling in now, for the first time in his life. He had just bought a nineteen-room house in London, and finally was able to afford paintings by Jack B. Yeats. Yet O'Toole was no more contented or secure now than he had been as an underfed drama student living on a barge, a barge that sank one night after too many people had come to a party.

He could still be wild and self-destructive, and the psychiatrists had been no help. All he knew was that within him, simmering in the smithy of his soul, were confusion and conflict, and they were probably responsible for his talent, his rebellion, his exile, his guilt. They were all linked somehow with Ireland and the Church, with his smashing up so many cars that his license had to be taken away, and with marching in Ban-the-Bomb parades, with becoming obsessed with Lawrence of Arabia, with detesting cops, barbed wire, and girls who shave under their arms; with being an aesthete, a horse player, a former altar boy, a drinker who now wanders through the streets at night buying the same book ("My life is littered with copies of *Moby Dick*") and reading the same sermon in that book (". . . and if we obey God, we must disobey ourselves . . ."); with being gentle, generous, sensitive, yet suspicious ("You're talking to an Irish bookie's son; you can't con me!"); with devotion to his wife, loyalty to old friends, great concern over the uncertain eyesight of his three-year-old daughter, now wearing very thick glasses ("Daddy, Daddy! I broke my eyes!" "Don't cry, Kate, don't cry—we'll get you a new pair"); with theatrical genius that is equally moving whether performing pantomime or Hamlet; with an anger that can be sudden ("Why should I tell *you* the truth? Who are you, Bertrand Russell?") and with anger that quickly subsides ("Look, I'd tell you if I knew why, but I don't know, just don't know . . ."); and with the as yet unrealized contradictions in the Peter O'Toole who, at this very moment, was about to land in Ireland . . . where he was born thirty-one years ago . . . where he would have his next drink.

Two bumps, and the plane was safely down, racing across the concrete, then spinning around and rolling toward the Dublin air terminal. When the door was opened, a crowd of photographers and reporters moved in, flash bulbs fixed, and soon they were popping away as Peter O'Toole, a thin, lanky man of six feet three inches, wearing a green corduroy jacket, a green bowtie, and green socks (he wears nothing *but* green socks, even with tuxedos), came down the steps, smiling and waving in the sun. He posed for pictures, gave a radio interview, bought everybody a drink; he laughed and backslapped, he was charming and suave, he was his public self, his airport self.

Then he got into a limousine that would take him into the city, and soon he riding through the narrow, winding roads past the farmhouses, past the goats and cows and green, very green land stretching for miles in the distance.

"A lovely land," O'Toole said, with a sigh. "God, you can love it! But you can't live in it. It's a frightening thing. My father, who lives in England, won't put a foot in Ireland any more. And yet, you mention one word against Ireland and he goes stark raving mad. . . .

"Oh, Ireland," O'Toole went on, "it's the sow that ate its own farrow. Tell me one Irish artist that ever produced here, just one! God, Jack Yeats couldn't sell a painting in this country, and *all the talent* . . . oh, daddy . . . You know what Ireland's biggest export is? It's men. Men . . . Shaw, Joyce, Synge, they couldn't stay here. O'Casey couldn't stay. Why? Because O'Casey preaches the Doctrine of Joy, daddy, that's why. . . . Oh, the Irish know despair, *by God they do!* They are Dostoyevskian about it. But Joy, dear love, in *this* land! . . . Oh, dear Father," O'Toole went on, pounding his breast, "forgive me, Father, for I have fucked Mrs. Rafferty. . . . Ten Hail Marys, son, five Our Fathers . . . But Father, Father, I didn't enjoy fucking Mrs. Rafferty. . . . Good, son, *good* . . .

"Ireland," O'Toole repeated, "you can love it . . . can't *live* in it."

Now he was at the hotel. It was near the Liffey River not far from the tower described by Joyce in *Ulysses*. O'Toole had a drink at the bar. He seemed very quiet and somber, so different from the way he had been at the airport.

"The Celts are, at rock bottom, deep pessimists," Peter O'Toole said, tossing down his Scotch. Part of his own pessimism, he added, springs from his birthplace, Connemara, "the wildest part of Ireland, famine country, a land without horizons"—a land that Jack Yeats paints so well into his Irish faces, faces that remind O'Toole so much of his seventy-five-year-old father, Patrick O'Toole, a former bookmaker, a dashing gentleman, tall and very slim, like Peter; who nearly always drank too much and fought with the police, like Peter; and who was not very lucky at the racetrack, like Peter; and people in the neighborhood back in Connemara used to shake their heads for Patty O'Toole's wife, Constance ("a saint"), and would say, "Oh, what would Patty O'Toole ever do without Connie?"

"When my father would come home from the track after a good day," said Peter O'Toole, leaning against the bar, "the whole room would light up; it was fairyland. But when he lost, it was black. In our house, it was always either a wake . . . or a wedding."

Later in his boyhood, Peter O'Toole was taken out of Ireland; his father, wishing to be closer to the racetracks clustered in northern England's industrial district, moved the family to Leeds, a slum of one-down, two-up houses.

"My first memory of Leeds as a child was being lost," said Peter O'Toole, tossing down another drink. "I remember wandering around the city . . . remember seeing a man painting a telephone pole *green* . . . And I remember him going away and leaving his paint brushes and things behind. . . . And I remember finishing the pole for him. . . . And I remember being brought to the police station. . . . And remember looking up at the desk, all white tile, white as a nun's hand, and then I remember seeing a big, fucking nasty looking down at me. . . ."

At thirteen, Peter O'Toole had quit school and had gone to work briefly in a warehouse and learned to break string without scissors, a talent he has never lost, and after that he worked as a copyboy and photographer's assistant at the *Yorkshire Evening News,* a job he liked very much until it occurred to him that newspapermen remain primarily along the sidelines of life recording the deeds of famous men, and rarely become famous themselves, and he very much wanted to become famous, he said. At eighteen years of age, he had copied in his notebook the lines that would be his credo, and now, in this bar in Dublin, tilting back on his barstool, he recited them aloud:

"I do not choose to be a common man . . . it is my right to be uncommon—if I can. . . . I seek opportunity—not security. . . . I want to take the calculated risk; to dream and to build, to fail and to succeed . . . to refuse to barter incentive for a dole. . . . I prefer the challenges of life to the guaranteed existence, the thrill of fulfillment to the stale calm of utopia. . . ."

After he finished, two drunken men at the far end of the bar clapped their hands, and O'Toole bought them, and himself, another drink.

His career as an actor, he said, began after his tour in the Navy and a year of study at the Royal Academy of Dramatic Art. One of his first acting jobs was with the Bristol Old Vic Company impersonating a Georgian peasant in a Chekhov play.

"I was supposed to lumber onto the stage and say, 'Dr. Ostroff, the horses have arrived,' and then walk off," O'Toole said. "But not *me*. I decided this Georgian peasant was really *Stalin!* And so I played it with a slight limp, like Stalin's, and fixed my make-up like Stalin . . . and when I came on the stage, smoldering with resentment for the aristocracy, I could hear a hush come over the audience. Then I glared at Dr. Ostroff . . . and said, 'Dr. Horsey, the Ostroffs have arrived!' "

In the next three years at the Bristol Old Vic, he played seventy-three roles, including Hamlet, but, until he got the movie role in *Lawrence of Arabia,* nobody had heard of Peter O'Toole, said Peter O'Toole, his voice hard.

"Lawrence!" O'Toole spat out, swallowing his Scotch. "I became obsessed by that man, and it was bad. A true artist should be able to jump into a bucket of shit and come out smelling of violets, but I spent two years and three months making that picture, and it was two years, three months of thinking about nothing *but* Lawrence, and you were him, and that's how it was day after day, day after day, and it became bad for me, personally, and it killed my acting later.

"After Lawrence, as you know, I did *Baal* and a close friend of mine, after my dress rehearsal, came back and said, 'What's the matter, Peter, what *is* it?' I asked what the hell he meant, and he said, 'There's no *give!'* . . . Christ, his words struck terror in me. Oh, it was bad acting! I was looking at the floor . . . couldn't get my voice going again. . . . I was flabby, diffuse. . . . Later I said, 'You're in trouble, daddy,' and I felt it in my fucking toes. I was emotionally bankrupt after that picture.

"On a BBC show, on Harry Craig's show—that mother dug too deep! —I said that after *Lawrence* I was afraid of being mutilated. That filming for that length of time, two years, three months, and having all the responsibility for the performance but none of the control . . . Christ, in one scene of the film I saw a close-up of my face when I was twenty-seven years old, and then, eight seconds later, there was another close-up of me when I was twenty-nine years old! *Eight goddamn seconds* and two years of my life had gone from me!

"Oh, it's painful seeing it all there on the screen, solidified, embalmed," he said, staring straight ahead toward the rows of bottles.

"Once a thing is solidified it stops being a living thing. That's why I love the theatre. It's the Art of the Moment. I'm in love with ephemera and I hate permanence. Acting is making words into flesh, and I love classical acting because . . . because you need the vocal range of an opera singer . . . the movement of a ballet dancer . . . you have to be able to *act* . . . it's turning your whole body into a musical instrument on which you yourself play. . . . It's more than behaviorism, which is what you get in the movies. . . . Chrissake, what *are* movies anyway? Just fucking moving photographs, that's all. But the theatre! Ah, there you have the *impermanence* that I love. It's a reflection of life somehow. It's . . . it's . . . like building a statue of snow. . . ."

Peter O'Toole looked at his watch. Then he paid the barman and waved good-bye to the drunks in the corner. It was 1:15 P.M.—time to be getting to the track.

The chauffeur, a fat and quiet man who had been dozing in the hotel lobby all this time, woke up when he heard O'Toole singing and sauntering out of the bar, and he quickly hopped up when O'Toole announced cheerfully, bowing slightly, "To the races, m'good man."

In the car on the way to Punchestown, O'Toole, who was in good spirits but not drunk by any means, recalled the joy he'd had as a boy when his father would take him to the racetrack. Sometimes, O'Toole said, his father would miscalculate the odds at his bookie stand, or would lose so heavily on one of his own bets that he would not have enough cash to pay off his winning customers; so, immediately after the race was over, but before the customers could charge toward the O'Toole bookie booth, Patrick O'Toole would grab Peter's hand and say, "C'm'on, son, let's be off!"—and the two of them would slip through the shrubbery and disappear quickly from the track, and could not return again for a long time.

Punchestown's grandstand was jammed with people when O'Toole's chauffeur drove toward the clubhouse. There were long lines of people waiting to buy tickets, too, well-dressed people in tweed suits and tweed caps, or Tyrolean hats with feathers sticking up. Beyond the people was the paddock, a paddock of soft, very green grass on which the horses pounded back and forth, circling and turning, nostrils flaring. And behind the paddock, making lots of noise, were rows and rows of bookies, all of them elderly men wearing caps and standing behind their brightly-painted wooden stands, all of them echoing the odds and waving little pieces of paper in the breeze.

Peter O'Toole watched them for a moment, silently. Then, suddenly, a woman's voice could be heard calling, "PEE-*tah*, Pee-*tah*, Pee-*tah* O'Toole, well, how *ah* you?"

O'Toole recognized the woman as one of Dublin society, a well-built woman of about forty whose husband owned race horses and lots of stock in Guinness.

O'Toole smiled and held her hand for a few moments, and she said, "Oh, you look better every day, Pee-tah, even better than you did on those bloody Arab camels. Come to our trailer behind the clubhouse and have drinks with us, dear, won't you?"

O'Toole said he would, but first wanted to place a bet.

He placed a five-pound bet on a horse in the first race but, before the horse could clear the final hedge, the rider was thrown. O'Toole lost the next five races, too, and the liquor was also getting to him. Between races he'd stopped in at the Guinness trailer, a big white van filled with rich men and champagne and elegant Irishwomen who brushed up very close to him, called him "Pee-tah" and saying he should come back to Ireland more often, and, as he smiled and put his long arms around them, he sometimes found that he was leaning on them for support.

Just before the final race, O'Toole wandered out into the fresh air and sun and placed a ten-pound bet on a horse about which he knew nothing; then, instead of going back into the Guinness van, he leaned against the rail near the track, his bloodshot blue eyes gazing at the row of horses lined up at the gate. The bell sounded, and O'Toole's horse, a big chestnut gelding, pulled out ahead, and, swinging around the turn, kicking divots of grass into the air, it maintained the lead, leaped over a hedge, pounded onward, leaped over another hedge, still ahead by two lengths. Now Peter O'Toole began to wake up, and seconds later he was waving his fist in the air, cheering and jumping, as the horse moved across the finish line—and galloped past, the jockey leaning up on the saddle, an easy victor.

"Pee-tah, Pee-tah, you've won!" came the cries from the van.

"Pee-tah, darling, let's have a drink!"

But Peter O'Toole was not interested in a drink. He rushed immediately to the ticket window before the bookie could get away. O'Toole got his money.

After the races, with the late afternoon sun going down and the air suddenly chilly, O'Toole decided he would avoid the parties in Dublin; instead he asked the chauffeur to take him to Glendalough, a quiet, beautiful, almost deserted spot along a lake between two small mountains in outer Dublin, not far from where the earliest O'Tooles were buried, and where he, as a boy, used to take long walks.

By 5:30 P.M. the driver was edging the big car around the narrow dirt roads at the base of the mountain, then he stopped, there being no more road. O'Toole got out, lifted the collar of his green corduroy jacket, and began to walk up the mountain, a bit uneasily, because he was still slightly dazed by all the drinking.

"Oh, Christ, what color!" he shouted, his voice echoing through the valley. "Just look at those trees, those young trees—they're *running,* for chrissake, they're not planted there—and they're so luscious, like pubic hair, and that *lake,* no fish in *that* lake! And no birds sing, it's so quiet, no birds singing in Glendalough on account of there being no fish . . . for them to sing for. . . ."

Then he slumped down on the side of the mountain, tossed his head back against the grass. Then he held his hands in the air, and said, "See that? See that right hand?" He turned his right hand back and forth, saying, "Look at those scars, daddy," and there were about thirty or forty little scars inside his right hand as well as on his knuckles, and his little finger was deformed.

"I don't know if there's any significance to it, daddy, but . . . but *I am a left-hander who was made to be right-handed.* . . . Oh, they would wack me over the knuckles when I used my left, those nuns, and maybe, just maybe that is why I hated school so much."

All his life, he said, his right hand has been a kind of violent weapon. He has smashed it through glass, into concrete, against other people.

"But look at my *left* hand," he said, holding it high. "Not a single scar on it. Long and smooth as a lily . . ."

He paused, then said, "You know, I can write absolutely backwards, mirror writing. . . . Look. . . ."

He pulled out his airplane ticket and, with a ballpoint pen, wrote out his name.

He laughed. Then, standing and brushing the dirt from his green jacket and trousers, he staggered down the mountain toward the car, and began to leave behind the eerie quiet of the lake, the running trees, and the island of those wizened white nuns.

VOGUEland

Each weekday morning a group of suave and wrinkle-proof women, who call one another "dear" and "dahling," and can speak in italics and curse in French, move into Manhattan's Graybar Building, elevate to the nineteenth floor, and then slip behind their desks at *Vogue*—a magazine that has long been the supreme symbol of sophistication for every American female who ever dreamed of being frocked by Balenciaga, shod by Roger Vivier, coiffed by Kenneth, or set free to swing from the Arc de Triomphe in maiden-form mink.

Not since Sappho has anybody worked up such a lather over women as have the editors of *Vogue*. With almost every issue they present stunning goddesses who seemingly become more perfect, more devastating with the flip of each page. Sometimes the *Vogue* model is leaping across the page in mocha-colored silk, or piloting a teak-tipped ketch through the Lesser Antilles, or standing, Dior-length, in front of the Eiffel Tower as racy Renaults buzz by—but never hit her—as she poses in the middle of the street, one leg kicking, mouth open, teeth agleam, two gendarmes winking in the background, all Paris in love with her and her dinner dress of mousseline de soie.

At other times the *Vogue* model is wearing "never-out-of-season black" on the Queensboro Bridge with a white cat crawling up her back, a cat she presumably leaves home when she later jets down to Puerto Rico to lunch with Casals while being watched from the hills by native women holding naked children—women who smile at her, admire her silk tussah skirt ("Nantucket nipped"), love her as she spikes up the nine-hole course inside the fortress of old El Morro.

While these fashion models in *Vogue* are merely stupendous, the socialites photographed for that magazine are rich, beautiful, indefatigable, vivid, vital, brilliant, witty, serve on more committees than Congressmen, know more about airplanes than Wolfgang Langewiesche, thrive on country air and yet are equally at home in the smart poker parlors of Cannes; they never age, fade, or get dandruff, and are also (in the words of *Vogue*'s battery of sycophantic caption writers) "amusable," "exquisite," "delicate," "fun," and "smashing."

In one *Vogue* issue, for instance, Mrs. Loel Guinness, photographed before she sashayed from Lausanne to Palm Beach, was described as "vivid, vital, amusing." And, in another issue, Mrs. Columbus O'Donnel possessed a "quick, amused sparkle," Queen Sirikit of Thailand was "amusable, exquisite," and the Countess of Dalkeith was "ravishing" and as effulgent as Lady Caroline Somerset—herself a "delicate moonbeam beauty." Mrs. Murray Vanderbilt, last year a "slender brunette with direct, heartbreaker eyes, and a soft, open laugh," this year is a "beauty with a strong sense of purpose"—her purpose being to fly to Paris to have her portrait painted by "jaunty, rakish" Kees Van Dongen on a Tuesday, and then fly back to New York the same night, "investing," as *Vogue* said, "only 23 hours, 45 minutes."

Should there be that extraordinary case when a celebrated woman in *Vogue* is not a "rare beauty"—as, for instance, when she is almost homely—she is then described as "wise" or "filled with wisdom" or reminiscent of heroines in exquisite, vital novels. Madame Helene Rochas "looks rather like the heroine of a novel by Stendhal." And, should *Vogue* make mention of a non-*Vogue* type, such as Ingrid Bergman, who spends little money in the cosmetic industry, she is credited with having a nose which is "rather generous."

The noses of *Vogue* heroines are usually long and thin, as are the noses of many *Vogue* editors—noses they can look down upon their generally shorter, younger, and less-sophisticated Condé Nast relatives on *Glamour* magazine, also located on the nineteenth floor of the Gray-bar Building. But it is usually quite simple to tell the two staffs apart because the *jeunes filles* at *Glamour,* in addition to possessing a high quota of noses that *Vogue* might dismiss as "eager, retroussé," are also given to wearing shirt dresses, college-girl circle pins, smiling in the elevator, and saying, "Hi." A *Vogue* lady once described the *Glamour* staff as "those peppy, Hi people."

One day a few years ago a wide-eyed, newly-hired *Vogue* secretary went bouncing into an editor's office with a package, and said, "Hi"—at which the editor is supposed to have cringed, and finally snapped, "We don't say *that* around *here!*"

"Everyone at *Glamour* of course hopes to work her way up to the *Vogue* staff of grim vigilantes," says the writer Eve Marriam, once a fashion copy editor at *Glamour.* "But it rarely happens. *Vogue* has to be careful. The upcomer might use the word *cute* instead of *panche;* she might talk about giving a *party* instead of a *dinner;* or describe a suède coat 'for weekending with the station-wagon set' rather than 'for your country home.' Or talk of going to a jewelry store instead of a *bijouterie.* Most maladroit of all, she might talk in terms of a *best buy* rather than an *investment,* or a *coup.* Or refer to a *ballgown* as—one shudders to think of it—a *formal.*"

One has only to leave the elevator and enter the nineteenth floor to experience a sudden sensation of being *in Vogue.* The floors are black and star-studded, and the spacious outer room is tastefully furnished with a "delicate, amusable" receptionist with a British accent—perchance in keeping with the magazine's policy of spelling many words the British way: "colour," "honour," "jewellery," and "marvellous" (pronounced *MAA*-vellous!).

To the rear of the receptionist is a curved corridor leading to *Vogue's* editorial offices. The first office, that of the Beauty Editor, smells of pomades and powders, rejuvenators and other fountains of youth. Beyond this point, and around a second curve, are a half-dozen offices of other editors, and dividing them is the large, noisy Fashion Room. From nine till five the Fashion Room and the offices around it throb with the shrill, exuberant voices of fifty women, the incessant ring of telephones, the blurred image of leggy silhouettes shooting past, their heels clacking with *élan.* In one corner, the Fabrics Editor picks at silk swatches; in another corner, near a window, the Shoe Editor ponders what's next in "smashing" footwear; in still another corner, the Model Procurer flips through a filing cabinet that contains such highly-classified data on models as which will pose for corset ads, which have the best legs, which have clawlike fingers (ideal for modeling gloves), and which have small, pretty hands (ideal for making small, expensive perfume bottles seem larger).

From the nearby offices of an editor named Carol Phillips ("delicate, amusable, pure-profiled beauty") can be heard the well-bred titters and talk of other *Vogue* tastemakers who stand, arms akimbo, toes pointed out, in front of Mrs. Phillips' desk. Inevitably their chatter blends with the dialogue that ricochets through the corridor, making it at times most difficult for the Baron De Gunzburg, a senior fashion editor, to concentrate fully on the London *Times* crossword puzzle that a messenger fetches for him each morning from the out-of-town newsstand in Times Square. The Baron, who is called "Nick-kee" by *Vogue* ladies, and who makes his 7's in the European style 7 is a former dancer with a Russian ballet and a one-time actor in a German film called *The Vampire*. (In the film he played a poet who spent two weeks in a casket before his chance to murder the Vampire; nowadays the Baron is rarely without a black tie, and it is said that once, while entering a Seventh Avenue elevator without specifying his choice of floors, he was immediately whisked up to the floor of a tailor who made uniforms for undertakers.)

Upstairs from the Baron, in one of the few offices occupied by *Vogue* on the twentieth floor, Feature Editor Allene Talmey, whom Crowninshield once described as a "Soufflé of Crowbars," bats out her famous column "People Are Talking About"—a collection of items that she and other *Vogue* ladies are talking about, and think *everybody* should be talking about. She writes:

PEOPLE ARE TALKING ABOUT . . . the present need for the Greek word, *bottologia,* meaning much speaking, or vain repetitions, as used by St. Matthew (6:7) . . .

PEOPLE ARE TALKING ABOUT . . . the christening presents given to the daughter of the great Austrian conductor, Herbert von Karajan . . .

PEOPLE ARE TALKING ABOUT . . . Takraw, a game beautiful to watch . . .

PEOPLE ARE TALKING ABOUT . . . Hummingbirds . . .
PEOPLE ARE TALKING ABOUT . . . the Eastern half of the world . . .

While some of *Vogue's* critics contend that the magazine's literary policy can be summed up with "When in Doubt, Reprint Colette," it must be said in *Vogue's* behalf that it has printed work by some excellent writers, among them Marianne Moore, Jacques Barzun, Rebecca West, and Allene Talmey. And yet one of *Vogue's* former art directors, the inimitable Dr. Mehemet Femy Agha, once said, "Although Allene is wonderful, I've often told her she's like a piano player in a whorehouse. She may be a very good piano player, but nobody goes there to hear music. Nobody buys *Vogue* to read good literature; they buy it to see the clothes."

Among the first to see the clothes is the Baron De Gunzburg, who, having finished the London *Times* crossword puzzle, is now in the Garment Center on Seventh Avenue reclining in a posh divan in the showroom of the clothier Herbert Sondheim, who is giving *Vogue* magazine a private preview of Sondheim's spring frocks. Sitting next to the Baron is another *Vogue* editor, Mildred Morton ("pure-profiled blonde with slightly bored, raised eyebrow").

"You are the first persons in the entire world to be seeing these," says Mr. Sondheim, a short, rather stout, gravel-voiced man who rubs his hands, smiles from ear to ear.

A moment later a blonde model appears from behind the curtain, prances toward the Baron and Mrs. Morton, and coos, "Number 628."

The Baron writes down the style number in his Hermes leather notebook, and watches her twirl around, and then walk back through the curtain.

"That's pomecia," says Mr. Sondheim.

"Expensive?" asks Mrs. Morton.

"Pomecia cotton is about $2.50 a yard," Mr. Sondheim says.

"Number 648," says a second model, a brunette, who slithers past Mr. Sondheim, dips, then twirls around in front of the Baron De Gunzburg.

"Awfully smart," says the Baron, letting his fingers give the model's pomecia evening dress a professional pinch. "I just *love* the slashed coat."

Mrs. Morton raises her right eyebrow.

"Are you getting away this winter?" the Baron asks Mr. Sondheim.

"Probably," he says. "Palm Beach."

The Baron seems unimpressed.

"Number 624," announces the brunette model, appearing again with a flourish of frock, a dip, a spin.

"Wonderful texture, pomecia," Mr. Sondheim says, quickly getting businesslike again. "Furthermore, it doesn't crease."

"Like the other two better, don't you, Nick-*kee?*" asks Mrs. Morton.

The Baron is silent. The model twirls in front of him again, then stands with her back to him.

"What is your number?" the Baron asks, in a clipped British tone.

"*Numba* 6 3 9," she shoots back over her shoulder. The Baron writes it down, and then watches the model disappear behind the curtain to the clatter of plastic hangers.

Five minutes later, Mr. Sondheim's collection has been shown, and the Baron gives him the style numbers of the dresses *Vogue* wishes to have photographed and shown exclusively. Mr. Sondheim is delighted to comply, for having clothes appear first in *Vogue's* editorial pages almost guarantees their successful sale.

It all started back on December 17, 1892, when "quiet, clubby" Arthur Baldwin Turnure (Princeton '76), husband of one of America's first lady golf bugs, founded *Vogue* magazine. By 1895 he had created a sensation by displaying in his magazine the dresses and underwear to be worn by Miss Consuelo Vanderbilt on the occasion of her marriage to the Duke of Marlborough.

In 1909 *Vogue* was purchased by Condé Nast, under whom it flourished as never before, and no other magazine in the fashion field has ever been able to challenge it. *Harper's Bazaar,* which has always been less conservative—"It goes one rhinestone too *far,*" a *Vogue* lady explains—does not provide its readers with quite so much of what Mary McCarthy calls "Democratic snobbery."

Some years ago Miss McCarthy, who did a rather extensive study of women's fashion magazines for *The Reporter,* concluded that as one descended through the less chichi magazines—such as *Charm, Glamour, Mademoiselle*—one found more genuine solicitude for the reader and her problems—"the pain of being a B.G. (Business Girl), the envy of superiors, self-consciousness, awkwardness, loneliness, sexual fears, timid friendliness to the Boss, endless evenings with the mirror and the tweezers, desperate Saturday social strivings ('Give a party and ask *everyone* you know'), the struggle to achieve any identity in the dead cubbyhole of office life."

And in another study of female magazines, this one done in *Social Forces* by two sociologists, Bernard Barber of Barnard College and Lyle S. Lobel, then of Harvard, it was stated that while the symbols of prestige in *Vogue* were "sophistication and chic," these same symbols were scorned by the respectable, PTA-types on the *Ladies' Home Journal,* where there "is a distaste for 'high style,' for what is 'daring' or 'unusual.' "

But above *Vogue*'s ultra-chic level, according to the sociologists, there looms an even more-envied class of women: the unfashionable "old money" rich.

"At this top-most level, where there is little need to compete for status through consumption," wrote Barber and Lobel, "women may even maintain a certain independence of current changeful 'fashion.' Their quality clothes can remain roughly the same for several years. . . . Even eccentric, like the old ladies on Beacon Street in Boston."

Describing the *Vogue* level, they continued: "In the social class just below the 'old money' families we find most of the 'high fashion,' Paris-conscious style leaders. Since they are aware of the class above, perhaps trying to gain entrance into it, these women seek to combine opulence with 'quiet elegance.' 'Fashion copy' for this group stresses the *pose* of assured distinction, effortless superiority, and inbred elegance."

Before *Vogue* magazine can display its pose of assured distinction and elegance, of course, it must summon its high-fashion models and have them photographed by fashion photographers, and on this particular afternoon *Vogue*'s colour photography sitting was being held in the penthouse studio of the noted photographer Horst Horst, a marvellous spot overlooking the East River. In the studio, while Horst Horst adjusts his German, Japanese, and Swedish cameras, his Chinese houseboy tacks enormous sheets of balmy skyblue cardboard to the wall, creating a summery background. In the middle of the floor, in front of a box of flowers, is a plush stool of warm, Hazelmu brown on which the model will sit. In the adjoining dressing room, *Vogue*'s Mrs. Simpson, while awaiting the arrival of the model, Dorothea McGowan, does needlepoint from a Matisse pattern.

"I'd go mad, *mad* without this," Mrs. Simpson says of her needlepoint.

In another corner of the dressing room, *Vogue*'s wardrobe mistresses press a half-dozen Galanos chiffon gowns that the model will wear. Finally, ten minutes later, Dorothea McGowan, a tall, pale girl, lunges in with her hair in curlers. Immediately she removes her coat, unhinges her hair, dashes for the mirror, and quickly begins to stroke her canvas-like facial skin with a Japanese paint brush.

"Which shoes, Mrs. Simpson?" she asks.

"Try the red ones, dear," Mrs. Simpson says, looking up from Matisse.

"Let's go," calls Horst from the other room.

Within a few minutes, after expert facial painting, Dorothea transforms herself from the pale, gangling Brooklyn girl she'd been upon entering the studio into a sophisticated ageless woman about to pose for her seventh *Vogue* cover. She walks confidently into the studio, stands fifteen feet in front of Horst, stretches her calf muscles, spreads her legs slightly, places hands on hips, and prepares for her love affair with the camera.

Horst Horst, hands caressing his tripod, crouches and is about to shoot when Mrs. Simpson, standing on the sidelines like a duenna, shouts, "Wait." And the trance is momentarily broken as Mrs. Simpson says, "Her nails look terrible."

"Do they?" asks Dorothea, no longer the confident woman, but now again the girl from Brooklyn.

"Yes, do you have your nails with you?"

The model goes into the dressing room to put on her false nails, and then returns in front of the camera. Mrs. Simpson, satisfied now, returns to her needlepoint in the next room, and the Chinese boy places a fan in front of Dorothea, blowing her chiffon dress into her thin, lean body.

Dorothea throws her head back.

"Oh, such a rich feeling when the fan blows," she titters.

"Do something with your leg," Horst says.

She bends it backward, opens her mouth. And Horst's camera goes *click.* Then she leans down against the stool, lips puckered. Horst goes *click.*

"Oh, that's good," Horst says. "Do it again" (click).

Dorothea smiles (click); opens her mouth (click); wider, a big O (click).

"Hat's coming off," she giggles.

"Just smile, don't grin," he says (click). "Make a long neck."

She stretches (click).

"That's my girl," he says (click).

"Yesss," he repeats slowly (click).

And now, without any directions from him, she automatically strikes different poses, each one punctuated with a click; her face now bitchy, now primed for love, now blazy-eyed, now as demure as a Vassar virgin's. And Horst all the while is saying, excitedly behind the camera,

"Yesss" (click), "Yesss" (click), "Yesss" (click).

"What are these little flowers?" Dorothea asks finally, breaking out of the mood.

"Azaleas," Horst says, lighting a cigarette. Dorothea pulls off a large rhinestone ring from her right hand, places it on her left, and then says, "You know, if you take a ring off one finger and put it on another finger, it still feels like you have it on the first finger."

Horst Horst looks at her in mild wonderment. Then Dorothea goes to change her dress. And the Chinese boy, built like a speed swimmer, turns off the fan and quickly changes the background from blue cardboard to pink. When Dorothea returns, Mrs. Simpson is back for another look.

"Dorothea," Mrs. Simpson says, "you have little hairs sticking out in the back of your neck."

"Oh?" Dorothea says, touching her neck.

Dorothea, turning toward the dressing room, notices the pink background, and her face becomes alive with anticipation.

"Oh," she exclaims, "I have pink . . . pink, PINK!"

Looking for
Hemingway

I remember very well the impression I had of Hemingway that first after-noon. He was an extraordinarily good-looking young man, twenty-three years old. It was not long after that that everybody was twenty-six. It became the period of being twenty-six. During the next two or three years all the young men were twenty-six years old. It was the right age apparently for that time and place.

—Gertrude Stein

Early in the Fifties another young generation of American expatriates in Paris became twenty-six years old, but they were not Sad Young Men, nor were they Lost; they were the witty, irreverent sons of a conquering nation and, though they came mostly from wealthy parents and had been graduated from Harvard or Yale, they seemed endlessly delighted in posing as paupers and dodging the bill collectors, possibly because it seemed challenging and distinguished them from American tourists, whom they despised, and also because it was another way of having fun with the French, who despised *them*. Nevertheless, they lived in happy squalor on the Left Bank for two or three years amid the whores, jazz musicians and pederast poets, and became involved with people both tragic and mad, including a passionate Spanish painter who one day cut open a vein in his leg and finished his final portrait with his own blood.

In July they drove down to Pamplona to run from the bulls, and when they returned they played tennis with Irwin Shaw at Saint-Cloud on a magnificent court overlooking Paris—and, when they tossed up the ball to serve, *there,* sprawled before them, was the whole city: the Eiffel Tower, Sacré-Coeur, the Opéra, the spires of Notre Dame in the distance. Irwin Shaw was amused by them. He called them "The Tall Young Men."

The tallest of them, at six feet four inches, was George Ames Plimpton, a quick, graceful tennis player with long, skinny limbs, a small head, bright blue eyes and a delicate, fine-tipped nose. He had come to Paris in 1952, at the age of twenty-six, because several other tall, young Americans—and some short, wild ones—were publishing a literary quarterly to be called *The Paris Review,* over the protest of one of their staff members, a poet, who wanted it to be called *Druids' Home Companion* and to be printed on birch bark. George Plimpton was made editor in chief, and soon he could be seen strolling through the streets of Paris with a long, woolen scarf flung around his neck, or sometimes with a black evening cape billowing from his shoulders, cutting a figure reminiscent of Toulouse-Lautrec's famous lithograph of Aristide Bruant, that dashing littérateur of the nineteenth century.

Though much of the editing of *The Paris Review* was done at sidewalk cafés by editors awaiting their turns on the pinball machine, the magazine nevertheless became very successful because the editors had talent, money and taste, and they avoided using such typical little-magazine words as "zeitgeist" and "dichotomous," and published no crusty critiques about Melville or Kafka, but instead printed the poetry and fiction of gifted young writers not yet popular. They also started a superb series of interviews with famous authors—who took them to lunch, introduced them to actresses, playwrights and producers, and everybody invited everybody else to parties, and the parties have not stopped, even though ten years have passed; Paris is no longer the scene, and the Tall Young Men have become thirty-six years old.

They now live in New York. And most of the parties are held at George Plimpton's large bachelor apartment on Seventy-second Street overlooking the East River, an apartment that is also the headquarters for what Elaine Dundy calls "The Quality Lit Set," or what Candida Donadio, the agent, calls "The East Side Gang," or what everybody else just calls *The Paris Review* Crowd." The Plimpton apartment today is the liveliest literary salon in New York—the only place where, standing in a single room on almost any night of the week, one may find James Jones; William Styron; Irwin Shaw; a few call girls for decoration; Norman Mailer; Philip Roth; Lillian Hellman; a bongo player; a junkie or two; Harold L. Humes; Jack Gelber; Sadruddin Aga Khan; Terry Southern; Blair Fuller; the cast from *Beyond the Fringe;* Tom Keogh; William Pène du Bois; Bee Whistler Dabney (an artist who descends from Whistler's mother); Robert Silvers; and an angry veteran of the Bay of Pigs invasion; and a retired bunny from the Playboy Club; John P. C. Train; Joe Fox; John Phillips Marquand; and Robert W. Dowling's secretary; Peter Duchin; Gene Andrewski; Jean vanden Heuvel; and Ernest Hemingway's former boxing coach; Frederick Seidel; Thomas H. Guinzburg; David Amram; and a bartender from down the street; Barbara Epstein; Jill Fox; and a local distributor of pot; Piedy Gimbel; Dwight Macdonald; Bill Cole; Jules Feiffer; *and* into such a scene one wintry night earlier this year walked another old friend of George Plimpton's—Jacqueline Kennedy.

"Jackie!" George called out, opening the door to greet the First Lady and also her sister and brother-in-law, the Radziwills. Mrs. Kennedy, smiling broadly between gleaming earrings, extended her hand to George, whom she has known since her dancing-school days, and they chatted for a few seconds in the hallway while George helped her with her coat. Then, peeking into the bedroom and noticing a mound of overcoats piled higher than a Volkswagen, Mrs. Kennedy said, in a soft, hushed, sympathetic voice, "Oh, *George*—your *b e d!*"

George shrugged, and then escorted them through the hall down three steps into the smoky scene.

"Look," said one hipster in the corner, "there's Lee Radziwill's sister!"

George first introduced Mrs. Kennedy to Ved Mehta, the Indian writer, and then slipped her skillfully past Norman Mailer toward William Styron.

"Why, hel*LO*, Bill," she said, shaking hands, "nice to see you."

For the next few moments, talking with Styron and Cass Canfield Jr., Mrs. Kennedy stood with her back to Sandra Hochman, a Greenwich Village poetess, a streaked blonde in a thick woolly sweater and partially unzipped ski pants.

"I think," Miss Hochman whispered to a friend, tossing a backward nod at Mrs. Kennedy's beautiful white brocade suit, "that I am a bit *déshabillée*."

"Nonsense," said her friend, flicking cigarette ashes on the rug. And, in truth, it must be said that none of the seventy other people in that room felt that Sandra Hochman's outfit contrasted unpleasantly with the First Lady's; in fact, some did not even notice the First Lady, and there was one who noticed her but failed to recognize her.

"My," he said, squinting through the smoke toward the elaborately teased coiffure of Mrs. Kennedy, "that *really* is the look this year, isn't it? And that chick has almost made it."

While Mrs. Kennedy conversed in the corner, Princess Radziwill talked with Bee Whistler Dabney a few feet away, and Prince Radziwill stood alone next to the baby grand piano humming to himself. He often hums to himself at parties. In Washington he is known as a great hummer.

Fifteen minutes later Mrs. Kennedy, expected soon at a dinner given by Adlai Stevenson, said good-bye to Styron and Canfield and, escorted by George Plimpton, headed for the steps toward the hall. Norman Mailer, who had meanwhile drunk three glasses of water, was standing by the steps. He looked hard at her as she passed. She did not return his glance.

Three quick steps, and she was gone—down the hall, her coat on, her long white gloves on, down two flights of steps to the sidewalk, the Radziwills and George Plimpton behind her.

"Look," squealed a blonde, Sally Belfrage, gazing down from the kitchen window at the figures below climbing into the limousine, "there's *George!* And *look* at that car!"

"What's so unusual about that car?" somebody asked. "It's only a Cadillac."

"Yes, but it's *black*, and so-o-o *un*chromed."

Sally Belfrage watched as the big car, pointed in the direction of another world, moved quietly away, but in the living room the party went on louder than before, with nearly everyone oblivious to the fact that the host had disappeared. But there was liquor to be consumed and, besides, by just casting an eye over the photographs on the walls throughout the apartment, one could easily feel the presence of George Plimpton. One photograph shows him fighting small bulls in Spain with Hemingway; another catches him drinking beer with other Tall Young Men at a Paris café; others show him as a lieutenant marching a platoon of troops through Rome, as a tennis player for King's College, as an amateur prizefighter sparring with Archie Moore in Stillman's Gymnasium, an occasion during which the rancid smell of the gym was temporarily replaced by the musk of El Morocco and the cheers of Plimpton's friends when he scored with a solid jab—but it quickly changed to *"Ohhhhhhh"* when Archie Moore retaliated with a punch that broke part of the cartilage in Plimpton's nose, causing it to bleed and causing Miles Davis to ask afterward, "Archie, is that black blood or white blood on your gloves?" to which one of Plimpton's friends replied, "Sir, *that* is blue blood."

Also on the wall is Plimpton's rebab, a one-stringed instrument of goatskin that Bedouin tribesmen gave him prior to his doing a walk-on in *Lawrence of Arabia* during a dust storm. And above his baby grand piano—he plays it well enough to have won a tie-for-third prize on Amateur Night at the Apollo theatre a couple of years ago in Harlem—is a coconut sent him by a lady swimmer he knows in Palm Beach, and also a photograph of another girl, Vali, the orange-haired Existentialist known to all Left Bank concierges as *la bête,* and also a major-league baseball that Plimpton occasionally hurls full distance across the living room into a short, chunky, stuffed chair, using the same windup as when he pitched batting practice against Willie Mays while researching his book, *Out of My League,* which concerns how it feels to be an amateur among pros—and which, incidentally, is a key not only to George Ames Plimpton but to many others on *The Paris Review* as well.

They are obsessed, so many of them, by the wish to know how the other half lives. And so they befriend the more interesting of the odd, avoid the downtown dullards on Wall Street, and dip into the world of the junkie, the pederast, the prizefighter, and the adventurer in pursuit of kicks and literature, being influenced perhaps by that glorious generation of ambulance drivers that preceded them to Paris at the age of twenty-six.

In Paris in the early Fifties, their great white hope was Irwin Shaw because, in the words of Thomas Guinzburg, a Yale man then managing editor of *The Paris Review,* "Shaw was a tough, tennis-playing, hard-drinking writer with a good-looking wife—the closest thing we had to Hemingway." Of course the editor in chief, George Plimpton, then as now, kept the magazine going, kept the group together, and set a style of romanticism that was—and is—infectious.

Arriving in Paris in the Spring of 1952 with a wardrobe that included the tails his grandfather had worn in the Twenties, and which George himself had worn in 1951 while attending a ball in London as an escort to the future Queen of England, he moved immediately into a tool shed behind a house owned by Gertrude Stein's nephew. Since the door of the shed was jammed, Plimpton, to enter it, had to hoist himself, his books, and his grandfather's tails through the window. His bed was a long, thin cot flanked by a lawn mower and garden hose, and was covered by an electric blanket that Plimpton could never remember to turn off—so that, when he returned to the shed at night and plopped into the cot, he was usually greeted by the angry howls of several stray cats reluctant to leave the warmth that his forgetfulness had provided.

One lonely night, before returning home, Plimpton took the walk through Montparnasse down the same streets and past the same cafés that Jake Barnes took after leaving Lady Brett in *The Sun Also Rises.* Plimpton wanted to see what Hemingway had seen, to feel what Hemingway had felt. Then, the walk over, Plimpton went into the nearest bar and ordered a drink.

In 1952 *The Paris Review*'s headquarters was a one-room office at 8 Rue Garancière. It was furnished with a desk, four chairs, a bottle of brandy, and several lively, long-legged Smith and Radcliffe girls who were anxious to get onto the masthead so that they might convince their parents back home of their innocence abroad. But so many young women came and went that Plimpton's business manager, a small, sharp-tongued

Harvard wit named John P. C. Train, decided it was ridiculous to try to remember all their names, whereupon he declared that they should henceforth all be called by one name—"Apetecker." And the Apetecker alumnae came to include, at one time or another, Jane Fonda, Joan Dillon Moseley (daughter of Treasury Secretary Dillon), Gail Jones (daughter of Lena Horne), and Louisa Noble (daughter of the Groton football coach), a very industrious but forgetful girl who was endlessly losing manuscripts, letters, dictionaries. One day, after John P. C. Train received a letter from a librarian complaining that Miss Noble was a year overdue on a book, he wrote back:

Dear Sir:
I take the liberty of writing to you in my own hand because Miss L. Noble took with her the last time she left this office the typewriter on which I was accustomed to compose these messages. Perhaps when she comes into your library you will ask if we might not have this machine.
Subscription blank enclosed.

Yours faithfully,
J. P. C. Train

Since *The Paris Review*'s one-room office obviously was too small to fulfill the staff's need for mixing business with pleasure, and since there was also a limit to the number of hours they could spend at cafés, everybody would usually gather at five p.m. at the apartment of Peter and Patsy Matthiessen on 14 Rue Perceval, where by that time a party was sure to be in progress.

Peter Matthiessen, then fiction editor of *The Paris Review,* was a tall, thin Yale graduate who as a youngster had attended St. Bernard's School in New York with George Plimpton, and who now was working on his first novel, *Race Rock.* Patsy was a small, lovely, vivacious blonde with pale blue eyes and a marvelous figure, and all the boys of twenty-six were in love with her. She was the daughter of the late Richard Southgate, one-time Chief of Protocol for the State Department, and Patsy had gone to lawn parties with Kennedy children, had chauffeurs and governesses and, in her junior year at Smith, in 1948, had come to Paris and met Peter. Three years later, married, they returned to Paris and acquired for $21 a month this apartment in Montparnasse that had been left vacant when Peter's old girl friend had gone off to Venezuela.

The apartment had high ceilings, a terrace and lots of sun. On one wall was a Foujita painting of a gigantic head of a cat. The other wall was all glass, and there were large trees against the glass and wild growth crawling up it, and visitors to this apartment often felt that they were in a monstrous fishbowl, particularly by six p.m., when the room was floating with Dutch gin and absinthe and the cat's head seemed bigger, and a few junkies would wander in, nod, and settle softly, soundlessly in the corner.

This apartment, in the Fifties, was as much a meeting place for the young American literati as was Gertrude Stein's apartment in the Twenties, and it also caught the atmosphere that would, in the Sixties, prevail at George Plimpton's apartment in New York.

William Styron, often at the Matthiessens', describes their apartment in his novel, *Set This House on Fire,* and other novelists there were John Phillips Marquand and Terry Southern, both editors on *The Paris Review,* and sometimes James Baldwin, and nearly always Harold L. Humes, a chunky, indefatigable, impulsive young man with a beard, beret and a silver-handled umbrella. After being dismissed from M.I.T. for taking a Radcliffe girl sailing several hours beyond her bedtime, and after spending an unhappy tour with the Navy making mayonnaise in Bainbridge, Maryland, Harold Humes burst onto the Paris scene in full rebellion.

He became a chess hustler in cafés, earning several hundred francs a night. It was in the cafés that he met Peter Matthiessen, and they both talked of starting a little magazine that would be *The Paris Review.* Before coming to Paris, Humes had never worked on a magazine, but had grown fond of a little magazine called *Zero,* edited by a small Greek named Themistocles Hoetes, whom everybody called "Them." Impressed by what Them had done with *Zero,* Humes purchased for $600 a magazine called *The Paris News Post,* which John Ciardi later called the "best fourth-rate imitation of *The New Yorker* I have ever seen," and to which Matthiessen felt condescendingly superior, and so Humes sold it for $600 to a very nervous English girl, under whom it collapsed one issue later. Then Humes and Matthiessen and others began a long series of talks on what policy, if any, they would follow should *The Paris Review* ever get beyond the talking and drinking stages.

When the magazine was finally organized, and when George Plimpton was selected as its editor instead of Humes, Humes was disappointed. He refused to leave the cafés to sell advertising or negotiate with French printers. And in the Summer of 1952 he did not hesitate to leave Paris with William Styron, accepting an invitation from a French actress, Mme. Nénot, to go down to Cap Myrt, near Saint-Tropez, and visit her fifty-room villa that had been designed by her father, a leading architect. The villa had been occupied by the Germans early in the war. And so when Styron and Humes arrived they found holes in its walls, through which they could look out to the sea, and the grass was so high and the trees so thick with grapes that Humes's little Volkswagen became tangled in the grass. So they went on foot toward the villa, but suddenly stopped when they saw, rushing past them, a young, half-naked girl, very brown from the sun, wearing only handkerchiefs tied bikini-style, her mouth spilling with grapes. Screaming behind her was a lecherous-looking old French farmer whose grape arbor she obviously had raided.

"*Styron,*" Humes cried, gleefully, "*we have arrived!*"

"Yes," he said, "we are *here!*"

More nymphets came out of the trees in bikinis later, carrying grapes and also half cantaloupes the size of cartwheels, and they offered some to Styron and Humes. The next day they all went swimming and fishing and, in the evening, they sat in the bombed-out villa, a breathtaking site of beauty and destruction, drinking wine with the young girls who seemed to belong only to the beach. It was an electric summer, with the nymphets batting around like moths against the screen. Styron remembers it as a scene out of Ovid, Humes as the high point of his career as an epicurean and scholar.

George Plimpton remembers that summer not romantically, but as it was—a long, hot summer of frustration with French printers and advertisers; and the other *Review* staff members, particularly John P. C. Train, were so annoyed at Humes' departure that they decided they would drop his name from the top of the masthead, where he belonged as one of the founders, down to near the bottom under "advertising and circulation."

When the first issue of *The Paris Review* came out, in the Spring of 1953, Humes was in the United States. But he had heard what they had done to him and, infuriated, he now planned his revenge. When the ship arrived at the Hudson River pier with the thousands of *Paris Reviews* that would be distributed throughout the United States, Harold Humes, wearing his beret and swearing, *"Le Paris Review c'est moi!"* was at the dock waiting for them; soon he had ripped the cartons open and, with a rubber stamp bearing his name in letters larger than any on the masthead, he began to pound his name in red over the masthead of each issue, a feat that took several hours to accomplish and which left him, in the end, totally exhausted.

"But . . . but . . . how *c-o-u-l-d* you have *done* such a thing?" George Plimpton asked when he next saw Humes.

Humes was now sad, almost tearful; but, with a final flash of vengeance, he said, "I am damned well not going to get shoved around!"

Rages of this sort were to become quite common at *The Paris Review.* Terry Southern was incensed when a phrase in one of his short stories was changed from "don't get your crap hot" to "don't get hot." Two poets wished to dissect John P. C. Train when, after a French printer had accidentally spilled the type from one poem into another, and the two poems appeared as one in the magazine, Train *casually* remarked that the printer's carelessness had actually improved the work of both poets.

Another cause for chaos was the Paris police force, which seemed ever in pursuit of John Train's nocturnal squad of flying poster plasterers, a union of Yale men and Arab youths who ran through Paris at night sticking large *Paris Review* advertising posters on every lamppost, bus, and *pissoir* they could. The ace of the squadron, a tall Yale graduate named Frank Musinsky, was so impressive that John Train decided to name all the other young men "Musinsky"—just as he had previously named the girls "Apetecker"—which Musinsky considered quite an honor, even though his real name was not Musinsky. Musinsky acquired the name because his grandfather, whose surname was Supovitch (sic), had switched names in Russia many years ago with a countryman named Musinsky who, for a price, agreed to take Frank's grandfather's place in the Russian army.

Nobody knows what became of him in the Russian army, but Frank's grandfather came to the United States where his son later prospered in the retail shoe business and his grandson, Frank, after Yale and his tour with Train's flying squad, got a job in 1954 with *The New York Times*— and soon lost it.

He had been hired as a copyboy in the *Times* sports department and, as such, was expected to devote himself to running galley proofs and filling pastepots, and was not expected to be sitting behind a desk, feet propped up, reading Yeats and Pound and refusing to move.

One night an editor shouted, "Musinsky, without doubt you're the worst copyboy in the history of the *Times*," to which Musinsky, rising haughtily, snapped, "Sir, to quote E. E. Cummings, whom I'm sure you have heard of, 'There is some shit I shall not eat.' " Frank Musinsky turned and left the *Times,* never to return.

Meanwhile, Frank's place in the Paris flying squad was taken by several other Musinskys—Colin Wilson was one—and they all helped to preserve *The Review*'s traditional irreverence for the bourgeoisie, the Establishment, and even for the late Aga Khan who, after offering to give a $1,000 prize for fiction, then submitted his own manuscript.

The editors quickly snapped up his money, but just as quickly returned the manuscript, making it clear that his prose style was not what they were seeking, even though the Aga's own son, Sadruddin Khan, a Harvard friend of Plimpton's, had just become publisher of *The Paris Review,* an offer that George proposed and Sadruddin accepted rather impulsively one day when they both were running from the bulls at Pamplona—a moment during which George suspected, correctly, that Sadruddin might agree to just about anything.

As improbable as it may seem, what with all the Musinskys and Apeteckers flying this way and that, *The Paris Review* did very well, publishing fine stories by such younger writers as Philip Roth, Mac Hyman, Pati Hill, Evan Connell, Jr. and Hughes Rudd, and, of course, distinguishing itself most of all by its "Art of Fiction" interviews with famous authors, particularly the one with William Faulkner by Jean Stein vanden Heuvel and the one with Ernest Hemingway by Plimpton, which began in a Madrid café with Hemingway asking Plimpton, "You go to the races?"

"Yes, occasionally."

"Then you read *The Racing Form*," Hemingway said. "There you have the true Art of Fiction."

But as much as anything else, *The Paris Review* survived because it had money. And its staff members had fun because they knew that, should they ever land in jail, their friends or families would always bail them out. They would never have to share with James Baldwin the experience of spending eight days and nights in a dirty French cell on the erroneous charge of having stolen a bed sheet from a hotelkeeper, all of which led Baldwin to conclude that while the wretched round of hotel rooms, bad food, humiliating concierges, and unpaid bills may have been the "Great Adventure" for the Tall Young Men, it was not for him because, he said, "there was a real question in my mind as to which would end soonest, the Great Adventure or me."

The comparative opulence of *The Paris Review,* of course, made it the envy of the other little magazines, particularly the staff members of a quarterly called *Merlin,* some of whose editors charged the *Review* people with dilettantism, resented their pranks, resented that the *Review* would continue to be published while *Merlin,* which had also discovered and printed new talent, would soon fold.

In those days *Merlin*'s editor was Alexander Trocchi, born in Glasgow of a Scotch mother and Italian father, a very exciting, tall and conspicuous literary figure with a craggy, satanic face, faun's ears, a talent for writing and a powerful presence that enabled him to walk into any room and take charge. He would soon become a friend of George Plimpton, John Phillips Marquand, and the other *Review* people, and years later he would come to New York to live on a barge, and still later in the back room of *The Paris Review*'s Manhattan office, but eventually he would be arrested on narcotics charges, would jump bail, and would leave the United States with two of George Plimpton's Brooks Brothers suits. But he would leave behind a good novel about drug addiction, *Cain's Book,* with its memorable line: "Heroin is habit-forming . . . habit-forming . . . rabbit-forming . . . Babbitt-forming."

Alexander Trocchi's staff at *Merlin* in those days was made up largely of humorless young men in true rebellion, which *The Paris Review* staff was not; the *Merlin* crowd also read the leftist monthly *Les Temps Modernes,* and were concerned with the importance of being *engagé.* Their editors included Richard Seaver, who was reared in the Pennsylvania coal-mine district and in whose dark, humid Paris garage *Merlin* held its staff meetings, and also Austryn Wainhouse, a disenchanted Exeter-Harvard man who wrote a strong, esoteric novel, *Hedyphagetica,* and who, after several years in France, is now living in Martha's Vineyard building furniture according to the methods of the eighteenth century.

While the entire *Merlin* staff was poor, none was so poor as the poet, Christopher Logue, about whom it was said that once, when playing a pinball machine in a café, he noticed a ragged old peasant lady staring at a five-franc piece lying on the floor near the machine, but before she could pick it up Logue's foot quickly reached out and stomped on it. He kept his foot there while the old lady screamed and while he continued, rather jerkily, to hold both hands to the machine trying to keep the ball bouncing—and *did,* until the owner of the café grabbed him and escorted him out.

Some time later, when Logue's girl friend left him, he came under the influence of a wild Svengali character then living in Paris, a pale, waxen-faced South African painter who was a disciple of Nietzsche and his dictum, "Die at the right time," and who, looking for kicks, actually encouraged Logue to commit suicide—which Logue, in his depressed state, said he would do.

Austryn Wainhouse, who had suspected that suicide was very much on Logue's mind, had spent the following week sitting outside of Logue's hotel each night watching his window, but one afternoon when Logue was late for a luncheon date with Wainhouse, the latter rushed to the poet's hotel and there, on the bed, was the South African painter.

"Where's Chris?" Wainhouse demanded.

"I am not going to tell you," the painter said. "You can beat me if you wish; you're bigger and stronger than I, and. . . ."

"I *don't* want to beat you," Wainhouse shouted. It then occurred to him how ridiculous was the South African's remark since he (Wainhouse) was actually much smaller and hardly stronger than the painter. "Look," he said, finally, "don't you leave here," and then he ran quickly to a café where he knew he would find Trocchi.

Trocchi got the South African to talk and admit that Christopher Logue had left that morning for Perpignan, near the Spanish border twelve hours south of Paris, where he planned to commit suicide in much the same way as the character in the Samuel Beckett story in *Merlin,* entitled "The End"—he would hire a boat and row out to sea, further and further, and then pull up the plugs and slowly sink.

Trocchi, borrowing 30,000 francs from Wainhouse, hopped on the next train for Perpignan, five hours behind Logue. It was dark when he arrived, but early the next morning he began his search.

Logue, meanwhile, had tried to rent a boat, but did not have enough money. He also carried with him, along with some letters from his former girl friend, a tin of poison, but he did not have an opener, nor were there rocks on the beach, and so he wandered about, frustrated and frantic, until he finally came upon a refreshment stand where he hoped to borrow an opener.

It was then that the tall figure of Trocchi spotted him and placed a hand on Logue's shoulder. Logue looked up.

"Alex," Logue said, casually handing him the tin of poison, "will you open this for me?"

Trocchi put the tin in his pocket.

"*Alex*," Logue then said, "what are *you* doing here?"

"Oh," Trocchi said lightly, "I've come down to embarrass you."

Logue broke down in tears, and Trocchi helped him off the beach and then they rode, almost in total silence, back to Paris on the train.

Immediately George Plimpton and several others on *The Paris Review* who were very fond of Logue, and proud of Trocchi, raised enough money to put Christopher Logue on a kind of monthly allowance. Later Logue returned to London and published books of poetry and his plays, *Antigone* and *The Lily-White Boys* were performed at the Royal Court Theatre in London. Still later he began to write songs for The Establishment, London's satirical nightclub act.

After the Logue episode, which, according to George Plimpton, sent at least a half-dozen young novelists to their typewriters trying to build a book around it, life in Paris at the *Review* was once more happy and ribald—but, a year later with the *Review* still doing well, Paris slowly seemed to pall.

John P. C. Train, then managing editor, put a sign on his in-basket reading, "Please Do Not Put Anything In The Managing Editor's Box," and one day when a pleasant, blue-eyed Oklahoman named Gene Andrewski wandered in with a manuscript and mentioned that he had once helped produce his college humor magazine, John Train quickly handed him a beer and said, "How would you like to run this magazine?" Andrewski said he would think it over. He thought it over for a few seconds, looked around at everybody else drinking beer, and agreed to become a kind of Assistant Managing Editor in Charge of Doing Train's

Job. "The main reason I took the job," Andrewski later explained, "was I wanted the freedom."

In 1956 Peter Duchin moved to Paris and lived on a barge on the Seine, and many *Paris Review* people made this their new headquarters. There was no water on the barge, and in the morning everybody had to shave with Perrier. But the attempt at merriment on the barge seemed futile because, by this time, most of the old crowd had left. Paris was, as Gertrude Stein suggested, the right place for twenty-six, but now most of them were thirty years old. And so they returned to New York—but not in the melancholy mood of Malcolm Cowley's exiles of the Twenties, who were forced home during the early currents of the crash, but rather with the attitude that the party would now shift to the other side of the Atlantic. Soon New York was aware of their presence, particularly the presence of Harold L. Humes.

After taking over a large apartment on upper Broadway with his wife, his daughters, and his unclipped wirehair terrier, and installing seven telephones and a large paper cutter that has the cracking eighteenth-century sound of a guillotine, Humes lashed out with a series of ideas and tall deeds: he hit on a theory of cosmology that would jolt Descartes, finished a second novel, played piano in a Harlem jazz club, began to shoot a movie called *Don Peyote,* a kind of Greenwich Village version of Don Quixote starring an unknown from Kansas City named Ojo de Vidrio, whose girl friend eventually grabbed the film and ran off with it. Humes also invented a paper house, an *actual paper house* that is water-proof, fireproof and large enough for people to live in; he set up a full-sized model on the Long Island estate of George Plimpton's family, and Humes's corporation, which included some backers from *The Paris Review* crowd, insured Humes's brain for $1,000,000.

During the Democratic National Convention in 1960, Humes led a phalanx of screaming Stevensonians onto the scene after employing the gate-crashing techniques of the ancient armies of Athens. When back in New York he called for an investigation of the New York police force, whereupon the police commissioner called for an investigation of *Humes* —and discovered fourteen unpaid traffic tickets. Humes went to jail just long enough to be discovered by the Commissioner of Corrections, Anna Kross, who upon recognizing him behind bars said, "Why, Mr. Humes, what are *you* doing in *there?*", to which he responded with Thoreau's line to Emerson, "Why, Miss Kross, what are *you* doing out *there?*"

When released on bail that was produced by Robert Silvers, another *Paris Review* editor, Harold Humes was asked by newspaper reporters how he liked the cell, and he replied, once more after Thoreau, "In a time of injustice, the place for an honest man is in jail."

Robert Silvers, one of the few quiet editors on the *Review,* a man with no apparent vices except smoking in bed, had no place to stay when he returned from Paris, and so he temporarily occupied the guest room in George Plimpton's apartment on East Seventy-second Street, where he proceeded to burn many holes in the mattress. He then plugged up the holes with peach pits. George Plimpton did not object. Robert Silvers was an old friend and, besides, the mattress did not belong to Plimpton. It belonged to a fashion model who had once occupied the apartment, and who surprised both Plimpton and Silvers one day with a letter asking if they would please send the mattress to her home in France. They did, pits and all, and, having heard no complaints, they both nurture some delight in the thought that somewhere in Paris, somewhere in the very chic apartment of a high-fashion model, there is a mattress stuffed with peach pits.

Fortunately for Plimpton, he did not have to buy a new mattress for his guest room because, at about that time, *The Paris Review,* which had an office in a tenement on Eighty-second Street, had been evicted; and so Plimpton took home the small bed that had been in the back room of *The Paris Review*'s office—a room that had been the locale of several parties that had reduced the premise to a collage of broken bottles, bent spoons, rats and chewed manuscripts.

After the eviction from the tenement, *The Paris Review*'s New York office shifted to the unlikely and quiet borough of Queens, where, in a large home between Grand Central Parkway and a cemetery, Lillian von Nickern Pashaian, when she is not tending to her three children, canaries and turtles, accepts manuscripts that are addressed to *The Paris Review* and forwards them for a reading to either Jill Fox in Bedford Village, New York, or to Rose Styron in Roxbury, Connecticut. If *they* like what they have read, they forward the manuscript to George Plimpton's apartment on Seventy-second Street where, between all his other activities, he gives a final reading and decides whether or not it will be accepted.

If it is accepted, the author usually becomes the recipient of a small check and all he can drink at the next Plimpton party.

A Plimpton party is often planned only a few hours before it begins. George will pick up the phone and call a few people. They, in turn, will call others. Soon there is the thunder of feet ascending the Plimpton staircase. The inspiration for the party may have been that Plimpton won a court-tennis match earlier that day at the Racquet and Tennis Club, or that one member of *The Paris Review* crowd has a book coming out (in which case the publisher is invited to share the expenses), or that a member has just returned to Manhattan from a trip—a trip that might have carried John P. C. Train, a financial speculator, to Africa, or Peter Matthiessen to New Guinea to live with Stone Age tribesmen, or Harold Humes to the Bronx to fight in court over a parking ticket.

And in giving so many parties, in giving out keys to his apartment, in keeping the names of old friends on *The Paris Review* masthead long after they have ceased to work for it, George Ames Plimpton has managed to keep the crowd together all these years, and has also created around himself a rather romantic world, a free, frolicsome world within which he, and they, may briefly escape the inevitability of being thirty-six.

It exudes charm, talent, beauty, adventure. It is the envy of the uninvited, particularly of some child-bearing Apeteckers in the suburbs who often ask, "When is that group going to settle down?" Some in the group have remained bachelors. Others have married women who like parties —or have been divorced. Still others have an understanding that, if the wife is too tired for a party, the husband goes alone. It is largely a man's world, all of them bound by their memories of Paris and the Great Adventure they shared, and it has very few exiles, although it has had some —one being the beautiful blonde who was very much on everyone's mind in Paris ten years ago, Patsy Matthiessen.

Patsy and Peter are divorced. She is now married to Michael Goldberg, an abstract painter, lives on West Eleventh Street, and moves in the little world of downtown intellectuals and painters. Recently she spent several days in a hospital after being bitten by the dog of the widow of Jackson Pollock. In her apartment she has a cardboard box full of snapshots of *The Paris Review* crowd of the Fifties. But she remembers those days with some bitterness.

"The whole life seemed after a while to be utterly meaningless," she said. "And there was something very *manqué* about them—this going to West Africa, and getting thrown in jail, and getting in the ring with Archie Moore. . . . And *I* was a Stepin Fetchit in that crowd, getting them tea at four, and sandwiches at ten. . . ."

A few blocks away, in a small, dark apartment, another exile, James Baldwin, said, "It didn't take long before I really was no longer a part of them. They were more interested in kicks and hashish cigarettes than I was. I had already done that in the Village when I was eighteen or seventeen. It was a little boring by then.

"They also used to go to Montparnasse, where all the painters and writers went, and where I hardly went. And they used to go there and hang around at the cafés for hours and hours looking for Hemingway. They didn't seem to realize," he said, "that Hemingway was long gone."

The Party's Over

Nothing is happening. It is a meaningless moment in history. I am standing here in a dark, noisy gymnasium on the East Side of Manhattan. Four hundred people are dancing here, beautiful girls in mini-skirts, hippies, honkies, the Sassoon set in pants suits, twisting, turning, and up on the stage a quintet is banging electric guitars and tossing banana peels up over their heads into the psychedelic light. It is an Andy Warhol party. It is spring, the weekend of the big Peace March to the United Nations, and thousands of protesters are in New York and many are massed here in this gymnasium-discothèque, including Stokely Carmichael, who has just come up from the riots in Nashville.

Carmichael is wearing his Bimini-blue sunglasses over his soft roving eyes and he is standing on the sidelines in his trench coat; and now I see him moving slowly toward a big blonde who, arms flailing and hips moving, is inviting him to dance. He stands facing her for a few moments, then his body and arms begin to imitate her movements, but he seems uncertain, awkward. He stops. No rhythm.

Dancing nearby is a big, middle-aged man dripping with sweat that even trickles from the tip of his white goatee. But he moves very well for a big, soft man, smiling, dipping his head, moving his hips, *Dwight Macdonald,* and he does not lose his cool when I, with unpardonable bad manners, slip up behind him and call out "Parajournalist!" This was a term he coined in *The New York Review of Books* to attack a clique from the New Journalism, but here he is, Mr. Midcult himself, encircled in the pop scene he had seemed to abhor, the sweat pouring out of him, his face flushed red and purple, but he does not remove the jacket of his suit as another dancing critic near him has done, Max Lerner.

Lerner's coat is on the floor, wrapped in a ball and resting next to the black leather handbag of a slim brunette who is his partner. Lerner's head is flung back, his mouth open, he seems older than his photograph in the New York *Post,* but he is a strong little man, particularly around the neck, a bulging muscular neck supporting a bouncing head of wiry grey hair, and his little body moves with a determined, definite thrust, it is not tentative or stiff like Stokely Carmichael's. Tomorrow, in his column, Lerner will be making lofty pronouncements about de Gaulle or Vietnam, or the problems of power, but tonight he is at a Warhol party dancing with his eyes closed.

But no need to carp. It is symptomatic of our time, truly the Age of the Party in America, and no one can resist. The Calvinist, James Reston, went to the Capote Ball; and Jules Feiffer, after walking out of Hubert Humphrey's speech at the National Book Awards, protesting Vietnam, walked into a party later where Humphrey was present. One must be *seen* to exist, for now there is no other proof. There is no longer an identity in craft, only in self-promotion. There are no acts, only scenes. Peace marches are masquerades, Selma was a minstrel. News is staged for camera crews. Critics dance with their eyes closed.

The Ethnics of
Frank Costello

From the 1880's through the early 1900's they crossed the Atlantic in filthy ships, because they were poor; and dug ditches, because they were ignorant; and hardly a day passed in New York without some Irishman across the street yelling down at them, "Hey, you dirty wop, why don't you go back where you came from?"

They were not from the Italy of da Vinci or the Medicis; they were mostly from Sicily and the South—the Italy of goats and mountain men, and of fat ladies with little mustaches who wore rosaries and black dresses down to their ankles.

They were people who, from pre-Roman times, seemed always to be mourning something: mourning the murders and rapes by the invading Saracens, Greeks, and French; mourning the erupting volcanoes, malaria, taxes, and endless poverty. And, finally, many of them had enough, and they sailed away to America. Two who did this were named Castiglia, and from their town of Cosenza near the toe of Italy they brought their four-year-old son, Francesco, who never dreamed he would someday have an Anglo-Saxon doorman.

He never dreamed that, as Frank Costello, he would someday spend $50 for a hat, $350 for a suit, and be capable of forgetting $27,200 in the back seat of a New York taxicab. Nor did he ever dream that the mere mention of his name would whet the appetites of crime busters, and make thousands of Italian-Americans slightly uncomfortable with *their* names, and hypersensitive to slurs and questions. . . .

> *You Italian?*
> "Half and half."
> *You Italian?*
> "French."
> *You Italian?*
> "None a your goddamn business."

"Hey, wop!"
"Who ya talking to, ya bastid!"

> "And how did you enjoy Rome, Mrs. Winfred?"
> "Fine, except too many Italians."

> "Look, Angelo, my son, don't ever let them push you around because you're Italian. Don't forget that America is named after an Italian, was discovered by an Italian, and Italians were giving art to the world when those goddamned English were living in caves like savages, and painting their faces blue. . . ."

Frank Costello grew up in a New York slum with other peasant children whose parents understood neither the language nor the law. Their mothers relied entirely upon God. And their fathers relied on those better-educated but unreliable countrymen, the *padrones,* with the same blind faith that in later years led them to believe that Primo Carnera would beat Max Baer. These fathers were short and humble men—too short ever to become cops, but just right for collecting garbage and building subways, although some preferred to tend farms upstate, and still others moved into Ohio and Pennsylvania and pushed wheelbarrows filled with rocks up hills to build homes. And when they would reach the top of a certain hill in Ambler, Pennsylvania, panting and sweating, a parrot at the window of a roadside home would shrill down at them: *"Dago-dago-dago-dago-dago-dago-dago!"* The desire to sneak in and murder the parrot at night was strong. But the men never did. Instead at night they drank wine, got sleepy.

Why couldn't you go straight, Frank Costello?
Why couldn't you get a shovel and identify with Christ in Concrete?

He never could. Like many sons of these peasants, Costello despised his father's humility and inadequacy, and sought easy money and escape from his father's grocery stand. In 1908, when he was sixteen and had run away from home and quit school, he was arrested for assault and robbery. In 1912 he was arrested for the same thing. On both occasions he gave his name as Castello. In 1914, when he got his marriage license, he said he was born Costello and was a "plumber" by trade. In 1915, when he served ten months for carrying a concealed weapon, he gave his name as Frank "Saverio" and his occupation as "steamfitter." But when he appeared before General Sessions Court for sentencing, he gave his name as "Stella." He had little capacity for the truth.

By 1923 he was a rum runner; he worked under the notorious ex-longshoreman, Big Bill Dwyer, and helped command a vast operation that illegally shipped liquor down from Canada via a dozen steel-plated speedboats armed with machine guns, and aided by corrupt Coast Guardsmen. Once Costello's swift vessels accidentally strayed into the path of a speedboat race—swished across the finish line first, and kept going. It was said that during Prohibition the Dwyer-Costello operation not only supplied most of the whisky for the Eastern Seaboard, but also made large shipments to Chicago and throughout the Midwest.

Detectives began to trail Costello. They visited Italian ghettos and asked questions about him. But the neighbors would not talk. Even if a murder had occurred in broad daylight before the eyes of fifty witnesses in that neighborhood, the explanation to the police would have been the same: *"We no see notting."*

These people would no more squeal on a countryman to the New York police in the twenties than they would to the Saracen conquerors in the ninth century, the Byzantine Greeks in the tenth century, or the cruel French in the thirteenth century. Suspicious of all alien authority, they had learned the art of silence—learned it through centuries of biting their lips. They had also learned to accept the worst because the worst had long been their heritage in both Sicily and around Costello's home town of Cosenza. More than 150 landslides were recorded in Cosenza alone in 1903, and almost simultaneously the vicious Phylloxera plant parasite attacked the grapevines of the region's wine makers, and soon Bordeaux monopolized the world's wine market. Malaria was so bad in Cosenza in 1807 that it even wiped out eight hundred of the French soldiers—just as, in 1173, it had eliminated one of Thomas à Becket's fleeing murderers, William de Tracy, and in 410 had cut down Alaric, King of the Visigoths, shortly after he had plundered Rome.

"Were statistics available," wrote historian Norman Douglas of Italy's wildly beautiful South, "I have not the slightest doubt that fever could be shown to be largely responsible for the withering of its spiritual life."

To survive here amid the pestilence, poverty, impossible taxes, and torture, the peasant had to live by his wits, often remain silent, and wait for revenge—as had that vengeful band of Sicilians in 1282 before butchering an entire French garrison after a soldier had raped and murdered a Palermo maiden on her wedding day. It is said that out of this incident, glorified in a Verdi opera, came the inspiration for the Mafia— a union pledged to avenge offenses to a brother, never appeal for police protection, and never, never—on pain of death—to reveal anything about the organization or its membership to the law.

This was Frank Costello's background, and even today a travel book on this poor Southern tip of Italy reads: "While at a hotel or *pension* in Calabria, dispute in 'friendly fashion' every item. It is a matter of principle. By this system, which must not be overdone, your position in the house gradually changes; from being a guest, you become a friend, a brother. For it is your duty to show, above all things, that you are not *scemo*—witless, soft-headed—the unforgivable sin in the South. You may be a forger or cut-throat—why not? It is a vocation like any other. . . ."

And so it was in New York in the twenties that the police encountered silence in Italian Harlem, Brooklyn, and on Mulberry Street in Manhattan. After the police had gone, the men would mutter among themselves, "We wanta no trouble." And they would agree that Costello had done no wrong—the law was merely picking on him because he was Italian. Their obedient wives over the stoves would nod. Then, pushing pasta and wine in front of their husbands, the women would plead, *"Eat-a, eat-a,"* in their white-washed apartments with madonnas atop the radio, and crosses everywhere. *"Eat-a."*

Frank Costello himself felt he had done no wrong. And, in 1925, he became an American citizen. When asked his occupation, he answered, with a straight face and clear voice, "Real estate."

Following Prohibition, Costello's diversified interests included slot machines, gambling, and a legitimate business in the distribution of Scotch whisky. When Mayor Fiorello La Guardia had the New York police junk the slots and dump them at sea, Costello moved machines into New Orleans with the cooperation of Senator Huey Long, who in 1936 said he wished to raise extra money for Louisiana orphans, widows, and the blind. As managers and collectors for his slot machines, Costello hired the two Geigerman boys, his brothers-in-law, both former cab drivers.

"Dudley Geigerman is probably the thriftiest man ever heard of anywhere," wrote one crime reporter. "At a time when he was paying $40 a month rent, buying furniture on the installment plan and worrying about paying a maid $6 a week, he was reporting to the government taxable income of more than $100,000 a year. The suspicious agents of the Internal Revenue Department said it was mostly Costello's money and that Dudley was helping to keep Costello away from the high tax brackets. But they were unable to prove it."

Costello, to be sure, was trying to live a quiet, inconspicuous life during the thirties. The ten months he'd spent in jail in 1915 for carrying a concealed weapon was the first and last time he'd been behind bars. And it was said in his behalf that in 1929, following the St. Valentine's Day massacre in Chicago, Frank Costello convinced a convention of gangsters at Atlantic City of the utter senselessness of carrying weapons and murdering rival gangs. He advocated instead that rival gangs respect one another's territorial rights. As for himself, he dabbled in New York politics and contributed to the campaigns of his favorite politicians. Among the politicians who allegedly visited Costello's penthouse in 1942 was William O'Dwyer, a future Mayor of New York City. But Costello's notoriety was not so well established then. The *New York Times* on July 17, 1942, identified Costello as a "sportsman." He was always polite and entertained graciously at his estate in Long Island. He was also a model husband. He gave his Jewish wife, the former Loretta Geigerman, charge accounts at leading Fifth Avenue shops, and uttered nary a word when she spent $241.91 for three hats and a handkerchief at Mr. John, Inc.

Thousands of dollars were given by Costello to charities, churches, and an endless procession of panhandlers. But he did not worry; he had money coming in from all sides. He was even listed as earning an $18,000-a-year salary from his work with Dandy Phil Kastel at the Beverly Club, a Louisiana restaurant and gambling house, although nobody knew precisely what Costello's job was.

"And what did you do for that salary, Mr. Costello?" a crime committeeman asked in a later investigation.

"Well," Costello said, "I helped to get different acts, and I solicited some business. In other words, if someone was going to Louisiana, I would recommend a place. I was just a goodwill man for them. And I would recommend different acts for the club."

"How did you go about looking for acts?"

"Well," he said, "if I would hear of a good act, I would go in there, have dinner, and watch it. If I thought it was good, I would call them up and say, 'Here is a good act.' "

"What acts did you recommend?"

"Well, Joe Louis, Sophie Tucker, and a lot of big acts."

"Would it take an expert to recommend headliners like that to a night club?"

"Yes, well, I don't consider myself an expert. But a good act can go bad, too. No material, they would go bad. If they have new material, you will recommend it."

"Did you do anything about preparing or reviewing the material of these acts?"

"No. I was just soliciting them. Then, if I would like them, I told them I liked them."

"And for that you got $18,000 a year?"

"That's right."

Frank Costello had them completely baffled. "Costello," wrote Herbert Asbury, "has succeeded in becoming as mysterious a figure as the American underworld has ever produced. Not that the cops, both city and Federal, haven't tried to find out. They've been trying, in fact, since the middle 1920's, but by and large Costello has been too clever; they've been led up so many blind alleys that he has become a symbol of frustration to policemen and G-men throughout the country."

Costello's telephone wires were tapped by the F.B.I.; the Federal Bureau of Narcotics printed his photo on its black list; Mayor La Guardia called him a "bum." But Costello, who never kept less than $50,000 in cash in his apartment on Central Park West, paid other hoods to do his chores. Somehow he remained clean, even though New York detectives trailed him throughout the city: into the Waldorf, where he often lunched with politicians and the finest people; into the steambaths at the Biltmore, where he sweated it out in the same room with James A. Farley, Hank Greenberg, Gene Tunney, Bernard Gimbel, and dozens of distinguished executives; into barbershops, where he was fawned upon, manicured, powdered, and surrounded by serfs who fell over themselves for the big tip; through Central Park, where they observed the stocky, well-tailored figure of Costello observing the wonders of nature, studying the sky, watching animals behind bars in the park's zoo; and then to the Wollman Memorial rink, about which a *New York Times*man wrote: "The Wollman Memorial rink in Central Park . . . has attracted a good many celebrities, including Frank Costello, the gambler, of whom it is reported that he did not skate, but merely looked on skeptically, grunted and walked away."

As for the other immigrants, life became a little better through the 1930's and into the 1940's. The parrot who shrilled "dago-dago-dago-dago-dago" in Ambler, Pennsylvania, was dead. There was much to cheer about. The DiMaggio brothers could do no wrong. Pinza was sensational. And Valli became the first Italian movie actress on the American screen with something more than just large breasts. In Manhattan, The Lambs Club, in a moment of magnanimity, honored its long-time bootblack, Biaggio Velluzzi, with a dinner and theatre tickets. Biaggio, known to all as "Murph," said, "Those-a Lambs a-lovea me, and I a-lovea those-a Lambs."

All around the nation, the sons of wheelbarrow pushers and bricklayers were prospering in their own construction firms. Former caddies were being promoted to club professionals, and were able to strut around country clubs on Sunday afternoons in white yachting jackets—and *sign* for their drinks. Italian-American schoolboys still were conscious of their long names, and perhaps even envied the shorter names of Negroes, but relatively few Italians changed them; it was a matter of family pride. Or a matter of realizing that changing names would fool nobody. Perhaps a lesson had been learned from the old Italian prizefighter, Joseph Carrora, who changed his name to Johnny Dundee, but was from then on called the "Scotch Wop."

World War II produced such heralded, but short-lived heroes as the ace pilot Captain Don Gentile; and Army life brought to many Italian-American boys a sense of belonging to something more than just a Catholic parish, a labor union, or a Brooklyn bowling team sponsored by an olive-oil importer.

"It's a funny thing," said Corporal DiAngelo of Ralph Avenue, Brooklyn, "but when we moved up into Naples and Rome, all the Italians there called me an *Americano*. It was the first time in my life I'd ever felt American before. . . ."

And finally, the sons of these Sicilian and Southern immigrants, some of whose parents had posed in 1910 for Jacob Riis's forlorn photos of Mulberry Street, were moving up in politics—some with Costello's help, and some with help from the large Italian-American voting bloc. Thus, in this era of American history, there existed a generation of politicians who were never quite sure whether they were elected *because* they were Italian, or *despite* it.

Nevertheless, it felt good to sit on a judicial bench and act like a priest in a long, black gown. And it was good, as an Assemblyman, to kiss the wife and kids good-bye and ride the trains to the state capital. Although, in their shiny dark suits, pointed black shoes, white-on-white shirts, and Windsor-knot ties, these politicians were rarely mistaken for Choate men.

Frank Costello's personal ambition during these years was respectability. And this seemed almost attainable in 1949 when he was asked to serve as vice-chairman of a Salvation Army fund-raising drive. Walter Hoving, president of Tiffany and then chairman of the committee, wrote Costello that "key people in New York" were being sought and that the committee was "most anxious" to have Mr. Costello's help.

Delighted and flattered, Costello showed the letter to his attorney, George Wolf. Wolf thought there had been a mistake. He called the committee and asked, "Do you know who this man Costello is? He's a former bootlegger."

Wolf recalled that the Salvation Army was fully aware of Costello's former occupation, but nonetheless would be "delighted" with any help he could give. So Costello threw a $100-a-plate party at the Copacabana and invited, among others, Manhattan Borough President Hugo E. Rogers, and many Supreme Court Justices and leading New York politicians. He was able to collect $3,500 from contributions this way and, adding $6,500 of his own money, sent $10,000 to the Salvation Army.

But when the newspapers learned of the party, and printed the names of those present, it became a *cause célèbre*. Those in attendance came off badly, it being inferred that they were Costello's pawns. Costello looked worse, and the indignant public's response made it mandatory that action be taken.

Frank Costello, seeing his public relations drive shattered, became so annoyed with the publicity that, according to Warren Moscow, writing in the Sunday *New York Times*, Costello "arranged for the ouster of Hugo E. Rogers as leader of Tammany Hall, and for the selection of Carmine G. De Sapio as his successor. He hoped that De Sapio would make a good, respectable leader, that the public would forget about Costello while Costello enjoyed his golf and his friends in respectable retirement, free from politics and racket connections." But Mr. Moscow continued, "The Senate Crime Investigation Committee in 1951 insisted on raking up Costello's past, even after his plea, at the start of the hearings, that 'I am only asking you to respect fundamental rights and principles, I am begging you to treat me as a human being.'"

So Frank Costello went before the committee. And when he insisted that his face not be exposed on television, the cameras focused on his fingers, which tapped and danced nervously, offering a grotesque ballet for the home-screen audience. For hours he sat under the questioning with the cameras nipping away at his fingers, and one evening he was promised a large sum by cigarette salesmen if he would display their brand of cigarettes before the camera. But Costello, ever loyal to English Ovals, refused. Yet he was sick of the exposure even to his fingers, and sick in the throat, too, he told the committee.

"For a sick man," the counsel retorted, "Mr. Costello is a very astute witness."

"When I testify," Costello said hoarsely, "I want to testify truthfully, and my mind don't function."

In addition to being a reluctant witness, Costello had also become short-tempered and listless.

"Mr. Costello," shouted the counsel, finally, "did you hear the testimony . . ."

Costello's gray eyes blazed; his steel-gray hair around his temples bristled. "I am not going to answer another question," he said, firmly. "I am going to walk out."

Behind his attorney, Frank Costello moved toward the exit, disappeared, and made page 1 headlines:

COSTELLO DEFIES SENATORS

WALKS OUT OF HEARING HERE;

FACES ARREST ON CONTEMPT

Pleads Ill Health

LIGHTS AND CAMERAS BAR

PROPER TESTIMONY, HIS

ATTORNEYS SAY

Walking out was unwise; he had gone too far. He had done it before a national television audience, and the Senate could never condone such public defiance. Costello was quickly found guilty of contempt and sentenced to eighteen months in jail.

But even in jail Costello baffled the law. He continued to smoke English Ovals, although nobody knew how he smuggled them in. He ate steak—ebony on the outside, claret on the inside, just as he'd ordered them at "21"—and yet it was impossible to uncover the source of the steaks. The unbelievable power that Costello was able to wield despite his imprisonment was demonstrated some years later when he performed a behind-bars miracle for his attorney, Edward Bennett Williams.

Williams, during a visit to Costello's jail, seemed concerned about something, and Costello, detecting it, asked, "What's bothering you, Mr. Williams?"

Williams explained that he and his wife were taking her parents out that night to celebrate their thirty-fifth wedding anniversary and that he had promised them tickets to *My Fair Lady;* but the particular agent who had promised Williams the tickets—a person who'd always been reliable in the past—had suddenly failed on this occasion.

"Mr. Williams," Costello said, "you shoulda told me; maybe I coulda helped."

Williams admitted it had never occurred to him that a man in jail could help get four tickets at the last minute to a hit Broadway show.

Costello shrugged.

It was then 5 P.M.

When Williams returned to his hotel room, he heard a soft rap on the door. Upon opening it, a broad-shouldered man under a slouch hat grunted something, handed over an envelope containing four tickets to that evening's performance of *My Fair Lady,* then quickly disappeared down the hall.

While Costello was in jail, the grandchildren of the immigrants were growing up and becoming aware of the subtle handicaps of their names, and becoming confused by some conflicts in their environment. What these children heard at home often differed from what they read in books by non-Italians, heard in church from Irish priests, learned in schools under Protestant deans, culled from editorials by Jewish liberals, and overheard on streets. . . .

> *"Those Italians, they're all alike. . . ." "Why don't they ship Costello back where . . ."*

And among Italians they heard . . .

> *"They're picking on Costello 'cause he's . . ."*
> *"God, if they pulled that stuff on the Jews, the Anti-Defamation League would . . ."*

Frank Costello rarely defended himself verbally. To newsmen's questions on how he made so much money, his stock answers usually were either "No comment" or "I don't sell Bibles." Although he once explained to a reporter, "Look, I'm a gambler, but I don't operate where I'm not wanted."

No sooner had he completed his year in prison for contempt than he was hauled back on charges of tax evasion. His high-priced attorneys tried hard to beat the case in court.

"Now for God's sake, Frank," one of them said, "when you appear in court tomorrow don't come in wearing one of your $350 suits, and appear so affluent."

"What do you want me to wear?" Costello asked.

"What you have on," the attorney said, nodding toward Costello's blue denim prison suit.

Costello thought it over for a second, then frowned and said, "I'm sorry, but I'd rather blow the goddamn case."

He did. On May 14, 1954, the headlines read: "Costello Guilty in Tax Fraud Case!" And the newspapers and magazines ran a photograph of Costello that was like so many other photos of him during his career: it showed him coming down the steps of the courthouse flanked by lawyers, his gray eyes lowered, his gray fedora squarely on his head, his nose long and rounded, his sullen face sucking in on a cigarette, his expression giving no clue as to how he felt or what he thought.

Before getting into an automobile on this May morning, he turned to reporters on the sidewalk and said, "I think this is a political thing. A lot of guys trying to get ahead by climbing on my back. And that's the way the world goes."

"What was the first mistake?" Walter Winchell asked.

"If you call it a mistake," Costello said, "I guess it was being born of poor parents and raised in a tough neighborhood. If things had been different I might have gone to college and been sitting up there with Mr. Kefauver. But I can say honestly that since I got old enough to know right from wrong I've tried to live a good life. I've been married to the same girl for thirty-five years. How many of my critics can match that?"

In 1956, rather than continue on in jail, Frank Costello volunteered to go into exile if the government would nullify his jail sentence. He might have even returned to Cosenza. But the Justice Department refused.

If Costello had been able to return, however, he would have encountered a lovely but mysterious land still in the Dark Ages—just as he'd left it when he was four, and just as it had been hundreds of years before his birth. He would have seen peasant women walking along the roads around Cosenza balancing clay pots on their heads. And the men riding donkeys there would have sun-baked, Biblical faces. He would have seen small, ancient white houses of stone studded in the vast green mountainside to the east, and to the west, in the blue-green Tyrrhenian Sea, swarthy boys would be swimming in the nude and making obscene gestures to the trains that passed.

Frank Costello would probably not have liked this land; it is not pleasant to see one's roots so exposed, nor to be reminded of such humble beginnings. If Costello were there, he would see few American tourists—except a few second-generation Italian-Americans who might now be of age to travel and visit any relatives in the South or to see the birthplace of their grandparents.

And every once in a while Frank Costello might hear a young grandson being greeted at the Cosenza train station by packs of jubilant relatives who would make the boy feel like a new Messiah, or a kind of Latin Lindbergh in a ticker-tape parade—except instead of confetti, the boy would be showered with wet kisses from endless uncles, aunts, and cousins who could not understand a word of English.

Nevertheless, with an 8-mm movie camera the boy would begin to click off scenes of these relatives in Costello country, and the films perhaps later would be shown in a kitchen back in Brooklyn where a bed-sheet, serving as a projection screen, would be tacked to the flowered wallpaper. And when the lights would go on in this Brooklyn kitchen, tears would be seen in the eyes of some of the older people seated around the room. . . .

In the latter part of 1956, after Edward Bennett Williams proved that the conviction had been based on illegal wiretap evidence, the gambler got out of jail for a while, and tried very hard to avoid publicity. But he was back in the nation's headlines soon because on the night of May 2, 1957, at 10:55 o'clock, as Costello was walking past his Anglo-Saxon doorman toward his penthouse apartment, a bullet whizzed toward his head, nicked his scalp, and whistled through his $50 gray fedora.

Frank Costello insisted to the police that he had no idea who did the shooting.

"Isn't it a fact, Mr. Costello, that you saw this man?" a detective asked. "Isn't it a fact?"

"No, I haven't seen no man."

"Do you know of any reason why anybody in the wide world should want to kill you, Mr. Costello?"

"No, I don't know of any human being that had a motive."

This was *typical* Costello cooperation, the investigators agreed. But Frederic Sondhern, Jr., the writer and Mafia expert, pointed out that Costello's silence was merely his adherence to the Mafia law prohibiting squealing on a countryman. And after the trial Mr. Sondhern quoted a Federal official as saying that Costello, faithful to his tradition, now saw himself as a "good soldier" from the Mafioso's viewpoint. "He'd be committing treason, high treason, by going over to the enemy, which is the way Costello sees us," the officer said. "He might be executed at the end of a .38, but he would certainly be punished by something which to him seems even worse—ostracism and the contempt of the brothers, who are the only people that he really knows. You've just seen the Mafia's *omertà* (silence) working, my friend; it's more than a code or a pattern of faith. It's almost a religion—with teeth in it."

Because Costello refused to cooperate, and refused to answer questions about certain numbers on slips of paper found in his pockets on the night he was shot, he was adjudged in contempt. And soon Costello was not only back in jail, but was also being divested of his citizenship on the grounds that, when he was naturalized in 1925 and was asked his occupation, he said "Real estate." He should have said "Bootlegging."

The deportation proceedings were protested throughout Italy.

"Why should he be deported to *Italy?*" they asked. "He is not Italian —he is a product of the corrupt American civilization!" The newspaper *Il Secolo D'Italia* called it a curious punishment—sending a man back to a country whose language he does not speak. The Italian government did not mind taking credit for such well-bred Italian-Americans as Vicenzo Botta, vice-president of the exclusive Union League Club from 1863 to 1894; or Count Luigi Palma di Cesnola, a Yankee general in the Civil War; or the scientist Enrico Fermi; or any of those thousands of other Italian immigrants who made good in America, and seemed to confirm the view that Italians, after all, are extremely cultured and attractive people—whether one regards them in their Roman role as conquerors, or their Reinaissance role as artists, or in their post-World War II role as cosmopolites driving Ferrari sports cars, or wearing

Simonetta gowns, or playing in Fellini films, or carrying Gucci handbags, or pounding Olivetti typewriters, or . . .

But when it came to taking credit for those unskilled Sicilian or Southern Italian peasants whose offspring became gangsters, the Italian government became very, very sensitive. And who could blame it? There seemed to be so many Italian gangsters in the United States. . . .

"That's a lie!" shouted former Congressman Alfred E. Santangelo of New York. "And I have figures to prove it." Recent figures from the six major prisons in the United States show that of 23,605 inmates, only 588 had Italian-sounding names, and the average prison population of those with Italian ancestry is 2.5 percent, Santangelo said. He had gathered these figures to support his demand that the ABC-TV show *The Untouchables* stop giving Italian-sounding names to the fictional criminal characters on the show. "*The Untouchables* is disgraceful," he said. "Kids were calling it *The Italian Family Hour* and saying, 'Let's go watch the Cops and Wops on teevee.' "

Mr. Santangelo, supported by many Italian-American organizations, protested the insults to Italian names, and enough pressure was put on ABC's sponsors, Liggett & Myers, to force a change in the script.

This is the big difference in the Italian-American of today—he is quick to defend himself, whereas his grandfather, who was illiterate, couldn't; and his father, often insecure, wouldn't. The evidence of this change in the present Italo-American generation's behavior can be found in such news items as:

New York Times—The Italian-American League Against Discrimination announced yesterday that it would seek to counteract by publicity campaigns recent tendencies to characterize Italians as criminals. . . .

UPI—The weekly newspaper, *The Pilot,* said in its lead editorial that there are also gangsters who are English, Irish, Dutch, Jewish, German, Negro. . . .

New York *Post*—Frank Sinatra almost came to blows with Desi Arnaz in an argument over the way Italians are depicted in some TV shows. . . . The result is that Sinatra moved his TV company out of the Desilu studios and into the Sam Goldwyn studios. . . .

Today the offspring of the immigrants who came to America at the turn of the century are gaining the respectability that eluded Frank

Costello. Like the peasant Irish before them, the peasant Italian's sons and grandsons are leaving the labor class and are moving into white-collared security: they are Civil Service workers, CPA's, they're solid union musicians—and their music is not "far out." These products of peasants try hard *not* to be different in America. They keep one foot on the bag, play it safe.

Many have switched from white-on-white shirts to Oxford button-downs, and have become aware of the hazards of garlic. On Sundays many of them drive to golf courses in long, low automobiles with plastic Christ figures on the dashboard. Some have daughters who, when they become engaged, will have a photo by Bachrach. They are not hungry enough to make good prizefighters any more; Marciano was the last of the great Italian heavyweights. They are successful as advertising and news writers, yet have established no literary tradition in the English language, and there is not a good novelist among them. On the radio and television they sing soft, soothing melodies, but most of the great opera voices are still imported. The Italo-Americans have not yet *arrived*, like the Irish, but the Italian masses are on the rise—aspiring to solid, middle-class status. Great numbers of them have moved out of the neighborhoods of their parents, and become "integrated." Quite a few have left the city altogether for suburban living. And when asked why they left the city, some become almost indignant, and exclaim, "What! And live next to the *Puerto Ricans!*"

Meanwhile, as Frank Costello approaches his seventy-fourth birthday, the present-generation Italians are celebrating his decline, in a sense, because his notoriety reminds them of an era they wish to forget. Costello never understood the rules of the New World because he was influenced by the tradition of a land that exists in the past. When he left it for America, and crossed the Atlantic in two weeks, he actually was crossing hundreds of years of civilization. He was moving into a world in which Robin Hoods were out of date. He was moving into a land that possessed hostility toward the most-recently-arrived peasant. While most immigrants accepted their lowly status, and worked patiently to overcome it, Costello did not.

He rebelled early against the society that called him "wop." His father, who might have dominated family life in Italy—as fathers do there—was illiterate and incapable here. His father was *scemo*—the unforgivable sin of the Southern peasant and Sicilian. Costello had no respect for him. At sixteen he ran away from his home in the slum and regarded those who were not his friends as Saracens. He justified his thievery by his kindness to his wife, and by giving money to panhandlers and for stained-glass windows to churches.

And he will die thinking he has done no wrong.

Joe Louis:
The King as a
Middle-Aged Man

"Hi, sweetheart!" Joe Louis called to his wife, spotting her waiting for him at the Los Angeles airport.

She smiled, walked toward him, and was about to stretch up on her toes and kiss him—but suddenly stopped.

"Joe," she said, "where's your tie?"

"Aw, sweetie," he said, shrugging, "I stayed out all night in New York and didn't have time—"

"All *night!*" she cut in. "When you're out here all you do is sleep, sleep, sleep."

"Sweetie," Joe Louis said, with a tired grin, "I'm an ole man."

"Yes," she agreed, "but when you go to New York you try to be young again."

They walked slowly through the airport lobby toward their car, being followed by a redcap with Joe's luggage. Mrs. Louis, the third wife of the forty-eight-year-old former fighter, always meets him at the airport when he is returning from a business trip to New York, where he is vice-president of a Negro public-relations firm. She is an alert, pleasingly plump woman in her forties who is a very successful trial lawyer in California. She had never known a prizefighter before she met Joe. Previously, she'd been married to a fellow lawyer, a Phi Beta Kappa— a man she once described as being "exposed to books, not to life." After her divorce, she vowed she wanted a man "exposed to life, not to books."

She met Joe in 1957 through an introduction from a West Coast lady friend and, two years later, to the surprise of her courtroom associates in Los Angeles, she married him. "How in the hell did *you* meet Joe Louis?" they kept asking, and she usually replied, "How in the hell did Joe Louis meet me?"

Arriving at the car, Joe Louis tipped the redcap and opened the door for his wife. Then he drove past palm trees and quiet neighborhoods for a few miles, and finally turned into a long driveway that flanks an impressive, ten-room, Spanish-style house that is worth $75,000. Mrs. Louis bought it a few years ago and filled it with Louis XV furniture— and eight television sets. Joe Louis was a television addict, she explained to her friends, adding that he even has a set in his bathroom above the tub; the set is placed at such an angle that Joe, when taking a shower across the room, can peek over the shower curtain and see a reflection of the TV screen through a strategically placed mirror.

"Television and golf," Mrs. Louis said, helping to carry her husband's things into the house, "that's Joe Louis today." She said this unruefully and, later kissing her husband on the cheek, she suddenly seemed a lot less formal than she had at the airport. After hanging his coat in the closet, she quickly put on a kettle for tea.

"Cookies, honey?" she asked.

"Nah," he said, sitting slope-shouldered at the breakfast table, his eyelids drooping from lack of sleep. Soon she was upstairs, turning down the covers of their gigantic bed, and five minutes later Joe Louis had plunged upon it and was fast asleep. When Mrs. Louis returned to the kitchen, she was smiling.

"In court, I'm a lawyer," she said, "but when I'm home, I'm *all* woman." Her voice was husky, suggestive. "I treat a man *right*, I treat a man like a *king*—if he treats *me* right," she added, pouring herself a glass of milk.

"Each morning I bring Joe breakfast in bed," she said. "Then I turn on Channel 4 so he can watch the Today show. Then I go down and get him the Los Angeles *Times*. Then I leave the house for court.

"By 11 a.m.," she continued, "it's time for him to tee off at the Hillcrest Country Club and, if he plays eighteen holes, he should be finished by 3 o'clock, and will probably drive over to the Fox Hills Country Club for eighteen more. But if he isn't hitting the ball right, he'll stop after eighteen and go buy a bucket of balls and hit 'em for hours. He don't buy *regular* balls—no, not Joe Louis!—he buys the Select balls, the best, which cost $1.25 a bucket. And he'll hit—if he's real mad—two, three, or four buckets full, $5 worth.

"Some nights he comes home, all excited, and says, 'Well, sweetheart, I *finally* got it today! After all these years playing golf, I just realized what I been doing wrong.'

"But," she said, "a day later he may come home, all mad from throwing clubs, and say, 'I'm never gonna play again!' I'll say, 'But, honey, you told me yesterday you *had* it!' He'll say, 'I *had* it, but I didn't *keep* it!'

"The next morning it might be raining, and I'll say, 'Sweetheart, you gonna play golf today? It's raining.' And he'll say, 'It rains on the course, but it don't rain on the players.' And off to the golf course he goes."

Joe Louis' present wife, Martha, is as different from his first two wives as he is from Martha's Phi Beta Kappa husband.

Joe's first wife, Marva, a sleek Chicago stenographer whom he married in 1935 and remarried in 1946, belonged to his lush years, to the years when he blew most of his $5,000,000 boxing fortune on trinkets, jewels, furs, trips abroad, gambling on the golf course, poor investments, lavish tips and clothes. In 1939, a year in which he had already purchased twenty suits, thirty-six shirts and two tuxedos, he also hired tailors to create clothing styles of his own invention, such as two-tone floppy green trousers, suit coats without lapels, and camel's-hair jackets with leather piping. When he was not training or fighting— he won the title by knocking out James J. Braddock in 1937—Joe Louis was doing the town with Marva ("I could make her laugh") or was gambling as much as $1,000 a hole at golf, a game that two sportswriters, Hype Igoe and Walter Stewart, introduced to him in 1936.

"One guy built a house in California with the money he took Joe for," an old friend of Louis' said.

Joe's second wife, Rose Morgan, the cosmetics and beauty expert to whom he was married from 1955 to 1958, is a stunning, curvesome woman dedicated to her prosperous business, and she refused to stay up all night with Joe. "I tried to make him settle down," she said. "I told him he couldn't sleep all day and stay out all night any more. Once he asked me why not, and I told him I'd worry and wouldn't be able to sleep. So he said he'd wait till I fell asleep before going out. Well, I stayed up till 4 a.m.—and then *he* fell asleep." Rose was also disenchanted with him in 1956 when, in an effort to make some money toward the $1,000,000 he owed the Government in back taxes, he began touring as a wrestler. "To me, Joe Louis was like the President of the United States," Rose said. "How would you like to see the President of the United States washing dishes? That's how I felt about Joe wrestling."

Joe's third wife, while having none of the obvious sex appeal of his first two, has succeeded where they had failed because she is wiser than they, and because Joe was ripe for taming when he fell in love with Martha. She seems to be many things to him: a combination lawyer, cook, mistress, press agent, tax consultant, valet de chambre, and everything but caddie. And she was obviously pleased recently when her friend, the singer Mahalia Jackson, noticed the closets bulging with Joe's belongings and remarked, "Well, Martha, I guess he's finally ready to settle down; this is the first time in his life he's got all his clothes under one roof."

It does not seem to matter to Martha that she got Joe Louis in his declining years—at a time when he weighs 240 pounds, is going bald, is somewhat less than prosperous, and no longer possesses the quick reflexes either to hit or pick up checks. "There's a soul about this man, and a quietness that I love," she said, adding that her love has been returned. Joe even goes to church with her on Sundays, she said, and often appears in court to watch her handle cases. Though he neither smokes nor drinks, Joe still goes to nightclubs occasionally to hear some of the many musicians and singers he lists among his friends, she says, and she is aware of the number of women who still find Joe Louis sexually appealing, and would consider a night with him time well spent. "If those sort of women like living on the side streets of a man's life," Martha said, "I wish them well. But I am his wife, and when I come on the scene they got to get the hell out."

Martha is aware, too, that Joe Louis still is friendly with his former wives—who, after getting divorced from him, went to polar extremes in choosing their future husbands. Marva, after leaving Joe, married a doctor in Chicago. Rose followed her divorce from Joe with a marriage to a lawyer. When Joe is in Chicago, he often calls Marva (the mother of his two children) and sometimes goes over for dinner. When in New York, he does the same thing with Rose. "Joe Louis never really cuts off a woman," Martha observed, more amused than piqued. "He just adds another to his list." Actually, Joe has been responsible for his three wives getting acquainted with each other, and he is delighted that they get along. He introduced his first wife to his present wife at the Patterson-Johansson title fight in New York and on another occasion he arranged to have his present wife's hair done by his second wife—free.

Joe Louis had told me all about this earlier in the day on the plane during our flight to Los Angeles from New York (where I'd spent some time following him around Manhattan and watching him function as a public-relations executive). "I called Rose on the phone," Joe had said, "and told her, 'Now Rose Morgan, don't you charge my wife.' She said, 'No, Joe, I won't.' That Rose Morgan is a wonderful woman," Joe mused, shaking his head.

"You know, I been married to three of the finest women in the world. My only mistake in life was getting divorced."

"Why did you then?" I asked.

"Oh," he said, "in those days I wanted to be free, and sometimes I just wanted to be alone. I was crazy. I'd go out of the house and stay weeks without coming home. Or maybe I'd stay home in bed for days watching television."

Just as he blames himself for the failure of his first two marriages, so does he accept the blame for all of his other difficulties, such as his inability to hold onto his money, and his negligence in paying taxes. During his last visit to New York, some old boxing friends were saying, "Joe, if only you were fighting today, you'd be making twice what you did in the old days, with the money fighters now get from closed-circuit TV and all." But Joe Louis shook his head and said, "I ain't sorry I fought when I did. In my time, I made $5,000,000, wound up broke, and owe the Government $1,000,000 in taxes. If I was fighting today, I'd earn $10,000,000, would still wind up broke, and would owe the Government $2,000,000 in taxes."

Such remarks, simple yet mixed with an almost absurd sense of humor, were delivered often by Joe Louis during the hours I followed him in New York—much to my surprise.

Rightly or wrongly, I had imagined that this middle-aged hero would merely be a flabby version of the rather dim-witted champion that Don Dunphy used to interview over the radio after the knockout of another Great White Hope—and I had assumed that Joe Louis, at forty-eight, would still hold his title as perhaps the most quiet athlete since Dummy Taylor, the Giant pitcher, who was a mute.

Of course, I was aware of those few, famous Joe Louis remarks— like the one about Billy Conn: "Maybe he kin run, but he can't hide"; and Pvt. Joe Louis' answer in World War II when somebody asked how he felt about fighting for nothing: "I ain't fighting for nothing, I'm fighting for my country." But I'd read, too, that Joe Louis was incredibly naïve—so naïve that in 1960 he agreed to do public-relations work for Fidel Castro. I'd also seen recent news photos of Joe posing outside courtrooms with Hulan E. Jack, the ex-Manhattan Borough President who tried to conceal gratuities concerning the remodeling of his apartment. And once Senator John L. McClellan hinted that Louis had received $2,500 for sitting for two hours at the bribery trial of James R. Hoffa; although there were denials all around, the undeniable image of Joe Louis then was that while he was a "credit to his race—the human race," he was now probably a debt to everybody else.

And so it was with some unexpected elation that I found Joe Louis to be an astute businessman in New York, a shrewd bargainer, and a man with a sense of humor often quite subtle. For instance, as we were boarding the plane at Idlewild Airport for Los Angeles and I had to exchange my tourist-class ticket for first class so I could sit next to Joe, I casually asked him how the airlines could justify the $45 difference in price. "First-class seats are up in front of the plane," Louis said, "and they get you to L.A. faster."

The day before, I'd seen Joe Louis argue some extra money out of

New York television executives who are doing a television show on his life.

"Hey," Joe said, carefully reading every word of the contract before signing it, "this says you'll pay my plane ticket from L.A. to New York and back, and my hotel bill, but what about my living expenses when I'm here?"

"But, Mr. Louis," one executive said, nervously, "we never discussed that."

"Who's gonna pay? How ma gonna eat?" Louis asked, his voice rising with irritation.

"But, but . . ."

Louis stood up, put the pen down, and would not have signed at all had not the president of the television company finally said, "Okay, Joe, I'm sure something can be worked out."

Assured that it would, Louis then signed, shook hands with everyone, and left the office.

"Well," he said, on the sidewalk, "I won that round."

Then he added, "I know what I'm worth, and I don't want less." He said the movie producers of *Requiem for a Heavyweight* wanted him to appear as a referee, but only offered him a fee of $500 plus $50-a-day living expenses. Though the whole part would have kept Louis on the screen only about forty-five seconds, Louis said it was worth a fee of $1,000. The producers said that was too much. But a few days later, Louis said, they called him back. He got his $1,000.

Though his tax difficulties have eradicated all his assets—including two trust funds he'd set up for his children—Joe Louis is still a man of great pride. He refused the money that hundreds of citizens sent him to help with his Government debt, although he still owes the Government thousands, and could have used the cash. Last year Joe Louis earned less than $10,000, most of it from refereeing wrestling matches (he earns between $750 and $1,000 a night), and from endorsements or appearances. The last big money he made was the $100,000-a-year guarantee he got in 1956 for wrestling. He won all his matches—except those in which he was disqualified for using his fists—but his career ended not long afterward when the 300-pound cowboy Rocky Lee accidentally stepped on Louis' chest one night, cracked one of his ribs and damaged some of his heart muscles.

Today Joe Louis is a matchmaker with a group of California boxing promoters he formed (United World Boxing Enterprises), and
still has his name used by a Chicago milk company; but the only
financial interests he has are with the Manhattan public-relations firm
of Louis-Rowe Enterprises, Inc., a swinging outfit on West Fifty-
seventh Street that handles Louis Armstrong and the new singer,
Dean Barlow, among other Negro entertainers, and would have had
a profitable thing going in Cuba had there not been such an uproar
over Joe Louis representing Castro and saying, as he did in 1960,
"There is no place in the world except Cuba where the Negro can
go in the wintertime with absolutely no discrimination."

Without being a racist, Joe Louis today is very much concerned
with the Negro's fight for equality and, possibly for the first time in
his life, is quite outspoken on the subject. Frankly, Joe Louis saw
nothing wrong in endorsing Cuba in 1960 as a vacationland for
American Negroes, and is also quick to point out that he canceled
his firm's $287,000-a-year contract with Cuba's National Institute of
Tourism *before* the United States severed diplomatic relations with
the Castro regime. Even now, Louis feels Castro is far, far better for
the Cuban people than the United Fruit Company.

When Joe Louis reads newspapers, I noticed that it was not the
sports page that got his first attention, but rather such stories as the
announcement that Lieut. Commander Samuel Gravely, Jr. had become the first Negro in United States naval history to command a
warship. "Things are getting better," Louis said. I noticed, too, that
one afternoon, as he was switching the television dial in search of a
golf match, he happened upon a panel show on which a delegate from
Ghana was speaking; Louis listened until the African finished before
switching to the golf tournament.

While the second Max Schmeling fight was billed by American
newspapers as a grudge match in which Louis sought revenge against
the "Super Race" that regarded Negroes an inferior breed, Joe Louis
said this was strictly a publicity stunt to build up the gate. Louis said
he never really felt hostility toward Schmeling, although he did not
like one of Schmeling's friends who strode about the fight camp wearing a Nazi armband. Louis said that he is far more bitter toward
Eastern Air Lines than he ever was at the Schmeling camp, having

never forgiven Eastern for refusing him limousine service in 1946 from a New Orleans hotel to the airport after Louis had fought an exhibition. Louis, who would have missed his plane had he not gotten there on his own, wrote a letter of protest to Eastern's Eddie Ricken-backer. "He never answered," Louis said.

As a result, Louis said he has never flown Eastern since, even when it would have been much more convenient; he also said he has told many of his friend to avoid the airline, and believes this has cost Eastern considerable revenue in the past sixteen years.

It is one of the aims of Joe Louis, and his public-relations partner, Billy Rowe, to convince big business executives that the Negro market, if discourage or ignored, can be hazardous to sales figures; but if properly encouraged, it can be very profitable. The Louis-Rowe agency claims that each year American Negroes pour $22,000,000,000 into big business, spend more than eighteen percent of America's travel dollar, and that Negroes in Harlem alone spend $200,000 a day gambling on sports events and the numbers game.

Negroes would spend much more, Louis and Rowe argue, if big business would increase its advertising budget for the Negro market and would make its advertising campaigns more specialized—i.e., would show more Negro models in Negro newspapers selling certain brands of soap, beer, and so forth. This is the message that Rowe delivers when he, accompanied by Louis, visits Madison Avenue ad agencies, insurance companies, stockbrokerages, and racetracks; Rowe, a fast-talking, endlessly articulate man who dresses like a Broadway dude and resembles Nat King Cole (but is handsomer), dom-inates most conversations, although Louis gets in a good line now and then.

Billy Rowe, who is forty-seven and was once a Deputy Police Com-missioner in New York—he still carries a pistol everywhere he goes—occupies a larger, fancier office than Joe at their agency. While Joe has only one of his plaques hanging on the wall—the "State of Michigan Hall of Fame" plaque—Billy Rowe has covered a wall with eighteen of *his* plaques and scrolls, including commendations for youth work from the Minisink Men's Guidance Council, letters from the Governor, and two gold trophies that do not even belong to him. Modesty is not his primary virtue.

Mr. Rowe, who lives in a fourteen-room house (with four television sets) in the suburbs of New Rochelle, arrives at the office a full hour ahead of Louis, and has the day's—and some of the week's—appointments all lined up by the time Louis strolls in, usually around 11 a.m., with a big wink for the girl at the switchboard.

"Hey, Dad," Rowe greets Louis, "we got an appointment with the Mayor on the 13th. We'd had it before, but he's fighting with the Governor."

Louis nodded, then yawned, then suddenly became wide-eyed when he noticed walking toward him a voluptuous Harlem nightclub singer named Ann Weldon. Without saying a word, Miss Weldon swished right up to Louis and wiggled close to him.

"You get any closer," Louis said, "I gonna have to marry you."

She swooned, and slithered away.

"Hey, Dad," Rowe said, "you gonna eat lunch at Lindy's?"

"Yeah."

"Who's picking up the check?"

"Yonkers Raceway."

"In that case," Rowe said, "I'll join you."

An hour later, headed for Lindy's, Rowe and Louis left the office and jammed into the crowded elevator, where nearly everyone grinned or winced as they recognized Joe Louis.

"Hi, champ," they said. "Hello, Joe."

"Sure wouldn't want to start a fight in this car," the elevator man said.

"No," Joe said, "not enough room for me to run."

"Joe," a man said, shaking Louis' hand, "you sure look in good shape."

"Only in shape for a steak," Louis said.

"Joe," another man said, "seems like only yesterday I seen you fight Billy Conn. Time sure flies."

"Yeah," said Louis. "It do, don't it?"

And on and on it went, as Louis walked down Broadway: cab drivers waved at him, bus drivers honked at him, and dozens of men stopped him and recalled how they'd once traveled a hundred thirty miles to get to one of his fights, and how they'd put their heads down to light a cigarette in the first round, then before they could look up Louis had flattened his opponent and they'd missed everything: or how they'd had guests at the house that night to hear the fight, and while they were struggling in the kitchen to get the ice out, somebody came in from the living room and said, "It's all over! Louis knocked 'im out with the first punch."

It was astonishing, most of all to Louis, that they had remembered him so—especially since he has not had a fight since his unwise comeback in 1951, when Rocky Marciano knocked him out. Two years before that Louis had retired undefeated, having defended his title twenty-five times, more than any other champion.

In Lindy's, the waiters, fussing over Louis, led him and Rowe to a table occupied by an official from Yonkers Raceway. Before the lunch was half over, Louis was making a pitch for the track's account, saying that a good public-relations campaign by Louis-Rowe would get more Negroes to the track than ever before. The official said he would present their proposal to the board of directors and would let Louis and Rowe know the result.

"Joe, we better get moving," Rowe said, looking at his watch. "We gotta see Joe Glaser. That Glaser's got so much money that the bank charges him storage." Rowe laughed at his joke and said, "Joe, tell that to Glaser when you see him."

Five minutes later, Louis and Rowe were escorted by Glaser's assistants into the new, plush quarters of Mr. Glaser, the talent-booking man, who pounded Joe on the back and said, loud enough for his assistants in the other offices to hear, "Joe Louis is one of the finest men in the world!"

And Billy Rowe said, because he could not resist, "Joe Glaser's got so much money that the bank charges him storage."

Everybody laughed, except Joe Louis, who glanced sideways at Rowe.

After leaving Glaser's, Louis and Rowe had appointments at the Investors Planning Corporation of America, where they submitted proposals for selling more mutual funds to Negroes; then visited the Cobleigh and Gordon, Inc. agency, where they discussed a Negro newsletter that Rowe and Louis wish to produce; then dropped into Toots Shor's, and finally went to dinner at La Fonda del Sol, where Rowe had arranged for a couple of Harlem nightclub starlets to join them.

"Oh, Joe," one of the girls said, as a Spanish guitar strummed behind her, "when you used to fight, I was a young girl, and in our house we all gathered around the radio—and I wasn't allowed to talk."

Joe winked.

"Joe," another said, "while I'm sitting so close, how's about autographing this menu—for my son."

Louis grinned, and playfully pulled from a pocket his hotel key, dangled it, then slid it across the table at her.

"You don't want to let your son down, do you?" he asked.

Everybody laughed, but she did not know whether or not Joe was kidding.

"If I do," she said primly, "I'm sure he'll understand—when he gets older." She slid the key back. Joe howled, and signed the menu.

After dinner, Louis and the rest planned to go nightclubbing in Harlem, but I had an appointment to see Louis' second wife, Rose Morgan. Rose now lives in the large, magnificent uptown apartment that overlooks the Polo Grounds and once was occupied by Joe and his first wife, Marva.

Opening the door, Rose Morgan was chic, impeccably groomed, almost exotic in a Japanese loll suit. She led the way across a sprawling, thick rug to a boomerang-shaped white sofa; there, sitting cross-legged and arms akimbo, she said, "Oh, I don't know what it was about Joe. He just got under your skin."

But being married to Joe was not as exciting as being courted by Joe, Rose observed, shaking her head. "When I'd come home from work, 6:30 or 7 p.m., Joe'd be there watching television and eating apples. But," she continued, after a pause, "we're now very good friends. In fact, I just wrote him a letter the other day telling him I found some things of his around and want to know if he wants them."

"Like what?"

"I have the robe he wore when he started boxing," she said, "and his road shoes, and also a film of the first Billy Conn fight. Would you like to watch it?"

Just then, Rose's husband, the lawyer, walked in, followed by some friends from Philadelphia. Rose's husband is a short, portly, manicured man who, after introducing everyone, suggested a round of drinks.

"I'm just showing Joe's fight film," Rose said.

"Hate to put you through all the trouble," I told her.

"Oh, it's *no* trouble," Rose said. "I haven't seen it in years, and I'd love to see it again."

"Is it all right with you if we watch it?" I asked Rose's husband.

"Yes, yes, it's all right with me," he said, quietly. It was obvious that he was just being polite, and would rather not have to sit through it; yet, there was no way of stopping Rose, for she quickly had the projector out of the closet and soon the lights were off and the fight was on.

"Joe Louis was definitely the greatest of all time," one of the men from Philadelphia said, clinking the ice in his glass. "There was a time when nothing was more important to colored people than God and Joe Louis."

The menacing, solemn image of Joe Louis, then twenty years younger than he is today, moved across the screen toward Conn; when he clouted Conn, Billy's bones seemed to shake.

"Joe didn't waste no punches," somebody said from the sofa.

Rose seemed excited at seeing Joe at his top form, and every time a Louis punch would jolt Conn, she'd go, "Mummmm" (sock). "Mummmm" (sock). "Mummmm."

Billy Conn was impressive through the middle rounds, but as the screen flashed Round 13, somebody said, "Here's where Conn's gonna make his mistake; he's gonna try to slug it out with Joe Louis." Rose's husband remained silent, sipping his Scotch.

When the Louis combinations began to land, Rose went, "Mummmm, mummmm," and then the pale body of Conn began to collapse against the canvas.

Billy Conn slowly began to rise. The referee counted over him. Conn had one leg up, then two, then was standing—but the referee forced him back. It was too late.

But Rose's husband in the back of the room disagreed.

"I thought Conn got up in time," he said, "but that referee wouldn't let him go on."

Rose Morgan said nothing—just swallowed the rest of her drink.

Mr. Bad News

Let's talk of graves, of worms and epitaphs,
Make dust our paper and with rainy eyes
Write sorrow on the bosom of the earth.
Let's choose executors and talk of wills. . . .
                    —*Richard II,* Shakespeare

"Winston Churchill gave you your heart attack," the wife of the obituary writer said, but the obituary writer, a short and rather shy man wearing horn-rimmed glasses and smoking a pipe, shook his head and replied, very softly, "No, it was not Winston Churchill."

"Then T. S. Eliot gave you your heart attack," she quickly added, lightly, for they were at a small dinner party in New York and the others seemed amused.

"No," the obituary writer said, again softly, "it was not T. S. Eliot."

If he was at all irritated by his wife's line of questioning, her assertion that writing lengthy obituaries for *The New York Times* under deadline pressure might be speeding him to his own grave, he did not show it, did not raise his voice; but then he rarely does. Only once has Alden Whitman raised his voice at Joan, his present wife, a youthful brunette, and

168

on that occasion he *screamed*. Alden Whitman does not recall precisely why he screamed. Vaguely he remembers accusing Joan of misplacing something around the house, but he suspects that in the end *he* was the guilty one. Though this incident occurred more than two years ago, lasting only a few seconds, the memory of it still haunts him—a rare occasion when he truly lost control; but since then he has remained a quiet man, a predictable man who early each morning, while Joan is asleep, slips out of bed and begins to make breakfast: a pot of coffee for her, one of tea for himself. Then he sits for an hour or so in his study smoking a pipe, sipping his tea, scanning the newspapers, his eyebrows raising slightly whenever he reads that a dictator is missing, a statesman is ill.

By midmorning he will dress in one of the two or three suits he owns and, looking briefly into a mirror, will tighten his bow tie. He is not a handsome man. He has a plain, somewhat round face that is almost always serious, if not dour, and it is topped by a full head of brown hair which, though he is fifty-two, is without a trace of grey. Behind his horn-rimmed glasses are small, very small, blue eyes that he douses with drops of pilocarpine every three hours for his case of controlled glaucoma, and he has a thick, reddish moustache beneath which protrudes, most of the day, a pipe held tightly between a full bridge of false teeth.

His real teeth, all thirty-two of them, were knocked out or loosened by three strong-arm men in an alley one night in 1936 in Alden Whitman's hometown, Bridgeport, Connecticut. He was twenty-three years old then, a year out of Harvard and full of verve, and his assailants apparently opposed opinions supported by Whitman. He bears no ill will toward those who attacked him, conceding they had their point of view, nor is he at all sentimental about his missing teeth. They were full of cavities, he says, a blessing to be rid of them.

After he is finished dressing, Whitman says good-bye to his wife, but not for long. She too works for the *Times,* and it was there, one spring day in 1958, that he spotted her walking through the large, noisy City Room on the third floor dressed in paisley and carrying an inky page proof down from the women's department on the ninth floor, where she works. After learning her name, he proceeded to send anonymous notes in brown envelopes up to her through the house mail, the first of which read, "You look ravishing in paisley," and was signed, "The American Paisley Association." Later he identified himself, and they dined on the night of May 13 at the Teheran Restaurant, on West Forty-fourth Street, and talked until the maître d' asked them to leave.

Joan was fascinated by Whitman, especially by his marvelous, magpie mind cluttered with all sorts of useless information—he could recite the list of Popes backward and forward; knew the names of every king's mistress and his date of reign; knew that the Treaty of Westphalia was signed in 1648, that Niagara Falls is 167 feet high, that snakes do not blink; that cats attach themselves to places, not people, and dogs to people, not places; he was a regular subscriber to the *New Statesman, Le Nouvel Observateur,* to nearly every journal in the Out-of-Town Newsstand in Times Square, he read two books a day, he had seen Bogart in *Casablanca* three-dozen times. Joan knew she had to see *him* again, even though she was sixteen years his junior and a minister's daughter, and he was an atheist. They were married on November 13, 1960.

After Whitman leaves his apartment, which is on the twelfth floor of an old brick building on West 116th Street, he walks slowly uphill toward the subway kiosk on Broadway. At this time of morning the sidewalk is rushing with youth—pretty Columbia co-eds in tight skirts clasping books to their breasts and walking quickly to class, young longhaired men distributing leaflets attacking American policies in Vietnam and Cuba—and yet this neighborhood near the Hudson River is also solemn with reminders of mortality: Grant's Tomb, the grave of St. Claire Pollock, the memorial statues to Louis Kossuth and Governor Tilden and Joan of Arc; the churches, the hospitals, the Fireman's Monument, the sign on the upper Broadway office building "The Wages of Sin is Death," the old-ladies' home, the two aging men who live near Whitman—a recently retired *Times* obituary writer, and the *Times* obituary writer who retired before *him*.

Death is on Whitman's mind as he sits in the subway that now races downtown toward Times Square. In the morning paper he has read that Henry Wallace is not well, that Billy Graham has visited the Mayo Clinic. Whitman plans, when he arrives at the *Times* in ten minutes, to go directly to the newspaper's morgue, the room where all news clippings and advance obituaries are filed, and examine the "condition" of the advance obituaries on Reverend Graham and former Vice-President Wallace (Wallace died a few months later). There are two thousand advance obituaries in the *Times'* morgue, Whitman knows, but many of them, such as the ones on J. Edgar Hoover and Charles Lindbergh and Walter Winchell, were written long ago and now require updating. Recently, when President Johnson was in the hospital for gallbladder surgery, his advance obituary was brought up-to-the-minute; so was Pope Paul's before his trip to New York; so was Joseph P. Kennedy's. For an obituary writer there is nothing worse than to have a world figure die before his obituary is up-to-date; it can be a harrowing experience, Whitman knows, requiring that the writer become an instant historian, assessing in a few hours the dead man's life with lucidity, accuracy, and objectivity.

When Adlai Stevenson died suddenly in London in 1965, Whitman, who was just beginning his new assignment as the *Times'* mortician and was anxious to make good, learned of it through a telephone call from Joan. Whitman broke into a cool sweat, slipped out of the City Room, went to lunch. He took the elevator up to the cafeteria on the eleventh floor. But soon he felt a soft tap on his shoulder. It was one of the Metropolitan Editor's assistants asking, "Will you be down soon, Alden?"

Whitman, his lunch finished, returned downstairs and was given a basket full of folders containing data on Adlai Stevenson. Then, carrying them to the back of the room, he opened them and spread them out on a table in the thirteenth row of the City Room, reading, digesting, making notes, his pipe tip tapping against his false teeth, *cluck-cluck*.

Finally he turned, facing his typewriter. Soon, paragraph by paragraph, the words began to flow: "Adlai Stevenson was a rarity in American public life, a cultivated, urbane, witty, articulate politician whose popularity was untarnished by defeat and whose stature grew in diplomacy. . . ." It ran forty-five hundred words and would have gone longer had there been time.

Difficult as it was, it was not nearly so demanding as a three-thousand-word deadline assignment he was given on Martin Buber, the Jewish philosopher, about whom he knew virtually nothing. Fortunately Whitman was able to reach by telephone a scholar who was very familiar with Buber's teachings and life, and this, together with the clippings in the *Times'* morgue, enabled Whitman to complete the job. But he was far from pleased with it, and that night Joan was constantly aware of the sound of his pacing up and down the floor of their apartment, drink in hand, and the words uttered in contempt and self-derision, "fraud . . . superficial . . . fraud." Whitman went to work the following day expecting to be criticized. But instead he was informed that there had been several congratulatory telephone messages from intellectuals around New York, and Whitman's reaction, far from relief, was to immediately suspect all those who had praised him.

The obituaries that leave Whitman untroubled are those that he is able to complete before the individual dies, such as the rather controversial one he did on Albert Schweitzer, which both paid tribute to "Le Grand Docteur" for his humanitarianism, yet damned him for his lofty paternalism; and the one on Winston Churchill, a twenty-thousand-word piece in which Whitman and several other *Times* men were involved and which was finished almost two weeks before Sir Winston's death. Whitman's obituaries on Father Divine, Le Corbusier, and T. S. Eliot *were* produced under deadline pressure, but caused him no panic because he was quite familiar with the work and lives of all three, particularly Eliot, who had been the poet-in-residence at Harvard during Whitman's student days there. His obituary on Eliot began: *"This is the way the world ends/ This is the way the world ends/ This is the way the world ends/ Not with a bang but a whimper,"* and it went on to describe Eliot as a most unlikely poetic figure, lacking "flamboyance or oddity in dress or manner, and there was nothing of the romantic about him. He carried no auras, cast no arresting eye and wore his heart, as nearly as could be observed, in its proper anatomical place."

It was while writing the Eliot obituary that a copyboy had dropped onto Whitman's desk a number of statements praising the poet's work, and one of these came from a fellow poet, Louis Untermeyer. When Whitman read Untermeyer's statement, he raised an eyebrow in disbelief. He had thought Louis Untermeyer was dead.

This is part of an occupational astigmatism that afflicts many obituary writers. After they have written or read an advance obituary about someone, they come to think of that person as being dead in advance. Alden Whitman has discovered, since moving from his copyreader's job to his present one, that in his brain have become embalmed several people who are *alive,* or were at last look, but whom he is constantly referring to in the *past* tense. He thinks, for example, of John L. Lewis as being dead and also E. M. Forster and Floyd Dell, Rudolf Hess and Rhode Island's former Senator Green, Ruth Etting and Gertrude Ederle, among many others.

Furthermore he admits that, after having written a fine advance obituary, his pride of authorship is such that he can barely wait for that person to drop dead so that he may see his masterpiece in print. While this revelation may mark him as something less than romantic, it must be said in his defense that he thinks no differently than most obituary writers; they are, even by City Room standards, rather special.

A former obituary writer for the *New York World-Telegram & Sun,* Edward Ellis, who is also the author of a book about suicides, admits that he enjoys seeing, from time to time, his old advance obituaries fulfilling their destiny in the *Telegram.*

At the Associated Press, Mr. Dow Henry Fonda announces with satisfaction that he is all set with up-to-date obituaries on Teddy Kennedy, Mrs. John F. Kennedy, John O'Hara, Grayson Kirk, Lammot du Pont Copeland, Charles Munch, Walter Hallstein, Jean Monnet, Frank Costello, and Kelso. The United Press International, which has a dozen four-drawer filing cabinets of "preparation stories—including one on five-year-old John F. Kennedy, Jr. and the children of Queen Elizabeth —does not have any full-time death specialist but passes the corpse copy around, some of the best of it going to a veteran reporter named Doc Quigg about whom it has been said, with pride, that he can "smooth 'em out, make 'em sing."

An obituarian's traditional eagerness about breaking into print is not exclusively based on author's pride, according to one antique in the trade, but it is also a holdover perhaps from the days when editors did not pay their obituary writers, whom they often hired on a free-lance basis, until the subject of the obit had died—or, as they sometimes phrased it in those days, "passed away," "departed from this earth," "gone to his reward." Occasionally, while waiting, those in the City Room would form a so-called "ghoul pool" in which everybody would put up $5 or $10 and try to select from the list of advance obituaries the name of the person who would go first. Karl Schriftgiesser, the *Times'* gravedigger about twenty-five years ago, recalls that some ghoul-pool winners in those days collected as much as $300.

There are no such pools in evidence around the *Times* today, but Whitman, for quite different reasons, does keep in his desk a kind of list of the living to whom he is giving *priority*. These individuals are included because he thinks their days are numbered, or because he believes their life's work is finished and sees no reason to delay the inevitable writing task, or because he merely finds the individual "interesting" and wishes to write the obituary in advance for his own enjoyment.

Whitman also has what he calls a "deferred list," which is composed of aging but durable world leaders, *monstres sacrés,* who are still in power or still making news in other ways, and to attempt a "final" obituary on such individuals would be not only difficult but would require continuous alterations or insertions in the future; so even if these "deferred" people may have out-of-date obituaries in the *Times* morgue— people like de Gaulle, Franco—Whitman still chooses to let them wait a while for a final polishing. Whitman realizes of course that any or all of these "deferred" customers may suddenly tap out, but he also has candidates that he thinks will die sooner or remain out of the news longer, and so he continues to give priority to those *not* on his deferred list, and should he be wrong—well, he has been wrong before.

There are, naturally, some people that Whitman may *think* will soon die, and for whom he has already tucked away a final tribute in the *Times'* morgue, that may *not* die for years and years; they may diminish in importance or influence in the world, perhaps, but they keep right on living. If this be the case—if the name dies before the man, as A. E. Housman would put it—then Whitman reserves the right to cut the obituary down. Vivisection. He is a precise, unemotional man. While death obsessed Hemingway and diminished John Donne, it provides Alden Whitman with a five-day-a-week job that he likes very much and he would possibly die sooner if they took the job away and put him back on the copydesk where he could no longer write about it.

And so each weekday morning, after riding the subway down to Times Square from his apartment on upper Broadway, Whitman anticipates another day at the *Times,* another session with men who are dead, men who are dying, or men who, if Whitman's guess is correct, will soon die. He arrives in the lobby of the Times Building usually at eleven, his soft rubber-soled shoes hardly making a sound against the glossy marble floor. In his mouth is his pipe, and in his left hand is a container of tea that he bought a moment ago across the street at a small lunch counter run by a large Greek whose face he has known for years, never his name.

Whitman then elevates to the third floor, says good-morning to the receptionist, swings into the City Room, says good-morning to all the other reporters who sit behind their desks, rows and rows of desks, and they greet him in turn, they know him well, they are happy it is *he,* not they, who must write for the obituary page—a page that is read very carefully, they know, maybe *too* carefully by readers with a morbid curiosity, readers searching for clues to life, readers searching for vacant apartments.

Occasionally all reporters must do their share of the smaller obituaries, which are bad enough, but the long ones are hard work, they must be accurate and interesting, they must be infallible in their analysis, and will be later judged, as will the *Times,* by historians; and yet for the writer there is no glory, no by-line, it being a policy of the newspaper to eliminate by-lines from such stories, but Whitman does not care. Anonymity superbly suits him. He prefers being everyman, anyman, nobody—*Times* Employee No. 97353, Library Card No. 663 7662, the possessor of a Sam Goody Courtesy Card, the borrower of his mother-in-law's 1963 Buick Compact on sunny weekends, an eminently unquotable man, a onetime manager for the Roger Ludlowe High School football, baseball, and basketball teams who is now keeping toll for the *Times.* All day long while his colleagues are running this way and that, pursuing the here and now, Whitman sits quietly at his desk near the back, sipping his tea, dwelling in his strange little world of the half-living, the half-dead in this enormous place called the City Room.

It is a room as large as a football field, maybe twice as large, and it is lined with rows and rows of grey metal desks, all the same shade, each with a telephone held by reporters who are talking to their news sources about the latest rumors, tips, reports, allegations, threats, robberies, rapes, accidents, crises, problems, problems—it is a Problem Room, and from all over the world via cable, telex, telegram, ticker or telephone the news reports on world problems are rocketed into this *one* room, hour after hour: disaster in the Danube, turmoil in Tanzania, peril in Pakistan, touchy Trieste, rumors in Rio, the Saigon scene, coups d'état, informed sources said, reliable sources said, African problems, Jewish problems, N.A.T.O., S.E.A.T.O., Sukarno, Sihanouk—and Whitman sits, sipping tea, in the back of this room paying little attention to all this; he is concerned with the *final* fact.

He is thinking of the words he will use when these men, these problem makers, finally die. He is leaning forward behind his typewriter now, shoulders forward, thinking of the words that will, bit by bit, build the advance obituaries of Mao Tse-tung, of Harry S Truman, of Picasso. He is also contemplating Garbo and Marlene Dietrich, Steichen and Haile Selassie. On one piece of paper, from a previous hour's work, Whitman has typed: ". . . Mao Tse-tung, the son of an obscure rice farmer, died one of the world's most powerful rulers. . . ." On another piece of paper: ". . . At 7:09 p.m., April 12, 1945, a man few people had ever heard of became President of the United States. . . ." On still another piece: ". . . there was Picasso the painter, Picasso the faithful and faithless lover, Picasso the generous man, even Picasso the playwright. . . ." And, from an earlier day's notes: ". . . As an actress, Mrs. Rudolph Sieber was nondescript, her legs were by no means as beautiful as Mistinguett's, but Mrs. Sieber as Marlene Dietrich was for years an international symbol of sex and glamour. . . ."

Whitman is not satisfied with what he has written, but he goes over the words and phrases with care, and then he pauses and thinks aloud, *Ah, what a wonderful collection of photographs will appear on the* Times' *obituary page when the great Steichen dies.* Then Whitman reminds himself that he must not forget to purchase the issue of the *Saturday Review* with its fine cover story on the white-haired British communications tycoon, Baron Roy Thomson, now seventy years old. This story may soon come in handy. Another man of interest, Whitman says, is the noted humorist, Frank Sullivan, who lives in Saratoga Springs, New York. A few days ago Whitman telephoned one of Mr. Sullivan's close friends, the playwright Marc Connelly, and almost began with, "You *knew* Mr. Sullivan, didn't you?" But he caught himself and said, instead, that the *Times* was "bringing its files up-to-date"—yes, that is the phrase —on Frank Sullivan and could a lunch be arranged with Mr. Connelly so that Mr. Whitman could learn something of Mr. Sullivan? A lunch was arranged. Next Whitman hopes to go up to Saratoga Springs and discuss the life of Marc Connelly over lunch with Mr. Sullivan.

When Whitman goes to concerts, as he so often does, he cannot resist looking around the hall and observing the distinguished members in the audience about whom he might be particularly curious someday soon. Recently, at Carnegie Hall, he noticed that one of the spectators seated up ahead was Artur Rubinstein. Quickly, Whitman lifted his opera glasses and brought Mr. Rubinstein's face into sharp focus, noticing the expression around the eyes, the mouth, the soft grey hair, and noticing, too, when Rubinstein stood up at intermission, how surprisingly short he was.

Whitman made notes on such details, knowing that someday they would help bring life to his work, knowing that masterful obituaries, like fine funerals, must be planned well in advance. Churchill himself had arranged his own funeral; and the relatives of Bernard Baruch, before he died, visited the Frank E. Campbell Funeral Chapel to arrange the details; and now Baruch's son, though in apparent good health, has done the same thing—as has a little charwoman who recently purchased a mausoleum for more than $6,000 and had her name put on it, and now every month or so she travels up to the cemetery in Westchester County to get a look at it.

"Death never takes a wise man by surprise," wrote La Fontaine, and Whitman agrees and keeps his "files up-to-date," although he never permits any man to read his own obituary; as the late Elmer Davis said, "A man who has read his own obituary will never be quite the same again."

Several years ago, after a *Times'* editor had recovered from a heart attack and returned to the office, the reporter who had done the editor's obituary showed it to him so that any errors or omissions might be corrected. The editor read it. That evening he had another heart attack. Ernest Hemingway, on the other hand, thoroughly enjoyed reading the newspaper accounts of his death during a plane crash in Africa. He had the newspaper clippings pasted up in a thick scrapbook and claimed to begin each day with "a regular morning ritual of a glass of cold champagne and a couple of pages of obituaries." Elmer Davis had twice been erroneously reported as having died in catastrophes, and while he conceded that "to turn up alive after you have been reported dead is an unwarrantable imposition on your friends," he nonetheless denied the rumor and was "more generally believed than is usually the case when people have to contradict something that the papers have said about them."

Some newspapermen, possibly not trusting their colleagues, have written their own advance obituaries and inconspicuously slipped them into the morgue to await the proper moment. One of these advance obituaries, written by a New York *Daily News* reporter named Lowell Limpus, appeared under his own by-line in that newspaper in 1957 and began: "This is the last of the 8,700 or more stories I've written to appear in the *News*. It must be the final one because I died yesterday. . . . I wrote this, my own obituary, because I know more about the subject than anybody else and I'd rather have it honest than flowery. . . ."

While the obituary page might have once been sodden with sentimentality, it is rarely so today except in that italicized column of death notices that usually appears on the right-hand side of the page above the flowered ads of the undertakers. The relatives of the deceased pay to have these notices published, and in them every dead man is invariably described as a "loving" father, a "beloved" husband, a "dear" brother, an "adored" grandfather, or a "revered" uncle. All the names of the dead are listed in alphabetical order and set in capital letters and bold type so that the casual reader may scan them quickly, like the baseball scores, and it is the rare reader that ponders over them. One such rarity is a seventy-three-year-old gentleman named Simon de Vaulchier.

Mr. de Vaulchier, a retired research librarian, was for a brief period a kind of professional reader of the obituary pages of New York's metropolitan dailies. And he compiled for the Jesuit magazine, *America,* the research for a study in which it was observed, among other things, that most of the dead in the *New York Post* were Jewish, most of those in the *New York World-Telegram & Sun* were Protestant, most of those in the *Journal-American* were Catholic. A rabbi added a footnote, after reading the survey, to the effect that they *all* seemed to die for the *Times.*

If one is to believe only what one reads in the *Times,* however, then the individuals with the highest fatality rate are chairmen of the board, Mr. de Vaulchier noted. Admirals usually got longer obits than generals in the *Times,* he continued, architects did better than engineers, painters did better than other artists and always seemed to die in Woodstock, New York. Women and Negroes hardly ever seemed to die.

Obituary writers never die. At least Mr. de Vaulchier said he has never read such an obituary in a newspaper, although early last year on the occasion of Whitman's heart attack he came quite close.

After Whitman had been taken to Knickerbocker Hospital in New York, a reporter in the City Room was assigned to "bring the files on him up-to-date." Whitman, since recovering, has never seen this advance obituary, nor does he expect to, but he imagines that it ran seven or eight paragraphs in length and, when it is finally used, will begin something like this:

"Alden Whitman, a member of *The New York Times* staff who wrote obituary articles on many of the world's notable personalities, died suddenly last night at his home, 600 West 116th Street, of a heart attack. He was fifty-two years old. . . ."

It will be very factual and verifiable, he is sure, and will record that he was born on October 27, 1913, in Nova Scotia and was brought to Bridgeport by his parents two years later; that he was twice married, had two children by the first wife, was active in the New York Newspaper Guild, and that in 1956 he, among other newsmen, was questioned by Senator James O. Eastland about his Leftist activities. The obituary will possibly list the schools he attended, but will not mention that during his elementary years he skipped *twice* (to his mother's delight; she was a schoolteacher and this happy event did her reputation with the school board no harm); it will list his places of employment, but will not report that in 1935 he got his teeth knocked out, nor that in 1937 he nearly drowned while swimming (an experience he found highly pleasant), nor that in 1940 he came within an inch of being crushed by part of a falling parapet; nor that in 1949 he lost control of his automobile and skidded helplessly to the very edge of a mountain in Colorado; nor that in 1965, after surviving his coronary thrombosis, he repeated what he had been saying most of his life: there is no God; I do not fear death because there is no God, there will be no Judgment Day.

"But what will happen to you then, after you die, Mr. Whitman?"

"I have no soul that is going anywhere," he said. "It is simply a matter of bodily extinction."

"If you had died during your heart attack, what, in your opinion, would have been the first thing your wife would have done?"

"She would first have seen to it that my body was disposed of in the way that I wanted," he said. "To be cremated without fuss or fanfare."

"And then what?"

"Then, after she'd gotten to that, she would have turned her attention to the children."

"And then?"

"Then, I guess, she would have broken down and had a good cry."

"Are you sure?"

Whitman paused.

"Yes, I would assume so," he said finally, puffing his pipe. "This is the formal outlet for grief under such circumstances."

Part Two
The Bridge

1.
The Boomers

They drive into town in big cars, and live in furnished rooms, and drink whiskey with beer chasers, and chase women they will soon forget. They linger only a little while, only until they have built the bridge; then they are off again to another town, another bridge, linking everything but their lives.

They possess none of the foundation of their bridges. They are part circus, part gypsy—graceful in the air, restless on the ground; it is as if the wide-open road below lacks for them the clear direction of an eight-inch beam stretching across the sky six hundred feet above the sea.

When there are no bridges to be built, they will build skyscrapers, or highways, or power dams, or anything that promises a challenge—and overtime. They will go anywhere, will drive a thousand miles all day and night to be part of a new building boom. They find boom towns irresistible. That is why they are called "the boomers."

In appearance, boomers usually are big men, or if not always big, always strong, and their skin is ruddy from all the sun and wind. Some who heat rivets have charred complexions; some who drive rivets are hard of hearing; some who catch rivets in small metal cones have blisters and body burns marking each miss; some who do welding see flashes at night while they sleep. Those who connect steel have deep scars along their shins from climbing columns. Many boomers have mangled hands and fingers sliced off by slipped steel. Most have taken falls and broken a limb or two. All have seen death.

They are cocky men, men of great pride, and at night they brag and build bridges in bars, and sometimes when they are turning to leave, the bartender will yell after them, "Hey, you guys, how's about clearing some steel out of here?"

Stray women are drawn to them, like them because they have money and no wives within miles—they liked them well enough to have floated a bordello boat beneath one bridge near St. Louis, and to have used up-turned hardhats for flowerpots in the red-light district of Paducah.

On weekends some boomers drive hundreds of miles to visit their families, are tender and tolerant, and will deny to the heavens any suggestion that they raise hell on the job—except they'll admit it in whispers, half proud, half ashamed, fearful the wives will hear and then any semblance of marital stability will be shattered.

Like most men, the boomer wants it both ways.

Occasionally his family will follow him, living in small hotels or trailer courts, but it is no life for a wife and child.

The boomer's child might live in forty states and attend a dozen high schools before he graduates, *if* he graduates, and though the father swears he wants no boomer for a son, he usually gets one. He gets one, possibly, because he really wanted one, and maybe that is why boomers brag so much at home on weekends, creating a wondrous world with whiskey words, a world no son can resist because this world seems to have everything: adventure, big cars, big money—sometimes $350 or $450 a week—and gambling on rainy days when the bridge is slippery, and booming around the country with Indians who are sure-footed as spiders, with Newfoundlanders as shifty as the sea they come from, with roaming Rebel riveters escaping the poverty of their small Southern towns, all of them building something big and permanent, something that can be revisited years later and pointed to and said of: "See that bridge over there, son—well one day, when I was younger, I drove twelve hundred rivets into that goddamned thing."

They tell their sons the good parts, forgetting the bad, hardly ever describing how men sometimes freeze with fear on high steel and clutch to beams with closed eyes, or admitting that when they climb down they need three drinks to settle their nerves; no, they dwell on the glory, the overtime, not the weeks of unemployment; they recall how they helped build the Golden Gate and Empire State, and how their fathers before them worked on the Williamsburg Bridge in 1902, lifting steel beams with derricks pulled by horses.

They make their world sound as if it were an extension of the Wild West, which in a way it is, with boomers today still regarding themselves as pioneering men, the last of America's unhenpecked heroes, but there are probably only a thousand of them left who are footloose enough to go anywhere to build anything. And when they arrive at the newest boom town, they hold brief reunions in bars, and talk about old times, old faces: about Cicero Mike, who once drove a Capone whiskey truck during Prohibition and recently fell to his death off a bridge near Chicago; and Indian Al Deal, who kept three women happy out West and came to the bridge each morning in a fancy silk shirt; and about Riphorn Red, who used to paste twenty-dollar bills along the sides of his suitcase and who went berserk one night in a cemetery. And there was the Nutley Kid, who smoked long Italian cigars and chewed snuff and used toilet water and, at lunch, would drink milk and beer—without taking out the snuff. And there was Ice Water Charley, who on freezing wintry days up on the bridge would send apprentice boys all the way down to fetch hot water, but by the time they'd climbed back up, the water was cold, and he would spit it out, screaming angrily, *"Ice water, ice water!"* and send them all the way down for more. And there was that one-legged lecher, Whitey Howard, who, on a rail bridge one day, did not hear the train coming, and so he had to jump the tracks at the last second, holding on to the edge, during which time his wooden left leg fell off, and Whitey spent the rest of his life bragging about how he lost his left leg twice.

Sometimes they go on and on this way, drinking and reminiscing about the undramatic little things involving people known only to boomers, people seen only at a distance by the rest of the world, and then they'll start a card game, the first of hundreds to be played in this boom town while the bridge is being built—a bridge many boomers will never cross. For before the bridge is finished, maybe six months before it is opened to traffic, some boomers get itchy and want to move elsewhere. The challenge is dying. So is the overtime. And they begin to wonder: "Where next?" This is what they were asking one another in the early spring of 1957, but some boomers already had the answer: New York.

New York was planning a number of bridges. Several projects were scheduled upstate, and New York City alone, between 1958 and 1964, planned to spend nearly $600,000,000 for, among other things, the double-decking of the George Washington Bridge, the construction of the Throgs Neck Bridge across Long Island Sound—and, finally, in what might be the most challenging task of a boomer's lifetime, the construction of the world's largest suspension span, the Verrazano-Narrows Bridge.

The Verrazano-Narrows, linking Brooklyn and Staten Island (over the futile objections of thousands of citizens in both boroughs), would possess a 4,260-foot center span that would surpass San Francisco's Golden Gate by 60 feet, and would be 460 feet longer than the Mackinac Bridge in upper Michigan, just below Canada.

It was the Mackinac Bridge, slicing down between Lake Huron and Lake Michigan and connecting the cities of St. Ignace and Mackinaw City, that had attracted the boomers between the years 1954 and 1957. And though they would now abandon it for New York, not being able to resist the big movement eastward, there were a few boomers who actually were sorry to be leaving Michigan, for in their history of hell-raising there never had been a more bombastic little boom town than the once tranquil St. Ignace.

Before the boomers had infiltrated it, St. Ignace was a rather sober city of about 2,500 residents, who went hunting in winter, fishing in summer, ran small shops that catered to tourists, helped run the ferry-boats across five miles of water to Mackinaw City, and gave the local police very little trouble. The land had been inhabited first by peaceful Indians, then by French bushrangers, then by missionaries and fur traders, and in 1954 it was still clean and uncorrupt, still with one hotel, called the Nicolet—named after a white man, Jean Nicolet, who in 1634 is said to have paddled in a canoe through the Straits of Mackinac and discovered Lake Michigan.

So it was the Nicolet Hotel, and principally its bar, that became the boomers' headquarters, and soon the place was a smoky scene of nightly parties and brawls, and there were girls down from Canada and up from

Detroit, and there were crap games along the floor—and if St. Ignace had not been such a friendly city, all the boomers might have gone to jail and the bridge might never have been finished.

But the people of St. Ignace were pleased with the big new bridge going up. They could see how hard the men worked on it and they did not want to spoil their little fun at night. The merchants, of course, were favorably disposed because, suddenly, in this small Michigan town by the sea, the sidewalks were enhanced by six hundred or seven hundred men, each earning between $300 and $500 a week—and some spending it as fast as they were making it.

The local police did not want to seem inhospitable, either, and so they did not raid the poker or crap games. The only raid in memory was led by some Michigan state troopers; and when they broke in, they discovered gambling among the boomers another state trooper. The only person arrested was the boomer who had been winning the most. And since his earnings were confiscated, he was unable to pay the $100 fine and therefore had to go to jail. Later that night, however, he got a poker game going in his cell, won $100, and bought his way out of jail. He was on the bridge promptly for work the next morning.

It is perhaps a slight exaggeration to suggest that, excepting state troopers, everybody else in St. Ignace either fawned upon or quietly tolerated boomers. For there were some families who forbade their daughters to date boomers, with some success, and there were young local men in town who despised boomers, although this attitude may be attributed as much to their envy of boomers' big cars and money as to the fact that comparatively few boomers were teetotalers or celibates. On the other hand, it would be equally misleading to assume that there were not some boomers who were quiet, modest men—maybe as many as six or seven—one of them being, for instance, a big quiet Kentuckian named Ace Cowan (whose wife was with him in Michigan), and another being Johnny Atkins, who once at the Nicolet drank a dozen double Martinis without causing a fuss or seeming drunk, and then floated quietly, happily out into the night.

And there was also Jack Kelly, the tall 235-pound son of a Philadelphia sailmaker, who, despite years of work on noisy bridges and despite getting hit on the head by so much falling hardware that he had fifty-two stitches in his scalp, remained ever mild. And finally there was another admired man on the Mackinac—the superintendent, Art "Drag-Up" Drilling, a veteran boomer from Arkansas who went West to work on the Golden Gate and Oakland Bay bridges in the thirties, and who was called "Drag-Up" because he always said, though never in threat, that he'd sooner drag-up and leave town than work under a superintendent who knew less about bridges than he.

So he went from town to town, bridge to bridge, never really satisfied until he became the top bridgeman—as he did on the Mackinac, and as he hoped to do in 1962 on the Verrazano-Narrows Bridge.

In the course of his travels, however, Drag-Up Drilling sired a son named John. And while John Drilling inherited much of his father's soft Southern charm and easy manner, these qualities actually belied the devil beneath. For John Drilling, who was only nineteen years old when he first joined the gang on the Mackinac, worked as hard as any to leave the boomer's mark on St. Ignace.

John Drilling had been born in Oakland in 1937 while his father was finishing on the Bay bridge there. And in the next nineteen years he followed his father, living in forty-one states, attending two dozen schools, charming the girls—marrying one, and living with her for four months. There was nothing raw nor rude in his manner. He was always extremely genteel and clean-cut in appearance, but, like many boomers' offspring, he was afflicted with what old bridgemen call "rambling fever."

This made him challenging to some women, and frustrating to others, yet intriguing to most. On his first week in St. Ignace, while stopped at a gas station, he noticed a carload of girls nearby and, exuding all the shy and bumbling uncertainty of a new boy in town, addressed himself politely to the prettiest girl in the car—a Swedish beauty, a very healthy girl whose boy friend had just been drafted—and thus began an unforgettable romance that would last until the next one.

Having saved a few thousand dollars from working on the Mackinac, he became, very briefly, a student at the University of Arkansas and also bought a $2,700 Impala. One night in Ola, Ark., he cracked up the car and might have gotten into legal difficulty had not his date that evening been the judge's daughter.

John Drilling seemed to have a charmed life. Of all the bridge builders who worked on the Mackinac, and who would later come East to work on the Verrazano-Narrows Bridge, young John Drilling seemed the luckiest—with the possible exception of his close friend, Robert Anderson.

Anderson was luckier mainly because he had lived longer, done more, survived more; and he never lost his sunny disposition or incurable optimism. He was thirty-four years old when he came to the Mackinac. He had been married to one girl for a dozen years, to another for two weeks. He had been in auto accidents, been hit by falling tools, taken falls—once toppling forty-two feet—but his only visible injury was two missing inside fingers on his left hand, and he never lost its full use.

One day on the north tower of the Mackinac, the section of catwalk upon which Anderson was standing snapped loose, and suddenly it came sliding down like a rollercoaster, with Anderson clinging to it as it bumped and raced down the cables, down 1,800 feet all the way to near the bottom where the cables slope gently and straighten out before the anchorage. Anderson quietly got off and began the long climb up again. Fortunately for him, the Mackinac was designed by David B. Steinman, who preferred long, tapering backspans; had the bridge been designed by O. H. Ammann, who favored shorter, chunkier backspans, such as the type he was then creating for the Verrazano-Narrows Bridge, Bob Anderson would have had a steeper, more abrupt ride down, and might have gone smashing into the anchorage and been killed. But Anderson was lucky that way.

Off the bridge, Anderson had a boomer's luck with women. All the moving around he had done during his youth as a boomer's son, all the shifting from town to town and the enforced flexibility required of such living, gave him a casual air of detachment, an ability to be at home anywhere. Once, in Mexico, he made his home in a whorehouse. The prostitutes down there liked him very much, fought over him, admired his gentle manners and the fact that he treated them all like ladies. Finally the madam invited him in as a full-time house guest and each night Anderson would dine with them, and in the morning he stood in line with them awaiting his turn in the shower.

Though he stands six feet and is broad-shouldered and erect, Bob Anderson is not a particularly handsome fellow; but he has bright alert eyes, and a round, friendly, usually smiling face, and he is very disarming, a sort of Tom Jones of the bridge business—smooth and swift, somewhat gallant, addicted to good times and hot-blooded women, and yet never slick or tricky.

He is also fairly lucky at gambling, having learned a bit back in Oklahoma from his uncle Manuel, a guitar-playing rogue who once won a whole carnival playing poker. Anderson avoids crap games, although one evening at the Nicolet, when a crap game got started on the floor of the men's room and he'd been invited to join, he did.

"Oh, I was drunk that night," he said, in his slow Southwestern drawl, to a friend some days later. "I was so drunk I could hardly see. But I jes' kept rolling them dice, and all I was seeing was sevens and elevens, sevens, and elevens, *Jee-sus Kee-rist,* all night long it went like that, and I kept winning and drinking and winning some more. Finally lots of other folks came jamming in, hearing all the noise and all, in this men's toilet room there's some women and tourists who also came in —jes' watching me roll those sevens and elevens.

"Next morning I woke up with a helluva hangover, but on my bureau I seen this pile of money. And when I felt inside my pockets they were stuffed with bills, crumpled up like dried leaves. And when I counted it all, it came to more than one thousand dollars. And that day on the bridge, there was guys coming up to me and saying, 'Here, Bob, here's the fifty I borrowed last night,' or, 'Here's the hundred,' and I didn't even remember they borrowed it. Jee-sus Kee-rist, what a night!"

When Bob Anderson finally left the Mackinac job and St. Ignace, he had managed to save five thousand dollars, and, not knowing what else to do with it, he bought a round-trip airplane ticket and went flying off to Tangier, Paris and Switzerland—"whoring and drinking," as he put it—and then, flat broke, except for his return ticket, he went back to St. Ignace and married a lean, lovely brunette he'd been unable to forget.

And not long after that, he packed his things and his new wife, and along with dozens of other boomers—with John Drilling and Drag-Up, with Ace Cowan and Jack Kelly and other veterans of the Mackinac and the Nicolet—he began the long road trip eastward to try his luck in New York.

2.
Panic in Brooklyn

"You sonamabitch!" the old Italian shoemaker cried, standing in the doorway of the Brooklyn real estate office, glaring at the men who sat behind desks in the rear of the room. "You *sonamabitch*," he repeated when nobody looked up.

"Hey," snapped one of the men, jumping up from his desk, "who are *you* talking to?"

"You," said the shoemaker, his small disheveled figure leaning against the door unsteadily, as if he'd been drinking, his tiny dark eyes angry and bloodshot. "You take-a my store . . . you no give-a me notting, you . . ."

"Now listen here," said the real estate man, quickly walking to where the shoemaker stood and looking down at him hard, "we will have none of *that* talk around here. In fact I am going to call the cops . . ."

He grabbed the phone nearest him and began to dial. The shoemaker watched for a moment, not seeming to care. Then he shrugged to himself and slowly turned and, without another word, walked out the door and shuffled down the street.

The real estate man, putting down the telephone, watched the shoemaker go. He did not chase him. He wanted nothing further to do with him—neither with him nor with *any* of those boisterous people who had been making so much noise lately, cursing or signing petitions or issuing threats, as if it had been the *real estate men's* idea to build the Verrazano-Narrows Bridge and the big highway leading up to it, the highway that would cut into the Bay Ridge section of Brooklyn where seven thousand people now lived, where eight hundred buildings now stood—including a shoestore—and would level everything in its path into a long, smooth piece of concrete.

No, it was not their idea, it was the idea of Robert Moses and his Triborough Bridge and Tunnel Authority to build the bridge and its adjoining highways—but the real estate men, hired by the Authority, were getting most of the direct blame because it was they, not Moses, who had to face the people and say, "Abandon your homes—we must build a bridge."

Some people, particularly old people, panicked. Many of them pleaded with the Authority's representatives and prayed to God not to destroy these homes where their children had been born, where their husbands had died. Others panicked with anger, saying this was *their* home, *their* castle, and Mr. Moses would have to drag them from it bodily.

Some took the news quietly, waiting without words to be listed among the missing—waiting for the moving van as if it meant death itself. With the money the Authority paid them for their old home, they went to Florida, or to Arizona, or to another home in Brooklyn, any home, not seeming to care very much because now they were old people and new homes were all the same.

The old shoemaker, nearly seventy, returned to Southern Italy, back to his native Cosenza, where he had some farmland he hoped to sell. He had left Cosenza for America when he was twenty-two years old. And now, in 1959, seeing Cosenza again was seeing how little it had changed. There were still goats and donkeys climbing up the narrow roads, and some peasant women carrying clay pots on their heads, and a few men wearing black bands on their sleeves or ribbons in their lapels to show that they were in mourning; and still the same white stone houses speckled against the lush green of the mountainside—houses of many generations.

When he arrived, he was greeted by relatives he had long forgotten, and they welcomed him like a returning hero. But later they began to tell him about their ailments, their poverty, all their problems, and he knew what was coming next. So he quickly began to tell them about *his* problems, sparing few details, recalling how he had fallen behind in the rent of his shoestore in Brooklyn, how the Authority had thrown him out without a dime, and how he now found himself back in Italy where he had started—all because this damned bridge was going to be built, this bridge the Americans were planning to name after an Italian explorer the shoemaker's relatives had never heard of: this Giovanni da Verrazano, who, sailing for the French in 1524, discovered New York Bay. The shoemaker went on and on, gesturing with his hands and making his point, making certain they knew he was no soft touch—and, a day or two later, he went about the business of trying to sell the farmland. . . .

On the Staten Island side, opposition to the bridge was nothing like it was in Brooklyn, where more than twice as many people and buildings were affected by the bridge; in fact, in Staten Island there had long been powerful factions that dreamed of the day when a bridge might be built to link their borough more firmly with the rest of New York City. Staten Island had always been the most isolated, the most ignored of New York's five boroughs; it was separated from Manhattan by five miles of water and a half-hour's ride on the ferry.

While New Yorkers and tourists had always enjoyed riding the Staten Island ferry—"a luxury cruise at a penny a mile"—nobody was ever much interested in getting to the other side. What was there to see? Sixty percent of the island's fifty-four square miles were underdeveloped as of 1958. Most of its 225,000 citizens lived in one-family houses. It was the dullest of New York's boroughs, and when a New York policeman was in the doghouse with headquarters, he was often transferred to Staten Island.

The island first acquired its rural quality when the British controlled it three hundred years ago, encouraging farming rather than manufacturing, and that was the way many Staten Islanders wanted it to remain— quiet and remote. But on the last day of 1958, after years of debate and doubt, plans for the building of the Verrazano-Narrows Bridge finally became definite and the way of those who cherished the traditional life was in decline. But many more Staten Island residents were overjoyed with the news; they had wanted a change, had grown bored with the provincialism, and now hoped the bridge would trigger a boom—and suddenly they had their wish.

The bridge announcement was followed by a land rush. Real estate values shot up. A small lot that cost $1,200 in 1958 was worth $6,000 in 1959, and larger pieces of property worth $100,000 in the morning often sold for $200,000 that afternoon. Tax-delinquent properties were quickly claimed by the city. Huge foreign syndicates from Brazil, Italy and Switzerland moved in for a quick kill. New construction was planned for almost every part of Staten Island, and despite complaints and suits against contractors for cheaply built homes (one foreman was so ashamed of the shoddy work he was ordered to do that he waited until night to leave the construction site) nothing discouraged the boom or deglamorized the bridge in Staten Island.

The bridge had become, in early 1959, months before any workmen started to put it up, the symbol of hope.

"We are now on our way to surmounting the barrier of isolation," announced the borough president, Albert V. Maniscalco—while other leaders were conceding that the bridge, no matter what it might bring, could not really hurt Staten Island. What was there to hurt? "Nothing has ever been successful in Staten Island in its entire history," said one resident, Robert Regan, husband of opera singer Eileen Farrell. He pointed out that there had been attempts in the past to establish a Staten Island Opera Company, a semi-professional football team, a dog track, a boxing arena, a symphony orchestra, a midget auto track, a basketball team—and all failed. "The only thing that might save this island," he said, "is a lot of new people."

Over in Brooklyn, however, it was different. They did not need or want new people. They had a flourishing, middle-class, almost all-white community in the Bay Ridge section, and they were satisfied with what they had. Bay Ridge, which is in western Brooklyn along the ridge of Upper New York Bay and Lower New York Bay, commands a superb view of the Narrows, a mile-wide tidal strait that connects the two Bays, and through which pass all the big ships entering or leaving New York. Among its first settlers were thousands of Scandinavians, most of them

Danes, who liked Bay Ridge because of its nearness to the water and the balmy breeze. And in the late nineteenth century, Bay Ridge became one of the most exclusive sections of Brooklyn.

It was not that now, in 1959, except possibly along its shorefront section, which was lined with trees and manicured lawns and with strong sturdy homes, one of them occupied by Charles Atlas. The rest of Bay Ridge was almost like any other Brooklyn residential neighborhood, except that there were few if any Negroes living among the whites. The whites were mostly Catholic. The big churches, some with parishes in excess of 12,000, were supported by the lace-curtain Irish and aspiring Italians, and the politics, usually Republican, were run by them, too. There were still large numbers of Swedes and Danes, and also many Syrian shopkeepers, and there were old Italian immigrants (friends of the shoemaker) who were hanging on, but it was the younger, second- and third-generation Italians, together with the Irish, who determined the tone of Bay Ridge. They lived, those not yet rich enough for the shorefront homes, in smaller brown brick houses jammed together along tree-lined streets, and they competed each day for a parking place at the curb. They shopped along busy sidewalks clustered with tiny neighborhood stores with apartments above, and there were plenty of small taverns on corners, and there was the Hamilton House for a good dinner at night—provided they wore a jacket and tie—and there was a dimly lit sidestreet supper-club on the front barstool of which sat a curvesome, wrinkled platinum blonde with a cigarette, but no match.

So Bay Ridge, in 1959, had things in balance; it was no longer chic, but it was tidy, and most people wanted no change, no new people, no more traffic. And they certainly wanted no bridge. When the news came that they would get one, the local politicians were stunned. Some women began to cry. A number of people refused to believe it. They had heard this talk before, they said, pointing out that as far back as 1888 there had been plans for a railroad tunnel that would link Brooklyn and Staten Island. And in 1923 New York's Mayor Hylan even broke ground for a combined rail-and-automobile tunnel to Staten Island, and all that happened was that the city lost a half-million dollars and now has a little hole somewhere going nowhere.

And there had been talk about this big bridge across the Narrows for *twenty years,* they said, and each time it turned out to be just talk. In

1950 there was talk that a bridge between Brooklyn and Staten Island was a good thing, but what if the Russians blew it up during a war: would not the United States Navy ships docked in New York harbor be trapped behind the collapsed bridge at the harbor's entrance? And a year later, there was more talk of a tunnel to Staten Island, and then more debate on the bridge, and it went on this way, on and on. So, they said, in 1959, maybe this is *still* all talk, no action, so let's not worry.

What these people failed to realize was that about 1957 the talk changed a little; it became more intense, and Robert Moses was getting more determined, and New York City's Fire Commissioner was so sure in 1957 that the bridge to Staten Island would become a reality that he quickly got in his bid with the City Planning Commission for a big new Staten Island firehouse, asking that he be given $379,500 to build it and $250,000 to equip it. They did not realize that the powerful Brooklyn politician Joseph T. Sharkey saw the bridge as inevitable in 1958, and he had made one last desperate attack, too late, on Robert Moses on the City Council floor, shouting that Moses was getting too much power and was listening only to the engineers, not to the will of the people. And they did not realize, too, that while they were thinking it was still *all talk,* a group of engineers around a drawing board were quietly inking out a large chunk of Brooklyn that would be destroyed for the big approach-way to the bridge—and one of the engineers, to his horror, realized that his plan included the demolition of the home of his own mother-in-law. When he told her the news, she screamed and cried and demanded he change the plan. He told her he was helpless to do so; the bridge was inevitable. She died without forgiving him.

The bridge was inevitable—and it was inevitable they would hate it. They saw the coming bridge not as a sign of progress, but as a symbol of destruction, as an enormous sea monster that soon would rise out of the water and destroy eight hundred buildings and force seven thousand Bay Ridge people to move—all sorts of people: housewives, bartenders, a tugboat skipper, doctors, lawyers, a pimp, teetotalers, drunks, secretaries, a retired light-heavyweight fighter, a former Ziegfeld Follies girl, a family of seventeen children (two dogs and a cat), a dentist who had just spent $15,000 installing news chairs, a vegetarian, a bank clerk, an assistant school principal, and two lovers—a divorced man of forty-one and an unhappily married woman who lived across the street. Each afternoon in his apartment they would meet, these lovers, and make love and wonder what next, wonder if she could ever tell her husband and leave her children. And now, suddenly, this bridge was coming between the lovers, would destroy their neighborhood and their quiet afternoons together, and they had no idea, in 1959, what they would do.

What the others did, the angry ones, was join the "Save Bay Ridge" committee which tried to fight Moses until the bulldozers were bashing down their doors. They signed petitions, and made speeches, and screamed, "This bridge—*who needs it?*" News photographers took their photographs and reporters interviewed them, quoting their impassioned pleas, and Robert Moses became furious.

He wrote letters to a newspaper publisher saying that the reporter had distorted the truth, had lied, had emphasized only the bad part, not the good part, of destroying people's homes. Most people in Brooklyn did not, in 1959, understand the good part, and so they held on to their homes with determination. But sooner or later, within the next year or so, they let go. One by one they went, and soon the house lights went out for the last time, and then moving vans rolled in, and then the bulldozers came crashing up and the walls crumbled down, and the roofs caved in and everything was hidden in an avalanche of dust—a sordid scene to be witnessed by the hold-out next door, and soon he, too, would move out, and then another, and another. And that is how it went on each block, in each neighborhood, until, finally, even the most determined hold-out gave in because, when a block is almost completely destroyed, and one is all alone amid the chaos, strange and unfamiliar fears sprout up: the fear of being alone in a neighborhood that is dying; the fear of a band of young vagrants who occasionally would roam through the rubble smashing windows or stealing doors, or picket fences, light fixtures, or shrubbery, or picking at broken pictures or leftover love letters; fear of the derelicts who would sleep in the shells of empty apartments or hanging halls; fear of the rats that people said would soon be crawling up from the shattered sinks or sewers because, it was explained, rats also were being dispossessed in Bay Ridge, Brooklyn.

One of the last hold-outs was a hazel-eyed, very pretty brunette divorced woman of forty-two named Florence Campbell. She left after the lovers, after the dentist, and after the former Ziegfeld Follies girl, Bessie Gros Dempsey, who had to pack up her 350 plumed hats and old scrapbooks; she left after the crazy little man who had been discovered alone in an empty apartment house because, somehow, he never heard the bulldozers beneath him and had no idea that a bridge was being built.

She left after the retired prizefighter, Freddy Fredericksen, who had only lost twice before, and after Mr. and Mrs. John G. Herbert, the parents of seventeen children—although Florence Campbell's leaving was nowhere as complex as the Herberts'. It had taken them twelve trips to move all their furniture, all the bicycles, sleds, dishes, dogs to their new house a little more than a mile away—twelve trips and sixteen hours; and when they had finally gotten everything there, Mr. Herbert, a Navy Yard worker, discovered that the cat was missing. So early the next morning he sent two sons back to the old house, and they discovered the cat beneath the porch. They also discovered an old axe there. And for the next hour they used the axe to destroy everything they could of the old house; they smashed windows, walls, the floors, they smashed their old bedroom, the kitchen shelves, and the banister of the porch, where they used to gather on summer nights, and they smashed without knowing exactly why, only knowing, as they took turns swinging, that they felt a little wild and gleeful and sad and mad as they smashed—and then, too tired to continue, they retrieved the cat from under the smashed porch and they left their old home for the last time.

In the case of Florence Campbell, it took more than even a murder to make her abandon her home. She had been living, since her divorce, with her young son in a sixty-four-dollar-a-month spacious apartment. It was difficult for her to find anything like it at a rental she could afford. The relocation agent, who had lost patience with her for turning down apartments he considered suitable but she considered too expensive, now forgot about her, and she was on her own to search alone at night after she had returned from her bookkeeping job with the Whitehall Club in Manhattan.

Then one morning she started smelling a strange odor in the apartment. She thought perhaps that her son had gone fishing the day before, after school, and had dumped his catch in the dumbwaiter. He denied it, and the next night, when the odor became worse, she telephoned the police. They soon discovered that the elderly man living on the first floor, the only other tenant in the house, had three days before murdered his wife with shotgun bullets and now, dazed and silent, he was sitting next to the corpse, empty whiskey bottles at his feet.

"Lady, do me a favor," the police sergeant said to Florence Campbell. "Get out of this block, will ya?"

She said she would, but she still could not find an apartment during her searchings. She had no relatives she could move in with, no friends within the neighborhood, because they had all moved. When she came home at midnight from apartment hunting, she would find the hall dark —somebody was always stealing the light bulb—or she might stumble over a drunken derelict sleeping on the sidewalk in front of the downstairs door.

A few nights after the sergeant's warning she was awakened from sleep by the sounds of shuffling feet outside her door and the pounding of fists against the wall. Her son, in the adjoining bedroom, jumped up, grabbed a shotgun he kept in his closet, and ran out into the hall. But it was completely dark, the light bulb had been stolen again. He tripped and Florence Campbell screamed.

A strange man raced up the steps to the roof. She called the police. They came quickly but could find no one on the roof. The police sergeant again told her to leave, and she nodded, weeping, that she would. The next day she was too nervous to go to work, and so she went to a nearby bar to get a drink and told the bartender what had happened, and, very excited, he told her he knew of an apartment that was available a block away for sixty-eight dollars month. She ran to the address, got the apartment—and the landlord could not understand why, after she got it, she began to cry.

3.
Survival of the Fittest

The bridge began as bridges always begin—silently. It began with underwater investigations and soil studies and survey sheets; and when the noise finally started, on January 16, 1959, nobody in Brooklyn or Staten Island heard it.

It started with the sound of a steam pile driver ramming a pipe thirty-six inches in diameter into the silt of a small island off the Brooklyn shore. The island held an old battered bastion called Fort Lafayette, which had been a prison during the Civil War, but now it was about to be demolished, and the island would only serve as a base for one of the bridge's two gigantic towers.

Nobody heard the first sounds of the bridge because they were soft and because the island was six hundred feet off the Brooklyn shore; but even if it had been closer, the sounds would not have risen above the rancor and clamor of the people, for when the drilling began, the people still were protesting, still were hopeful that the bridge would never be built. They were aware that the city had not yet formally condemned their property—but that came three months later. On April 30, 1959, in Brooklyn Supreme Court, Justice J. Vincent Keogh—who would later go to jail on charges of sharing in a bribe to fix another case—signed

200

the acquisition papers, and four hundred Bay Ridge residents suddenly stopped protesting and submitted in silence.

The next new noise was the spirited, high-stepping sound of a marching band and the blaring platitudes of politicians echoing over a sun-baked parade ground on August 14, 1959—it was ground-breaking day for the bridge, with the ceremony held, wisely, on the Staten Island side. Over in Brooklyn, when a reporter asked State Senator William T. Conklin for a reaction, the Bay Ridge representative snapped, "It is not a ground-breaking—to many it will be heartbreaking." And then, slowly and more emotionally, he continued: "Any public official attending should always be identified in the future with the cruelty that has been inflicted on the community in the name of progress."

Governor Nelson Rockefeller of New York had been invited to attend the ceremony in Staten Island, but he sent a telegram expressing regret that a prior engagement made it impossible for him to be there. He designated Assembly Speaker Joseph Carlino to read his message. But Mr. Carlino did not show up. Robert Moses had to read it.

As Mr. Moses expressed all the grand hope of the future, a small airplane chartered by the Staten Island Chamber of Commerce circled overhead with an advertising banner that urged: "Name it the Staten Island Bridge." Many people opposed the name Verrazano—which had been loudly recommended by the Italian Historical Society of America and its founder, John N. La Corte—because they could not spell it. Others, many of them Irish, did not want a bridge named after an Italian, and they took to calling it the "Guinea Gangplank." Still others advocated simpler names—"The Gateway Bridge," "Freedom Bridge," "Neptune Bridge," "New World Bridge," "The Narrows Bridge." One of the last things ever written by Ludwig Bemelmans was a letter to the *New York Times* expressing the hope that the name "Verrazano" be dropped in favor of a more "romantic" and "tremendous" name, and he suggested calling it the "Commissioner Moses Bridge." But the Italian Historical Society, boasting a large membership of emotional voters, was not about to knuckle under, and finally after months of debate and threats, a compromise was reached in the name "Verrazano-Narrows Bridge."

The person making the least amount of noise about the bridge all this time was the man who was creating it—Othmar H. Ammann, a lean, elderly, proper man in a high starched collar, who now, in his eightieth year, was recognized as probably the greatest bridge engineer in the world. His monumental achievement so far, the one that soared above dozens of others, was the George Washington Bridge, the sight of which had quietly thrilled him since its completion in 1931. Since then, when he and his wife drove down along the Hudson River from upstate New York and suddenly saw the bridge looming in the distance, stretching like a silver rainbow over the river between New York and New Jersey, they often gently bowed and saluted it.

"That bridge is his firstborn, and it was a difficult birth," his wife once explained. "He'll always love it best." And Othmar Ammann, though reluctant to reveal any sentimentality, nevertheless once described its effect upon him. "It is as if you have a beautiful daughter," he said, "and you are the father."

But now the Verrazano-Narrows Bridge presented Ammann with an even larger task. And to master its gigantic design he would even have to take into account the curvature of the earth. The two 693-foot towers, though exactly perpendicular to the earth's surface, would have to be one and five eighths inches farther apart at their summits than at their bases.

Though the Verrazano-Narrows Bridge would require 188,000 tons of steel—three times the amount used in the Empire State Building— Ammann knew that it would be an ever restless structure, would always sway slightly in the wind. Its steel cables would swell when hot and contract when cold, and its roadway would be twelve feet closer to the water in summer than in winter. Sometimes, on long hot summer days, the sun would beat down on one side of the structure with such intensity that it might warp the steel slightly, making the bridge a fraction lower on its hot side than on its shady side. So, Ammann knew, any precision measuring to be done during the bridge's construction would have to be done at night.

From the start of a career that began in 1902, when he graduated from the Swiss Federal Polytechnic Institute with a degree in civil engineering, Ammann had made few mistakes. He had been a careful student, a perfectionist. He had witnessed the rise and fall of other men's creations, had seen how one flaw in mathematics could ruin an engineer's reputation for life—and he was determined it would not happen to him.

Othmar Hermann Ammann had been born on March 26, 1879, in Schaffhausen, Switzerland, into a family that had been established in Schaffhausen since the twelfth century. His father had been a prominent manufacturer and his forebears had been physicians, clergymen, lawyers, government leaders, but none had been engineers, and few had shared his enthusiasm for bridges.

There had always been a wooden bridge stretching from the village of Schaffhausen across the Rhine, the most famous of them being built at a length of 364 feet in the 1700's by a Swiss named Hans Ulrich Grubenmann. It had been destroyed by the French in 1799, but had been replaced by others, and as a boy Othmar Ammann saw bridges as a symbol of challenge and a monument to beauty.

In 1904, after working for a time in Germany as a design engineer, Ammann came to the United States—which, after slumbering for many decades in a kind of dark age of bridge design, was now finally experiencing a renaissance. American bridges were getting bigger and safer; American engineers were now bolder than any in the world.

There were still disasters, but it was nothing like it had been in the middle 1800's, when as many as forty bridges might collapse in a single year, a figure that meant that for every four bridges put up one would fall down. Usually it was a case of engineers not knowing precisely the stress and strain a bridge could withstand, and also there were cases of contractors being too cost-conscious and willing to use inferior building materials. Many bridges in those days, even some railroad bridges, were made of timber. Others were made of a new material, wrought iron, and nobody knew exactly how it would hold up until two disasters—one in Ohio, the other in Scotland—proved its weakness.

The first occurred on a snowy December night in 1877 when a train from New York going west over the Ashtabula Bridge in Ohio suddenly crumbled the bridge's iron beams and then, one by one, the rail cars fell into the icy waters, killing ninety-two people. Two years later, the Firth of Tay Bridge in Scotland collapsed under the strain of a locomotive pulling six coaches and a brakeman's van. It had been a windy Sunday night, and seventy-five people were killed, and religious extremists blamed the railroad for running trains on Sunday. But engineers realized that it was the wrought iron that was wrong, and these two bridge failures hastened the acceptance of steel—which has a working strength twenty-five percent greater than wrought iron—and thus began the great era that would influence young Othmar Ammann.

This era drew its confidence from two spectacular events—the completion in 1874 of the world's first steel bridge, a triple arch over the Mississippi River at St. Louis designed and built by James Buchanan Eads, and the completion in 1883 of the Brooklyn Bridge, first steel cable suspension span, designed by John Roebling and, upon his tragic death, completed by his son, Washington Roebling. Both structures would shape the future course in American bridge-building, and would establish a foundation of knowledge, a link of trial and error, that would guide every engineer through the twentieth century. The Roeblings and James Buchanan Eads were America's first heroes in high steel.

James B. Eads was a flamboyant and cocky Indiana boy whose first engineering work was raising sunken steamers from the bottom of the Mississippi. He also was among the first to explore the river's bed in a diver's suit, and he realized, when it came time for him to start constructing the foundations for his St. Louis bridge, that he could not rely on the Mississippi River soil for firmness, because it had a peculiar and powerful shifting movement.

So he introduced to America the European pneumatic caisson—an air-tight enclosure that would allow men to work underwater without being hindered by the shifting tides. Eventually, as the caisson sank deeper and deeper and the men dug up more and more of the river bed below, the bridge's foundation could penetrate the soft sand and silt and could settle solidly on the hard rock beneath the Mississippi. Part of this delicate operation was helped by Eads' invention—a sand pump that could lift and eject gravel, silt and sand from the caisson's chamber.

Before Eads' bridge would be finished, however, 352 workmen would suffer from a strange new ailment—caisson's disease or "the bends"—and twelve men would die from it, and two would remain crippled for life. But from the experience and observations made by James Eads' physician, Dr. Jaminet, who spent time in the caisson with the men and became temporarily paralyzed himself, sufficient knowledge was obtained to greatly reduce the occurrence of the ailment on future jobs.

When the St. Louis steel bridge was finished, James Eads, to show its strength, ran fourteen locomotives across each of the bridge's three arches. Later a fifteen-mile parade marched across it, President Grant applauded from the reviewing stand, General Sherman drove in the last spike on the Illinois side, and Andrew Carnegie, who had been selling bonds for the project, made his first fortune. The bridge was suddenly instrumental in the development of St. Louis as the most important city on the Mississippi River, and it helped develop the transcontinental railroad systems. It was credited with "the winning of the West" and was pictured on a United States stamp in 1898; and in 1920 James Buchanan Eads became the first engineer elected to the American Hall of Fame.

He died an unhappy man. A project he envisioned across the Isthmus of Tehuantepec did not work out.

John Augustus Roebling was a studious German youth born in 1806, in a small town called Mühlhausen, to a tobacco merchant who smoked more than he sold and to a mother who prayed he would someday amount to more than his father. Largely through her ambition and thrift he received a fine education in architecture and engineering in Berlin, and later he worked for the Prussian government building roads and bridges.

But there was little opportunity for originality, and so at the age of twenty-five he came to America and soon, in Pennsylvania, he was working as a surveyor for the railroads and canals. And one day, while observing how the hemp rope that hauled canal boats often broke, John Roebling began to experiment with a more durable fiber, and soon he was twisting iron wire into the hemp—an idea that would eventually lead him and his family into a prosperous industry that today, in Trenton, N.J., is the basis for the Roebling Company—world's largest manufacturers of wire rope and cable.

But in those days it led John Roebling toward his more immediate goal, the construction of suspension bridges. He had seen smaller suspensions, hung with iron chains, during his student days in Germany, and he wondered if the suspension bridge might not be more graceful, longer and stronger with iron wire rope, maybe even strong enough to support rail cars.

He had his chance to find out when, in 1851, he received a commission to build a suspension bridge over Niagara Falls. This opportunity arose only because the original engineer had abandoned the project after a financial dispute with the bridge company—this engineer being a brilliant but wholly unpredictable and daring man named Charles Ellet. Ellet, when confronted with the problem of getting the first rope across Niagara, found the solution by offering five dollars to any boy who could fly a kite across it. Ellet later had a basket carrier made and he pulled himself over the rushing waters of Niagara to the other side; and next he did the same thing accompanied by his horse, as crowds standing on the cliffs screamed and some women fainted.

Things quieted down when Ellet left Niagara, but John Roebling, in his methodical way, got the job done. "Engineering," as Joseph Gies, an editor and bridge historian, wrote, "is the art of the efficient, and the success of an engineering project often may be measured by the absence of any dramatic history."

In 1855, Roebling's 821-foot single span was finished, and on March 6 of that year a 368-ton train crossed it—the first train in history to cross a span sustained by wire cables. The success quickly led Roebling to other bridge commissions, and in 1867 he started his greatest task, the Brooklyn Bridge.

It would take thirteen years to complete the Brooklyn Bridge, and both John Roebling and his son would be its victims.

One summer morning in 1869, while standing on a pier off Manhattan, surveying the location of one of the towers, and paying no attention to the docking ferryboat that was about to bump into the pier, John Roebling suddenly had his foot caught and crushed between the pier floor and piles; tetanus set in, and two weeks later, at the age of sixty-three, he died.

At the death of his father, Washington Roebling, then thirty-two years old and the chief engineering assistant for the bridge, took over the job. Roebling had previously supervised the construction of other bridges that his father had designed, and had served as an engineering officer for the Union Army during the Civil War. During the war he had also been one of General Grant's airborne spies, ascending in a balloon to watch the movement of Lee's army during its invasion of Pennsylvania.

When he took over the building of the Brooklyn Bridge, Washington Roebling decided that since the bridge's tower foundations would have to be sunk forty-four feet into the East River on the Brooklyn side and seventy-six feet on the New York side, he would use pneumatic caissons —as James Eads had done a few years before with his bridge over the Mississippi. Roebling drove himself relentlessly, working in the caissons day and night and he finally collapsed. When he was carried up, he was paralyzed for life. He was then thirty-five years old.

But Washington Roebling, assisted by his wife Emily, continued to direct the building of the bridge from his sickbed; he would watch the construction through field glasses while sitting at the window of his home on the Brooklyn shore; and then his wife—to whom he had taught the engineer's language, and who understood the problems involved—would carry his instructions to the superintendents on the bridge itself.

Washington Roebling was the first bridge engineer to use steel wire for his cables—it was lighter and stronger than the iron wire cables used by his father on the Niagara bridge—and he had every one of the 5,180 wires galvanized as a safeguard against rust. The first wire was drawn across the East River in 1877, and for the next twenty-six months, from one end of the bridge to the other, the small traveling wheels—looking like bicycle wheels with the tires missing—spun back and forth on pulleys, crossing the East River 10,360 times, each time bringing with them a double strand of wire which, when wrapped, would form the four cables that would hold up the center span of 1,595 feet and its two side spans of 930 feet each. This technique of spinning wire, and the use of a cowbell attached to each wheel to warn the men of its ap-proaches, is still used today; it was used, in a more modern form, even by O. H. Ammann in the cable-spinning phase of his Verrazano-Narrows Bridge in the 1960's.

The Brooklyn Bridge was opened on May 24, 1883. Washington Roebling and his wife watched the celebrations from their windows through field glasses. It was a great day in New York—business was suspended, homes were draped with bunting, church bells rang out, steamships whistled. There was the thunder of guns from the forts in the harbor and from the Navy ships docked near the bridge, and finally, in open carriages, the dignitaries arrived. President Chester A. Arthur, New York's Governor Grover Cleveland, and the mayors of every city within several miles of New York arrived at the bridge. Later that night there was a procession in Brooklyn that led to Roebling's home, and he was congratulated in person by President Arthur.

To this day the Brooklyn Bridge has remained the most famous in America, and, until the Williamsburg Bridge was completed over the East River between Brooklyn and Manhattan in 1903, it was the world's longest suspension. In the great bridge boom of the twentieth century nineteen other suspension spans would surpass it—but none would cast a longer shadow. It has been praised by poets, admired by aesthetes, and sought by the suicidal. Its tower over the tenement roofs of the Lower East Side so electrified a young neighborhood boy named David Steinman that he became determined to emulate the Roeblings, and later he would become one of the world's great bridge designers; he alone, until his death in 1960, would challenge Ammann's dominance.

David Steinman at the age of fourteen had secured a pass from New York's Commissioner of Bridges to climb around the catwalks of the Williamsburg Bridge, then under construction, and he talked to bridge builders, took notes, and dreamed of the bridges he would someday build. In 1906, after graduating from City College in New York with the highest honors, he continued his engineering studies at Columbia, where, in 1911, he received his doctor's degree for his thesis on long-span bridges and foundations. Later he became consulting engineer on the design and construction of the Florianopólis Bridge in Brazil, the Mount Hope Bridge in Rhode Island, the Grand Mère in Quebec, the Henry Hudson arch bridge in New York. It was Dr. David Steinman who was called upon to renovate the Brooklyn Bridge in 1948, and it was he who was selected over Ammann to build the Mackinac Bridge —although it was Ammann who emerged with the Verrazano-Narrows commission, the bridge that Steinman had dreamed of building.

The two men were never close as friends, possibly because they were too close in other ways. Both had been assistants in their earlier days to the late Gustav Lindenthal, designer of the Hell Gate and the Queensboro bridges in New York, and the two men were inevitably compared. They shared ambition and vanity, and yet possessed dissimilar personalities. Steinman was a colorfully blunt product of New York, a man who relished publicity and controversy, and who wrote poetry and had published books. Ammann was a stiff, formal Swiss gentleman, well-born and distant. But that they were to be lifelong competitors was inevitable, for the bridge business thrives on competition; it exists on every level. There is competition between steel corporations as they bid for each job, and there is competition between even the lowliest apprentices in the work gangs. All the gangs—the riveters, the steel connectors, the cable spinners—battle throughout the construction of every bridge to see who can do the most work, and later in bars there is competition to see who can drink the most, brag the most. But here, on the lower level, among the bridge workers, the rivalry is clear and open; on the higher level, among the engineers, it is more secret and subtle.

Some engineers quietly go through life envying one another, some quietly prey on others' failures. Every time there is a bridge disaster, engineers who are unaffiliated with its construction flock to the site of the bridge and try to determine the reason for the failure. Then, quietly, they return to their own plans, armed with the knowledge of the disaster, and patch up their own bridges, hoping to prevent the same thing. This is as it should be. But it does not belie the truth of the competition. When a bridge fails, the engineer who designed it is as good as dead. In the bridge business, on every level, there is an endless battle to stay alive—and no one has stayed alive longer than O. H. Ammann.

Ammann was among the engineers who, in 1907, investigated the collapse of a cantilever bridge over the St. Lawrence River near Quebec. Eighty-six workmen, many of them Indians, who were just learning the high-construction business then, fell with the bridge, and seventy-five drowned. The engineer whose career ended with his failure was Theodore Cooper, one of America's most noted engineers—the same man who had been so lucky years before when, after falling one hundred feet into the Mississippi River while working on James Eads' bridge, not only survived but went back to work the same day.

But now, in 1907, it was the opinion of most engineers that Theodore Cooper did not know enough about the stresses involved in the cantilever bridge. None of them did. There is no way to know enough about bridge failure until enough bridges have failed. "This bridge failed because it was not strong enough," one engineer, C. C. Schneider, quipped to the others. Then they all returned to their own bridges, or to their plans for bridges, to see if they too had made miscalculations.

One bridge that perhaps was saved in this manner was Gustav Lindenthal's Queensboro Bridge, which was then approaching completion over the East River in Manhattan. After a re-examination, it was concluded that the Queensboro was inadequate to safely carry its intended load. So the four rapid-transit tracks that had been planned for the upper deck were reduced by two. The loss of the two tracks was compensated by the construction of a subway tunnel a block away from the bridge—the BMT tunnel at Sixtieth Street under the East River, built at an additional cost of $4,000,000.

In November of 1940, when the Tacoma Narrows Bridge fell into the waters of Puget Sound in the state of Washington, O. H. Ammann was again one of the engineers called in to help determine the cause. The engineer who caught the blame in this case was L. S. Moisseiff, a man with a fine reputation throughout the United States.

Moisseiff had been involved in the design of the Manhattan Bridge in New York, and had been the consulting engineer of the Ambassador Bridge in Detroit and the Golden Gate in California, among many others, and nobody had questioned him when he planned a lean, two-lane bridge that would stretch 2,800 feet over the waters of Puget Sound. True, it was a startlingly slim, fragile-looking bridge, but during this time there had been an aesthetic trend toward slimmer, sleeker, lovelier suspension bridges. This was the same trend that led David Steinman to paint his Mount Hope Bridge over Narragansett Bay a soft green color, and to have its cables strung with lights and approaches lined with evergreens and roses, costing an additional $70,000 for landscaping.

There was also a prewar trend toward economizing on the over-all cost of bridge construction, however, and one way to save money without spoiling the aesthetics—and supposedly without diminishing safety —was to shape the span and roadway floor with solid plate girders, not trusses that wind could easily pass through. And it was partially because of these solid girders that, on days when the wind beat hard against its solid mass of roadway, the Tacoma Narrows Bridge kicked up and down. But it never kicked too much, and the motorists, far from becoming alarmed, actually loved it, enjoyed riding over it. They knew that all bridges swayed a little in the wind—this bridge was just livelier, that was all, and they began calling it, affectionately, "Galloping Gertie."

Four months after it had opened—on November 7—with the wind between thirty-five and forty-two miles an hour, the bridge suddenly began to kick more than usual. Sometimes it would heave up and down as much as three feet. Bridge authorities decided to close the bridge to traffic; it was a wise decision, for later it began to twist wildly, rising on one side of its span, falling on the other, rising and falling sometimes as much as twenty-eight feet, tilting at a forty-five-degree angle in the wind. Finally, at 11 A.M., the main span ripped away from its suspenders and went crashing into Puget Sound.

The factors that led to the failure, the examining engineers deduced, were generally that the tall skinny bridge was too flexible and lacked the necessary stiffening girders; and also they spoke about a new factor that they had previously known very little about—"aerodynamic instability."

And soon, on other bridges, on bridges all over America and elsewhere, adjustments were made to compensate for the instability. The Golden Gate underwent alterations that cost more than $3,000,000. The very flexible Bronx-Whitestone Bridge in New York, which Leon Moisseiff had designed—with O. H. Ammann directing the planning and construction—had holes punched into its plate girders and had trusses added. Several other bridges that formerly had been slim and frail now became sturdier with trusses, and twenty years later, when Ammann was creating the Verrazano-Narrows Bridge, the Tacoma lesson lived on. Though the lower second deck on the Verrazano-Narrows was not yet needed, because the anticipated traffic could easily be accommodated by the six-lane upper deck, Ammann made plans for the second deck to go on right away—something he hadn't done in 1930 with his George Washington Bridge. The six-lane lower deck of the Verrazano will probably be without an automobile passenger for the next ten years, but the big bridge will be more rigid from its opening day.

After the Tacoma incident, Moisseiff's talents were no longer in demand. He never tried to pass off any of the blame on other engineers or the financiers; he accepted his decline quietly, though finding little solace in the fact that with his demise as an influential designer of bridges the world of engineering knowledge was expanded and bigger bridges were planned, bringing renown to others.

And so some engineers, like Leon Moisseiff and Theodore Cooper, go down with their bridges. Others, like Ammann and Steinman, remain high and mighty. But O. H. Ammann is not fooled by his fate.

One day, after he had completed his design on the Verrazano-Narrows Bridge, he mused aloud in his New York apartment, on the thirty-second floor of the Hotel Carlyle, that one reason he has experienced no tragedy with his bridges is that he has been blessed with good fortune.

"I have been lucky," he said, quietly.

"Lucky!" snapped his wife, who attributes his success solely to his superior mind.

"Lucky," he repeated, silencing her with his soft, hard tone of authority.

4.

Punks and Pushers

Building a bridge is like combat; the language is of the barracks, and the men are organized along the lines of the noncommissioned officers' caste. At the very bottom, comparable to the Army recruit, are the apprentices—called "punks." They climb catwalks with buckets of bolts, learn through observation and turns on the tools, occasionally are sent down for coffee and water, seldom hear thanks. Within two or three years, most punks have become full-fledged bridgemen, qualified to heat, catch, or drive rivets; to raise, weld, or connect steel—but it is the last job, connecting the steel, that most captures their fancy. The steel connectors stand highest on the bridge, their sweat taking minutes to hit the ground, and when the derricks hoist up new steel, the connectors reach out and grab it with their hands, swing it into position, bang it with bolts and mallets, link it temporarily to the steel already in place, and leave the rest to the riveting gangs.

Connecting steel is the closest thing to aerial art, except the men must build a new sky stage for each show, and that is what makes it so dangerous—that and the fact that young connectors sometimes like to grandstand a bit, like to show the old men how it is done, and so they

213

sometimes swing on the cables too much, or stand on unconnected steel, or run across narrow beams on windy days instead of straddling as they should—and sometimes they get so daring they die.

Once the steel is in place, riveting gangs move in to make it permanent. The fast, four-man riveting gangs are wondrous to watch. They toss rivets around as gracefully as infielders, driving in more than a thousand a day, each man knowing the others' moves, some having traveled together for years as a team. One man is called the "heater," and he sweats on the bridge all day over a kind of barbecue pit of flaming coal, cooking rivets until they are red—but not so red that they will buckle or blister. The heater must be a good cook, a chef, must think he is cooking sausages not rivets, because the other three men in the riveting gang are very particular people.

Once the rivet is red, but not too red, the heater tong-tosses it fifty, or sixty, or seventy feet, a perfect strike to the "catcher," who snares it out of the air with his metal mitt. Then the catcher relays the rivet to the third man, who stands nearby and is called the "bucker-up"—and who, with a long cylindrical tool named after the anatomical pride of a stud horse, bucks the rivet into the prescribed hole and holds it there while the fourth man, the riveter, moves in from the other side and begins to rattle his gun against the rivet's front end until the soft tip of the rivet has been flattened and made round and full against the hole. When the rivet cools, it is as permanent as the bridge itself.

Each gang—whether it be a riveting gang, connecting gang or raising gang—is under the direct supervision of a foreman called a "pusher." (One night in a Brooklyn bar, an Indian pusher named Mike Tarbell was arrested by two plainclothesmen who had overheard his occupation, and Tarbell was to spend three days in court and lose $175 in wages before convincing the judge that he was not a pusher of dope, only of bridgemen.)

The pusher, like an Army corporal who is bucking for sergeant, drives his gang to be the best, the fastest, because he knows that along the bridge other pushers are doing the same thing. They all know that the bridge company officials keep daily records of the productivity of each gang. The officials know which gang lifted the most steel, drove the most rivets, spun the most cable—and if the pusher is ambitious, wants to be promoted someday to a better job on the bridge, pushing is the only way.

But if he pushes too hard, resulting in accidents or death, then he is in trouble with the bridge company. While the bridge company encourages competition between gangs, because it wants to see the bridge finished fast, wants to see traffic jams up there and hear the clink of coins at toll gates, it does not want any accidents or deaths to upset the schedule or get into the newspapers or degrade the company's safety record with the insurance men. So the pusher is caught in the middle. If he is not lucky, if there is death in his gang, he may be blamed and be dropped back into the gang himself, and another workman will be promoted to pusher. But if he is lucky, and his gang works fast and well, then he someday might become an assistant superintendent on the bridge—a "walkin' boss."

The walkin' boss, of which there usually are four on a big bridge where four hundred or five hundred men are employed, commands a section of the span. One walkin' boss may be in charge of the section between an anchorage and a tower, another from that tower to the center of the span, a third from the center of the span to the other tower, the fourth from that tower to the other anchorage—and all they do all day is walk up and down, up and down, strutting like gamecocks, a look of suspicion in their eyes as they glance sideways to see that the pushers are pushing, the punks are punking, and the young steel connectors are not behaving like acrobats on the cables.

The thing that concerns walkin' bosses most is that they impress *the* boss, who is the superintendent, and is comparable to a top sergeant. The superintendent is usually the toughest, loudest, foulest-mouthed, best bridgeman on the whole job, and he lets everybody know it. He usually spends most of his day at a headquarters shack built along the shore near the anchorage of the bridge, there to communicate with the engineers, designers, and other white-collar officers from the bridge company. The walkin' bosses up on the bridge represent him and keep him informed, but about two or three times a day the superintendent will leave his shack and visit the bridge, and when he struts across the span the whole thing seems to stiffen. The men are all heads down at work, the punks seem petrified.

The superintendent selected to supervise the construction of the span and the building of the cables for the Verrazano-Narrows Bridge was a six-foot, fifty-nine-year-old, hot-tempered man named John Murphy, who, behind his back, was known as "Hard Nose" or "Short Fuse."

He was a broad-shouldered and chesty man with a thin strong nose and jaw, with pale blue eyes and thinning white hair—but the most distinguishing thing about him was his red face, a face so red that if he ever blushed, which he rarely did, nobody would know it. The red hard face—the result of forty years' booming in the high wind and hot sun of a hundred bridges and skyscrapers around America—gave Murphy the appearance of always being boiling mad at something, which he usually was.

He had been born, like so many boomers, in a small town without horizons—in this case, Rexton, a hamlet of three hundred in New Brunswick, Canada. The flu epidemic that had swept through Rexton in the spring of 1919, when Murphy was sixteen years old, killed his mother and father, an uncle and two cousins, and left him largely responsible for the support of his five younger brothers and sisters. So he went to work driving timber in Maine, and, when that got slow, he moved down to Pennsylvania and learned the bridge business, distinguishing himself as a steel connector because he was young and fearless. He was considered one of the best connectors on the George Washington Bridge, which he worked on in 1930 and 1931, and since then he had gone from one job to another, booming all the way up to Alaska to put a bridge across the Tanana River, and then back east again on other bridges and buildings.

In 1959 he was the superintendent in charge of putting up the Pan Am, the fifty-nine-story skyscraper in mid-Manhattan, and after that he was appointed to head the Verrazano job by the American Bridge Company, a division of United States Steel that had the contract to put up the bridge's span and steel cables.

When Hard Nose Murphy arrived at the bridge site in the early spring of 1962, the long, undramatic, sloppy, yet so vital part of bridge construction—the foundations—was finished, and the two 693-foot towers were rising.

The foundation construction for the two towers, done by J. Rich Steers, Inc., and the Frederick Snare Corporation, if not an aesthetic operation that would appeal to the adventurers in high steel, nevertheless was a most difficult and challenging task, because the two caissons sunk in the Narrows had been among the largest ever built. They were 229 feet long and 129 feet wide, and each had sixty-six circular dredging holes—each hole being seventeen feet in diameter—and, from a distance, the concrete caissons looked like gigantic chunks of Swiss cheese.

Building the caisson that would support the pedestal which would in turn bear the foundation for the Staten Island tower had required 47,000 cubic yards of concrete, and before it settled on firm sand 105 feet below the surface, 81,500 cubic yards of muck and sand had to be lifted up through the dredging holes by clamshell buckets suspended from cranes. The caisson for the Brooklyn tower had to be sunk to about 170 feet below sea level, had required 83,000 cubic yards of concrete, and 143,600 cubic yards of muck and sand had to be dredged up.

The foundations, the ones that anchor the bridge to Staten Island and Brooklyn, were concrete blocks the height of a ten-story building, each triangular-shaped, and holding, within their hollows, all the ends of the cable strands that stretch across the bridge. These two anchorages, built by The Arthur A. Johnson Corporation and Peter Kiewit Sons' Company, hold back the 240,000,000-pound pull of the bridge's four cables.

It had taken a little more than two years to complete the four foundations, and it had been a day-and-night grind, unappreciated by sidewalk superintendents and, in fact, protested by two hundred Staten Islanders on March 29, 1961; they claimed, in a petition presented to Richmond County District Attorney John M. Braisted, Jr., that the foundation construction between 6 P.M. and 6 A.M. was ruining the sleep of a thousand persons within a one-mile radius. In Brooklyn, the Bay Ridge neighborhood also was cluttered with cranes and earth-moving equipment as work on the approachway to the bridge continued, and the people still were hating Moses, and some had cried foul after he had awarded a $20,000,000 contract, without competitive bidding, to a construction company that employs his son-in-law. All concerned in the transaction immediately denied there was anything irregular about it.

But when Hard Nose Murphy arrived, things were getting better; the bridge was finally crawling up out of the water, and the people had something to *see*—some visible justification for all the noise at night— and in the afternoons some old Brooklyn men with nothing to do would line the shore watching the robin-red towers climb higher and higher.

The towers had been made in sections in steel plants and had been floated by barge to the bridge site. The Harris Structural Steel Company had made the Brooklyn tower, while Bethlehem made the Staten Island tower—both to O. H. Ammann's specifications. After the tower sections had arrived at the bridge site, they were lifted up by floating derricks anchored alongside the tower piers. After the first three tiers of each tower leg had been locked into place, soaring at this point to about 120 feet, the floating derricks were replaced by "creepers"—derricks, each with a lifting capacity of more than one hundred tons, that crept up the towers on tracks bolted to the sides of the tower legs. As the towers got higher, the creepers were raised until, finally, the towers had reached their pinnacle of 693 feet.

While the construction of towers possesses the element of danger, it is not really much different from building a tall building or an enormous lighthouse; after the third or fourth story is built, it is all the same the rest of the way up. The real art and drama in bridge building begins after the towers are up; then the men have to reach out from these towers and begin to stretch the cables and link the span over the sea.

This would be Murphy's problem, and as he sat in one of the Harris Company's boats on this morning in May, 1962, idly watching from the water as the Staten Island tower loomed up to its tenth tier, he was saying to one of the engineers in the boat, "You know, every time I see a bridge in this stage, I can't help but think of all the problems we got coming next—all the mistakes, all the cursing, all the goddamned sweat and the death we gotta go through to finish this thing. . . ."

The engineer nodded, and then they both watched quietly again as the derricks, swelling at the veins, continued to hoist large chunks of steel through the sky.

5.
Keeping the Wheel
from Benny

After the towers had been finished in the winter of 1962, the cable spinning would begin—and with it the mistakes, the cursing, the sweat, the death that Murphy had anticipated.

The spinning began in March of 1963. Six hundred men were up on the job, but Benny Olson, who had been the best cableman in America for thirty years, was not among them. He had been grounded. And though he had fumed, fretted, and cursed for three days after he'd gotten the news, it did not help. He was sixty-six years old—too old to be climbing catwalks six hundred feet in the sky, and too slow to be dodging those spinning wheels and snapping wires.

So he was sent four miles up the river to the bridge company's steel-yard near Bayonne, N.J., where he was made supervisor of a big tool shed and was given some punks to order around. But each day Olson would gaze down the river and see the towers in the distance, and he could sense the sounds, the sights, the familiar sensation that pervades a bridge just before the men begin to string steel thread across the sea. And Benny Olson knew, as did most others, that he had taught the cable experts most of what *they* knew and had inspired new techniques in the

219

task, and everybody knew, too, that Benny Olson, at sixty-six, was now a legend securely spun into the lore and links of dozens of big bridges between Staten Island and San Francisco.

He was a skinny little man. He weighed about 135 pounds, stood five feet six inches; he was nearly bald on the top of his head, though some strands grew long and loose down the back of his neck, and he had tiny blue eyes, rimmed with steel glasses, and a long nose. Everybody referred to him as "Benny the Mouse." In his long career he had been a pusher, a walkin' boss, and a superintendent. He compensated for his tiny stature by cutting big men down to size, insulting them endlessly and ruthlessly as he demanded perfection and speed on each cable-spinning job. At the slightest provocation he would fire anyone. He would fire his own brother. In fact, he had. On a bridge in Poughkeepsie in 1928, his brother, Ted, did not jump fast enough to one of Benny Olson's commands, and that was all for Ted.

"Now look, you idiots," Olson then told the other men on the bridge, "things around here will be done *my* way, hear? Or else I'll kick the rest of you the hell off, too, hear?"

Very few men would ever talk back to Benny Olson in those days because, first, they respected him as a bridgeman, as a quick-handed artist who was faster than anybody at pulling wires from a moving wheel and at inspiring a spinning gang to emulate him, and also because Olson, when enraged, was wholly unpredictable and possibly dangerous.

In Philadelphia one day, shortly after he had purchased a new car and was sitting in it at an intersection waiting for the red light to change, a jalopy filled with Negro teenagers came screeching up from behind and banged into the rear bumper of Olson's new car. Quickly, but without saying a word, Olson got out of his car and reached in the back seat for the axe he knew was there. Then he walked back to the boys' car and, still without saying a word, he lifted the axe into the air with both hands and then sent it crashing down upon the fender of the jalopy, chopping off a headlight. Two more fast swings and he had sliced off the other headlight and put a big incision in the middle of the hood. Finally he chopped off a chunk of the aerial with a wide sweep of his axe, and then he turned and walked back to his car and drove slowly away. The boys just sat in their jalopy. They were paralyzed with fear, stunned with disbelief.

Olson was in Philadelphia then because the Walt Whitman Bridge was going up, and the punks hired to work on that bridge were incessantly tormented by Olson, especially the larger ones, and particularly one six-foot two-inch, 235-pound Italian apprentice named Dominick. Every time Benny Olson saw him, he would call him "a dumb bastard" or, at best, a "big, stupid ox."

Just the mere sight of Olson walking down the catwalk would terrorize Dominick, for he was a very high-strung and emotional type, and Olson could get him so nervous and shaky that he could barely light a cigarette. One day, after Olson had hurled five minutes' worth of abuse at Dominick, the big Italian, turning red, lunged toward Olson and grabbed him by the scrawny neck. Then Dominick lifted Olson into the air, carried him toward the edge of the catwalk and held him out over the river.

"You *leetle preek*," Dominick screamed, "now I throw you off."

Four other bridgemen rushed up from behind, held Dominick's arms, pulled him back and tried to calm him. Olson, after he'd been let loose, said nothing. He just rubbed his neck and smoothed out his shirt. A moment later he turned and walked idly up the catwalk, but after he had gotten about fifty feet away, Benny Olson suddenly turned and, with a wild flare of fury, yelled to Dominick, "You know, you really *are* a big, dumb stupid bastard." Then he turned again and continued calmly up the catwalk.

Finally, a few punks on the Walt Whitman Bridge decided to get revenge on Benny Olson. One way to irritate him, they decided, was to stop the spinning wheels, which they could do merely by clicking one of the several turn-off switches installed along the catwalk—placed there in case an accident to one of the men or some flaw in the wiring demanded an instant halt.

So this they did—and, at first, Olson was perplexed. He would be standing on one end of the bridge with everything going smoothly, then, suddenly, a wheel would stop at the other end.

"Hey, what the hell's the matter with that wheel?" he'd yell, but nobody knew. So he would run toward it, running the full length of the catwalk, puffing and panting all the way. Just before he would reach the wheel, however, it would begin to move again—a punk at the other end of the bridge would have flipped the switch back on. This conspiracy went on for hours sometimes, and the game became known as "Keeping the Wheel from Benny." And at 3 A.M. a few punks in a saloon would telephone Benny Olson at his hotel and shout, "Who's got the wheel, Benny?"—and then hang up.

Benny Olson responded without humor, and all day on the bridge he would chase the wheel like a crazy chimpanzee—until, suddenly, he came up with an idea that would stop the game. With help from an engineer, he created an electrical switchboard with red lights on top, each light connected with one of the turn-off switches strung along the bridge. So now if any punk turned off a switch he would give away his location. Olson also appointed a loyal bridge worker to do nothing but watch the switchboard, and this bridgeman was officially called the "tattletale." If the wheel should stop, all Benny Olson had to do was pick up the telephone and say, "Who's got the wheel, Tattletale?" The tattletale would give the precise switch that had been flipped off, and Olson, knowing who was working nearest that spot, could easily fix the blame. But this invention did more than just put an end to the game; it also created a new job in bridge building—the tattletale—and on every big bridge that has been built since the Walt Whitman Bridge, there has been a bridge worker assigned to do nothing but watch the switchboard and keep track of the location of the wheels during the cable-spinning phase of construction. There was a tattletale on the Verrazano-Narrows Bridge, too, but he did little work, for, without Benny Olson to irritate, the demonic spirit had died—there was just no point any more to "Keeping the Wheel from Benny." And besides, the men involved in spinning the cables on the Verrazano were very serious, very competitive men with no time for games. All they wanted, in the spring of 1963, was to get the catwalks strung up between the towers and the anchorages, and then to get the spinning wheels rolling back and forth across the bridge as quickly and as often as possible. The number of trips that the wheels would make between the anchorages during the daily workshift of each gang would be recorded in Hard Nose Murphy's office—and it would be a matter of pride for each gang to try to set a daily mark that other gangs could not equal.

Before the spinning could begin, however, the men would have to build a platform on which to stand. This platform would be the two catwalks, each made of wire mesh, each twenty feet wide, each resembling a long thin road of spider web or a mile-long hammock. The catwalks would each be held up by twelve horizontal pieces of wire rope, each rope a little more than two inches thick, each more than a mile long. The difficult trick, of course, would be in getting the first of these ropes over the towers of the bridge—a feat that on smaller bridges was accomplished by shooting the rope across with a bow and arrow or, in the case of Charles Ellet's pedestrian bridge, by paying a boy five dollars to fly a rope across Niagara on the end of a kite.

But with the Verrazano, the first rope would be dragged across the water by barge, then, as the Coast Guard temporarily stopped all ship movements, the two ends of the rope would be hoisted out of the water by the derricks on top of the two towers, more than four thousand feet apart. The other ropes would be hoisted up the same way. Then all would be fastened between the towers, and from the towers back to the anchorages on the extremities of the bridge, following the same "sag" lines that the cables would later follow. When this was done, the catwalk sections would be hauled up. Each catwalk section, as it was lifted, would be folded up like an accordion, but once it had arrived high up on the tower, the bridgemen standing on platforms clamped to the sides of the tower would hook the catwalk sections onto the horizontal ropes, and then shove or kick the catwalk sections forward down the sloping ropes. The catwalks would glide on under the impetus of their own weight and unfurl—as a rolled-up rug might unfurl if pushed down the steep aisle of a movie theatre.

Once all the catwalk sections glided, bumper to bumper, in place, they would be linked end to end, and would be further stiffened by crossbeams. A handrail wire "banister" would also be strung across the catwalks, as would several wooden cross planks to give the men better footing in places where the catwalk was quite steep.

After the two catwalks were in place, another set of wires would be strung above each catwalk, about fifteen feet above, and these upper wires would be the "traveling ropes" that would pull the wheels back and forth, powered by diesel engines mounted atop the anchorages.

Four spinning wheels, each forty-eight inches in diameter and weighing a few hundred pounds apiece, would run simultaneously along the bridge—two wheels atop each of the two catwalks. Each wheel, being double-grooved, would carry two wires at once, and each wheel would take perhaps twelve minutes to cross the entire bridge, averaging eight miles per hour, although it could be speeded up to thirteen miles an hour downhill. As the wheels passed overhead, the men would grab the wires and clamp them down into the specified hooks and pulleys along the cat-walk; when a wheel arrived at the anchorage, the men there would re-move the wire, hook it in place, reload the wheel and send it back as quickly as possible in the opposite direction.

After the wheel had carried 428 wires across the bridge, the wires would be bound in a strand, and when the wheel had carried across 26,018 wires—or sixty-one strands—they would be squeezed together by hydraulic jacks into a cylindrical shape. This would be a cable. Each cable—there would be four cables on the Verrazano—would be a yard thick, 7,205 feet long, and would contain 36,000 miles of pencil-thin wire. The four cables, collectively, would weigh 38,290 tons. From each cable would later be hung, vertically, 262 suspender ropes—some ropes as long as 447 feet—and they would hold the deck more than two hun-dred feet above the water, holding it high enough so that no matter how hot and limp the cables got in summer the deck would always be high enough for the *Queen Mary* to easily pass beneath.

From the very first day that the wheels began to roll—March 7, 1963 —there was fierce competition between the two gangs working alongside one another on the two catwalks. This rivalry existed both between the gangs on the early-morning shift as well as the gangs on the late-after-noon shift. The goal of each gang, of course, was to get its two wheels back and forth across the bridge more times than the other gang's wheels. The result was that the cable-spinning operation turned into a kind of horse race or, better yet, a dog race. The catwalks became a noisy arena lined with screaming, fist-waving men, all of them looking up and shout-ing at their wheels—wheels that became mechanical rabbits.

"Com'on, you mother, move your ass," they yelled as their wheel skimmed overhead, grinding away and carrying the wire to the other end. *"Move* it, com'on, *move* it!" And from the other catwalk, there came the same desperate urgings, the same wild-eyed competition and anger when their wheel—their star, their hope—would drag behind the other gang's wheel.

The men from one end of the catwalk to the other were all in rhythm with their wheels, all quick at pulling down the wire, all glancing sideways to study the relative position of the other gang's wheels, all hoping that the diesel engines propelling their wheels would not conk out, all very angry if their men standing on the anchorages were too slow at re-loading their wheel once it had completed the journey across. It was in such competition as this that Benny Olson had excelled in his younger days. He used to stand on the catwalk in front of an anchorage inspiring his gang, screaming insults at those too slow at pulling down the wire, or too sluggish at reloading the wheel, or too casual about the competi-tion. Olson was like a deck master hovering over a shipload of slave oarsmen.

On Wednesday, June 19, to the astonishment of the engineers who kept the "score" in Hard Nose Murphy's office, one gang had moved its wheels back and forth across the bridge fifty times. Then, on June 26, a second gang also registered fifty trips. Two days later, in the heat of battle, one of the wheels suddenly broke loose from its moorings and came bouncing down onto the catwalk, skipping toward a bridgeman named John Newberry. He froze with fright. If it hit him, it might knock him off the bridge; if he jumped out of its path too far, he might lose his balance and fall off himself. So he held his position, waiting to see how it jumped. Fortunately, the wheel skimmed by him, he turned slightly like a matador making a pass, and then it stopped dead a few yards down the catwalk. He breathed relief, but his gang was angry because now their daily total was ruined. The other gang would win.

On July 16, one gang got the wheels back and forth fifty-one times, and on July 22, another gang duplicated it. A few days later, the gang under Bob Anderson, the boomer who had been so irresistible to women back on the Mackinac Bridge, was moving along with such flawless pre-cision that with an hour to go of working time it had already registered forty-seven trips. If all went well in the remaining hour, six more trips could be added—meaning a record total of fifty-three.

"Okay, let's move it," Anderson yelled down the line to his gang, all of them focusing on what they hoped would be the winning wheel.

They watched it move smoothly along the tramway overhead, then it rolled higher to the tower, then down, down faster to the anchorage, then up again, quickly reloaded, up the tramway—"Keep moving, you mother!"—closer and closer to the tower now . . . then it stopped.

"*Bitch!*" screamed one of the punks.

"What the hell's wrong?" shouted Anderson.

"The engine's conked out," someone finally yelled.

"Those goddamn idiots!" said the punk.

"Let's go beat their asses," yelled another punk, quite serious and ready to run down the catwalk.

"Calm down," Anderson said, with resignation, looking up at the stilled wheel, shaking his head. "Let me go down and see what can be done."

He went down to the anchorage, only to learn that the engine failure could not be fixed in time to continue the race within the hour. So Anderson walked back up, sadly giving the news to his men, and when they walked down the catwalk that night, their hardhats under their arms, their brows sweaty, they looked like a losing football team leaving the field after the game. In the remaining two months, no gang could top the mark of fifty-one, but in September, when the gangs started to place the two-thousand-pound castings over the cables (the castings are metal saddles which would help support the 262 suspender ropes that would stream down vertically from each cable to hold up the deck), a new kind of competition began: a game to see who could bolt into position the most castings, and this got to be dangerous. Not only were bolts dropping off the bridge in this frenzied race—bolts that could pepper the decks of passing vessels and possibly kill anybody they hit—but the castings themselves were unwieldy, and if one of them fell . . .

"Chrissake, Joe, let's get the bolts out and put that mother on," one pusher yelled to Joe Jacklets, who was being cautious with the casting.

The pusher, noticing that another gang working down the catwalk had already removed the bolts and were clamping the casting into place, was getting nervous—his gang was behind.

"Take it easy," Joe Jacklets said, "this thing might not hold."

"It'll hold."

So Joe Jacklets removed the last bolt of the two-section casting and, as soon as he did, one half of the casting—weighing one thousand pounds—toppled off the cable and fell from the bridge.

"Jes-sus!"

"Ohhhhhhh."

"Kee-*rist*."

"Noooooooooo!"

"Jes-*SUS*."

The gang, their hardhats sticking out over the catwalk, watched the one-thousand-pound casting falling like a bomb toward the sea. They noticed, too, a tiny hydrofoil churning through the water below, almost directly below the spot where it seemed the casting might hit. They watched quietly now, mouths open, holding their breaths. Then, after a loud plopping sound, they saw a gigantic splash mushroom up from the water, an enormous fountain soaring forty feet high.

Then, swishing from under the fountain, fully intact, came the hydrofoil, its skipper turning his head away from the splashing spray and shooting his craft in the opposite direction.

"Oh, that lucky little bastard," one of the men said, peering down from the catwalk, shaking his head.

Nobody said anything else for a moment. They just watched the water below. It was as if they hated to turn around and face the catwalk—and later confront Hard Nose Murphy's fiery face and blazing eyes. They watched the water for perhaps two minutes, watched the bubbles subside and the ripples move out. And then, moving majestically into the ripples, moving slowly and peacefully past, was the enormous gray deck of the United States aircraft carrier *Wasp*.

"Holy God!" Joe Jacklets finally said, shaking his head once more.

"You silly bastard," muttered the pusher.

Jacklets glared at him.

"What do you mean? I told you it might not hold."

"Like hell you did, you . . ."

Jacklets stared back at the pusher, disbelieving; but then he knew it was no use arguing—he would collect his pay as soon as he could and go back to the union hall and wait for a new job . . .

But before he could escape the scene, the whole line of bridgemen came down the catwalk, some cursing, a few smiling because it was too ridiculous.

"What are you stupid bastards laughing at?" said the walkin' boss.

"Aw, com'on, Leroy," said one of the men, "can't you take a little joke?"

"Yeah, Leroy, don't take it so hard. It's not as if we lost the casting. If we know where a thing is, we ain't lost it."

"Sure, that's right," another said. "We know where it is—it's in the river."

The walkin' boss was just too sick to answer. It was *he* who would later have to face Murphy.

Across on the other catwalk, the rival gang waved and a few of the younger men smiled, and one yelled out, "Hey, we set ten castings today. How many did you guys set?"

"Nine and a half," somebody else answered.

This got a laugh, but as the workday ended and the men climbed down from the bridge and prepared to invade Johnny's Bar, Joe Jacklets was seen walking with his head down.

If a casting had to fall, it could not have fallen on a better day—September 20, a Friday—because, with work stopped for the weekend anyway, the divers might be able to locate the casting and have it pulled up out of the water before the workers returned to the bridge on Monday. There was no duplicate of the casting, and the plant where it was made was on strike, and so there was no choice but to fish for it—which the divers did, with no success, all day Saturday and Sunday. They saw lots of other bridge parts down there, but no casting. They saw riveting guns, wrenches and bolts, and there was a big bucket that might have been the one that had fallen with four bolt machines, each worth eight hundred dollars.

Even if it was, the machines as well as the other items were now unserviceable, having been ruined either by the water or the jolt they received when hitting the sea from such high altitudes. Anyway, after a brief inspection of all the tools down there, the divers could easily believe the old saying, "A bridgeman will drop everything off a bridge but money."

Yet this is not precisely true; they drop money off, too. A few five-dollar and ten-dollar bills, even twenty-dollar bills, had been blown off the bridge on some windy Fridays—Friday is payday. And during the cable-spinning months, inasmuch as the men were working long hours, they received their pay *on* the bridge from four clerks who walked along the catwalks carrying more than $200,000 in bundles of cash in zippered camera cases. The cash was sealed in envelopes with each bridgeman's name printed on the outside, and the bridgeman would have to sign a receipt as he received his envelope from the clerk. Some bridgemen, however, after signing the receipt slip, would rip open the envelope and count the money—and that is when they would lose a few bills in the wind. More cautious men would rip off a corner of the envelope, clutching it tight, and count the tips of the bills. Others would just stuff the envelope into their pockets without counting. Still others seemed so preoccupied with their work, so caught up in the competitive swing of spinning, that when the pay clerk arrived with the receipt slip, a pencil, and the envelope, the bridgeman would hastily scribble his name on the slip, then turn away without taking the envelope. Once, as a joke, a clerk named Johnny Cothran walked away with a man's envelope containing more than four hundred dollars, wondering how far he could get with it. He got about twenty feet when he heard the man yelling, *"Hey!"*

Cothran turned, expecting to face an angry bridgeman. But instead the bridgeman said, "You forgot your pencil." Cothran took the pencil, then handed the bridgeman his envelope. "Thanks," he said, stuffing it absently into his pocket and then quickly getting back to the cable-spinning race.

On Monday, September 23, shortly before noon, the casting was discovered more than one hundred feet below the surface of the Narrows, and soon the cranes were swooping over it and pulling it up out of the water. The whole bridge seemed, briefly, to breathe more easily, and Murphy (who had been swearing for three straight days) suddenly calmed down. But two days later, Murphy was again shaking his head in disgust and frustration. At 3:15 P.M. on Wednesday, September 25, somebody on the catwalk had dropped a six-inch steel bolt and, after it had fallen more than one hundred feet, it had hit a bridgeman named Berger Hanson in the face and gone four inches through his skin right under his left eye.

Berger had been standing below the bridge at the time and had been looking up. If he hadn't been looking up the fallen bolt might have hit his hardhat and merely jarred him, instead of doing the damage it did—lifting his eyeball upward, crushing his jawbone, getting stuck in his throat.

Rushed to Victory Memorial Hospital in Brooklyn, Berger was met by the surgeon, Dr. S. Thomas Coppola, who treated all injuries to the bridgemen. Quickly, Dr. Coppola removed the bolt, stopped the bleeding with stitches, then realigned by hand the facial bones and restitched the jaw.

"How do you feel?" Dr. Coppola asked.

"Okay," said Berger.

Dr. Coppola was flabbergasted.

"Don't you have any pain?"

"No."

"Can I give you anything—an aspirin or two?"

"No, I'm okay."

After plastic surgery to correct the deformation of his face, and after a few months' recuperation, Berger was back on the bridge.

Dr. Coppola was amazed not only by Berger but by the stoicism he encountered in so many other patients among bridgemen.

"These are the most interesting men I've ever met," Dr. Coppola was telling another doctor shortly afterward. "They're strong, they can stand all kinds of pain, they're full of pride, and they live it up. This guy Berger has had five lives already, and he's only thirty-nine. . . . Oh, I'll tell you, it's a young man's world."

True, the bridge is a young man's world, and old men like Benny Olson leave it with some bitterness and longing, and hate to be deposited in the steelyard on the other side of the river—a yard where old men keep out of trouble and younger men, like Larry Tatum, supervise them.

Larry Tatum, a tall, broad-shouldered, daring man of thirty-seven, had been spotted years ago by Murphy as a "stepper," which, in bridge parlance, means a comer, a future leader of bridgemen.

Tatum had started as a welder when he was only seventeen years old, and had become a riveter, a fine connector, a pusher. He had fallen occasionally, but always came back, and had never lost his nerve or enthusiasm. He had four younger brothers in the business, too—three working under Murphy on the bridge, one having died under Murphy after falling off the Pan Am building. Larry Tatum's father, Lemuel Tatum, had been a boomer since the twenties, but now, pushing seventy, he also was in the steelyard, working under his son, the stepper, watching the boy gain experience as a walkin' boss so that, quite soon, he would be ready for a promotion to the number-one job, superintendent.

It was just a little awkward for Larry Tatum, though it was not obvious, to be ordering around so many old boomers—men with reputations, like Benny the Mouse, and Lemuel Tatum, and a few dozen others who were in the yard doing maintenance on tools or preparing to load the steel links of the span on barges soon to be floated down to the bridge site. But, excepting for some of Olson's unpredictable explosions, the old men generally were quiet and cooperative—and none more so than the former heavyweight boxing champion, James J. Braddock.

Once they had called Braddock the "Cinderella Man" because, after working as a longshoreman, he won the heavyweight title and earned almost $1,000,000 until his retirement in 1938, after Joe Louis beat him.

Now Braddock was nearly sixty, and was back on the waterfront. His main job was to maintain a welding machine. His clothes were greasy, his fingernails black, and his arms so dirty that it was hard to see the tattoos he had gotten one night in the Bowery, in 1921, when he was a frolicsome boy of sixteen.

Now Braddock was earning $170 a week as an oiler, and some men who did not know Braddock might say, as men so often *like* to say of former champions, "Well, easy come, easy go. Now he's broke, just like Joe Louis."

But his was not another maudlin epic story about a broken prizefighter. Braddock, as he walked slowly around the steelyard, friendly to everyone, his big body erect and his chest out, still was a man of dignity and pride—he was still doing an honest day's work, and this made him feel good.

"What the hell, I'm a working man," he said. "I worked as a longshoreman before I was a fighter, and now I need the money, so I'm working again. I always liked hard work. There's nothing wrong with it."

He lost $15,000 on a restaurant, Braddock's Corner, once on West Forty-ninth Street in Manhattan, and the money he had put into a marine supply house, which he operated for ten years, proved not to be a profitable venture. But he still owns the $14,000 home he bought in North Bergen, N.J., shortly after the Joe Louis fight, he said, and he still loves his wife of thirty-three years' marriage, and still has his health and a desire to work hard, and has two sons who work hard, too.

One son, Jay, who is thirty-two, weighs 330 pounds and stands six feet five inches. He works in a Jersey City powerhouse; the other, thirty-one-year-old Howard, is a 240-pounder who is six feet seven inches and is in road construction.

"So don't feel sorry for me," James J. Braddock, the former Cinderella Man, said, inhaling on a cigarette and leaning forward on a big machine. "Don't feel sorry for me one bit." But he did admit that bridge building, like boxing, was a young man's game.

And of all the eager young men working on the Verrazano-Narrows Bridge under Hard Nose Murphy in the fall of 1963, few seemed better suited to the work or happier on a bridge job than the two men working together atop the cable 385 feet over the water behind the Brooklyn tower.

One was very small, the other very large. The small man, standing five feet seven inches and weighing only 138 pounds—but very sinewy and tough—was named Edward Iannielli. He was called "The Rabbit" by the other men because he jumped the beams and ran across wires, and everybody said of the twenty-seven-year-old Iannielli that he would never live to be thirty.

The big boy was named Gerard McKee. He was a handsome, wholesome boy, about two hundred pounds and six feet three and one-half inches. He had been a Coney Island lifeguard, had charm with women and a gentle disposition, and all the men on the bridge immediately took to him, although he was not as friendly and forward as Iannielli.

On Wednesday morning, October 9, the two climbed the cables as usual, and soon, amid the rattling of the riveters and clang of mallets, they were hard at work, heads down, tightening cable bolts, barely visible from the ground below.

Before the morning was over, however, the attention of the whole bridge would focus on them.

6.
Death on a Bridge

It was a gray and windy morning. At 6:45 A.M. Gerard McKee and Edward Iannielli left their homes in two different parts of Brooklyn and headed for the bridge.

Iannielli, driving his car from his home in Flatbush, got there first. He was already on the catwalk, propped up on a cable with one leg dangling 385 feet above the water, when Gerard McKee walked over to him and waved greetings.

The two young men had much in common. Both were the sons of bridgemen, both were Roman Catholics, both were natives of New York City, and both were out to prove something—that they were as good as any boomer on the bridge.

They quietly resented the prevailing theory that boomers make the best bridgemen. After all, they reasoned, boomers were created more out of necessity than desire; the Indian from the reservation, the Southerner from the farm, the Newfoundlander from the sea, the Midwesterner from the sticks—those who composed most of the boomer population—actually were escaping the poverty and boredom of their birthplaces when they went chasing from boom town to boom town. Iannielli and McKee, on the other hand, did not have to chase all over America for the big job; they could wait for the job to come to them, and did, because the New York area had been enjoying an almost constant building boom for the last ten years.

And yet both were impressed with the sure swagger of the boomer, impressed with the fact that boomers were hired on jobs from New York to California, from Michigan to Louisiana, purely on their national reputations, not on the strength of strong local unions.

This realization seemed to impress Iannielli a bit more than McKee. Perhaps it was partly due to Iannielli's being so small in this big man's business.

He, like Benny Olson, desperately wanted to prove himself, but he would make his mark not by cutting big men to size, or by boasting or boozing, but rather by displaying cold nerve on high steel—taking chances that only a suicidal circus performer would take—and by also displaying excessive pride on the ground.

Iannielli loved to say, "I'm an *iron*worker." (Bridges are now made of steel, but iron was the first metal of big bridges, and the first bridgemen were called "ironworkers." There is great tradition in the title, and so Iannielli—and all bridgemen with pride in the past—refer to themselves as *iron*workers, never *steel*workers.)

When Edward Iannielli first became an apprentice ironworker, he used to rub orange dust, the residue of lead paint, into his boots before taking the subway home; he was naïve enough in those days to think that passengers on the subway would associate orange dust with the solution that is coated over steel during construction to make it rustproof.

"When I was a little kid growing up," he had once recalled, "my old man, Edward Iannielli, Sr., would bring other ironworkers home after work, and all they'd talk about was ironwork, ironwork. That's all we ever heard as kids, my brother and me. Sometimes my old man would take us out to the job, and all the other ironworkers were nice to us because we were Eddie's sons, and the foreman might come over and ask, 'You Eddie's sons?' and we'd say, 'Yeah,' and he'd say, 'Here, take a quarter.' And that is how I first started to love this business.

"Later, when I was about thirteen or fourteen, I remember going out to a job with the old man and seeing this big ladder. And I yelled to my father, 'Can I climb up?' and he said, 'Okay, but don't fall.' So I began to climb up this thing, higher and higher, a little scared at first, and then finally I'm on the top, standing on this steel beam way up there, and I'm all alone and looking all around up there, looking out and seeing very far, and it was exciting, and as I stood up there, all of a sudden, I am thinking to myself, *'This* is what I want to do!' "

After his father had introduced him to the business agent of Local 361, the ironworkers' union in Brooklyn, Edward Iannielli, Jr., started work as an apprentice.

"I'll never forget the first day I walked into that union hall," he had recalled. "I had on a brand-new pair of shoes, and I saw all those big men lined up, and some of them looked like bums, some looked like gangsters, some just sat around tables playing cards and cursing.

"I was scared, and so I found a little corner and just sat there, and in my pocket I had these rosaries that I held. Then a guy walked out and yelled, 'Is young Iannielli here?' and I said, 'Here,' and he said, 'Got a job for you.' He told me to go down and report to a guy named Harry at this new twelve-story criminal court building in downtown Brooklyn, and so I rushed down there and said to Harry, 'I'm sent out from the hall,' and he said, 'Oh, so you're the new apprentice boy,' and I said, 'Yeah,' and he said, 'You got your parents' permission?' and I said, 'Yeah,' and he said, 'In writing?' and I said, 'No,' and so he said, 'Go home and get it.'

"So I get back on the subway and go all the way back, and I remember running down the street, very excited because I had a job, to get my mother to sign this piece of paper. Then I ran all the way back, after getting out of the subway, up to Harry and gave him the piece of paper, and then he said, 'Okay, now I gotta see your birth certificate.' So I had to run all the way back, get another subway, and then come back, and now my feet in my new shoes are hurting.

"Anyway, when I gave Harry the birth certificate, he said, 'Okay, go up that ladder and see the pusher,' and when I got to the top, a big guy asked, 'Who you?' I tell 'im I'm the new apprentice boy, and he says, 'Okay, get them two buckets over there and fill 'em up with water and give 'em to the riveting gang.'

"These buckets were two big metal milk cans, and I had to carry them down the ladder, one at a time, and bring them up, and this is what I did for a long time—kept the riveting gangs supplied with drinking water, with coffee and with rivets—no ifs and buts, either.

"And one time, when I was on a skyscraper in Manhattan, I remember I had to climb down a ladder six floors to get twenty coffees, a dozen sodas, some cake and everything, and on my way back, holding everything in a cardboard box, I remember slipping on a beam and losing my balance. I fell two flights. But luckily I fell in a pile of canvas, and the only thing that happened was I got splashed in all that steaming hot coffee. Some ironworker saw me laying there and he yelled, 'What happened?' and I said, 'I fell off and dropped the coffee,' and he said, '*You dropped the coffee!* Well, you better get the hell down there fast, boy, and get some more coffee.'

"So I go running down again, and out of my own money—must have cost me four dollars or more—I bought all the coffee and soda and cake, and then I climbed back up the ladder, and when I saw the pusher, before he could complain about anything, I told him I'm sorry I'm late."

After Edward Iannielli had become a full-fledged ironworker, he fell a few more times, mostly because he would run, not walk across girders, and once—while working on the First National City Bank in Manhattan— he fell backward about three stories and it looked as if he was going down all the way. But he was quick, light and lucky—he was "The Rabbit," and he landed on a beam and held on.

"I don't know what it is about me," he once tried to explain, "but I think it all has something to do with being young, and not wanting to be like those older men up there, the ones that keep telling me, 'Don't be reckless, you'll get killed, be careful.' Sometimes, on windy days, those old-timers get across a girder by crawling on their hands and knees, but I always liked to run across and show those other men how to do it. That's when they all used to say, 'Kid, you'll never see thirty.'

"Windy days, of course, are the hardest. Like you're walking across an eight-inch beam, balancing yourself in the wind, and then, all of a sudden, the wind stops—and you *temporarily lose your balance.* You quickly straighten out—but it's some feeling when *that* happens."

Edward Iannielli first came to the Verrazano-Narrows job in 1961, and while working on the Gowanus Expressway that cut through Bay Ridge, Brooklyn, to the bridge, he got his left hand caught in a crane one day.

One finger was completely crushed, but the other, cleanly severed, remained in his glove. Dr. Coppola was able to sew it back on. The finger would always be stiff and never as strong as before, of course; yet the surgeon was able to offer Edward Iannielli two choices as to how the finger might be rejoined to his hand. It could either be set straight, which would make it less conspicuous and more attractive, or it could be shaped into a grip-form, a hook. While this was a bit ugly, it would mean that the finger could more easily be used by Iannielli when working with steel. There was no choice, as far as Iannielli was concerned; the finger was bent permanently into a grip.

When, in the fall of 1963, Gerard McKee met Edward Iannielli and saw the misshapen left hand, he did not ask any questions or pay any attention. Gerard McKee was a member of an old family of construction workers, and to him malformation was not uncommon, it was almost a way of life. His father, James McKee, a big, broad-shouldered man with dark hair and soft blue eyes—a man whom Gerard strongly resembled —had been hit by a collapsing crane a few years before, had had his leg permanently twisted, had a steel plate inserted in his head, and was disabled for life.

James McKee had been introduced to ironwork by an uncle, the late Jimmy Sullivan, who had once been Hard Nose Murphy's boss in a gang. The McKee name was well known down at Local 40, the union hall in Manhattan, and it had been quite logical for James McKee, prior to his accident, to take his three big sons down to the hall and register them in the ironworkers' apprentice program.

Of the three boys, Gerard McKee was the youngest, tallest and heaviest—but not by much. His brother John, a year older than Gerard, was 195 pounds and six feet two inches. And his brother Jimmy, two years older than Gerard, was 198 pounds and six feet three inches.

When the boys were introduced to union officials of Local 40, there were smiles of approval all around, and there was no doubt that the young McKees, all of them erect and broad-shouldered and seemingly eager, would someday develop into superb ironworkers. They looked like fine college football prospects—the type that a scout would eagerly offer scholarships to without asking too many embarrassing questions about grades. Actually, the McKee boys had never even played high school football. Somehow in their neighborhood along the waterfront of South Brooklyn, an old Irish neighborhood called Red Hook, the sport of football had never been very popular among young boys.

The big sport in Red Hook was swimming, and the way a young boy could win respect, could best prove his valor, was to jump off one of the big piers or warehouses along the waterfront, splash into Buttermilk Channel, and then swim more than a mile against the tide over to the Statue of Liberty.

Usually, upon arrival, the boys would be arrested by the guards. If they weren't caught, they would then swim all the way back across Buttermilk Channel to the Red Hook side.

None of the neighborhood boys was a better swimmer than Gerard McKee, and none had gotten back and forth through Buttermilk Channel with more ease and speed than he. All the young boys of the street respected him, all the young girls who sat on the stoops of the small frame houses admired him—but none more than a pretty little Italian redhead named Margaret Nucito, who lived across the street from the McKees.

She had first seen Gerard in the second grade of the parochial school. He had been the class clown—the one the nuns scolded the most, liked the most.

At fourteen years of age, when the neighborhood boys and girls began to think less about swimming and more about one another, Margaret and Gerard started to date regularly. And when they were eighteen they began to think about marriage.

In the Red Hook section of Brooklyn, the Catholic girls thought early about marriage. First they thought about boys, then the Prom, then marriage. Though Red Hook was a poor neighborhood of shanties and small two-story frame houses, it was one where engagement rings were nearly always large and usually expensive. It was marriage before sex in this neighborhood, as the Church preaches, and plenty of children; and, like most Irish Catholic neighborhoods, the mothers usually had more to say than the fathers. The mother was the major moral strength in the Irish church, where the Blessed Virgin was an omnipresent figure; it was the mother who, after marriage, stayed home and reared the children, and controlled the family purse strings, and chided the husband for drinking, and pushed the sons when they were lazy, and protected the purity of her daughters.

And so it was not unusual for Margaret, after they tentatively planned marriage and after Gerard had begun work on the bridge, to be in charge of the savings account formed by weekly deductions from his ironworker's earnings. He would only fritter the money away if he were in control of it, she had told him, and he did not disagree. By the summer of 1963 their account had reached $800. He wanted to put this money toward the purchase of the beautiful pear-shaped diamond engagement ring they had seen one day while walking past Kastle's jewelry window on Fulton Street. It was a one-and-one-half carat ring priced at $1,000. Margaret had insisted that the ring was too expensive, but Gerard had said, since she had liked it so much, that she would have it. They planned to announce their engagement in December.

On Wednesday morning, October 9, Gerard McKee hated to get out of bed. It was a gloomy day and he was tired, and downstairs his brothers were yelling up to him, "Hey, if you don't get down here in two minutes, we're leaving without you."

He stumbled down the steps. Everyone had finished breakfast and his mother had already packed three ham-and-cheese sandwiches for his lunch. His father, limping around the room, was quietly cross at his tardiness.

He had not been out late the night before. He had gone over to Margaret's briefly, then had had a few beers at Gabe's, a neighborhood saloon with a big bridge painted across the back-bar. He had been in bed by about midnight, but this morning he ached, and he suspected he might be getting a cold.

They all left the house at 6:45 A.M. and caught a bus near the corner; then at Forty-ninth Street they got a cab and rode it to One Hundred and First Street in Bay Ridge, and then they walked, with hundreds of other ironworkers, down the dirt road toward the Brooklyn anchorage of the Verrazano-Narrows Bridge.

"Wait, let me grab a container of coffee," Gerard said, stopping at a refreshment shack along the path.

"Hurry up."

"Okay," he said. He gulped down the coffee in three swallows as they walked, and then they all lined up to take the elevator up to the catwalk. That morning Jimmy and John McKee were working on the section of the catwalk opposite Gerard, and so they parted on top, and Gerard said, "See you tonight." Then he headed off to join Iannielli.

Edward Iannielli seemed his spry self. He was sitting up there on the cable, whistling and very chipper.

"Good morning," he said, and McKee waved and forced a smile. Then he climbed up on the cable, and soon they began to tighten the seven bolts on the top of the casting.

After they had finished, Iannielli slid down from the cable and McKee handed the ratchet wrench down to him. Iannielli then fitted the wrench to the first of the seven lower bolts.

It was now about 9:30 A.M. It was cloudy and windy, though not as windy as it had been in the first week of October. Iannielli pushed his hardhat down on his head. He gazed down the catwalk and could see hundreds of men, their khaki shirts and jackets billowing in the breeze, all working on the cable—bolting it, banging it with tools, pushing into it. Iannielli took the big wrench he held, fixed it to a bolt, and pressed hard. And then, suddenly, from the bottom of the cable he heard a voice yelling, *"Eddie, Eddie . . . help me, Eddie, help me . . . please, Eddie . . ."*

Iannielli saw, hanging by his fingers from the south edge of the catwalk, clutching tightly to thin lower wires of the hand rail, the struggling figure of Gerard McKee.

"God," Iannielli screamed, "dear God," he repeated, lunging forward, lying across the catwalk and trying to grab onto McKee's arms and pull him up. But it was very difficult.

Iannielli was only 138 pounds, and McKee was more than 200. And Iannielli, with one finger missing on his left hand from the crane accident, and with the resewn second finger not very strong, could not seem to pull McKee's heavy body upward even one inch. Then McKee's jacket and shirt came loose, and he seemed to be just hanging there, dead weight, and Iannielli kept pleading, "Oh, God, God, please bring him up . . . bring him up . . ."

Other men, hearing the screams, came running and they all stretched down, grabbing wildly for some part of McKee's clothing, and Gerard kept saying, "Hurry, hurry please, I can't hold on any longer." And then, a few moments later, he said, "I'm going to go . . . I'm going to go . . ." and he let go of the wire and dropped from the bridge.

The men watched him fall, feet first for about one hundred feet. Then his body tilted forward, and Iannielli could see McKee's shirt blowing off and could see McKee's bare back, white against the dark sea, and then he saw him splash hard, more than 350 feet below, and Iannielli closed his eyes and began to weep, and then he began to slip over, too, but an Indian, Lloyd LeClaire, jumped on top of him, held him tight to the catwalk.

Not far from where Gerard McKee hit the water, two doctors sat fishing in a boat, and also nearby was a safety launch. And for the next thirty seconds, hysterical and howling men's voices, dozens of them, came echoing down from the bridge, "Hey, grab that kid, grab that kid . . . hurry, grab that kid . . ."

Even if Gerard McKee had landed within a yard of the safety boat, it would have been no use; anyone falling from that altitude is sure to die, for, even if his lungs hold out, the water is like concrete, and bodies break into many pieces when they fall that far.

The remains of Gerard McKee were taken out of the water and put into the safety launch and taken to Victory Memorial Hospital. Some of the men up on the bridge began to cry, and, slowly, all of them, more than six hundred of them, removed their hardhats and began to come down. Work was immediately suspended for the day. One young apprentice ironworker, who had never seen a death like this before, froze to the catwalk and refused to leave; he later had to be carried down by three others.

Jimmy and John McKee went home to break the news and be with their parents and Margaret, but Edward Iannielli, in a kind of daze, got into his automobile and began to drive away from the bridge, without any destination. When he saw a saloon he stopped. He sat at the bar between a few men, shaking, his lips quivering. He ordered one whiskey, then another, then three beers. In a few minutes he felt loose, and he left the bar and got into his car and began to drive up the Belt Parkway. He drove about fifty miles, then, turning around, he drove fifty miles back, seeing the bridge in the distance, now empty and quiet. He turned off the Belt Parkway and drove toward his home. His wife greeted him, very excitedly, at the door, saying that the bridge company had called, the safety officer had called, and what had happened?

Iannielli heard very little of what she was saying. That night in bed all he could hear, over and over, was "Eddie, Eddie, help me . . . help me." And again and again he saw the figure falling toward the sea, the shirt blowing up and the white back exposed. He got out of bed and walked through the house for the rest of the night.

The next day, Thursday, October 10, the investigation was begun to determine the cause of McKee's death. Work was again suspended on the bridge. But since nobody had seen how McKee had gotten off the cable, nobody knew whether he had jumped onto the catwalk and bounced off it or whether he had tripped—and they still do not know. All they knew then was that the morale of the men was shot, and Ray Corbett, business agent for Local 40, began a campaign to get the bridge company to string nets under the men on the bridge.

This had not been the first death around the bridge. On August 24, 1962, one man fell off a ladder inside a tower and died, and on July 13, 1963, another man slipped off the approach road and died. But the death of Gerard McKee was somehow different—different, perhaps, because the men had watched it, had been helpless to stop it; different, perhaps, because it had involved a very popular young man, the son of an ironworker who had himself been crippled for life.

Whatever the reason, the day of Gerard McKee's death was the blackest day on the bridge so far. And it would have made little difference for any company official to point out that the Verrazano-Narrows' safety record—just three deaths during thousands of working hours involving hundreds of men—was highly commendable.

McKee's funeral, held at the Visitation Roman Catholic Church in Red Hook, was possibly the largest funeral ever held in the neighborhood. All the ironworkers seemed to be there, and so were the engineers and union officials. But of all the mourners, the individual who seemed to take it the worst was Gerard's father, James McKee.

"After what I've been through," he said, shaking his head, tears in his eyes, "I should know enough to keep my kids off the bridge."

7.
Stage in the Sky

Gerard McKee's two brothers quit the bridge immediately, as their father had requested, but both were back within the month. The other ironworkers were a bit nervous when the McKees climbed up that first day back, but the brothers assured everyone that it was far more comfortable working up on the bridge, busy among the men, than remaining in the quietude of a mournful home.

Though nobody could ever have imagined it then, the death of Gerard McKee was just the beginning of a long, harsh winter—possibly the worst in Hard Nose Murphy's career. There would be a tugboat strike and a five-day ironworkers' strike to force management to put nets under the bridge; there would be freezing weather, powerful winds that would swing the bridge, careless mistakes that would result in a near disaster while the men were lifting a four-hundred-ton piece of steel; and, hovering over everything else, there would be the assassination on November 22 of President Kennedy, an event that demoralized men nowhere in the world more than it did on the bridge, where the majority of workers were of Irish ancestry.

All of this would occur while Hard Nose Murphy and the American

Bridge engineers were facing their greatest challenge—the span across the sea.

If construction was to remain on schedule, permitting the bridge to open in late November of 1964, then the steel skeleton of the span would have to be linked 6,690 feet across the sky by spring—a feat that now, in the winter of 1963, seemed quite impossible.

The task would involve the hoisting off barges of sixty separate chunks of steel, each the size of a ten-room ranch house (but each weighing four hundred tons), more than 220 feet in the air. Each of these steel pieces, in addition to several smaller ones, would then be linked to the suspender ropes dangling from the cables and would finally be locked together horizontally across the water between Brooklyn and Staten Island.

If one of these pieces dropped, it would set the bridge's schedule back at least six months, for each piece was without a duplicate. The sixty larger pieces, all of them rectangular in shape, would be about twenty-eight feet high, 115 feet wide, almost as long, and would be floated to the bridge, one at a time, from the American Bridge Company's steel-yard four miles up the river in New Jersey, where Benny Olson, James Braddock, and the other old champs were working. The loaded barges, pulled by tugboats, would take an hour to make the trip. Once the steel pieces were lifted off the barges by two tremendous hoisting machines on the lower traverse strut of each tower, the whole bridge would sag under the pressure of weight; for instance, the first piece, when lifted up, would pull the main cables down twenty inches. The second and third pieces would lower the cables an additional four feet six inches. The fifth and sixth pieces would pull the cables down another four feet three inches. When all the pieces were hanging, the cables would be as much as twenty-eight feet lower than before. (All this was as O. H. Ammann had designed it—in fact, his design allowed for as much as a thirty-five-foot cable defection—but he did not take into account human and mechanical frailty, this being Murphy's problem.)

Murphy's problems did not begin with the lifting of the first few steel pieces. This was conducted in the presence of a boatload of television and news cameras, and all the workers were very much on the ball. His troubles began when the initial excitement was tempered by the rote of repetition and the coming of colder weather. One freezing day a small barge holding suspender ropes was tied too tightly to the pier and sank that night when the tide came in, and the guard not only slept through this but also permitted vagrants to ransack the tool shed.

Murphy, in his shack the next morning, pounding his fist against the desk, was on the phone screaming to one of the dock supervisors. "Jessus Kee-rist, I'm sick of this crap! That stupidbastardguard just stood in that warm shanty, sleeping instead of watching. Now that guard isn't supposed to be sleeping where it's warm, goddammit, he's supposed to be watching, and I'm not taking any more of this crap, so you get that goddam guard up here and I'll tell that stupidbastard a thing or two . . ."

In the outer office of the shack, Murphy's male secretary, a slim, dapper, well-groomed young man named Chris Reisman, was on the switchboard answering calls with a very polite, "Good *morn*ing, American Bridge . . ." and covering his ears to Murphy's profanity in the next room.

Male secretaries are the only sort that would survive in this atmosphere; a female secretary would probably not be safe around some of the insatiable studs who work on bridges, nor would any woman condone the language very long. But Chris Reisman, whose uncle was a riveter and whose stepfather died on a bridge six years before, worked out well as a secretary, although it took a while for the bridgemen to accustom themselves to Chris Reisman's polite telephone voice saying, "Good *morn*ing, American Bridge" (instead of "Yeah, whatyawant?"), and to his style of wearing slim, cuffless trousers, a British knee-length raincoat, and, sometimes in wet weather, high soft leather boots.

The day after Reisman had been hired by the American Bridge Company and sent to Murphy's shack on the Staten Island shore, Murphy's welcoming words were, "Well, I see we got another ass to sit around here." But soon even Murphy was impressed with twenty-three-year-old Reisman's efficiency as a secretary and his cool manner over the telephone in dealing with people Murphy was trying to avoid.

"Good *morn*ing, American Bridge . . ."

"Yeah, say, is Murphy in?"

"May I ask who's calling?"

"Wha?"

"May I ask who's calling?"

"Yeah, dis is an old friend, Willy . . . just tell 'im Willy . . ."

"May I have your last name?"

"Wha?"

"Your *last* name?"

"Just tell Murphy, well, maybe you can help me. Ya see, I worked on the Pan Am job with Murphy, and . . ."

"Just a minute, please," Chris cut in, then switched to Murphy on the intercom and said, "I have a Willy on the phone that worked for you . . ."

"I don't want to talk to that bastard," Murphy snapped back.

Then, back on the phone, Reisman said, "I am sorry, sir, but Mr. Murphy is not in."

"Wha?"

"I said I do not expect Mr. Murphy to be in today."

"Well, okay, I'll try tomorrow."

"Fine," said Chris Reisman, clicking him off, then picking up another call with, "Good *morn*ing, American Bridge . . ."

On Thursday, November 21, there was a hoisting engine failure, and a four-hundred-ton steel unit, which was halfway up, could not go any farther, so it dangled there all night. The next day, after the engine trouble was corrected, there was union rumbling over the failure of the bridge company to put nets under the bridge. This fight was led by Local 40's business agent, Ray Corbett, himself a onetime ironworker —he helped put up the television tower atop the Empire State—and on Monday, December 2, the men walked off the bridge because of the dispute.

The argument against nets was not so much money or the time it would take to string them up, although both of these were factors, but mainly the belief that nets were not really a safeguard against death. Nets could never be large enough to cover the whole underbelly of the bridge, the argument went, because the steel had to be lifted up into the bridge through the path of any nets. It was also felt that nets, even small ones strung here and there, and moved as the men moved, might induce a sense of false security and invite more injury than might otherwise occur.

The strike lasted from December 2 to December 6, ending with the ironworkers' unions victorious—they got their nets, small as they seemed, and Ray Corbett's strong stand was largely vindicated within the next year, when three men fell off the bridge and were saved from the water by dropping into nets.

By January, with barges arriving every day with one and sometimes two four-hundred-ton steel pieces to be lifted, about half of the sixty box-shaped units were hanging from the cables, and things seemed, at least for the time being, to be under control. Each day, if the sun was out, the old bridge buffs with binoculars would shiver on the Brooklyn shoreline, watching and exchanging sage comments and occasionally chatting with the ironworkers who passed back and forth through the gate with its sign:

> BEER OR ANY ALCOHOLIC BEVERAGES NOT PER-
> MITTED ON THIS JOB. APPRENTICES WHO BRING
> ALCOHOLIC BEVERAGES ON JOB FOR THE MEN
> WILL BE TERMINATED.

"You *never* drink on the bridge, right?" a man near the gate asked an Indian ironworker named Bronco Bill Martin.

"Who?"

"You."

"No, I only drink beer."

"Well, doesn't beer ruin your sense of balance?"

"I donno," Bronco Bill said. "I just go to job, drink beer, climb bridge, and I feel better on bridge than I do on ground. I can drink a dozen can of beer and still walk a straight line on that bridge."

"A *dozen?*"

"Yeah," he said, "easy."

A few yards away, a group of white-haired men, some of them retired engineers or construction workers, all of them now "seaside superintendents," were peering up at the bridge, listening to the grinds of the hoisting machines and the echoes of "Red" Kelly shouting instructions up through his bullhorn from a barge below the rising four-hundred-ton steel unit. It was a fascinating water show, very visual and dramatic, even for these elderly men who only saw the finale.

The show had its beginning more than an hour earlier up the river on the Jersey side. There, along the waterfront of the American Bridge Company's yard, a four-hundred-ton chunk of steel (steel that had been made in smaller sections at U.S. Steel plants in other states, and then shipped by rail to the New Jersey yard for assembly) was resting on a gigantic twin barge and was now just being pulled away by one tug, pushed by another.

The ironworkers, about seventy of them, waved from the yard to the tugs—another four hundred tons was off. The tug pilot, a thin, blond Norwegian-American named Villy Knutsen, carefully churned through New York Harbor—crisscrossing with oil tankers, ferryboats, luxury cruisers, aircraft carriers, fishing boats, driftwood, floating beer cans— squinting his pale blue eyes in the sun and splashing spray. On this day he was talking to a deckhand, Robert Guerra, telling him how he had hated the bridge when it first began. The Knutsens had been one of the families in Bay Ridge whose homes had been threatened by the approaches to the bridge. Villy Knutsen and his wife had joined the protests and signed many petitions before finally moving to Port Jefferson, Long Island.

"But I really hated that bridge then, I'll tell ya," he repeated.

"Well, don't hate it any more," Guerra said, "it's making you a day's pay."

"Yeah," agreed Knutsen, cutting his tugboat wheel around quickly to skirt past an oncoming tanker, then swinging his head around to observe the barges still slapping the sea under the big red steel; all was well.

Forty minutes later, Knutsen was bringing his tug with its big steel caboose toward the bridge. The old men on the shore lifted their binoculars, and the ironworkers on the bridge got ready, and under one of the towers a fat pusher, with a telephone pressed to his left ear, was looking up at the crane on the tower and frowning and saying, "Hello, Eddie? Eddie? Hello, Eddie?"

Eddie, the signal man on top, did not answer.

"Hello, Eddie?" Still no answer.

Gimme that phone," said another pusher, grabbing it.

"Hello, Eddie? Hello, Eddie?"

"Hello," came a thin voice through the static.

"Hello, Eddie?"

"No, Burt."

"Burt, this is Joe down the bottom. Eddie in the cab?"

Silence.

"Hello, *Burt?* Hello, *Burt?*"

"Christsakes!" the pusher with the phone shouted, holding it away from his ear and frowning at it again. Then he put it to his mouth again. "Hello, Burt? Burt, hello, Burt . . . ?"

"Yeah?"

"Whatthehell's wrong, Burt?"

"You got a goddam broken splice in your hand down there."

"Well, keep talking, Burt."

"Okay, Joe,"

"Keep talking, Burt . . . keep . . ." The phone went dead again.

"Christsakes," Joe shouted. "Hello, Burt? Hello? Hellohellohello? Nuthin' . . . Hello? . . . Nuthin'. Hello, Burt?"

"Hello," came the voice from the top.

"Burt?"

"No, this is Eddie."

"Keep talkin', Eddie . . ."

Finally the telephone system between the pusher on the ground and the man on top who controlled the movements of the crane was re-established. Soon Villy Knutsen's tug had bumped the barge into position, and the next step was to link the hauling ropes to the steel piece and prepare to hoist it from the barge up 225 feet to the span.

This whole operation would be under the direct supervision of one man, who now stepped out of a workboat onto the barge—onto the stage. He was a big, barrel-chested man of 235 pounds who stood six feet two inches, and he was very conspicuous, even from the shore, because he wore a red checkered jacket and a big brown hardhat tilted forward over his red hair and big ruddy nose, and because he carried in his right hand a yellow bullhorn through which his commands could be heard by all the men on top of the bridge. He was Jack "Red" Kelly, the number-two bridgeman, second only to Hard Nose Murphy himself.

Suddenly all the men's attention, and also the binoculars along the shore, were focused on Kelly as he carefully watched a dozen ironworkers link the heavy hoisting ropes to the four upper extremities of the steel piece as it gently rocked with the anchored barge. When the ropes had been securely bound, the men jumped off the barge onto an-

other barge, and so did Kelly, and then he called out, "Okay, ease now
. . . up . . . *UP* . . ."

Slowly the hauling machines on the tower, their steel thread strung
up through the cables and then down all the way to the four edges of
the steel unit on the sea, began to grind and grip and finally lift the
four hundred tons off the barge.

Within a few minutes, the piece was twenty feet above the barge, and
Kelly was yelling, "Slack down . . ." Then, "Go ahead on seven," "Level
it up," "Go ahead on seven"; and up on the bridge the signal man,
phones clamped to his ears, was relaying the instructions to the men
inside the hauling vehicles.

Within twenty-five minutes, the unit had climbed 225 feet in the air,
and the connectors on top were reaching out for it, grabbing it with
their gloves, then linking it temporarily to one of the units already
locked in place.

"Artfully done," said one of the old men with binoculars.

"Yes, good show," said another.

Most of the sixty pieces went up like this one—with remarkable
efficiency and speed, despite the wind and bitter cold, but just after New
Year's Day, a unit scheduled to be lifted onto the Brooklyn backspan,
close to the shoreline, caused trouble, and the "seaside superintendents"
had a good view of Murphy's temper.

As the steel piece was lifted a few feet off the barge, a set of hold-
back lines that stretched horizontally from the Brooklyn tower to the
rising steel unit broke loose with a screech. (The hold-back lines were
necessary in this case because the steel unit had to rise at an oblique
angle, the barge being unable to anchor close enough to the Brooklyn
shoreline to permit the unit a straight ride upward.)

Suddenly, the four-hundred-ton steel frame twisted, then went hurt-
ling toward the Brooklyn shore, still hanging on ropes, but out of control. It swished within a few inches of a guard-rail fence beneath the
anchorage, then careened back and dangled uneasily above the heads of
a few dozen workmen. Some fell to the ground; others ran.

"*Jes-sus,*" cried one of the spectators on shore. "Did you see that?"

"Oh, my!"

"Oh, if old man Ammann were here now, he'd have a fit!"

Down below, from the pier and along the pedestals of the tower, as well as up on the span itself, there were hysterical cries and cursing and fist waving. A hurried telephone call to Hard Nose Murphy brought him blazing across the Narrows in a boat, and his swearing echoed for a half-hour along the waterfront of Bay Ridge.

"Which gang put the clamps on that thing?" Murphy demanded.

"Drilling's gang," somebody said.

"And where the hell's Drilling?"

"Ain't here today."

Murphy was probably never angrier than he was on this particular Friday, January 3. John Drilling, who had led such a charmed life back on the Mackinac Bridge in Michigan, and who had recently been promoted to pusher though he was barely twenty-seven years old, had called in sick that day. He was at his apartment in Brooklyn with his blonde wife, a lovely girl whom he'd met while she was working as a waitress at a Brooklyn restaurant. His father, Drag-Up Drilling, had died of a heart attack before the cable spinning had begun, and some people speculated that if he had lived he might have been the American Bridge superintendent in place of Hard Nose Murphy. The loss of his father and the responsibility of a new wife and child had seemed to change John Drilling from the hell-raiser he had been in Michigan to a mature young man. But now, suddenly, he was in trouble. Though he was not present at the time of the accident that could have caused a number of deaths, he was nevertheless responsible; he should have checked the clamps when they were put on by his gang the day before.

When John Drilling returned to the bridge, not yet aware of the incident, he was met by his friend and fellow boomer, Ace Cowan, a big Kentuckian who was walkin' boss along the Brooklyn backspan.

"What you got lined out for today, Ace?" Drilling said cheerfully upon arrival in the morning.

"Er, well," Cowan said, looking at his feet, "they . . . the office made me put you back in the gang."

"The gang! What, for taking a lousy day off?"

"No, it was those clamps that slipped . . ."

Drilling's face fell.

"Anybody hurt?"

"No," Cowan said, "but everybody is just pissed . . . I mean Ammann and Whitney, and Murphy, and Kelly, and everybody."

"Whose gang am I in?"

"Whitey Miller's."

Whitey Miller, in the opinion of nearly every bridgeman who had ever worked within a mile of him, was the toughest, meanest, pushiest pusher on the Verrazano-Narrows Bridge. Drilling swallowed hard.

8.
The Indians

That night in Johnny's Bar near the bridge, the men spoke about little else.

"Hear about Drilling?"

"Yeah, poor guy."

"They put him in Whitey Miller's gang."

"It's a shame."

"That Whitey Miller's a great ironworker, though," one cut in. "You gotta admit that."

"Yeah, I admit it, but he don't give a crap if you get killed."

"I wouldn't say that."

"Well, *I* would. I mean, he won't even go to your goddam funeral, that Whitey Miller."

But in another bar in Brooklyn that night, a bar also filled with iron-workers, there was no gloom—no worries about Whitey Miller, no anguish over Drilling. This bar, The Wigwam, at 75 Nevins Street in the North Gowanus section, was a few miles away from Johnny's. The Wigwam was where the Indians always drank. They seemed the most casual, the most detached of ironworkers; they worked as hard as any-body on the bridge, but once the workday was done they left the bridge behind, forgot all about it, lost it in the cloud of smoke, the bubbles of beer, the jukebox jive of The Wigwam.

This was their home away from home. It was a mail drop, a club. On weekends the Indians drove four hundred miles up to Canada to visit their wives and children on the Caughnawaga reservation, eight miles from Montreal on the south shore of the St. Lawrence River; on week nights they all gathered in The Wigwam drinking Canadian beer (sometimes as many as twenty bottles apiece) and getting drunk to-gether, and lonely.

On the walls of the bar were painted murals of Indian chiefs, and there also was a big photograph of the Indian athlete, Jim Thorpe. Above the entrance to the bar hung a sign reading: THE GREATEST IRON-WORKERS IN THE WORLD PASS THRU THESE DOORS.

The bar was run by Irene and Manuel Vilis—Irene being a friendly, well-built Indian girl born into an ironworkers' family on the Caughna-waga reservation; Manuel, her husband, was a Spanish card shark with a thin upturned mustache; he resembled Salvadore Dali. He was born in Galicia, and after several years in the merchant marine, he jumped ship and settled in New York, working as a busboy and bottle washer in some highly unrecommended restaurants.

During World War II he joined the United States Army, landed at Normandy, and made a lot of money playing cards. He saved a few thousand dollars this way, and, upon his discharge, and after a few years as a bartender in Brooklyn, he bought his own saloon, married Irene, and called his place The Wigwam.

More than seven hundred Indians lived within ten blocks of The Wigwam, nearly every one of them ironworkers. Their fathers and grandfathers also were ironworkers. It all started on the Caughnawaga reservation in 1886, when the Dominion Bridge Company began con-structing a cantilever bridge across the St. Lawrence River. The bridge was to be built for the Canadian Pacific Railroad, and part of the con-struction was to be on Indian property. In order to get permission to trespass, the railroad company made a deal with the chiefs to employ Indian labor wherever possible. Prior to this, the Caughnawagas—a tribe of mixed-blood Mohawks who had always rejected Jesuit efforts to turn them into farmers—earned their living as canoemen for French fur traders, as raft riders for timbermen, as traveling circus performers, anything that would keep them outdoors and on the move, and that would offer a little excitement.

When the bridge company arrived, it employed Indian men to help the ironworkers on the ground, to carry buckets of bolts here and there, but not to risk their lives on the bridge. Yet when the ironworkers were not watching, the Indians would go walking casually across the narrow beams as if they had been doing it all their lives; at high altitudes the Indians seemed, according to one official, to be "as agile as goats." They also were eager to learn the bridge business—it offered good pay, lots of travel—and within a year or two, several of them became riveters and connectors. Within the next twenty years dozens of Caughnawagas were working on bridges all over Canada.

In 1907, on August 29, during the erection of the Quebec Bridge over the St. Lawrence River, the span collapsed. Eighty-six workmen, many Caughnawagas, fell, and seventy-five ironworkers died. (Among the engineers who investigated the collapse, and concluded that the designers were insufficiently informed about the stress capability of such large bridges, was O. H. Ammann, then twenty-seven years old.)

The Quebec Bridge disaster, it was assumed, would certainly keep the Indians out of the business in the future. But it did just the opposite. The disaster gave status to the bridgeman's job—accentuated the derring-do that Indians previously had not thought much about—and consequently more Indians became attracted to bridges than ever before.

During the bridge and skyscraper boom in the New York metropolitan area in the twenties and thirties, Indians came down to New York in great numbers, and they worked, among other places, on the Empire State Building, the R.C.A. Building, the George Washington Bridge, Pulaski Skyway, the Waldorf-Astoria, Triborough Bridge, Bayonne Bridge, and Henry Hudson Bridge. There was so much work in the New York City area that Indians began renting apartments or furnished rooms in the North Gowanus section of Brooklyn, a centralized spot from which to spring in any direction.

And now, in The Wigwam bar on this Friday night, pay night, these grandsons of Indians who died in 1907 on the Quebec Bridge, these sons of Indians who worked on the George Washington Bridge and Empire State, these men who were now working on the biggest bridge of all, were not thinking much about bridges or disasters: they were thinking mostly about home, and were drinking Canadian beer, and listening to the music.

"Oh, these Indians are crazy people," Manuel Vilis was saying, as he sat in a corner and shook his head at the crowded bar. "All they do when they're away from the reservation is build bridges and drink."

"Indians don't drink any more than other ironworkers, Manny," said Irene sharply, defending the Indians, as always, against her husband's criticism.

"The hell they don't," he said. "And in about a half-hour from now, half these guys in here will be loaded, and then they'll get in their cars and drive all the way up to Canada."

They did this every Friday night, he said, and when they arrived on the reservation, at 2 A.M., they all would honk their horns, waking everybody up, and soon the lights would be on in all the houses and everybody would be drinking and celebrating all night—the hunters were home, and they had brought back the meat.

Then on Sunday night, Manuel Vilis said, they all would start back to New York, speeding all the way, and many more Indians would die from automobile accidents along the road than would ever trip off a bridge. As he spoke, the Indians continued to drink, and there were ten-dollar and twenty-dollar bills all over the bar. Then, at 6:30 P.M., one Indian yelled to another, "Com'on, Danny, drink up, let's move." So Danny Montour, who was about to drive himself and two other Indians up to the reservation that night, tossed down his drink, waved goodbye to Irene and Manuel, and prepared for the four-hundred-mile journey.

Montour was a very handsome young man of twenty-six. He had blue eyes, sharp, very un-Indian facial features, almost blond hair. He was married to an extraordinary Indian beauty and had a two-year-old son, and each weekend Danny Montour drove up to the reservation to visit them. He had named his young son after his father, Mark, an ironworker who had crippled himself severely in an automobile accident and had died not long afterward. Danny's paternal grandfather had fallen with the Quebec Bridge in 1907, dying as a result of injuries. His maternal grandfather, also an ironworker, was drunk on the day of the Quebec disaster and, therefore, in no condition to climb the bridge. He later died in an automobile accident.

Despite all this, Danny Montour, as a boy growing up, never doubted that he would become an ironworker. What else would bring such money and position on the reservation? To not become an ironworker was to become a farmer—and to be awakened at 2 A.M. by the automobile horns of returning ironworkers.

So, of the two thousand men on the reservation, few became farmers or clerks or gas pumpers, and fewer became doctors or lawyers, but 1,700 became ironworkers. They could not escape it. It got them when they were babies awakened in their cribs by the horns. The lights would go on, and their mothers would pick them up and bring them downstairs to their fathers, all smiling and full of money and smelling of whiskey or beer, and so happy to be home. They were incapable of enforcing discipline, only capable of handing dollar bills around for the children to play with, and all Indian children grew up with money in their hands. They liked the feel of it, later wanted more of it, *fast*— for fast cars, fast living, fast trips back and forth between long weekends and endless bridges.

"It's a good life," Danny Montour was trying to explain, driving his car up the Henry Hudson Parkway in New York, past the George Washington Bridge. "You can *see* the job, can see it shape up from a hole in the ground to a tall building or a big bridge."

He paused for a moment, then, looking through the side window at the New York skyline, he said, "You know, I have a name for this town. I don't know if anybody said it before, but I call this town the City of Man-made Mountains. And we're all part of it, and it gives you a good feeling—you're a kind of mountain builder . . ."

"That's right, Danny-boy, old kid," said Del Stacey, the Indian ironworker who was a little drunk, and sat in the front seat next to Montour with a half-case of beer and bag of ice under his feet. Stacey was a short, plump, copper-skinned young man wearing a straw hat with a red feather in it; when he wanted to open a bottle of beer, he removed the cap with his teeth.

"Sometimes though," Montour continued, "I'd like to stay home more, and see more of my wife and kid . . ."

"But we can't, Danny-boy," Stacey cut in, cheerfully. "We gotta build them mountains, Danny-boy, and let them women stay home alone, so they'll miss us and won't get a big head, right?" Stacey finished his bottle of beer, then opened a second one with his teeth. The third Indian, in the back seat, was quietly sleeping, having passed out.

Once Montour had gotten the car on the New York Thruway, he began to speed, and occasionally the speedometer would tip between ninety and one hundred miles per hour. He had had three or four drinks at The Wigwam, and now, in his right hand, he was sipping a gin that Stacey had handed him; but he seemed sober and alert, and the expressway was empty, and every few moments his eyes would peer into the rear-view mirror to make certain no police car was following.

Only once during the long trip did Montour stop; in Malden, New York, he stopped at a Hot Shoppe for ten minutes to get a cup of coffee—and there he saw Mike Tarbell and several other Indians also bound for Canada. By 11 P.M. he was speeding past Warrensburg, New York, and an hour or so later he had pulled off the expressway and was on Route 9, a two-lane backroad, and Stacey was yelling, "Only forty miles to go, Danny-boy."

Now, with no radar and no cars coming or going, Danny Montour's big Buick was blazing along at 120 miles per hour, swishing past the tips of trees, skimming over the black road—and it seemed, at any second, that a big truck would surely appear in the windshield, as trucks always appear, suddenly, in motion-picture films to demolish a few actors near the end of the script.

But, on this particular night, there were no trucks for Danny Montour.

At 1:35 A.M., he took a sharp turn onto a long dirt road, then sped past a large black bridge that was silhouetted in the moonlight over the St. Lawrence Seaway—it was the Canadian railroad bridge that had been built in 1886, the one that got Indians started as ironworkers. With a screech of his brakes, Montour stopped in front of a white house.

"We're home, you lucky Indians," he yelled. The Indian in the back seat who had been sleeping all this time woke up, blinked. Then the lights went on in the white house; it was Montour's house, and everybody went in for a quick drink, and soon Danny's wife, Lorraine, was downstairs, and so was the two-year-old boy, Mark. Outside, other horns were honking, other lights burned; and they remained alive, some of

them, until 4 A.M. Then, one by one, they went out, and the last of the
Indians fell asleep—not rising again until Saturday afternoon, when they
would be awakened, probably, by the almost endless line of bill collectors knocking on doors: milkmen, laundrymen, newsboys, plumbers,
venders of vacuum cleaners, encyclopedia salesmen, junk dealers, insurance salesmen. They all waited until Saturday afternoon, when the ironworker was home, relaxed and happy, to separate him from his cash.

The reservation itself is quiet and peaceful. It consists of a two-lane
tar road that curves for eight miles near the south shore of the St. Lawrence River. Lined along both sides of the road and behind it are hundreds of small white frame houses, most of them with porches in front—
porches often occupied by old Indian men. They slump in rocking chairs,
puffing pipes, and quietly watch the cars pass or the big ships float
slowly through the St. Lawrence Seaway—ships with sailors on deck
who wave at any Indian women they see walking along the road.

Many of the younger Indian women are very pretty. They buy their
clothes in Montreal shops, have their hair done on Friday afternoons.
There is little about their style of clothing or about their homes that
is peculiarly Indian—no papooses, no totems, no Indian gadgets on
walls. Some Indian homes do not have running water, and have out-
houses in the back, but all seem to have television sets. The only sounds
heard on Saturday afternoon are the clanging bells of the Roman Catholic church along the road—most Indians are Catholics—and occasionally the honking of an Indian motorcade celebrating a wedding or
christening.

The only road signs bearing Indian symbols are CHARLIE MOHAWK'S
SNACK BAR and, on the other side of the road up a bit, the CHIEF POKING
FIRE INDIAN MUSEUM. The snack bar's sign is hung principally to amuse
the tourists who pass in a yellow bus each day; inside, however, the
place looks like any soda fountain, with the booths cluttered with teen-
aged boys sporting ducktail haircuts and smoking cigarettes, and teen-
aged girls in skin-tight dungarees and ponytails, all of them twisting or
kicking to the rock 'n' roll music blaring from the jukebox.

At Chief Poking Fire's museum, things are different; here it's strictly
for the tourists, with the Chief and his family assembling in full regalia
a few times each day to dance, whoop and holler for the tourists and

wave tomahawks so that the tourists, clicking their 16-mm. cameras, will have something to show for their visit to an Indian reservation.

The Indian mayor of Caughnawaga is John Lazare, who believes he might be a Jewish Indian. He succeeded his brother, Matthew, as mayor, and Matthew succeeded their father. The Lazares run a gas station on the same side of the road as Chief Poking Fire's museum, and they also sell liquid gas to Indians for home use.

The political viewpoint that has kept the Lazares popular with other Indians all these years is Mayor Lazare's speeches that usually include the sentence, "The Indian should be allowed to do whatever he wants," and also the Lazares' long-time denunciation of the license plate on automobiles. Indians hate to drive with license plates on their cars and would like to remove them, presumably so they'll get fewer speeding tickets (although many Indians ignore all tickets on the grounds that they are not valid documents, having never been agreed to by treaty).

On Saturday afternoons, when the Indian men get out of bed (if they get out of bed), they usually play lacrosse, if it is not too cold. In summer months they might spend their afternoons skimming along the St. Lawrence Seaway in a motorboat they themselves built, or fishing or watching television. On Sunday morning they have their traditional breakfast of steak and cornbread, and usually loll around the house all morning and visit friends in the afternoon.

Then, anywhere from 8 P.M. to 11 P.M., the big cars filled with iron-workers will begin to rumble down the reservation's roads, and then toward the routes to the expressway back to New York. It is a sad time for Indian women, these Sunday evenings, and the ride back to New York seems twice as long to the men as did the Friday-night ride coming up. The alcohol that many of them sip all the way back to New York is the only thing that helps make the trip endurable—and the thing that may help kill them.

And so on this Sunday evening, Danny Montour kissed his wife goodbye, and hugged his son, and then went to pick up the others for the long ride back.

"Now be careful," Lorraine said from the porch.

"Don't worry," he said.

And all day Monday she, and other Indian women, half-waited for the phone calls, hoping they would never come. And when they did not come on this particular Monday, the women were happy, and by mid-week the happiness would grow into a blithe anticipation of what was ahead—the late-Friday sounds of the horns, the croaking call of Cadillacs and Buicks and Oldsmobiles, the sounds that would bring their husbands home . . . and will take their sons away.

9.

Back to Bay Ridge

In the spring of 1964, to the astonishment of nobody in this neighborhood that had long suspected it, there was discovered behind the black curtains and awnings and white brick wall at 125 Eighty-sixth Street, in the plush Colonial Road section of Bay Ridge, a whorehouse.

Some people, of course, blamed the boomers, recalling the sight of those slinky blondes who lingered along the shore behind the bridge. But the *Brooklyn Spectator,* which broke the story on March 20, after the police finally had sufficient evidence to make arrests, reported that there were some prominent Bay Ridge citizens among the clientele, although it gave no names. The story caused a sensation—"the first story of its kind to appear in this paper in its thirty-two-year history," announced the *Spectator*—and not only was every copy suddenly sold out, but the newspaper office was left with none for its files, and it hastily had to announce that it would re-purchase, at the regular price of ten cents, any copies of the March 20 issue in good condition.

After arresting a thirty-six-year-old blonde madam who swore she was a "real estate broker," and two other blonde women who gave their occupations as "baby nurse" and "hostess," the police revealed that

262

even the kitchen of the house had been converted into a boudoir, that the wallpaper was "vivid," and that there were mirrors on the ceilings.

Many respectable, old-time Bay Ridge residents were shocked by the disclosure, and there was the familiar lament for yesteryear. And a few people, apprehensively gazing up at the almost-finished bridge, predicted that soon the bridge might bring many more changes for the worse—more traffic through residential streets, more and cheaper apartment houses (that might be crowded with Negroes), and more commercialism in neighborhoods traditionally occupied by two-family houses.

It had been five years since the bridge first invaded Bay Ridge, and, though the protestors were now quiet and the eight hundred buildings that stood in the path of the bridge's approachways had now all disappeared, many people had long memories, and they still hated the bridge.

Monsignor Edward J. Sweeney, whose parish at St. Ephrem's had lost two thousand of its twelve thousand parishioners, thus diminishing the Sunday collection considerably, still became enraged at the mere mention of the bridge. The dentist, Henry Amen, who had put on forty pounds in the last five years, and was now prosperous in a new office one mile north of his old office, was nevertheless still seething, saying, "I strongly resent the idea of being forced to move."

In some cases the anger in Bay Ridge was as alive in 1964 as it was back in 1959 when "Save Bay Ridge" banners flew; when people screamed "That bridge—who needs it?"; when an undertaker, Joseph V. Sessa, claimed he would lose 2,500 people "from which to draw"; and when the anti-bridge faction included the disparate likes of housewives, bartenders, a tugboat skipper, doctors, lawyers, a family of seventeen children (two dogs and a cat), a retired prizefighter, a former Ziegfeld Follies girl, two illicit lovers, and hundreds of others who reacted generally as people might react anywhere if, suddenly, the order was delivered: "Abandon your homes—we must build a bridge."

In all, it had taken eighteen months to move out the seven thousand people, and now, in 1964, though a majority of them had been relocated in Bay Ridge, they had lost touch with most of their old neighbors, and had nothing in common now but the memories.

"Oh, those were depressing days," recalled Bessie Gros Dempsey, the former Follies girl who now lives four blocks from the spot where her old home had stood. "When those demolition men moved into the neighborhood, you'd have flower pots full of dust on your window sills at night, and all day long you'd see them smashing down those lovely homes across the street.

"That crane was like the jaw of a monster, and when it cracked into those buildings, into the roof and ceiling and shingles, everything would turn into powder, and then the dogs would start barking because of all the strange sounds a building makes when it is falling.

"I remember back of where I used to live was this big brownstone— an artist lived there, and the place was built like an Irish castle. When the crane hit into it, it was a horrible sound I'll never forget. And I remember watching them tear down that colonial house that was directly across the street from me. It had columns in front, and a screened-in porch, and it was lived in by a nice elderly couple that had twin daughters, and also an uncle, Jack, a crippled fellow who used to trim those hedges. Such pride was in that home, and what a pity to see that crane smash it all down."

The couple with the twin daughters now lives in upstate New York, Mrs. Dempsey said, adding that she does not know what became of the crippled uncle named Jack. The artist who lived in the brownstone behind her old home is now dead, she said, along with five other people she used to know in her neighborhood in the pre-bridge days.

Mrs. Dempsey and many others in Bay Ridge in 1964 were citing the bridge as an accomplice in the death of many residents of the old neighborhood; they said that the tension and frustration in losing one's home and the uncertainty of the future had all contributed to the death of many since 1959. One woman pointed out that her husband, never ill before, suddenly had a heart attack and died after a "Save Bay Ridge" rally, and another woman blamed the bridge for her faltering eyesight, saying she never had to wear glasses until the announcement that her home would be destroyed by "that bridge."

Most of the older people who had owned their homes, particularly those on pensions or small fixed incomes, said that the relocation caused them financial hardships because they could not match the price of a new home of comparable size in a comparable neighborhood.

There were, to be sure, a minority who said they were happy that the bridge had forced them to move, or who felt that they had been unjustifiably pessimistic about the changes the Verrazano-Narrows Bridge would bring. Mrs. Carroll L. Christiansen, who had moved from Bay Ridge to Tenafly, New Jersey, into a suburban home with a quarter-acre of land around it, said, "It's a lot better here than in Brooklyn." She added, "In Brooklyn the people didn't mix socially—and never had too much to do with one another. But here it is entirely different. I've learned to play golf since coming here. And my husband and I play cards with other couples in the evenings, and we go to dances at the country club. My daughter, who is seventeen now, felt uprooted for about a year or so, but since then she's also made lots of new friends and the whole life is much easier here."

The undertaker, Joseph Sessa, who had feared he would lose thousands of people, was surviving nicely in Bay Ridge five years later; and the two lovers—the divorced man and the unhappily married woman who used to live across the street from him—have gone their separate ways (she to Long Island, he to Manhattan) and neither blames the bridge for coming between them. "It was just a passing fancy," she says of her old affair, now being moderately contented with her new home, her husband and children. The lover, a forty-six-year-old insurance company executive, has met a girl at the office, unmarried and in her middle thirties, and each evening they meet in a dimly lit cocktail lounge on Park Avenue South.

Florence Campbell, the divorcee who with her young son had held out in her old apartment until 1960, despite the murder on the floor below, now believes the bridge has changed her life for the better. In her new block, she was introduced by a friend to a merchant mariner, and a year later they were married and now live in a comfortable home on Shore Road.

The old shoemaker who had screamed *"sonamabitch"* at the bridge authorities for tearing down his little store five years ago, and who returned disillusioned to Cosenza in Southern Italy, has since come back to Brooklyn and is working in another shoe store. He became restless in Italy, and found life among his relatives unbearable.

Mr. and Mrs. John G. Herbert, parents of seventeen children, all of whom once lived in a noisy and tattered frame house on the corner of Sixty-seventh and Seventh Avenue in Bay Ridge before the bridge intruded, now live on Fifty-second Street in a three-story, nine-room house that they own, and, in a sense, they are better off than when they were only renting at the old place.

This newer house is two rooms larger than the other one, but it is not any more spacious, and it is also jammed in the middle of a block of teeming row houses. The Herbert children miss the rambling grass yard and trees that used to surround the old property.

Mr. Herbert, a short, muscular Navy Yard worker with blue eyes and a white crew cut, sometimes escapes the clatter and confusion of his home by drinking heavily, and when guests arrive he often greets them by pounding them on the back, pouring them a drink, and shouting, "Com'on, relax—take off your coat, sit down, have a drink, *relax*," and Mrs. Herbert, shaking her head sadly, half moans to the guests, "Oh, you're lucky *you* don't live here," and then Mr. Herbert, downing another drink, pounds the guests again and repeats, "Com'on, relax, have another drink, *relax!*"

Two of the Herbert boys—Eugene, who is twenty, and Roy, who is nineteen—are very sensitive to such scenes, and both recall how happy, how hopeful they'd been five years before when they had first heard that their old house would be torn down. Finally, they thought, they'd be out of the city altogether, and moving into the country as their father had so often said they would.

When this did not happen, the family being unable to afford any home except the one they now have, the boys felt a bit cheated; even five years afterward, they missed their old home, yearned for another like it. One day in the early spring of 1964, Eugene and Roy took a nostalgic journey back to their old neighborhood, a mile and a half away, and revisited the land upon which their old home had stood.

Now all was flattened and smoothed by concrete—it was buried by the highway leading to the bridge, the path toward the tollgates. The highway was three months away from completion, and so it was without automobiles. It was quiet and eerie. Eugene walked around in the middle of the empty highway and then stopped and said, "It was about here, Roy—this is where the house was."

"Yeah, I guess you're right," Roy said, "because over there's the telephone pole we used to climb . . ."

"And over here was where the porch was . . ."

"Yeah, and remember how we used to sit out there at night in the summertime with the radio plugged in, and remember when I'd be on that swinging sofa at night with Vera?"

"Boy, I remember that Vera. What a built!"

"And remember when on Friday nights we all used to sit on the steps waiting for Dad to come home from the Navy Yard with a half-gallon of ice cream?"

"I remember, and he never failed us, did he?"

"Nope, and I remember what we used to sing, all of us kids, as we waited for him . . . You remember?"

"Yeah," said Roy. Then both of them, in chorus, repeated their familiar childhood song:

> *You scream, I scream,*
> *We all scream*
> *For ice cream.*
>
> *You scream, I scream,*
> *We all scream*
> *For ice . . .*

They looked at one another, a little embarrassed, then remained quiet for a moment. Then they walked away from where the house had stood, crossed the empty highway, and, turning around slowly, they rediscovered, one by one, other familiar sights. There was the sidewalk upon which they used to roller-skate, the cement cracks as they had remembered them. There were some of the homes that had not been destroyed by the new highway. There was Leif Ericson Park, where, as boys, they played, and where they once had dug a deep hole in the grass within which to bury things—Scout knives, rings, toys, new baseballs—anything that they had wanted to keep away from their brothers and sisters, because at home nothing was private, nobody respected another's ownership.

They searched along the grass for the hole that they had covered with a metal plate, but could not find it. Then they crossed the street to one of the few houses left on the block, and an elderly woman was shaking a mop outside of a window, and Eugene called up to her, "Hello, Mrs. Johnson, we're the Herbert boys. Remember, we used to live across the street?"

"Why, *yes,*" she said, smiling. "Hardly would have recognized you. How are you?"

"Fine. We're over on Fifty-second Street now."

"Oh," she said, softly. "And how's your mother?"

"Fine, Mrs. Johnson."

"Well, give her my regards," the woman said, smiling, then she pulled the mop in and closed the window.

The boys walked on through the vacated neighborhood, past the yellow bulldozers and cement mixers that were quiet on this Saturday afternoon; past the long dirt road that would soon be paved; past the places that had once been alive with part of them.

"Roy, remember that barking dog that used to scare hell out of us?"

"Yeah."

"And remember that candy store that used to be here?"

"Yeah, Harry's. We used to steal him blind."

"And remember . . ."

"Hey," Roy said, "I wonder if Vera is still around?"

"Let's get to a phone booth and look her up."

They walked three blocks to the nearest sidewalk booth, and Roy looked up the name and then called out, "Hey, here it is—SHore 5–8486."

He put in a dime, dialed the number, and waited, thinking how he would begin. But in another second he realized there was no need to think any longer, because there was only a click, and then the coldly proper voice of a telephone operator began: "I am sorry. The number you have reached is not in service at this time . . . This is a recording . . ."

Roy picked out the dime, put it in his pocket. Then he and his brother walked quietly to the corner, and began to wait for the bus—but it never came. And so, without saying anything more, they began to walk back to their other home, the noisy one, on Fifty-second Street. It was not a long walk back—just a mile and a half—and yet in 1959, when they were young teenagers, and when it had taken the family sixteen hours to move all the furniture, the trip to the new house in a new neighborhood had seemed such a voyage, such an adventure.

Now they could see, as they walked, that it had been merely a short trip that had changed nothing, for better or for worse—it was as if they had never moved at all.

10.
Ramblin' Fever

A disease common among ironworkers—an itchy sensation called "ram-blin' fever"—seemed to vibrate through the long steel cables of the bridge in the spring of 1964, causing a restlessness, an impatience, a tingling tension within the men, and many began to wonder: "Where next?"

Suddenly, the bridge seemed finished. It was not finished, of course—eight months of work remained—but all the heavy steel units were now linked across the sky, the most dangerous part was done, the challenge was dying, the pessimism and cold wind of winter had, with spring, been swept away by a strange sense of surety that nothing could go wrong: a punk named Roberts slipped off the bridge, fell toward the sea—and was caught in a net; a heavy drill was dropped and sailed down directly toward the scalp of an Indian named Joe Tworivers—but it nipped only his toes, and he grunted and kept walking.

The sight of the sixty four-hundred-ton units all hanging horizontally from the cables, forming a lovely rainbow of red steel across the sea from Staten Island to Brooklyn, was inspiring to spectators along the shore, but to the ironworkers on the bridge it was a sign that boredom

270

was ahead. For the next phase of construction, referred to in the trade as "second-pass steel," would consist primarily of recrossing the entire span while lifting and inserting small pieces of steel into the structure—struts, grills, frills—and then tightening and retightening the bolts. When the whole span had been filled in with the finishing steel, and when all the bolts had been retightened, the concrete mixers would move in to pave the roadway, and next would come the electricians to string up the lights, and next the painters to cover the red steel with coats of silver.

And finally, when all was done, and months after the last ironworker had left the scene for a challenge elsewhere, the bridge would be opened, bands would march across, ribbons would be cut, pretty girls would smile from floats, politicians would make speeches, everyone would applaud—and the engineers would take all the bows.

And the ironworker would not give a damn. He will do his boasting in bars. And anyway, he will know what he has done, and he would somehow not feel comfortable standing still on a bridge, wearing a coat and tie, showing sentimentality.

In fact, for a long time afterward he will probably not even think much about the bridge. But then, maybe four or five years later, a sort of ramblin' fever in reverse will grip him. It might occur while he is driving to another job or driving off to a vacation; but suddenly it will dawn on him that a hundred or so miles away stands one of his old boom towns and bridges. He will stray from his course, and soon he will be back for a brief visit: maybe it is St. Ignace, and he is gazing up at the Mackinac Bridge; or perhaps it's San Francisco, and he is admiring the Golden Gate; or perhaps (some years from now) he will be back in Brooklyn staring across the sea at the Verrazano-Narrows Bridge.

Today he will doubt the possibility, most of the boomers will, but by 1968 or '69 he probably will have done it: he may be in his big car coming down from Long Island or up from Manhattan, and he will be moving swiftly with all the other cars on the Belt Parkway, but then, as they approach Bay Ridge, he will slow up a bit and hold his breath as he sees, stretching across his windshield, the Verrazano—its span now busy and alive with auto traffic, bumper-to-bumper, and nobody standing on the cables now but a few birds.

Then he will cut his car toward the right lane, pulling slowly off the Belt Parkway into the shoulder, kicking up dust, and motorists in the cars behind will yell out the window, "Hey, you idiot, watch where you're driving," and a woman may nudge her husband and say, "Look out, dear, the man in that car looks drunk."

In a way, she will be right. The boomer, for a few moments, will be under a hazy, heady influence as he takes it all in—the sights and sounds of the bridge he remembers—hearing again the rattling and clanging and Hard Nose Murphy's angry voice; and remembering, too, the cable-spinning and the lifting and Kelly saying, "Up on seven, easy now, *easy*"; and seeing again the spot where Gerard McKee fell, and where the clamps slipped, and where the one-thousand-pound casting was dropped; and he will know that on the bottom of the sea lies a treasury of rusty rivets and tools.

The boomer will watch silently for a few moments, sitting in his car, and then he will press the gas pedal and get back on the road, joining the other cars, soon getting lost in the line, and nobody will ever know that the man in this big car one day had knocked one thousand rivets into that bridge, or had helped lift four hundred tons of steel, or that his name is Tatum, or Olson, or Iannielli, or Jacklets, or maybe Hard Nose Murphy himself.

Anyway, this is how, in the spring of 1964, Bob Anderson felt—he was a victim of ramblin' fever. He was itchy to leave the Verrazano job in Brooklyn and get to Portugal, where he was going to work on a big new suspension span across the Tagus River.

"Oh, we're gonna have a ball in Portugal," Anderson was telling the other ironworkers on his last working day on the Verrazano-Narrows Bridge. "The country is absolutely beautiful, we'll have weekends in Paris . . . you guys gotta come over and join me."

"We will, Bob, in about a month," one said.

"Yeah, Bob, I'll sure be there," said another. "This job is finished as far as I'm concerned, and I got to get the hell out. . . ."

On Friday, June 19, Bob Anderson shook hands with dozens of men on the Verrazano and gave them his address in Portugal, and that night many of them joined him for a farewell drink at the Tamaqua Bar in Brooklyn. There were about fifty ironworkers there by 10 P.M. They gathered around four big tables in the back of the room, drank whiskey with beer chasers, and wished Anderson well. Ace Cowan was there, and so was John Drilling (he had just been promoted back to pusher after three hard months in Whitey Miller's gang), and so were several other boomers who had worked with Anderson on the Mackinac Bridge in Michigan between 1955 and 1957.

Everyone was very cheerful that night. They toasted Anderson, slapping him on the back endlessly, and they cheered when he promised them a big welcoming binge in Portugal. There were reminiscing and joke-telling, and they all remembered with joy the incidents that had most infuriated Hard Nose Murphy, and they recalled, too, some of the merry moments they had shared nearly a decade ago while working on the Mackinac. The party went on beyond midnight, and then, after a final farewell to Anderson, one by one they staggered out.

Prior to leaving for Lisbon, Bob Anderson, with his wife, Rita, and their two children, packed the car and embarked on a brief trip up to St. Ignace, Michigan. It was in St. Ignace, during the Mackinac Bridge job, that Bob Anderson had met Rita. She still had parents and many friends there, and that was the reason for the trip—that and the fact that Bob Anderson wanted to see again the big bridge upon which he had worked between 1955 and 1957.

A few days later he was standing alone on the shore of St. Ignace, gazing up at the Mackinac Bridge from which he had once come bumping down along a cable, clinging to a disconnected piece of catwalk for 1,800 feet, and he remembered how he'd gotten up after, and how everybody then had said he was the luckiest boomer on the bridge.

He remembered a great many other things, too, as he walked quietly at the river's edge. Then, ten minutes later, he slowly walked back toward his car and drove to his mother-in-law's to join his wife, and later they went for a drink at the Nicolet Hotel bar, which had been boomers' headquarters nine years ago and where he had won that thousand dollars shooting craps in the men's room.

But now, at forty-two years of age, all this was behind him. He was very much in love with Rita, his third wife, and he had finally settled down with her and their two young children. They both looked forward to the job in Portugal—and the possibility of tragedy there never could have occurred to them.

In Portugal while looking for a house, the Andersons stayed at the Tivoli Hotel in Lisbon. Bob Anderson's first visit to the Tagus River Bridge was on June 17. At that time the men were working on the towers, and the big derricks were hoisting up fifty-ton steel sections that would fit into the towers. Anderson apparently was standing on the pier when, as one fifty-ton unit was four feet off the ground, the boom buckled and suddenly the snapped hoisting cable whipped against him with such force that it sent him crashing against the pier, breaking his left shoulder and cracking open his skull, damaging his brain. Nobody saw the accident, and the bridge company could only guess what had happened. Bob Anderson remained unconscious all day and night and two months later he was still in a coma, unable to recognize Rita or to speak. His booming days were over, the doctors said.

When word got back to the Verrazano in Brooklyn, it affected every man on the bridge. Some were too shocked to speak, others swore angrily and bitterly. John Drilling and other boomers rushed off the bridge and called Rita in Portugal, volunteering to fly over. But she assured them there was nothing they could do. Her mother had arrived from St. Ignace and was helping care for the children.

For the boomers, it was a tragic ending to all the exciting time in New York on the world's longest suspension span. They were proud of Bob Anderson. He had been a daring man on the bridge, and a charming man off it. His name would not be mentioned at the Verrazano-Narrows dedication, they knew, because Anderson—and others like him—were known only within the small world of the boomers. But in *that* world they were giants, they were heroes never lacking in courage or pride—men who remained always true to the boomer's code: going wherever the big job was

. . . and lingering only a little while . . .

then off again to another town, another bridge . . .

linking everything but their lives.

Part Three
New York—
A Serendipiter's
Journey

New York Is
a City
of Things Unnoticed

New York is a city of things unnoticed. It is a city with cats sleeping under parked cars, two stone armadillos crawling up St. Patrick's Cathedral, and thousands of ants creeping on top of the Empire State Building. The ants probably were carried up there by wind or birds, but nobody is sure; nobody in New York knows any more about the ants than they do about the panhandler who takes taxis to the Bowery; or the dapper man who picks trash out of Sixth Avenue trash cans; or the medium in the West Seventies who claims, "I am clairvoyant, clairaudient and clairsensuous."

New York is a city for eccentrics and a center for odd bits of information. New Yorkers blink twenty-eight times a minute, but forty when tense. Most popcorn chewers at Yankee Stadium stop chewing momentarily just before the pitch. Gum chewers on Macy's escalators stop chewing momentarily just before they get off—to concentrate on the last step. Coins, paper clips, ballpoint pens, and little girls' pocketbooks are found by workmen when they clean the sea lions' pool at the Bronx Zoo.

Each day New Yorkers guzzle 460,000 gallons of beer, swallow 3,500,000 pounds of meat, and pull 21 miles of dental floss through

277

their teeth. Every day in New York about 250 people die, 460 are born, and 150,000 walk through the city wearing eyes of glass or plastic.

A Park Avenue doorman has parts of three bullets in his head—there since World War I. Several young gypsy daughters, influenced by television and literacy, are running away from home because they do not want to grow up and become fortunetellers. Each month one hundred pounds of hair is delivered to Louis Feder at 545 Fifth Avenue, where blonde hairpieces are made from German women's hair; brunette hairpieces from French and Italian women's hair; but no hairpieces from American women's hair which, says Mr. Feder, is weak from too-frequent rinses and permanents.

Some of New York's best-informed men are elevator operators, who rarely talk, but always listen—like doormen. Sardi's doorman listens to the comments made by Broadway's first-nighters walking by after the last act. He listens closely. He listens carefully. Within ten minutes of the curtain's fall he can tell you which shows will flop and which will be hits.

On Broadway in the evening, a big, dark 1948 Rolls-Royce pulls in—and out hops a little lady armed with a Bible and a sign reading "The Damned Shall Perish." She proceeds to stand on the corner screaming at the multitudes of Broadway sinners sometimes until 3 A.M., when the chauffeur-driven Rolls picks her up, and drives her back to Westchester.

By this time Fifth Avenue is deserted by all but a few strolling insomniacs, some cruising cab drivers, and a group of sophisticated females who stand in store windows all night and day wearing cold, perfect smiles—smiles formed by lips of clay, eyes of glass, and cheeks that will glow until the paint wears off. Like sentries they line Fifth Avenue—these window mannequins who gaze onto the quiet street with tilted heads and pointed toes and long, rubber fingers reaching for cigarettes that aren't there. At 4 A.M., some store windows become a strange fairyland of gangling goddesses, all of them frozen in the act of dashing to a party, diving into a swimming pool, or sashaying skyward in a billowy blue negligee.

While this wild illusion is partly due to the runaway imagination, it is also partly due to the incredible skill of mannequin makers, who have endowed mannequins with certain individual characteristics—the theory being that no two females, not even plastic or plaster females, are quite alike. As a result, the mannequins at Peck & Peck are made to look young and prim, while at Lord & Taylor they seem wiser and wind-blown. At Saks they are demure but mature, while at Bergdorf's they look agelessly elegant and quietly rich. The profiles of Fifth Avenue's mannequins have been fashioned after some of the world's most alluring women—women like Suzy Parker, who posed for the Best & Co. man-nequins, and Brigitte Bardot, who inspired some mannequins at Saks. The preoccupation with making mannequins almost human, and equip-ping them with curves, is perhaps responsible for the rather strange fascination so many New Yorkers have for these synthetic virgins. This is why some window decorators frequently talk to mannequins and give them pet names, and why naked mannequins in windows inevitably at-tract men, disgust women, and are banned in New York City. This is why some mannequins are attacked by perverts, and why the svelte mannequin in a White Plains shop was discovered in the basement not long ago with her clothes torn off, her make-up smeared and her body possessing evidence of attempted rape. The police laid a trap one night and caught the attacker—a shy little man: the porter.

When street traffic dwindles and most people are sleeping, some New York neighborhoods begin to crawl with cats. They move quickly through the shadows of buildings; night watchmen, policemen, garbage collectors and other nocturnal wanderers see them—but never for very long. A majority of them hang around the fish markets, in Greenwich Village, and in the East and West Side neighborhoods where garbage cans abound. No part of the city is without its strays, however, and all-night garage attendants in such busy neighborhoods as Fifty-fourth Street have counted as many as twenty of them around the Ziegfeld Theatre early in the morning. Troops of cats patrol the waterfront piers at night searching for rats. Subway trackwalkers have discovered cats living in the darkness. They seem never to get hit by trains, though some are occasionally liquidated by the third rail. About twenty-five cats live 75 feet below the west end of Grand Central Terminal, are fed by the underground workers, and never wander up into the daylight.

The roving, independent, self-laundering cats of the streets live a life strangely different from New York's kept, apartment-house cats. Most are flea-bitten. Many die of food poisoning, exposure and malnutrition; their average life span is two years, whereas the stay-at-home cats live ten to twelve years or more. Each year the ASPCA kills about 100,000 New York street cats for whom no homes can be found.

Social climbing among the stray cats of Gotham is not common. They rarely acquire a better mailing address out of choice. They usually die within the blocks of their birth, although one flea-bitten specimen picked up by the ASPCA was adopted by a wealthy woman; it now lives in a luxurious East Side apartment and spends the summer at the lady's estate on Long Island. The American Feline Society once moved two strays into the headquarters of the United Nations after having heard that some rodents had infested UN filing cabinets. "The cats took care of 'em," says Robert Lothar Kendell, Society president. "And they seemed happy at the UN. One of the cats used to sleep on a Chinese dictionary."

In every New York neighborhood the strays are dominated by a "boss"—the largest, strongest tomcat. But, except for the boss, there is not much organization in the street cat's society. Within the society, however, there are three "types" of cats—wild cats, Bohemians, and part-time grocery store (or restaurant) cats.

The wild cats rely on an occasional loose garbage lid or on rats for food, and will have little or nothing to do with people—even those who would feed them. These most unkempt of strays have a recognizable haunted look, a wide-eyed, wild expression, and they usually are found around the waterfront.

The Bohemian, however, is more tractable. It does not run from people. Often, it is fed in the streets daily by sensitive cat-lovers (mostly women) who call the strays "little people," "angels," or "darlings," and are indignant when the objects of their charity are referred to as "alley cats." So punctual are most Bohemians at feeding time that one cat-lover has advanced the theory that cats can tell time. He cited a gray tabby that appears five days a week, precisely at 5:30 P.M., in an office building at Broadway and Seventeenth Street, where the elevator men feed it. But the cat never shows up on Saturday or Sundays; it seems to know people don't work on those days.

The part-time grocery store (or restaurant) cat, often a reformed Bohemian, eats well and keeps rodents away, but it usually uses the store as a hotel and prefers to spend the nights prowling in the streets. Despite its liberal working schedule, it still assumes most of the privileges of a related breed—the full-time, or wholly nonstray, grocery store cat—including the right to sleep in the window. A reformed Bohemian at a Bleecker Street delicatessen hides behind the door and chases away all other Bohemians looking for handouts.

The number of full-time cats, incidentally, has diminished greatly since the decline of the small food store and the rise of supermarkets in New York. With better rat-proofing methods, improved packaging of foods and more sanitary conditions, such chain stores as the A&P rarely keep a cat full-time.

On the waterfront, however, the great need for cats remains unchanged. Once a longshoreman who was allergic to cats poisoned them. Within a day rats were all over the place. Every time the men turned around they'd find rats on crates. And on Pier 95 the rats began stealing the longshoremen's lunch, and even attacking the men. So the street cats were recruited from nearby neighbors, and now most of the rats are controlled.

"But cats don't get much sleep around here," said one longshoreman. "They can't. Rats would overrun them. We've had cases here where the rat has torn up the cat. But it doesn't happen often. Most waterfront cats are mean bastards."

At 5 A.M. Manhattan is a town of tired trumpet players and homeward-bound bartenders. Pigeons control Park Avenue and strut unchallenged in the middle of the street. This is Manhattan's mellowest hour. Most *night* people are out of sight—but the *day* people have not yet appeared. Truck drivers and cabs are alert, yet they do not disturb the mood. They do not disturb the abandoned Rockefeller Center, or the motionless night watchmen in the Fulton Fish Market, or the gas-station attendant sleeping next to Sloppy Louie's with the radio on.

At 5 A.M. the Broadway regulars have gone home or to all-night coffee shops where, under the glaring light, you see their whiskers and wear. And on Fifty-first Street a radio press car is parked at the curb with a photographer who has nothing to do. So he just sits there for a few nights, looks through the windshield, and soon becomes a keen observer of life after midnight.

"At 1 A.M.," he says, "Broadway is filled with wise guys and with kids coming out of the Astor Hotel in white dinner jackets—kids who drive to dances in their fathers' cars. You also see cleaning ladies going home, always wearing kerchiefs. By 2 A.M., some of the drinkers are getting out of hand, and this is the hour for bar fights. At 3 A.M. the last show is over in the night clubs, and most of the tourists and out-of-town buyers are back in hotels. At 4 A.M., after the bars close, you see the drunks come out—and also the pimps and prostitutes who take advantage of drunks. At 5 A.M., though, it is mostly quiet. New York is an entirely different city at 5 A.M."

At 6 A.M. the early workers begin to push up from the subways. The traffic begins to move down Broadway like a river. And Mrs. Mary Woody jumps out of bed, dashes to her office and phones dozens of sleepy New Yorkers to say in a cheerful voice, rarely appreciated: "Good morning. Time to get up." For twenty years, as an operator of Western Union's Wake-Up Service, Mrs. Woody has gotten millions out of bed.

At 7 A.M. a floridly robust little man, looking very Parisien in a blue beret and turtle-necked sweater, moves in a hurried step along Park Avenue visiting his wealthy lady friends—making certain that each is given a brisk, before-breakfast rubdown. The uniformed doormen greet him warmly and call him either "Biz" or "Mac" because he is Biz Mackey, a ladies' masseur extraordinaire.

Mr. Mackey is spry and straight-spined, and always carries a black leather grip containing liniments, creams and the towels of his trade. Up the elevator he goes; then, half an hour later, he is down again, and off to another lady—an opera singer, a movie actress, a lady police lieutenant.

Biz Mackey, a former featherweight prizefighter, started rubbing women the right way in Paris, in the twenties. He'd lost a fight during a Euopean tour and decided he'd had enough. A friend suggested he go to a school for masseurs, and six months later he had his first customer —Claire Luce, the actress then starring in the *Folies-Bergère*. She liked him, and sent him more clients—Pearl White, Mary Pickford, and a beefy Wagnerian soprano. It took World War II to get Biz out of Paris.

When he returned to Manhattan, his European clientele continued to patronize him when they visited here and, though he is now pushing seventy, he is still going strong. Biz handles about seven women a day. His muscular fingers and thick arms have a miraculously soothing touch. He is discreet, and that is why New York ladies prefer him. He visits each of them in her apartment, and has special keys to the bedrooms; he is often the first man they see in the morning, and they lie in bed waiting for him. He never reveals the names of his customers, but most of them are middle-aged and rich.

"Women don't want other women to know their business," Biz explains. "You know women," he adds, offhandedly, leaving no doubt that he does.

The doormen that Biz passes each morning are generally an obliging, endlessly articulate group of sidewalk diplomats who list among their friends some of Manhattan's most powerful men, most beautiful women and snootiest poodles. More often than not the doormen are big, slightly Gothic in design, and possessors of eyes sharp enough to spot big tippers a block away in the year's thickest fog.

Some East Side doormen are as proud as grandees, and their uniforms, heavily festooned, seem to have come from the same tailor who outfitted Marshal Tito. Most hotel doormen are superb at small talk, big talk and back talk, at remembering names and appraising luggage leather. (They size up a guest's wealth by the luggage he has, not by the clothes he wears.)

In Manhattan today there are 650 apartment-house doormen; 325 hotel doormen (fourteen at the Waldorf-Astoria); and an unknown, but formidable, number of restaurant and theater doormen, night-club doormen, barking doormen, and doorless doormen.

Doorless doormen, who are nonunion vagabonds, usually without uniforms (but with rented hats), pussyfoot about town opening car doors when traffic is thick—on nights of the opera, concerts, championship fights, and conventions. The Brass Rail doorman, Christos Efthimiou, says that doorless doormen know when he is off (Mondays and Tuesdays) and that on these days they free-lance off his spot on Seventh Avenue at Forty-ninth Street.

Barking doormen, who sometimes wear rented uniforms (but own their hats), post themselves in front of jazz clubs with floor shows, such as along Fifty-second Street. In addition to opening doors and lassoing cab drivers, the barking doormen might whisper to passing pedestrians, softly but distinctly, "Psssst! No cover charge—girls inside . . . the new Queen of Alaska!"

Though there is hardly a doorman in town who does not swear up and down that he is underpaid and underrated, many hotel doormen admit that on some good, rainy weeks they have made close to $200 in tips alone. (More people desire cabs when it is raining, and doormen who provide umbrellas and cabs rarely go untipped.)

When it rains in Manhattan automobile traffic is slow, dates are broken and, in hotel lobbies, people slump behind newspapers or walk aimlessly about with no place to sit, nobody to talk to, nothing to do. Taxis are harder to get; department stores do between 15 to 25 per cent less business, and the monkeys in the Bronx Zoo, having no audience, slouch grumpily in their cages looking more bored than the lobby loungers.

While some New Yorkers become morose with rain, others prefer it, like to walk in it, and say that on rainy days the city's buildings seem somehow cleaner—washed in an opalescence, like a Monet painting. There are fewer suicides in New York when it rains; but when the sun is shining, and New Yorkers seem happy, the depressed person sinks deeper into depression and Bellevue Hospital gets more attempted suicides.

Yet a rainy day in New York is a bright day for umbrella and raincoat salesmen, for hat-check girls, bellhops and for members of the British Consulate General's office, who say rain reminds them of home. Consolidated Edison claims New Yorkers burn $120,000 worth more electricity than they do on bright days; thousands of trouser creases lose their sharpness in rain, and Norton Cleaners on Forty-fifth Street presses an average of 125 more pants on such days.

Rain ruins the mascara on the eyes of fashion models who cannot find cabs; and rain makes it a lonely day for Times Square's recruiting sergeants, demonstrators, bootblacks and burglars—who all tend to lose their enthusiasm when wet.

Shortly after 7:30 each morning, while most New Yorkers still are in a bleary-eyed slumber, hundreds of people are lined along Forty-second Street waiting for the 8 A.M. opening of the ten movie houses that stand almost shoulder to shoulder between Times Square and Eighth Avenue.

Who are these people who go to the movies at 8 A.M.? They are the city's night watchmen, derelicts, or people who can't sleep, can't go home, or have no home. They are truck drivers, homosexuals, cops, hacks, cleaning ladies and restaurant men who have worked all night. They are also alcoholics who are waiting at 8 A.M. to pay 40 cents to get a soft seat and sleep in the cool, dark, smoky theater.

And yet, aside from being smoky, each Times Square theater has a special quality, or lack of quality, about it. At the Victory Theatre one finds only horror films, while at the Times Square Theatre they feature only cowboy films. There are first-run films for 40 cents at the Lyric, while at the Selwyn there are always second-run films for 30 cents. At both the Liberty and the Empire are reissues, and at the Apollo they run only foreign films. Foreign films have been making money at the Apollo for twenty years, and William Brandt, one of the owners, never could understand why. "So one day I investigated the place," he said, "and saw people in the lobby talking with their hands. I realized they were mostly deaf and dumb. They patronize the Apollo because they read the subtitles that go with foreign films; the Apollo probably has the biggest deaf-and-dumb movie audience in the world."

* * *

New York is a town of 8,485 telephone operators, 1,364 Western Union messenger boys, and 112 newspaper copyboys. An average base-ball crowd at Yankee Stadium uses over ten gallons of liquid soap per game—an unofficial high mark for cleanliness in the major leagues; the Stadium also has the league's top number of ushers (360), sweepers (72), and men's rooms (34).

In New York there are 500 mediums, from semi-trance to trance to deep-trance types. Most of them live in New York's West Seventies, Eighties and Nineties, and on Sundays some of these blocks are communicating with the dead, vibrating to trumpets, and solving all problems.

In New York the Fifth Avenue Lingerie Shop is on Madison Avenue; the Madison Pet Shop is on Lexington Avenue; the Park Avenue Florist is on Madison Avenue, and the Lexington Hand Laundry is on Third

Avenue. New York is the home of 120 pawnbrokers and it is where Bishop Sheen's brother, Dr. Sheen, shares an office with one Dr. Bishop.

Within a serene brownstone on Lexington Avenue, on the corner of Eighty-second Street, a pharmacist named Frederick D. Lascoff for years has been selling leeches to battered prizefighters, catnip oil to lion hunters and thousands of strange potions to people in exotic places around the world.

Within a somber West Side factory each month a long, green line of cardboard crawls like an endless reptile up and down a printing press until it is chopped into thousands of little, annoying pieces. Each piece is designed to fit into a policeman's pocket, decorate the windshield of an illegally parked car, and relieve a motorist of $15. About 500,000 $15 tickets are printed for New York's police each year on West Nineteenth Street by the May Tag and Label Corp., whose employees sometimes see their workmanship boomerang on their own windshields.

New York is a city of 200 chestnut venders, 300,000 pigeons, and 600 statues and monuments. When the equestrian statue of a general has both front hoofs off the ground, it means the general died in battle; if one hoof is off the ground, he died of wounds received in battle; if all four hoofs are on the ground, the general probably died in bed.

*   *   *

In New York from dawn to dusk to dawn, day after day, you can hear the steady rumble of tires against the concrete span of the George Washington Bridge. The bridge is never completely still. It trembles with traffic. It moves in the wind. Its great veins of steel swell when hot and contract when cold; its span often is ten feet closer to the Hudson River in summer than in winter. It is an almost restless structure of graceful beauty which, like an irresistible seductress, withholds secrets from the romantics who gaze upon it, the escapists who jump off it, the chubby girl who lumbers across its 3,500-foot span trying to reduce, and the 100,000 motorists who each day cross it, smash into it, short-change it, get jammed up on it.

Few of the New Yorkers and tourists who breeze through it are aware of the workmen riding elevators through the twin towers 612 feet above, and few people know that wandering drunks occasionally have climbed blithely to the top and fallen asleep up there. In the morning they are petrified and have to be carried down by emergency crews.

Few people know that the bridge was built in an area where Indians used to roam, battles were fought, and where, during early colonial times, pirates were hanged along the river as a warning to other adventurous sailors. The bridge now stands where Washington's troops fell back before the British invaders who later captured Fort Lee, New Jersey, and who found kettles still on the fire, the cannon abandoned, and clothing strewn along the path of Washington's retreating garrison.

The roadway at the George Washington Bridge is more than 100 feet above the little red lighthouse that became obsolete when the bridge went up in 1931; its Jersey approach is two miles from where Albert Anastasia lived behind a high wall guarded by Doberman pinschers; its Jersey tollgate is twenty feet from where a truck driver without a license tried to drive four elephants across in his trailer—and would have if one elephant hadn't fallen out. The upper span is 220 feet from where a Port Authority guard once climbed up to tell an aspiring suicide, "Listen, you s.o.b., if you don't come down, I'm going to shoot you down"—and the man crawled quickly down.

Around the clock the bridge guards stay alert. They have to. At any moment there may be an accident, breakdown, or a suicide. Since 1931, a hundred people have jumped from the bridge. More than twice that number have been stopped. Bridge jumpers intent on committing suicide go quickly and quietly. On the edge of the roadway they leave automobiles, jackets, eyeglasses, and sometimes a note reading, "I wish to take the blame for everything" or "I don't want to live any more."

*　　*　　*

A lonely out-of-town buyer who'd had a few drinks checked into a Broadway hotel near Sixty-fourth Street one night, went to bed, and awoke in the middle of the night to a shocking view. He saw, floating past his window, the shimmering image of the Statue of Liberty.

Immediately he imagined himself shanghaied—sailing past Liberty Island toward certain disaster on the high seas. But then, after a closer look, he found that he was actually seeing New York's *second* Statue of Liberty—the obscure, almost unnoticed statue that stands on top of the Liberty-Pac warehouse at 43 West Sixty-fourth Street.

This reasonable facsimile, erected in 1902 at the request of William H. Flattau, a patriotic warehouse owner, stands 55 feet high above its pedestal as compared with Bartholdi's 151-footer on Liberty Island. This smaller Liberty also had a lighted torch, a spiral staircase, and a hole in the head through which Broadway could be seen. But in 1912 the staircase became weakened, the torch blew off in a storm, and school children were no longer permitted to run up and down inside. Mr. Flattau died in 1931, and with him went much of the information on the history of this statue.

From time to time, however, employees in the warehouse, as well as people in the neighborhood, are asked by tourists about the statue. "People usually come over and say, 'Hey, what's *that* doing up *there?'*" said a Kinney parking-lot attendant who works across from the statue. "The other day a Texan pulls in, looks up and says, 'I thought that Statue was supposed to be in the water somewhere.' But some people are really interested in the statue, and take pictures of it. I consider it a privilege to work under it, and when tourists come I always remind them that this is the 'Second Largest Statue of Liberty in the World.'"

But most neighborhood folks pay no attention to the Statue. The gypsy fortunetellers who work to the left of it do not; the habitués of Mrs. Stern's tavern below it do not; the soup slurpers in Bickford's restaurant across the street do not. A New York cabby, David Zickerman (Cab No. 2865), has whizzed by the Statue hundreds of times and never knew it existed. "Who the hell looks up in this town?" he asks.

For decades this Statue has carried a burned-out torch over this neighborhood of punchball players, short-order cooks and warehouse watchmen; over undertipped bellhops and cops and high-heeled transvestites who leave their fire-escaped walls after midnight and stroll through this town of perhaps too much liberty.

*   *   *

New York is a city of movement. Artists and beatniks live in Greenwich Village, where the Negroes first settled. Negroes live in Harlem, where the Jews and Germans once lived. The wealth has moved from the West to the East Side. Puerto Ricans cluster everywhere. Only the Chinese have stability in their enclave around the ancient angle of Doyer Street.

To some people, New York is best remembered by the smile of an airline stewardess at LaGuardia, or the patience of a shoe salesman on Fifth Avenue; to others the city represents the smell of garlic in the rear of a Mulberry Street church, or a hunk of "turf" for juvenile gangs to fight over, or a chunk of real estate to be bought and sold by Zeckendorf.

But beyond the New York City guidebooks and the Chamber of Commerce, New York is no Summer Festival. For most New Yorkers it is a town of hard work, too many cars, too many people. Many of the people are anonymous, like busmen, charwomen, and those creepy pornographers who mark up advertising posters and are never caught. Many New Yorkers seem to have only one name, like barbers, doormen, bootblacks. Some New Yorkers go through life with the wrong name—like Jimmy Buns, who lives across from Police Headquarters on Centre Street. When Jimmy Buns, whose real surname is Mancuso, was a little boy, the cops sitting across the street would yell to him, "Hey, kid, how 'bout going down the corner and getting us some coffee and buns?" Jimmy always obliged, and soon they called him "Jimmy Buns," or just "Hey Buns." Now Jimmy is a white-haired, elderly man with a daughter named Jeannie. But Jeannie never had a maiden name; everybody just calls her "Jeannie Buns."

New York is the city of Jim Torpey, who has been flashing headlines around Times Square's electric sign since 1928 without burning a bulb for himself; and of George Bannan, Madison Square Garden's official time-keeper, who has held up like an imperishable grandfather's clock through 7,000 prizefights and has rung the bell two million times. It is the city of Michael McPadden, who sits behind a microphone in a subway booth near the Times Square shuttle train yelling in a voice wavering between futility and frustration, "Watch your step getting off, please, watch your step." He delivers this advice 500 times a day, and sometimes would like to ad-lib. Yet he rarely tries. He has long been convinced that his is a forgotten voice lost in the clamor of slamming doors and pushing bodies; and before he can think of anything witty to say another train has arrived from Grand Central, and Mr. McPadden must say (one more time!), "Watch your step getting off, please, watch your step."

When it begins to get dark in New York, and all the shoppers have left Macy's, ten black Doberman pinschers begin to tip-tap up and down the aisles sniffing for prowlers who may be hiding behind counters or lurking in clothes racks. They wander through all twenty floors of the big store, and are trained to climb ladders, jump through window frames, leap over hurdles, and bark at anything unusual—a leaky radiator, broken steamline, smoke, or a thief. Should a thief try to escape, the dogs can easily overtake him, run between his legs—and trip him. Their barks have alerted Macy's guards to many minor hazards, but never to a thief —none has dared remain in the store after closing hours since the dogs arrived in 1952.

New York is a city in which large, cliff-dwelling hawks cling to sky-scrapers and occasionally zoom to snatch a pigeon over Central Park, or Wall Street, or the Hudson River. Bird watchers have seen these peregrine falcons circling lazily over the city. They have seen them perched atop tall buildings, even around Times Square.

About twelve of these hawks patrol the city, sometimes with a wing span of thirty-five inches. They have buzzed women on the roof of the St. Regis Hotel, have attacked repairmen on smokestacks, and, in August, 1947, two hawks jumped women residents in the recreation yard of the Home of the New York Guild for the Jewish Blind. Mainte-nance men at the Riverside Church have seen hawks dining on pigeons in the bell tower. The hawks remain there for only a little while. And then they fly out to the river, leaving pigeons' heads for the Riverside mainte-nance men to clean up. When the hawks return, they fly in quietly— *unnoticed,* like the cats, the ants, the doorman with three bullets in his head, the ladies' masseur, and most of the other off-beat wonders in this town without time.

New York Is a City of the Anonymous

New York is a city of headless men who sit obscurely in subway booths all day and night selling tokens to people in a hurry. Each weekday over 4,000,000 riders pass these money-changers who seem to have neither heads, faces, nor personalities—only fingers. Except when giving directions, their vocabulary consists largely of three words: "How many, please?"

But down on Fourteenth Street there is a money-changer named William DeVillis who is openly rebelling against obscurity. Outside his IND booth, on Eighth Avenue, he has posted this sign: "Please Smile. This job is tough enough."

They smile.

He says "Good morning" to everyone. Some New Yorkers are shocked. He writes directions for them on slips of paper, and even lends them tokens when they have forgotten their money. And he is quite talkative. When his phone rings in his booth, he picks it up and says,

"Good morning, this is booth 78, Fourteenth Street and Eighth Avenue, Independent Branch of the New York Rapid Transit System, Rail-

291

road Clerk William F. DeVillis, Pass No. 216680, speaking. May I help you?"

As one who spends eight hours a day watching New Yorkers come and go, push and shove, and lunge ahead for the door that is closing, Mr. DeVillis has been in a position to see, if not to understand, a large portion of human nature in action.

"One of the things I've noticed," he says, "is that most New Yorkers are in the habit of walking through a certain turnstile each morning and they will never change to any other. I've also noticed that many will buy just two tokens at a time. And other people who have invested in full token-holders will, after they've spent one token, quickly buy one more token to replace it."

Mr. DeVillis, who has been in the subway system since 1939, believes that his friendly campaign has been eminently successful. Each day, after customers read the signs he posts on his booth, they go away smiling. But once on the train, their smiles are gone. And they are pushing and shoving again; or staring iron-eyed for a seat, hiding behind newspapers, or sneaking peeks at a pretty girl—wondering "How can I meet her?"

He'd first noticed her on Lexington Avenue as she crossed over from Bloomingdale's, and he fell in step easily behind her as she descended the subway kiosk, spun through the turnstile, and then stood on the platform between a chewing-gum machine and a large, toothy poster of a man who got his job through the New York Times.

The girl was probably around twenty-five. Her legs were long and sun-tanned, her blonde hair was short and pushed carelessly back— probably with her fingers. She wore a simple yellow dress, white gloves and no make-up. She had a lean, angular body and was the wholesome type that is often seen around the East Side shopping at Bloomingdale's, or carrying bags out of expensive delicatessens, or riding the Fifth Avenue bus home after work. Such girls usually avoided the subway, but occasionally one would slip through, and when she did he'd watch her.

Other men were looking at her, too. She probably noticed, but never let on. This was part of the game. The men tried to be subtle, pacing the platform casually, occasionally catching her reflection in a chewing-

gum mirror. Often they caught each other at this game, and sometimes they would exchange a wry smile. Sometimes they would become very righteous. When the train arrived, he followed a few paces behind her, and watched her sit across the aisle from him with her knees very close together, her gloved hands primly in her lap, and her blue eyes fixed innocently ahead.

The subway began to grind swiftly over the tracks toward Fifth Avenue, the lights in the dark tunnel flashing by, a fat lady with a Macy's shopping bag swaying like a tug, the men's eyes peeking over newspapers at the pretty girl; she not daring to look back—not daring to disturb her image of innocence in the subway.

If something would only happen—if only the subway would fail, the lights would go out, or the fat lady would topple over—then perhaps there would be an excuse for talking to this goddess sitting five feet across the aisle. But nothing happened. The train rolled flawlessly on, as trains inevitably do when you don't want them to.

It stopped at Fifth Avenue.

Then to Forty-ninth Street.

Then to Forty-second Street, where the girl quickly stood up, held onto the pole for a few seconds, and then was gone—like all the other bewitching and lovely girls he'd seen in New York and never spoken to, and probably would never see again.

*   *   *

New York's 10,000 bus drivers each day battle the world's worst traffic while being abused by old ladies, short-changed by schoolboys, cut off by cabs, truncated by trucks; all while driving with one hand and making change with the other, and issuing transfers, answering questions, making green lights, meeting a time schedule, avoiding Con Edison's holes in the ground, moving riders to the rear, listening to the incessant ding-ding-ding of the stop bell and suffering from a bad back, ulcers, hemorrhoids, or an almost uncontrollable desire to ram the bus into a stone wall and walk away.

Despite all this harassment and toil, New York's bus driver remains largely anonymous and goes through life with only half of his face showing in the rear-view mirror. Never does he attain the prestige of those dashing Greyhound drivers, who wear ninety-mission crush hats and zoom away like pilots; or suburban bus drivers, who are on a first-name basis with commuters and receive gifts at Christmas; or charter-bus drivers, who escort people to picnics and usually are asked to join in; or school-bus drivers, who can occasionally clout a noisy passenger and get away with it if the Board of Education is not too progressive.

The New York bus driver is taken for granted, and if he looks up into his rear-view mirror he can see the 15-cent multitudes ignoring him. He can see them looking out the window, or at their feet, or trying to read other people's newspapers. He can see a disheveled messenger squinting at a brown envelope and a fat lady clutching her shopping bag while trying to outstare a man for the only empty seat in the bus. He can see standees hanging from the straps like sides of beef and can hate them when they refuse to budge after he groans, for the umpteenth time:

"Move to da rear of da bus, please; plenty a room in the rear."

They ignore him, and will continue to ignore him until he disturbs their comfort—suddenly hitting his brake, not answering a question, or overshooting their stops while they're pulling the bell. Day after day the drivers go through this endlessly repetitive routine, and they know what to expect—and when—from the 3,000,000 New Yorkers who ride the buses each weekday.

At 6 A.M., for instance, the bus drivers pick up telephone operators, nurses, domestics and hotel workers; they are followed, at 7 A.M., by store clerks, longshoremen, elevators operators and an endless variety of other tabloid readers who must be on the job before eight o'clock. During these hours one hears the uninterrupted sound of coins jingling down into the coin machine, because these early passengers, being of the working class themselves, try to accommodate the driver by having the exact fare. The bus driver's job does not really become unpleasant until 8 A.M., when the students, books under arm, come plunging in and elbow their way to the seats.

At 9 A.M. the bus is filled with secretaries and receptionists and the smell of perfume. At ten o'clock, there are executive secretaries (who'll work until six) and whitecollar workers not yet ready to splurge on cabs and also the first waves of the busman's chief *bête noire*—lady shoppers.

"The lady shopper will have her pocketbook jingling with coins, and yet she'll hand me a five-dollar bill," says Barney O'Leary, who started as a trolley man in New York thirty-four years ago and looks as though he'd stepped out of *The Informer*. "Or she'll have a lady friend with her, and she'll say 'Oh, that's okay, Sophie, I have it.' Then she'll put her glove in her mouth and hunt for change—and everybody is waiting outside in the rain.

"When I pull into a crowded stop it never fails that the lady with a package is first in line. She puts her package on the floor when she gets in, fumbles through her purse and, after I've given her change, she asks for a three-cent transfer. So I have two transactions with her! Of course, when she's asking for a transfer, she whispers, and you can hardly hear her, but when she's chewing you out she can be heard all over the bus.

"Ladies are so bad that men no longer give up their seats to them in New York. Men always sit in the rear of the bus and pretend they don't see the ladies standing in the aisle. Or men'll put newspapers up to their faces, or take a piece of paper from a pocket and pretend they're writing up some big business deal. Men are so interested in keeping their seat sometimes that they go right past their stop."

For the drivers who can take it, the job holds a certain amount of security and an average salary of close to $120 a week, including overtime. The drivers cover about sixty miles during their eight-hour rides and collect about $100 in fares, every penny of which they must account for. Although there are some iron men like Barney O'Leary who can spend a lifetime trying to move people to the rear of the bus, there are others who have *had* it after ten or fifteen years. These drivers switch to less harassing jobs in the companies, becoming maintenance men or mechanics, for example, and here many of them are quite happy, even quite friendly—here, far from the madding crowd and the dinging bell, far from the traffic jams and complaining letter writers, far from the snippy shoppers who for 15 cents think they control a busman's destiny.

Early in the evening, as thousands of New York secretaries go heel-clacking and swishing out of office buildings, another large army of women prepare to move in. And from twilight to sunrise these women will seemingly control New York: they will occupy seats on the Stock Exchange, preside over abandoned board meetings, and pound their fists at invisible admen. They will walk unannounced into the plush quarters of tycoons, and deliver silent speeches into dictaphones. They will keep skyscraper lights burning all night, and along the windows their silhouettes and brooms will be reaching and touching like a ballet of witches.

Then, as daylight begins to fall on the city, their buckets will clatter in the halls, and downstairs their hollow voices will echo through the

marble corridors. Moments later they will be lined along the curb outside, bundled in heavy coats and smiling, waiting to fill buses with ba-
bushkas.

This is how they come and go in New York—these 12,000 unionized
cleaning ladies whose dustpan hands each night caress a thousand feet
of space and sleeping telephones, and give a quick brush-off to the desk-
top photos of other women. By 6 P.M., 200 cleaning ladies, flat-heeled
and garbed in peasant-blue cotton, are moving quickly through the 3,000
rooms of the Empire State, where each year they find about $5,000 in
bills and coins along the floor, and sometimes discover silent lovers behind furniture. The ladies dutifully turn in all money, and report all
lovers—a thankless gesture in either case.

By 7:30 P.M., 350 other charwomen have moved into Rockefeller
Center where, after all the wastepaper has been dumped into baskets, it
is stored for forty-eight hours in warehouses. Even vacuum cleaners are
held for twelve hours before being emptied, a practice that has paid off
in the recovery of jeweler's gold dust, diamond rings and many tiny
gems.

By midnight thousands more ladies have moved onto the ticker-taped
floors of Wall Street. They are ever careful to throw away only scrap
paper that is on the floor and will touch nothing on desks or tables. Often
some executive will deliberately leave scraps tottering temptingly on the
edge of desks to test the charwomen's adherence to rules.

The women, many of them Ukrainian, Czechoslovakian or Polish,
work thirty-five hours a week and earn $54.95 to start. They work either
to help support large families, supplement their alimony, or get away
from home at night. Often, however, they are secretive about their work,
telling neighbors they have nighttime clerical jobs.

Sometimes their own children know as little about charwomen as do
those ungrateful 9-to-5 chain smokers—who come bouncing in each
morning and proceed to fill up ashtrays, load wastebaskets, and stir up
more dust and dirt for these unheralded nocturnal ladies of the bucket
brigade.

*   *   *

Each Friday and Saturday night some gypsies, derelicts and a few
unwashed pickpockets are among those who converge on 133 Allen
Street for their weekly visit to Manhattan's last public bathhouse. To

them, and to thousands of other poor people who patronize it, the public
bath is a kind of tiled Taj Mahal.

All approach it quietly and sit with almost bowed heads in rows of
chairs until they are admitted to one of the ninety private shower stalls.
They pay nothing for a shower if they bring their own soap and towel.
Otherwise they are charged 25 cents, of which a nickel is refunded if
they do not steal the towel.

More than 130,000 persons shower in the Allen Street bathhouse each
year, and among them are ex-prizefighters, hung-over hobos, and some
withered little ladies who say they once were Floradora girls.

They are allowed twenty minutes to shower. When the time is up, bath
attendants ring an alarm, and then scream through the foggy shower
rooms until everybody is out—and in the dirt again.

*   *   *

Each day in New York 90,000 people dial WE 6–1212 for the latest
weather report; 70,000 dial ME 7–1212 for the correct time, and 650,-
000 dial 411 because they don't know what else to dial. It takes the information operator maybe fifteen seconds to find them a number to dial,
and then, after looking up about 130 numbers during a two-hour sitting,
she takes a 15-minute smoke or coffee break. Even when off duty she
continues to e-*nun*-ci-ate, and sometimes she wishes she could stop pro-
nouncing numbers as fo-wer,

> fi-yiv,

> > sev-ven,

> > > ni-yen

> > > > But it is not easy.

If only people would look numbers up . . .

If only people would look numbers up, her job could be so much
easier, she thinks, as she dashes out her cigarette and returns to the
switchboard to look numbers up

> for New York's 4,100,000 telephones and
its phonebook-phobiad psychopaths who need numbers, who need answers, who are just lonely and want to talk, who just want to make a
date with the operator, and seduce her . . .

But they do not want to look numbers up in the Manhattan telephone directory, which has 780,000 names, 1,830 pages, weighs five pounds, and is too thick to be torn apart nowadays even by Charles Atlas and Vic Tanny tigers, who say they are tired of the trick anyhow, and seem to ask: Who *needs* it?

Who needs the 1,795,000 Manhattan directories that are printed each year?

—a quarter of which are lost, destroyed or page-ripped on Wall Street and flipped out of skyscrapers, along with ticker tape and toilet paper, down upon dignitaries who are given trumped-up parades along lower Broadway to City Hall; the other

—three-quarters of which are collected each year by men who leaf through them and find leftover love letters, stamps, insurance policies, neckties, money, and then ship the books on a barge up the Hudson to a cardboard mill that reincarnates them into backboards for shirt laundries, boxes for eggs, covers for pocket novels, and other gewgaws for New Yorkers who will

> or will not
> look numbers up.

"Shine, mistah?"

"Shine, mistah?"

"Hey, mistah, shine?"

This is what you hear along New York's sidewalks when the sun is shining and when the city's roving bootlacks are lined up like buzzards for business—sometimes lurking in corners, sometimes perched at the curb, sometimes wandering through the crowds whispering *"shine, shine"* like a peddler of dirty postcards.

In New York there are 800 unlicensed bootblacks who are ever fearful of the police and who, because they must work fast, are more likely to get polish on your socks than the 1,500 indoor bootblacks who work in shops and hotels and sit, like royalty, on high, ornamented chairs.

These older, upper-crust bootblacks are also not so anonymous as the young street boys, and they frequently reach such heights as David the Bootblack King who worked in Bronx Magistrate's Court; or the late Biaggio Velluzzi, The Lambs Club's bootblack known as Murph; or Charlie, the bootblack-firebuff who traveled with Engine Ladder Company 8; or James Rinaldi, the United Nations bootblack who could ask *"shine?"* in twenty-seven languages. And sometimes they become as distinguished as Silk-hat Tony, the dapper bootblack at Broadway and Canal Street who casts an accusing eye at every passing pair of dirty shoes and who, like many mysterious types in this town, is suspected of being very, very rich.

But it is impossible to know how much the average bootblack earns each week. They're usually a close-mouthed clique (when they've finished shining a customer's shoes, they'll announce it by tapping once on the customer's heel or ankle—but they'll not look up and speak).

At any rate, the price of a shine and rhythmic rag-snap has gone up recently in New York to 20 cents in the city's railroad terminals. But it is still 15 cents in most places. And on Forty-ninth and Broadway there is an ambitious teenager who has written on his box: "Shine 5¢, Tax 20¢ —Total 25¢." He has competition, however, from a young Third Avenue bootblack who carries a large sign reading: *"Free Shine!—tip 25¢"*

As a group, hotel bootblacks are believed to be the most prosperous, earning between $60 and $80 a week. Tourists and transients are fair game for them, even though many tourists wipe their shoes with hotel towels and blankets. "But we can always tell when they do that," an Astor hotel bootblack says. "People who shine their own shoes in hotel rooms, or at home, usually smear too much polish on, and you can see it caked around the sole. It's sloppy."

When Albert Anastasia was murdered by gunmen as he sat for a haircut in the Park Sheraton Hotel in 1957, eleven persons (besides Anastasia) were in the barbershop—five barbers, two other customers, a manicurist, a valet, and two bootblacks. The bootblacks had little use for Anastasia, who polished his own shoes—a fact that did not go unobserved by reporter Meyer Berger. In describing the scene for the *Times* the next morning, Mr. Berger wrote:

"Anastasia . . . stolled into the hotel barbershop at about 10:15 and . . . hung up his topcoat and stripped open his white shirt. He was dressed all in brown—brown shoes with rather an amateur polish, brown suit . . ."

It is not possible for New York bootblacks to have compassion for people like Anastasia.

When it is hot in New York women stroll by in billowy dresses, tops of convertibles are down, and elbows stick out like fins from the open windows of buses. Sun worshipers bake on hotel rooftops and waterfront benches, and construction steelworkers toddle over high beams wearing T-shirts, undershirts—and no shirts.

Central Park and Fifth Avenue are crowded with people who do not wish to hurry. They walk in the shade. They paddle languidly in the Park's lake. Some try to encourage the Central Park sea lions to move from slumber into the cold water, but fail. From the windows of Manhattan tenements can be seen blubbery-armed women, hands under chins, watching the people below burn up energy. The boccie players take it slow in Greenwich Village. Merchants advertise drip-dry dresses and wash-and-wear suits. And in neighborhood stores customers mark the heat by exchanging the usual cliché: "Hot enough for you?"

"Hot enough for you?"

"You bet."

"Hot enough for you?"

"Yeah."

"Hot enough for you?"

"Sí."

"Yessuh."

"Yeah,"

"Yeah,"

"Yeah."

And on and on it goes in New York, day after day; people have only the same thing to say to one another. New York, as Hamilton Basso said, is a city of neighborhoods in which nobody has any neighbors.

If only something unusual would happen . . .

If only something unusual would happen—then the boy could talk to the pretty girl in the subway . . .

If only people would look numbers up, then the telephone operator could sneak in an extra smoke and take another breath . . .

If only . . .

Something unusual did happen at 2:49 P.M. on Wednesday, May 12, 1959, in a large portion of Manhattan: the electrical power failed and, in many neighborhoods, it was a dark town of stopped clocks, warm beer, soft butter and intimate, candlelit conversation in saloons without television. It was wonderful. People had something *else* to talk about.

It was possible to have a quiet drink and walk through imaginary red lights. Elevator-spoiled tenants had to walk upstairs for a change. People took showers and dried in the dark. Men shaved whiskers they could not see.

Only the blind were undaunted. At 3:10 P.M., at 1880 Broadway, in the dark four-story building of the New York Guild for the Jewish Blind, 200 blind workers, who knew every inch of the place by touch, led seventy sighted workers down the steps and safely onto Broadway.

But the next day the lights were on. The blind were forgotten in this big city of Conversation About The Weather. Things in New York City's neighborhoods would remain predictable, too, until something else happened—another blackout, a fire, perhaps a murder. A murder! Nothing like a murder in New York to shake up the neighborhood, if only for a few hours.

And there was a murder on the sunny Monday morning of August 10, 1959. An assistant city editor, having had his second cup of coffee and wishing to impress the boss with his imagination, was shuffling through news dispatches on his desk when he came upon a wire-service story reading: "BULLETIN! Residents of New York's Lower East Side are up in arms today over the robbery and murder of Philip Schickler, a kindly, 65-year-old owner of a small restaurant at 207 East Broadway. Police said . . ."

The assistant city editor quickly sent a reporter to 207 East Broadway with instructions to describe the "color" of the neighborhood, and when the reporter arrived he saw, clustered solemnly in front of the restaurant, dozens of neighbors listening to a short, stout woman saying: "They had to kill him? He gave them the money. They had to kill?"

Neither she nor anyone else could understand why anyone would want to rob and murder kindly Mr. Schickler. This was once a peaceful community, the lady said. Laundry is still hung from fire escapes, used suits still sell for as little as $2.50. This still is a noticeably Jewish community of bagels and whiskered men clinging to tradition, but the tradition is being challenged.

Housing projects are replacing the familiar tenements, and Puerto Ricans are moving in steadily. Such changes breed conflict, and the conflict occasionally reaches a point where there is a robbery or a murder— and on this August 10 there was the murder of a restaurant owner named

Schickler who used to sell coffee for a nickel and give bagels away to those too poor to pay.

Television cameramen and reporters flooded the block with hot lights and questions.

"What happened?" they asked.

"Who do you think did it?"

The neighbors, resenting questions from strangers, shook their heads. The reporters and cameramen rushed up to the apartment above the restaurant, and were met by Mr. Schickler's survivors, who were crying, cursing, and saying go-away, go-away.

"Can you tell our NBC-TV audience who happened, Mr. Greene?"

The television cameramen and reporters were consoling, and spoke softly and politely, because if they didn't the relatives would not talk, and the first edition might be missed and there would be no taped on-the-scene voices to go between the commercials for filter tips on the 11 o'clock news.

But they got nowhere with the relatives, and so they ran down to the street again and quoted and recorded the hushed voices of Jewish-Americans saying, "They had to kill?"

"Such a nice man, Philip Schickler."

"Who's going to be next, that's the question."

"This neighborhood—we must move."

"What happened, Mr. Cooperman?"

"What happened, Miss Rosenbloom?"

Miss Rosenbloom said, "Puerto Ricans began to move in about six years ago, and I first noticed the big change in this neighborhood when the politicians' trucks went by and, instead of speaking Yiddish, the loudspeakers were speaking Spanish, and . . ."

Witnesses told the police that the attackers were Puerto Rican, and Deputy Chief Inspector Edward Feeley, in charge of East Side detectives, quickly assigned fifty detectives to the case, a dozen of them Spanish-speaking.

Puerto Rican leaders were infuriated, and charged that everybody was picking on Puerto Ricans. Social workers, also hating this type of publicity, denied there was "conflict" in the neighborhood. How could there be after they'd worked so hard trying to mix up the Puerto Ricans and the Jews, the Italians, the Poles, the Irish, the gypsies, the homosexuals into one blend of happiness? The social workers wrote irate letters to the newspaper's managing editor, who forwarded them to the city editor, who forwarded them to the assistant city editor, who now wished the story had not made page 1 because his $8,500-a-year job did not seem so secure the next morning after his second cup of coffee.

By twilight the reporters and television lights no longer cluttered the sidewalk of the neighborhood. The relatives of the dead restaurant man were left with their grief. Within months the murderers were caught and justice was done. The newspapers that carried the sensational story have long since been wrapped around garbage and burned in a sanitation dump, and totaled and recorded with tons of other trash so that the Sanitation Department's press agent will have impressive annual figures to support his chief's annual plea to the Mayor for more sanitation workers.

If you return to 207 East Broadway today you will not be reminded of the murder, except that the restaurant has never reopened. It is not that the people have forgotten the murdered man, but they talk mainly of the weather . . . and ask, "Hot enough for you?"

New York Is
a City
of Characters

In New York there is a professional dog-walker in the East Seventies, a cat psychologist at 141 Lexington Avenue, and a little lady who shares her apartment on Forty-sixth Street with two peg-legged pigeons. On Sutton Place a man fishes out his eighteenth-story window for eels, and at 880 Fifth Avenue a woman is employed to investigate ghosts, and other paranormal happenings, for the American Society for Psychical Research. In various parts of the city there are clubs for odd-balls, eight-balls, and even a Pimps' Ball is thrown annually by tarts, in a midtown hotel.

Things go on in New York that probably go on nowhere else.

Each day people go up to a Fifty-eighth Street psychodrama studio to scream and curse at two masked dummies standing against the wall; the dummies represent bosses, rent collectors, parents, spouses, or various other tyrants that some people cannot yet face with courage.

In Cartier's you see a lady and gentleman scrutinizing jewelry, and suddenly he spots a diamond bracelet, buys it, and fits it around the lady's wrist. She smiles and dangles a key chain in the air. He snatches it, and they then leave together and disappear on Fifth Avenue.

At 608 West Forty-eighth Street you can rent a lion for $250 a day, and at 410 West Forty-seventh there are bona fide skeletons for $35 a day. At 155 Lexington Avenue the Plumb Trading and Sales Company sells beads to Indians, who sell them to tourists, and a teacher at the New School, Charlotte Selver, frequently gives courses in "Walking, Standing, Sitting, Lying."

One lady in Murray Hill has had a battered boat shipped up from Florida and now she keeps it on her roof. When neighbors ask why she keeps an old boat on her roof, she simply answers, "I like to look at it." In the summertime a man hangs his sails to dry in his one-room apartment and checks into a hotel for the night, and each warm morning a lovely Swedish blonde governess, Eivor Bergstrom, leaves the River House, strolls down to Franklin D. Roosevelt Drive, sprawls along the walkway and takes a sun bath. This is how she meets people in New York.

In New York you can meet all kinds. There are bars that cater either to men looking for women, women looking for men, men looking for men who look like women, or women looking for women who look like men. New York is habitated by an estimated 5,000 prostitutes and 250,000 homosexuals. And on Thanksgiving night each year at 155th Street, 1,000 men in expensive gowns and high heels attend Phil Black's Ball. Mr. Black, whose wardrobe includes a dozen ultra-chic gowns, climaxes the evening by presenting a prize to the "Queen of the Ball"— the man who acts most like a woman.

New York is a great city for committees. There is a Committee for a Free Estonia, a Committee for a Sane Nuclear Policy, a Committee for French American Wives, and committees to Protect Our Children's Teeth, Preserve American Art, Aid Heidelberg Students, and Secure Justice for Morton Sobell—not to mention the Cooperative for American Remittances to Everywhere, Inc. New York is the favorite city of the voodoo authority, Maya Deren, who lives at 61 Morton Street with nineteen cats and a husband, Teiji Ito, who plays thirty-nine musical instruments—mostly at night. It is the town of hope for Billy Klenosky, a song writer whose masterpiece, "April in Siberia," was voted "Bomb of the Month" by radio station WINS.

Some people in New York are paid to be nice; some are paid to be despised. Larry Hamilton, one of the most uncouth vertebrates this side of the Bronx Zoo, is paid about $35,000 a year to be a villain wrestler. Being constantly hated is not always easy for Larry, but he works at it. Four nights a week he spends sticking his finger into hero wrestlers' eyes, twisting their ears, destroying their pompadours, removing their dandruff. Like all villains, Larry soon gets crushed by the hero, but Larry never loses graciously. He curls his lip, protests to the referee; then, glaring up at the crowd in Madison Square Garden, he shakes his fist threateningly. The fans respond by hitting him with rotten fruit, whisky bottles and, occasionally, a chair. After the match is over, the naïve wrestling customers wait outside the arena for Larry, hoping to pelt him once more. But he crashes through them, dashes for a taxi, and soon is at the King Edward Hotel, off Broadway, resting for the following night's brawl.

New York is a zany, captivating, most unusual town. It is where a Pennsylvania lady visits periodically to recruit clients for her summer "Theater in the Nude," and where a certain personnel consultant sizes up job applicants by the shapes of their heads. It is where a homeless, panhandling clown, Pathétique, makes up his face in the subway, and where a former adman, Stuart Bart, has made a fortune by cleaning only ties. He calls himself a "tie-coon."

In mid-Manhattan is a school for unemployed gag writers; on the West Side is a school for up-and-coming belly dancers; on the East Side is a school that floats. It is the S.S. *John W. Brown,* an ex-liberty ship on Pier 22 that is used to train over 300 students in nautical skills as well as the usual high school subjects.

In Brooklyn the "Wigwam" bar caters mostly to Indian steelworkers, and there are certain blocks in New York that sell practically only jewelry, another that sells mostly flowers, and one that sells mostly wedding gowns.

In New York there is a Beigel Bakers Union, an Italian Actors Union, and the Russian Bath Rubbers Union. But the Russian bath rubbers, the only union advocating sweatshops, appear headed for their last rubdown. Most of the union members are now pushing seventy and are deaf—from all the water and hot temperatures.

There are women in New York who sometimes come to the window in blue negligees, sometimes in white negligees, and sometimes in no negligees at all. New York is a city of scantily clad women in windows—and of voyeurs who watch them. One woman on West Fourth Street used to be watched regularly as she stood naked on hot nights in front of her open refrigerator door—until one day she received in the mail a photograph of her naked self taken by a neighbor.

In New York there are water cabs that rush people to the ships they've missed, and on Ninth Avenue the Swift Laundry keeps a marine ticker running in the back room all day so it'll know exactly when the ships return. When they do return, Swift's men are waiting to collect any laundry the crew may have.

Whenever a prizefighter in New York gets banged on the mouth, hit in the teeth, or butted on the gums, Dr. Walter H. Jacobs immediately begins to worry—not about the fighter, but about the fighter's mouthpiece. Dr. Jacobs is a dentist who makes mouthpieces for fighters, and nothing disturbs him more than to see somebody knock his dental work.

New York is a town of fifteen midget wrestlers. They all can squeeze into the Hotel Holland's elevator, six can sleep in one bed, eight can be comfortably transported about in their chauffeur-driven limousine. New York is where Moshe Pumpernickel, a professional mourner, is paid to cry at funerals, and where Nathan Groob collects American flags with 48 or 49 stars—believing they someday will be valuable collectors' items. Each springtime at Yankee Stadium there appears a small, odd group of fans who like to collect foul balls; they attend games that are not too popular, and thus they have more room to run around in the stands retrieving foul balls. Some of these "foulball hawks" know how to play every hitter in the league.

New York can be a temporary blend of irritating sights and unexpected sounds. The irritant can be the sight of an Alfa Romeo double-parked in front of the Colony Restaurant with "MD" plates; the joy can be from the noise of a Negro pounding a piano in the middle of Sixty-first Street. The Negro is ecstatic for a few moments, and residents in brownstones peek out to listen. But then, regrettably, he must stop playing and push the piano up a ramp into the huge Dard's Van Company truck. He is a moving man first, a musician second.

New York is a schizophrenic town for the glamorous model who poses next to a Cadillac in the Waldorf lobby and wears a Simonetta gown with $100,000 worth of jewelry—and then, at 4:30 P.M., quickly changes clothes, boards the BMT, and hastens to prepare dinner for her family in a three-room apartment in Queens.

New York is an endlessly dirty town for the window washers at the United Nations, and a frustrating town for hotel managers who each day remain helpless as hundreds of ashtrays and towels are stolen by transients. There are times when it seems the whole city of New York is capable of going mad, of exploding into riot.

On Tuesday, September 20, 1960, when Khrushchev, Castro and other foreign leaders visited the UN, everybody in New York seemed mad at everybody else. The Ukrainians demonstrated against the presence of Khrushchev, Khrushchev complained of police brutality, many of the police were mad because they had to work through the Jewish holidays; New York's rabbis blamed it all on Police Commissioner Kennedy, who blamed it on Khrushchev. Outside the UN the Greeks cursed the Albanians, nihilists blasted pacifists, British Guiana students scorned England, and a group of rioting anti-Castro Cubans paraded up and down shouting, "Fi-del-ista . . . Com-mun-ista!" Outside the Waldorf, staff members of the *Catholic Worker* picketed against the American Banking Association's convention, and on East Fifty-fifth Street a truck driver named Tom Horch denounced the National Biscuit Company and demanded higher wages. All over town sirens blared, plainclothesmen stood like gargoyles on rooftops, and cab drivers insulted everybody. And on Forty-fourth Street, Mrs. Sylvia Kraus of 25 East Seventy-seventh Street carried a placard reading: "Americans Awake—Germ Warfare Has Begun."

"I know that people are putting things in my food," she told crowds in the street. "They've been trying to eliminate me since 1956, but I know how to combat it." Then she disappeared into the crowd without telling how.

New York is a city of 38,000 cab drivers, 10,000 bus drivers, but of only one chauffeur who has a chauffeur. The wealthy chauffeur is Roosevelt Zanders. He earns $100,000 a year, is a gentleman of impeccable taste and, although he owns a $23,000 Rolls-Royce, he does not scorn his friends who own Bentleys. For $150 a day, Mr. Zanders will drive anyone anywhere in his big, silver Rolls. Diplomats patronize him, models pose next to him, and each day he receives cables from around the world urging that he be waiting at Idlewild, on the docks, or outside the Plaza Hotel.

Doormen all over Manhattan's East Side know him. Taxi drivers honk at him. His Rolls stops traffic. Everywhere he drives he is watched by dreamers—like himself.

Roosevelt Zanders, born without money forty-five years ago in Ohio, dreamed of the day he would own a big car. He worked in a drugstore, in a locker room, in a hotel—and saved. Ten years ago he had saved enough to buy a Cadillac. He decided to become a chauffeur—a de luxe chauffeur who catered to the dreams and whims of people pursuing elegance. His first client was the late Gertrude Lawrence. She liked him, and boasted to her friends about his efficiency and charm. Other celebrities also hired him for special occasions, and eventually he owned five Cadillacs and a thriving chauffeur's business.

But his boyhood dream was unfulfilled. He wanted a custom-built Rolls-Royce, and three years ago he ordered it. Two years ago it arrived. It was equipped with wall-to-wall fur rugs, two separate high-fidelity sets, and a jack the size of a midget wrestler. Sometimes at night, however, he is too tired to drive any more. So Bob Clarke, his chauffeur, takes over and Mr. Zanders relaxes in the back.

The courtrooms in New York's Foley Square are crowded each day with a quaint group of spectators whose ubiquity (and genius for finding a seat) has launched them on brilliant careers in second-guessing the judge. These individuals are called "court buffs." They can be seen each day wandering from courtroom to courtroom scrutinizing juries, appraising lawyers, quoting wildly from Cardozo, and handing decisions down to each other.

"Court buffs usually are retired men who have nothing to do," said a 77-year-old buff named William Higgins. "So we come down and listen to court cases. It's entertaining and education. It keeps us out of trouble. Only a fool goes to the movies; we visit courts and see real actors in the flesh."

There are about a hundred "regulars" in Foley Square. They frequently know each other, dine together, and are connoisseurs of gavels. But the "regulars" rarely all go to the same court building.

Federal Court buffs prefer only federal cases, and they will have little or nothing to do with General Sessions buffs, who go for murder, rape, and robbery cases.

Still other regulars are Supreme Court buffs, and they even further classify themselves into Divorce buffs, Accident buffs, and Negligence buffs.

"Used to be lots of Hijacking buffs," says another aged kibitzer. "These hijacking cases used to be good. But the FBI cleaned them up and there are no more around."

In addition to the buffs who are lured by certain types of cases, there are other buffs who are more interested in watching a certain lawyer or judge perform. They claim they go to hear Judge Sidney Sugarman for his eloquence, Irving R. Kaufman for his fine baritone, and Thomas F. Murphy for his sighs. Judge Mitchell J. Schweitzer even has a fan club of buffs, headed by Louis Schwartz, who has had a special reserved seat in the judge's court for years.

Being a privileged class, court buffs—they're occasionally also called "corridor lawyers"—do not hesitate to assert their influence over high and low courts. They have even been known to get Judge Ed Weinfeld to close the window occasionally even though he is known as a "fresh-air judge" to the buffs, and therefore open to criticism by those buffs wishing only to come in out of the cold.

As for what some court buffs do at night, the answer is simple: Night Court.

*   *   *

On the door of Bernard A. Young's tiny office, on Broadway at Fifty-first Street, are lettered the names of fourteen firms over which he wields great and unchallenged power—because he is their president, board member, or only member. Mr. Young admits that having fourteen names on his door has aroused the curiosity of strangers and has infuriated the mailman. "The mail carrier dumps all questionable mail in my office," Mr. Young says. "And he's usually right."

The latest firm over which Mr. Young has won control, in a hard-fought victory over the only two other New Yorkers who had heard of it, is the Bird Research Foundation, Ltd. This is a corporation that Mr. Young started with two ladies, both bird-lovers, and it is dedicated to the care of caged birds.

"Ours is a nonprofit corporation," says Mr. Young, a 50-year-old Harvard man who has had a long history with nonprofit. "We disseminate information on the care, housing and conservation of pet birds in people's homes, and care nothing about birds in the street, who are cared for by Audubon societies, and such . . ."

Many of Mr. Young's firms are on his door only temporarily. As he quits one business and goes into another, he has the firm names changed, and each time it costs him $10 for a new printing and erasing job. Of the firms currently on his door, a dozen are either record companies or sheet music firms, one is a greeting card establishment, and the other is for the birds.

"I don't know what you'd call me," he says. "I got a law degree from Harvard, but never practiced. I'm a bachelor. I'm a Phi Beta Kappa and was magna cum laude. I've published and recorded music, but have always loved birds. I'm a bird in my own right. My chief gripe has been that song writers don't get paid whenever their songs are played. Song writers are like birds. They get handouts and crumbs."

*   *   *

The Manhattan telephone directory has 780,000 names, of which 3,277 are Smith, 2,811 are Brown, 2,446 are Williams, 2,073 are Cohen —and one is Mike Krasilovsky. Anyone who doubts this last fact has only to look at the top of page 894 where, in large black letters, is this sign:

There is *only* one	Remember	There is *only* one
Mike Krasilovsky	Mike	Mike Krasilovsky
STerling 3—1990	STerling 3—1990	STerling 3—1990

In order to get a close look at Mr. Krasilovsky, a journey must be taken to Brooklyn where, on 426 Lafayette Avenue, he runs a large trucking firm that specializes in moving heavy machinery, safes, huge statues and small mountains. He employs forty-three riggers and millwrights; owns thirty-two trucks and, on the front of his two-story building, he has posted a sign reading, "We Move Anything Anyplace Anytime."

Mr. Krasilovsky is a virile-looking man of fifty-eight with a crew cut, round face, big arms and dirty fingernails.

"I can dismantle, move and set up anything—no matter how big, small, or intricate—faster than any man in New York," Mr. Krasilovsky says, modestly. And in no time at all he is telling how he moved the twelve-ton Thomas Jefferson statue from Astoria to Washington, D.C.; the eight-ton George Washington statue from Providence to Mount Vernon; an atom smasher into the Mount Sinai Hospital; twelve tons of bells into Grace Church; a 53-foot Christmas tree onto Wall Street, and four Univacs through a third-story window at Remington Rand after some skeptics said it couldn't be done.

Mr. Krasilovsky began to learn the machinery-moving business in Brooklyn at the age of nine from his wise, but not entirely literate uncle named Samuel Krasilovsky, who made his mark with an "X" but was known to all his friends as Charley. In those days Uncle Charley hauled safes around town in a horse and wagon with some assistance from his brother, David, and, of course, from his young nephew, Mike Krasilovsky. The firm was officially called "S. Krasilovsky & Bro." And the three of them coexisted for about twenty years; but when David decided to bring into the firm his two sons, Monroe and Harry, Mike objected. And in 1939 he quit and opened his own moving firm. And now this story becomes complicated.

The two Krasilovsky firms began to steal each other's customers and run propaganda campaigns against each other. And the confused customers rarely knew with which Krasilovsky they were dealing, talking, cursing, or paying. So, to get matters straight in the telephone book, Mike began to advertise:

Remember Mike. There is *only* one Mike Krasilovsky.

He also began spelling his name Krasilo*U*sky—so he would jump alphabetically ahead of Krasilo*V*sky & Bro. in the telephone listings.

Then into the machinery moving business in 1957 came David's third son, Milton Krasilovsky. Milton, a bright young man out of Brooklyn College, decided to change his telephone name from Milton to Mick, and to drop the "v" from his last name: thus, his firm became "Mick Krasil*O*sky"—and he not only moved right ahead of Mike Krasilo*U*sky in the book, but he also began to steal many of Mike's customers.

This infuriated Mike. So he took over the "Atlas-York Safe Corp." and moved to the head of the book.

Then one of Milton's cousins took over the "Acme Safe Co."

So Mike started the "Ace Trucking Co."

Then Milton's other cousin, Marvin, inspired the "'AAA Acme Krasilovsky Safe Co."

Nobody knows how Mike plans to become the first name in the telephone book, but all he must do is step over an answering service at 237 First Avenue that is called "A."

At any rate, on page 894 alone, Mike has managed to get his telephone number listed eighteen times—under Krasilovsky Mike, KrasiloUsky Mike, and Krasilovsky Bros., and not counting Ace Trucking or Atlas-York Safe Corp.

Milton's number has crashed the pages thirteen times—as Krasilovsky Milton Inc., KrasilOsky Mick, Krasilovsky D. & S. (for his father, David, and the late Uncle Samuel who was known as Charley); and/or by alternating the last four letters of his surname from -vsky to -osky, but not yet -usky.

"All this silly routine has not helped any of our businesses," Milton Krasilovsky admits at his office on Brooklyn's Green Street. "Customers are now sending their business to places where there is less confusion."

Meanwhile, while half the Krasilovsky clan is trying to outdo each other in the moving business, the other half is moving out of the business altogether.

One of Mike's sons has become a lawyer. And the other son is off in Vienna learning to become a Congregationalist minister. Mike's daughter, Phyllis Krasilovsky, has become a successful New York writer of children's books. Mike's wife, a lecturer at the New School for Social Research in Greenwich Village, has changed her name to Harriet Krass. (Incidentally, Mike Krasilovsky's brother, Monroe, also has a wife who changed her name to Harriet Krass.)

Monroe II, David's son, who was largely responsible for the split in the Krasilovsky dynasty in the first place, has since shifted his talents to the body-collision business. His brother, Harry, is unemployed. Their father, David, has retired.

But Mike Krasilovsky is undismayed. Nothing can bother him—just so long as in New York there is *only* one Mike Krasilovsky.

* * *

With a cape draped over his shoulders, and a wig on his bald head, Henry W. Dubois has managed to make a living in New York by impersonating George Washington. During the past nineteen years Mr. Dubois has impersonated Washington hundreds of times at New York benefits, schools, churches and clubs. Thousands know him only as "Mr. Washington," and this is how he often gets his mail—at his home in Washington Heights.

About forty times a year an organization will hire Mr. Dubois to play Washington. Sometimes he'll be at the Christian Arts Fellowship meeting; at other times in Public School 115, or P.S. 83, or at the Masonic Veterans of Foreign Wars hall. He has repeated the Washington Prayer dozens of times at the Broadway Temple, at Rockland State Hospital, and at children's wards in hospitals throughout the city. Through it all, Mr. Dubois is august and solemn, a man of historic significance.

Mr. Dubois, in his seventies and never prone to chopping things down, was admittedly unsuccessful as an animal impersonator in the early days of radio. He was traditionally unemployed, he recalls, and finally took a job as a church watchman at St. Paul's Chapel downtown, where George Washington himself once worshiped. Suddenly, Mr. Dubois said, all his boyhood reverence for Washington was revived. He began repeating Washington's Prayer (which he had memorized in school) to his friends, and when asked to perform during a Washington's Birthday ceremony at the John Street Methodist Church, he was delighted.

"There suddenly seemed to be some mystical significance to my life," Mr. Dubois said. "I repeated the prayer, and somehow felt the spirit of Old George. After I finished the prayer the preacher slipped me a dollar—and there was George's photo on it."

Mr. Dubois acquired from an actor friend a colonial uniform, but from his constant assignments he barely gets it back from the cleaner's in time for his next job. Since playing Washington is year-round work for him—Dubois is hired through Flag Day, Constitution Day, and on many other holidays—he rarely relaxes.

But he always has time to visit the hospitals at night. At the hospitals he tries to cheer up the patients with his sounds impersonating dogs, cars, steamships and airplanes; children at Bellevue love his impersonations, and are much more appreciative than his old radio sponsors were. They have also given him a name—"Dr. Sunshine"—and have no idea that thousands of New Yorkers regard him as the nation's first President.

*   *   *

Joe Barbagallo, chief barber at the United Nations, has continued to coexist happily with the East and West by following a policy of no debating, no chopping and no waiting. Some of the world's foremost diplomats swear by his scissors, marvel at his speed, and relax comfortably under his razor. They have phoned from Washington to make appointments, and, once in his chair, they rarely tell him how the job should be done; Mr. Barbagallo does not tell them how to run the United Nations, and he doesn't expect them to tell him how to cut hair.

Twelve years of cutting up at the United Nations have taught him, among other things, that hair usually should be cut short above the ears for Russians, long on top and short on the neck for the French, long on the neck and full at the sideburns for the British, and very short on the top, sides and neck for the Chinese.

"Some people give instructions on how they wish to have their hair cut," Mr. Barbagallo acknowledged, "but nine times out of ten their instructions are wrong. I agree with them, but I use my own judgment. By always cutting off less hair than the customer tells me, I hardly ever go wrong."

He has listed among his devotees such leaders as Trygve Lie ("just a trim"); Dag Hammarskjöld ("hair very thin, go light"); Andrew W. Cordier ("short on sides and back"); Dr. Ralph J. Bunche ("just a little all around"); and Henry Cabot Lodge ("trim lightly around ears, but not too short").

Political issues are rarely, if ever, discussed in Mr. Barbagallo's chair. Since he wishes to maintain his policy of splendid isolationism, he deliberately talks to the British mostly about cricket, to the Americans mostly about the weather, to the Italians mostly about women.

When the United Nations opened at Lake Success, Joe Barbagallo, who had been working in Queens, applied for work and was hired "on trial." No one has ever officially taken him off "trial" and he has hung around all these years as inconspicuously as possible in his small shop in the Secretariat building.

One of his two assistants is his brother Gus. Gus cuts Joe's hair and Joe cuts Gus's, but both prefer to shave themselves.

No one has ever paid more tribute to Joe Barbagallo's skill than Pakistan's former Foreign Minister, Muhammed Zafrulla Khan, who often phoned from Washington for an appointment and then flew in for a haircut. A few years ago, during the Kashmir dispute, newspapermen spotted the Pakistani spokesman slipping out of the United Nations. They thought a hot story was forthcoming, and calls were quickly made to the Pakistani delegation. But reporters were told: "Muhammed went to have his beard trimmed. That's the only place his beard has ever been properly done."

*   *   *

The tallest man in New York, Edward Carmel, stands 8 feet 2 inches, weighs 475 pounds, eats like a horse, and lives in the Bronx. His knuckles are like golf balls and, when he shakes your hand, he envelops your wrist in lukewarm flesh. He pays $150 for each pair of shoes, $275 for each tailor-made suit, and sleeps at right angles on a seven-foot bed. At the movies he either sits or stands in the rear, or tries to get a front-row seat so he can extend his legs. He was born twenty-five years ago in Tel Aviv, and at birth weighed 15 pounds. At 11 years of age, he was a 6-footer; at 14, a 7-footer; at 18, an 8-footer. "I never recall being shorter than my father," he says.

The father of the Tallest Man in New York, an insurance salesman, is 5 feet 6 inches. His mother is 5 feet 5 inches. But his great-grandfather, Emanuel, stood 7 feet 6 inches, and was billed the Tallest Rabbi in the World.

So far, Ed Carmel has earned his living from six sources, although his yearly income from all is probably less than $10,000. He has acted in monster movies, been hired as a Happy Clown, appeared as a wrestler, delivered deep-voiced radio commercials, played the "World's Tallest Cowboy" in the Garden for Ringling Bros., and sold Mutual Funds. His office at Mutual Funds is on Forty-second Street, not far from the hotel patronized by the midget wrestlers—whom he has seen, but not tripped over. In his latest film, *The Head That Would Not Die,* which did not win an Oscar, Ed played the Son of Frankenstein. In this picture he chewed on a doctor's arm, hurled a half-naked girl over a table, burned down a house, and would have committed even more mayhem except, he said, "it was a low-budget film."

"A year ago," he said, "a wrestling promoter spotted me and they immediately billed me as 'Eliezer Har Carmel—World's Wrestling Champion from Israel.' I'd never wrestled before I became champion. All they asked me to do was appear at some wrestling shows, strangle the ring announcer, make like a real lunatic, and watch as all the other wrestlers jumped out of my way. So I put in a few appearances, but never did get a match. I retired undefeated."

Ed Carmel came to America with his parents when he was three and a half. "My childhood," he said, "was awfully, awfully rough." He was the butt of jokes, was reticent in school and reclusive out of it.

"I never laid a hand on anybody," he said, "until I was attacked. I knew that if I ever lost my temper and belted somebody, I'd get no sympathy from the judge. So, all my life I took lots of ribbing—either from drunken little people, or from those gutless bastards in subways: juvenile gangs, who insult me only when they're in a group."

After his graduation from Taft High School in 1954, he attended City College, where he acted in the dramatic group, wrote sports for the campus newspaper, ran for vice-president of his class—and won. "After two years at CCNY, I thought I could go out into the cold world and get a job as an announcer or actor," he said. "So I quit school, but everywhere I went they asked, 'What have you done?' I tried out for the lead in the Broadway show, *The Tall Story,* which was about a basketball player, but I was *too* tall."

The only employment he could find on television was in monster roles, and his acting lines thus far have consisted of a series of grunts and groans. If he gets any comfort at all from his life, it is perhaps in his conviction that it's better to be very conspicuous in New York than not be conspicuous at all. "In New York," said the Tallest Man, "I feel I'm somebody. I feel I have to give an illusion of prosperity in the subway, that I can't go out without wearing a suit and tie. I know that everybody I meet in New York is going to be attracted to me—or repelled by me—because of my size."

The Tallest Man in New York has a wry smile, is extremely intelligent, and possesses a sense of humor dipped in vitriol. "New York," he mused, "is an exciting town. Every day represents a new challenge—a new step forward on the road to getting an ulcer. In this city you're invariably waiting for some son-of-a-bitch to call—and he doesn't."

New York Is
a City
of Odd Occupations

Each afternoon in New York a rather seedy saxophone player, his cheeks blown out like a spinnaker, stands on the sidewalk playing "Danny Boy" in such a sad, sensitive way that he soon has half the neighborhood peeking out of windows, tossing nickels, dimes, and quarters at his feet. Some of the coins roll under parked cars, but most of them are caught in his outstretched hand.

The saxophone player is a street musician named Joe Gabler; for the past thirty years he has serenaded every block in New York and has sometimes been tossed as much as $100 a day in coins. He is also hit with buckets of water, empty beer cans, and chased by children and wild dogs. Sometimes accompanied by his brother, Carl, a lean guitarist who usually smells of beer, Joe walks about twenty miles a day, seven days a week. Both Joe and Carl were reared on the Lower East Side, and went up to the third grade in school. Joe later went on to reform school. But before they were in their teens they were strolling through saloons playing tunes.

"We've been roaming through the streets ever since," Joe says. "Carl keeps track of the streets we hit each day, and we never go back to the

318

same street twice in one year. The East Side of Manhattan is the best for tips, except in summertime, when the rich people go away. Whenever we go to the Puerto Rican sections on the West Side we play Spanish tunes and wear straw hats. There's a lady on Forty-ninth Street who gives us $5 whenever we play 'When Irish Eyes Are Smiling.' "

"What do you do with all your money?" Joe was asked.

"It goes," said Joe.

"Will you two ever quit the streets and get a job?"

"Till the day we die we're going to stay on streets," Joe said, dramatically.

"We have no choice," said Carl, quietly.

*   *   *

The strongest stomachs in the Department of Sanitation belong to two little men who operate New York City's only "dead horse wagon." Each week an average of four horses will drop dead in the city, and it's the job of Matthew Di Angelo and Philip Tortorici to haul away their carcasses—and also the carcasses of any other dead animals that may have fallen at zoos, race tracks, or stables.

In an average year, Di Angelo and Tortorici will handle over 200 horses, 50 steers, 30 lambs, 20 bulls, 10 deer, five cows, two donkeys and, almost invariably, a lion, elephant, or ape. And in recent years they were called upon to hoist a two-ton hippopotamus out of the Prospect Park Zoo, fish a 1,000-pound turtle out of Bowery Bay, and remove a nine-foot shark that someone left one night on Park Avenue and 150th Street in the Bronx.

"Our job," Mr. Tortorici explains, "is like Graves Registration in the Army. Nobody wants it." Nobody wants it, possibly, except Messrs. Tortorici and Di Angelo, who volunteered for the job and admit that it offers more variety than garbage collecting and less walking than street sweeping.

These Charons of New York's animal kingdom station themselves each morning at the Sanitation Department's Pier 70, Twenty-second Street on the East River, and wait for the three-bell signal that means an animal has dropped dead somewhere in New York. A Sanitation Department officer comes down with the address, and then Tortorici and Di Angelo jump into their truck equipped with cables and cranks, and putter away.

"We have to get to sheep fast before maggots get to them," Tortorici said. "Dead sheep really have a horrible odor, much worse than horses. Sheep take your appetite away. And at night, if I *am* hungry, I hardly ever want lamb."

After the two men throw half-hitches around the animals' hind legs and draw them into the truck, they drive to the Van Iderstein rendering company in Long Island City. They often drive to Van Iderstein's via Fifth Avenue and Park Avenue, and none of the shoppers pay any attention to the large Sanitation truck—although they surely get small, passing whiffs of it.

The dead animals are New York City's gift to Van Iderstein which, in addition to using the hides, also converts bones into glue and fertilizer; meat scraps into chicken feed and pet food; and even salvages nails from horses' hoofs.

Although nobody could estimate the wholesale value of a dead horse, Van Iderstein's butchers consider a brokendown horse from a peddler's wagon much more valuable, steak for steak, than a swift thoroughbred from Belmont. "We get lots more fat from an old peddler horse, and this fat produces a lot more tallow," a Van Iderstein man said. "Race horses are too lean."

After Di Angelo and Tortorici have emptied their load at Van Iderstein's, their truck is sprayed with a perfumy substance. The two men inhale deeply and smile. And then they hop into the truck and drive back to Pier 70 smelling like two under-arm deodorant salesmen.

*   *   *

Friday, July 15, 1960, was a typical day in New York City. Seven new "Littering Prohibited" signs were added in Central Park. John T. Jackson became Vice-President in Charge of Management Planning at Remington Rand and got his picture on page 26 of the *Times*. The Home for Aged and Infirm Hebrews of New York announced that it received $2,000,000 under the will of Solomon Friedman, a cotton merchant. John's Bargain Stores leased a building at 184 West 231 Street, near Broadway, from one Louis Cella. The Fifth Avenue Coach Lines, Inc., brought a $500,000 damage suit against Michael J. Quill's union for an unauthorized bus strike. At 11:15 A.M., Joseph J. Marinello, 77, whizzed into Times Square on his bicycle, asked for a tomato juice, and remarked, "I just knocked off 671 miles on this bike." (A sleepy-eyed counter clerk was very impressed.) Nitrous oxide seeped through gas masks and overcame twenty firemen at a blaze in the twelve-story loft at 107–109 West Thirty-eighth Street. At 8 P.M. it was 79 degrees. Eleanor Steber sang *Il Trovatore* at Lewisohn Stadium and everybody liked it. A Polish cleaning lady was stuck for five minutes in a Wall Street elevator on the 37th floor. A car plunged 40 feet down into the East River with a man and woman after speeding over the Tiffany Street pier shortly before midnight. Nobody saw either of them again until Saturday night, July 16, when a stocky deep-sea diver, wading through the slippery slime, felt the bodies, attached a hook to the car's rear bumper, and then sent it up toward the surface again.

The diver, Barney Sweeney, is New York's most prolific retriever of wet objects. For twenty-five years he has explored the deep waters of New York in search of dead bodies, murder weapons, diamond rings, and even the false teeth of a sea captain. He has been hired to unplug the drainage system under a Bronx Zoo lake, burn tangled cable off steamship propellers, and relocate cargo that has fallen off piers. His New York is not the city of skyscrapers; it is the cold, murky water 50 feet below the Statue of Liberty, 90 feet under Hell Gate, 180 feet beneath the George Washington Bridge.

The paths of his world are blocked by barnacle-bitten cars, corroded motorcycles, and tires nobody wants. There is a sunken plane on the river bottom off Brooklyn's Navy Yard, an Army Engineers' vessel (with two skeletons aboard) under Hell Gate, a $6,000 hunk of stainless steel beneath New York Bay off Fifty-seventh Street in Brooklyn, and a $25,000 diamond ring off Shelter Island. Barney Sweeney spent a week looking for the diamond before giving up, and has never been able to get close enough to get a hook on the steel; it has sunk into soft mud and every time he gets close to it, the $6,000 item sinks further and further down. "When things sink away from us divers, we have an expression for it," Barney says. "We say they've 'Gone to China.'"

Barney's New York is a floor of mud, and usually he must stomp through it up to his knees. He rarely can see a foot ahead of him when he's below, and when tugs pass overhead, they swirl up the river's silt even more, and Barney is temporarily blind. So he must feel his way. Yet he still is able to attain some deep insights into human behavior— insights into how people die.

"That man who drove off the Tiffany Street pier was, according to the police, mad at his wife," Barney said. "Well, when I reached the bodies, I found that he'd changed his mind about the plunge just before he hit the water. He was trying desperately to get out of the car. I noticed some skid marks on the edge of the pier, and I found him halfway out the window."

The car was upside down, as cars almost always are when they settle on the bottom. This is so, according to Barney, because the heavy automobile motor drags the vehicle nose first to the bottom and, upon reaching it, the momentum flips the car over on its roof. There were four other cars on their roofs in the same location off Tiffany Street on the night of July 16. He felt the other cars and, from the number of barnacles on them, knew they'd been down there at least eight months. "This area off Tiffany Street was, I imagine, an insurance dumping grounds," he said. "People'd push their cars off there and collect insurance."

Barney Sweeney, who is forty-eight, weighs 400 pounds when he's dresed for work and 225 when he is naked. He usually charges clients $125 a day, although sometimes he'll dive for a percentage of the salvage, or he might also dive on the "double-or-nothing" deal: if he retrieves the missing item, you pay him double—$250; if he doesn't, no charge. He averages 150 days of work a year, mainly on assignment for the Police Department, Port Authority, stevedores or private citizens; on such assignments he has retrieved a $20,000 diamond ring that a lady dropped off a fishing boat (collecting $1,000), tons of rock sulphate that had sunk when a barge struck a concrete pier, and the upper dental plate of a skipper. The plate, which had fallen into the East River, was worth $165, and Barney returned it without charge.

Since it is extremely cold beneath, and the work is very debilitating, Barney stays down only about an hour and a half a day. He sinks from a small float on which his two-man crew tends the airlines. Aside from eels and dirty New York fish, there is very little life in Barney's New York. He talks over his diver-to-tender phone to his son, Jack, a teenager who frequently assists him—just as Barney once assisted *his* father. "My father was killed in a diving accident," Barney said. "His heart gave out. He had no business being down there at his age. When we pulled him up for the last time, he was seventy-two."

Barney has little hope that his son Jack will continue the family tradition. "I ain't sending Jack to college to be a diver," Barney says. Last summer Jack worked part time as his father's helper and part time as a Chase Manhattan Bank clerk. One day, when workmen were laboring on the foundation for a new building, a valuable diamond drill was dropped down a 30-inch hole, descending 100 feet. Barney Sweeney was called. But Barney, who drinks eight bottles of ale a day—"it keeps me warm in winter, cool in summer"—was far too fat for the job. And young Jack was too inexperienced. So a skinny diver from a rival firm was hired to fetch the drill, and it marked one of the few times in New York that the Sweeneys were unable to capitalize on their motto: "Your Loss Is Our Gain."

*   *   *

David Amerman, a short, round man who works in a dark basement on the Lower East Side, is New York's master builder of pushcarts. His late father and grandfather before him also were pushcart makers, and their fine craftsmanship has given the family name a kind of Stradivari status with the city's most discriminating junkmen, fruit venders, and hot-dog peddlers.

"My grandfather, Benny, started making pushcarts with wooden axles in Russia," Mr. Amerman said. "And my father, Max, made carts in a basement on 193 East Houston Street. People used to walk by and say, 'Hey, Max, when you going to get out of the basement?' And my father would say, 'This is where I started; this is where I'm stayin'.' My father was too ashamed to give out bad work," he went on, leaning against a cart at his basement on 541 East Eleventh Street. "He would cry to my mother when my brother and I did a bad job, and he was always yelling, 'Why not one more nail?' And I'd say, 'Pop, don't worry; when you be dead the pushcarts will be still alive.' "

Mr. Amerman paused for a second, and then added, with a touch of both sentimentality and the dramatique, "You go down to Bleecker Street today and you'll see men pushing carts my father made forty years ago—the carts are still alive. And go over to Avenue C, and even to Brooklyn, and you'll see my father's work—still alive . . ."

He says that his carts "stay alive" for at least forty years, and from them generations of venders have survived good and bad times. He takes two weeks on each pushcart, makes his own hickory wood wheels, and sells a fully equipped hot-dog cart for $350, a fruit wagon for $125, junk carts for $105, grocery carts for $75.

"My father used to make carts for $12 each during the Depression," Mr. Amerman said. "That's when there were 8,000 pushcarts in New York. But when Mayor LaGuardia left, the city made peddlers get licenses, and now we have to keep walking. Since nobody can walk from 7 A.M. to 6 P.M., lots of peddlers can't take the job any more, and they've dropped out."

Mr. Amerman has not made much money from his craft, but, like his ancestors, takes pride in creating the finest pushcarts in town. His one regret, though minor, is that his sons have no interest in the tradition.

*   *   *

In some parts of New York City the air is worth nearly a dollar a whiff, the ground sells for $700 a square foot, and a certain hot-dog stand on Thirty-fourth Street cannot even be bought for a million dollars. There are some New York hotels that do not seem as fashionable as some others—yet they are worth more; in fact, throughout the city there are hotels and office buildings, chunks of earth and hunks of air that are precious gems in the real estate business—not because they always *seem* so, but because a spry little man on Wall Street *says* so.

The man, Gordon I. Kyle, is regarded by most plutocrats and speculators as the final word when it comes to evaluating land, space or buildings—particularly tall buildings. He essentially is a skyscraper appraiser. He is paid a small fortune by bankers, builders and insurance men to stand on sidewalks and gaze up at skyscrapers. Often he is mistaken for a tourist. But he appraises with the discerning eye of a pawnbroker and, according to William Zeckendorf, "Kyle has never been wrong."

In Mr. Kyle's latest decree of worth he declared that the 59-story Pan Am Building, scheduled to rise in 1962 over Grand Central Terminal, will be "over twice" as valuable as the 102-story Empire State Building, which he appraised at $45,000,000 in 1951. He came to this conclusion after only a weekend's work with Pan American fact sheets and floor plans, and charged the builders, Edwin S. Wolfson and some British partners, $50,000 for the opinion. But forty years' experience was behind Mr. Kyle's appraisal—forty years in which he has permitted nothing to ruffle the tedium of his correctness.

Such appaisers hardly can afford miscalculation. Banks and insurance firms depend on them to evaluate property accurately before it is bought, sold or mortgaged. Every large bank and insurance company in New York has hired Mr. Kyle for appraisals. On his word they have lent a client as much as $60,000,000. Gordon Kyle is said to have appraised 70 per cent of Manhattan's buildings that soar twenty stories or more. These include the Empire State, Chrysler and dozens of office buildings and hotels, as well as such diverse items as Carnegie Hall, Brooklyn's Bush Terminal, Saks Fifth Avenue, the Metropolitan Club, Grossinger's, the Stock Exchange, the Cleveland Welding Plant, Knickerbocker Village, and the late William Woodward, Jr.'s Belair stud farm near Baltimore.

Years of legwork as a New York rent collector, a later career as a real estate broker, and finally the presidency of both the Cruikshank Company and the New York Real Estate Board all have helped to provide the 63-year-old Gordon I. ("Jimmy") Kyle with the background that now enables him to say, "I know every square foot of Manhattan" and "You name any block and I'll tell you what's on it."

He also knows how much each square foot was worth ten years ago and how much it should be worth ten years from now. He knows that the air and sunlight flanking a certain Fifth Avenue office building is assured because the owner pays $35,000 annually for the "air rights" atop the small building next door, and this guarantees against any other skyscraper shooting up to blot out the view and disenchant tenants who pay fancy prices for sunlight. He knows that the land on No. 1 Wall Street, site of the Irving Trust Company, has sold for $700 a foot, and he says this is the most valuable land in Manhattan. The busiest corner in Manhattan, he says, is occupied by Nedick's stand at Thirty-fourth and Broadway, which is passed daily by 300,000 people.

With such facts at his fingertips, and with an astounding knowledge of real estate under his snap-brim hat, Mr. Kyle was thus able to evaluate the Pan Am Building even though it was not standing for him to see. But the building plans showed that the Pan Am had the largest rentable area in New York City—2,400,000 square feet—and would have 70 elevators, 21 escalators, and working space for 25,000 people. Since he had appraised the Grand Central neighborhood many times before, it was a relatively simple matter for him to size up the missing skyscraper.

But when the building he is appraising is standing, Mr. Kyle always tours it from roof to basement, and in action and appearance he resembles an inspector general. He is a short, chesty man who walks with his shoulders back, chin out, and an almost perpetual frown on his face. His nose, a finely tipped instrument, seems ever ready to sniff out a flaw; his eyes, pale blue, are forever roving around in a clockwise direction when he is scanning a skyscraper. His manner is direct, his wordage short and to the point.

"How many seats can we get in here?" he asked the manager of a mid-Manhattan hotel recently, while standing in the main restaurant.

"Twelve hundred and forty-four," the man said.

"Get your heat from the railroad?"

"Yes. Steam."

"I'd like to see a couple of bedrooms," Mr. Kyle said.

"Yes, sir."

"You don't have automatic cars any place?" Kyle asked in the elevator.

"No, sir," the man said, and then led him into a bedroom.

"These bedrooms are the cheapest?"

"Yes."

"Are they undesirable?" Kyle asked.

"No, *sir*," the man said. "Why?"

"Poor light," said Kyle.

The hotelman shrugged his shoulders. Kyle made notes.

"Are you full?" Kyle asked.

"We're pulling 78 per cent occupancy," the man said. "We pull as low as 55 or 60 in the summer."

Kyle's eyes scanned the furniture, peered out the windows, observed the bathroom tiling, then focused on the floor.

"Is this carpet typical?" he asked, raising an eyebrow.

"I'm sure it isn't," the man said.

On their way out, Kyle ran a hand along the wall to determine whether it was cheap or expensive wallpaper. Then they were in Room 1701.

"Fairly new, but I don't see any TV," Kyle said.

"This is a single $8 room," the man said.

"It needs painting," Kyle said.

"It's got good closets," the man said.

Kyle took more notes, then ran his fingers behind the door for dirt. Five minutes later, after saying good-bye to the hotel manager, Kyle roamed around the roof, and talked to elevator operators, who are great sources of information for him, especially when he is appraising apartment houses or office buildings. The elevator men know all the latest gossip, how many rooms are vacant, the wealth of tenants, the sobriety of superintendents, and other bits of intelligence they hear because people talk freely behind them.

While on the roof, Kyle examined the tar paper, the copper flashing, the brickwork, and then stuck his fingernail between bricks to see if the cement was weak, worn or pervious to rain. "If there is leakage," he said, "you're always in trouble with tenants." Then he examined the air-conditioning unit on the roof, banged it with his fist, and scribbled more notes.

"It's very important to inspect these buildings in person," he said. "You form impressions, you spot deficiencies and deterrent factors. First you go through the place with the owner or manager, and then continue on alone. Owners will give you the run of the place, usually. They're anxious to please. Should I get an adverse opinion that they are, shall we say, secretive, I'll begin to look into things even more thoroughly. There are times, of course, when they give me incorrect figures on the cost of operation or rental. Or they'll put 'estimated' before the figure. 'Estimated' could mean anything. But I know the value of space." And he added, emphatically, "I know rents."

He left the roof and started downward, spot-checking rooms and offices on his way. As he descended, the ground on which he trod was becoming less expensive; upper floors, sometimes worth $6.50 a foot, are invariably more expensive than lower floors because they offer more light and air.

"Everybody is buying light and air these days," Mr. Kyle said.

Two hours later he arrived in the basement, where, under the defensive stares of the superintendent, he examined the pipes and heating system. And then he was on the street again—crossing Park Avenue, which is worth between $200 and $250 a square foot; then to Fifth Avenue, worth up to $300 a square foot. He said that Fifth Avenue was worth more than Park Avenue because the railroad tracks under the latter eliminated basement space, and the rumble of Grand Central's trains often could be heard in many Park Avenue apartments.

An hour later Mr. Kyle was back at his office on 48 Wall Street scanning the fact sheets spread over his desk. The phones were ringing with long-distance and local calls from bankers and builders asking Kyle to look at this, look at that. At this particular moment, William Zeckendorf, leaning back in Webb & Knapp's plush penthouse, was shouting to his secretary for Kyle's line. The switchboard girl on Wall Street said,

"Mr. Kyle's line is busy."

"Will he be long?" Zeckendorf asked.

"I don't know," the girl said.

"See if he'll be long," Zeckendorf said.

A minute later Kyle was on the phone.

"Hello."

"Jimmy?"

"Yes, Bill."

"How's your brain today?"

"Weaker every day, Bill."

"Well, look, Jimmy, you read in the papers about the Astor . . . and I wonder if you'll take a look-see . . ."

"Bill, I will, but I have the real estate people tomorrow . . ."

"Hell with 'em," Zeckendorf said.

"I shall do it after," Kyle said more firmly.

"Okay, kid," Zeckendorf said, more softly.

"You'll be in tomorrow?"

"Why not?" Zeckendorf said.

"See you then," Kyle said.

"Okay, kid," Zeckendorf said.

(Click.)

Such conversations between real estate tycoons and Kyle are typically informal. And once Kyle has made known his appraisal figure, they usually do not question him. Although occasionally one or two will mumble that the building is worth more (especially if they want to sell it) or less (if they want to buy it). But Kyle doesn't budge. "Can't be convenient in this business," he says. "You can't do what people ask of you. I am able to prove everything I sign. I assume that I'm going to court to testify on every one of my appraisals."

Much of Mr. Kyle's judgment was developed during his days as a rent collector, a job he took shortly after his discharge from the Army and after he left Wesleyan University in Middletown, Connecticut. He collected rents for the United Cigar Company, then one of the largest property owners in New York City. "They had almost every prominent corner in town," Kyle recalled. "And I spent two years running up and down dark tenement halls and dusty lofts with my pockets full of cash. People who paid the lowest rents often kept their money in milk bottles. Once, after collecting rent from a man who was angry, he kicked me in the pants as I was going down the steps. I'll never forget it. I was just a kid. But those years were the most important of my life. They taught me, without my even knowing it, the value of space."

In 1921 he left rent collecting to open his own general brokerage and assessing firm. In the early thirties he was hired by the New York State Superintendent of Banks to appraise the real estate holdings of banks throughout the state. In 1936 he joined the Cruikshank Company, and two years ago became its president. He charges anywhere between $15,000 and $20,000 for appraising a skyscraper, and usually takes no more than a week on any of them. He took two weeks going from tower to toe of the Empire State Building in 1951 before its sale, and charged $25,000. The $50,000 he charged for the Pan Am job is believed the highest fee ever paid an appraiser—a price all the more astounding when one remembers that the building did not even exist.

"I am in," Mr. Kyle says, inhaling on a filter-tip, "a highly specialized and lucrative business."

* * *

A beefy lady, holding a Macy's shopping bag with one hand and her son with the other, waited impatiently for a moment at Nedick's counter. Then she looked down at her son and asked, "What you want, Maa-vin?"

"Hamburger," he said.

"Take a hot dog," she said.

"I wanna hamburger," he shouted.

Wham! She belted him across the head with her purse. He screamed, but she again said, "Take a hot dog."

Marvin took a hot dog.

Nobody in Nedick's paid any attention; they were all too busy stuffing their faces and, besides, this sort of commotion goes on nearly every day at Nedick's on Thirty-fourth Street and Broadway—the busiest hot-dog stand in the world.

Each day, as Mr. Kyle noted, 300,000 people pass this corner. And 8,000 of them drop (or are pushed) into Nedick's for about four minutes to gulp down a daily average of 700 hamburgers, 1,000 cups of coffee, 5,000 hot dogs and 5,500 orange drinks. Nedick's occupies only 1,000 square feet of floor space, and snuggles into one corner of R. H. Macy's. "But we always claim that Macy's is next to Nedick's," says Nedick's president, Lewis H. Phillips.

This hot-dog stand has prospered on that corner since 1947, and grosses an estimated $400,000 annually from 10-cent orange drinks, 20-cent hot dogs, and 40-cent hamburgers. Day and night the cash registers ring, frankfurters twirl over hot rollers, orangeade gushes forth into glasses, and the air is filled with sizzling pork and tangling tension, and with flashing bits of short-sentence dialogue between customers and employees.

"Yes, miss?" the waitress asks.

"Burger," says the customer.

"Burger!" shouts the waitress to the cook.

"Pick-up," he yells back.

"Glasses!" announces the washer to the waitress.

Almost with exception, Nedick's 84 other stores—59 of them in Manhattan—seem soothing by comparison.

"But we gotta get people in and out of the Thirty-fourth Street Nedick's in less than four minutes, or else we lose money," says Mr. Phillips, who worked his way to the presidency from counter clerk. "That's why we don't have stools. If we did, people would smoke a cigarette and dally too long. We stop serving coffee at Thirty-fourth Street at 10:30 A.M. in summertime because it takes customers too long to drink it. Once we had an executive who wanted to add fruit salad and cheese sandwiches to our menu, but I knew it would take customers about fourteen minutes to eat it. Too long, too long. I said no."

It has been estimated that if a customer smoked a cigarette in Nedick's on Thirty-fourth, the store would lose about $2 in turnover. Nedick's is believed to pay $95,000 rent annually for the tiny corner stand and, with its salaries and other expenses, it must sell thousands of hot dogs and orange drinks each day to break even. All this food is pushed over a 61-foot-long counter, and only thirty-two customers can be crushed against it at one time. Behind the counter, Nedick's twenty-six employees sidestep each other, collect coins, flip hamburgers, jab hot dogs, and pour orange drink into coolers. The famous drink is 20 per cent orange juice mixed with water, lemon and sugar.

Every once in a while the employees are visited by Mr. Phillips, who is regarded as the bourgeoisie king of the quick-lunch trade, and a man who is ever ready to hand his friends a card that reads: "One Frankfurter. One Drink. (At No Charge) L. H. Phillips."

"When I walk into a store, all my people know I started as an $18-a-week clerk stuffing hot dogs at Twenty-seventh and Broadway," Mr. Phillips says, puffing a cigar. "I came up the hard way. No relatives, no friends. No this, no that. I minded my P's and Q's. And I wrote some suggestions on how Nedick's could have faster service. For instance, I thought up the idea of packing orange concentrate in two-quart containers; we eliminated those gallon tin cans, which were a storage and disposal problem, and often employees would cut their fingers opening them. I thought up the idea to package hot dogs in cardboard flaps, and I had many other ideas I can't recall now. But I'll tell you this. If I'd been president around here fifteen or twenty years ago, there would be no Chock Full o' Nuts in New York today."

Although most of Nedick's twitching trade is not aware of it, the hot-dog stand occupies an ancient, narrow five-story building. Nedick's uses only the first two floors—the second floor has lockers for employees, and a small office for the manager, Thomas F. Magee. The top three floors are empty, and serve no purpose. This old building has long been a hot issue between the Smith family, which owns it and rents it to Nedick's, and the Straus family, proprietors of Macy's. The discord between the Smiths and Strauses goes back more than a half century when a dry-goods merchant, Robert S. Smith, had a department store on West Fourteenth Street next to Macy's. There was no-holds-barred competition between the two stores in those days, and Mr. Smith sometimes would erect on his store front a sign reading "Annex" or "Main Entrance"—and many Macy's-bound customers were thus lured into R. Smith & Co. by mistake.

When Macy's decided to move uptown to Thirty-fourth Street, Mr.

Smith, as well as other Fourteenth Street merchants, realized that much of the customer traffic would be taken away from their neighborhood. Macy's, meanwhile, was quietly trying to buy up every plot on the Thirty-fourth Street block so as to build its gigantic store. There was one small plot, however, that eluded Macy's—the corner plot, which was owned by a clergyman, Alfred Duane Pell, who was then traveling in Spain and refused to accept Macy's $250,000 offer until he returned to the United States. Upon his return, Mr. Smith quickly got to him and offered him $375,000 for the corner plot. Mr. Smith's precise motives are still debatable; Macy's version is that it was a spiteful move, while Mr. Smith's heirs say it was strictly an attempt to keep up with the times. Anyway, the Rev. Mr. Pell accepted the $375,000 offer from Smith, which the Strauses refused to match. And the Strauses proceeded to build the big store around the little plot. The land was too small for Mr. Smith to build a dry-goods store upon it, and so he rented the old Pell house to various tenants and, in 1947, Nedick's came along and converted the first floor into a lucrative hot-dog stand.

In addition to the rent from Nedick's, the Smith heirs also charge Macy's a fat sum for the privilege of clamping an advertising sign over the upper floors of the five-story building.

"We're making money from that land," said Robert Smith Kiliper, treasurer of the Smith family corporation. "And it remains as a kind of monument to granddad. Also, I have often been enchanted with the idea of some day renting that big sign to Gimbel's," he added, with a surly smile in keeping with the traditional Smith-Straus friendship. "So don't be surprised if you look up one day and see a Gimbel's sign up there—don't be surprised."

*   *   *

Early each morning, a little, bow-tied gentleman hastens to the city's freight yards and begins to sniff carloads of hay with the perception (and raised eyebrow) of a punctilious teataster. John Muhlhan sniffs hay by the hour, and he is believed to be one of the nation's top connoisseurs of hay for horses. The odd thing is that he has been selling hay in the heart of Forty-second Street for forty-five years—and hardly any of his neighbors know about it.

Mr. Muhlhan, on the other hand, cannot understand why anyone should think it odd for a hay merchant to be thriving on Madison Avenue. "I have my offices at Forty-second and Madison because it's convenient," he says. "You see, from here I can easily travel by train, subway or taxi to the docks in Brooklyn, the Hudson River, or to any other spot where barges or trains arrive with hay."

When the hay arrives, Mr. Muhlhan leans over and begins to inhale. "Without even opening the freight-car door I can tell if the hay is good or bad," he says. He imports about 500 tons of hay a week from Michigan, Ohio and Upstate New York, and then, after he sniffs and approves it, he sells it to retail dealers around the city and nation. This hay is later fed to race horses, policemen's horses, and various breeds of stock that can stomach it.

Mr. Muhlhan's father before him sold hay and straw to horse owners in the Bronx. In fact, in 1923 there were twenty-eight hay and grain merchants in New York City who belonged to the National Hay Association. Now there is only Mr. Muhlhan. At his office on 50 East Forty-second Street he keeps a foul-smelling bag of hay handy, which he is forever sniffing to keep his nose attuned to what bad hay smells like. When guests visit him, he often passes the bag around, as if it were hors d'oeuvres, and when you wince at its odor he goes into a lengthy tirade against farmers who produce such garbage—and he sounds almost like any other high-pressure pitchman on Madison Avenue.

*   *   *

The hides of a surprisingly large number of New Yorkers are decorated by tattoo artists, a durable breed of craftsmen whose interest in mankind may be only skin deep, but whose impressions usually last a lifetime. In New York there are a half dozen professional tattooists, and their work has been spotted from the chorus line at the Copacabana to the shower room at the New York Racquet and Tennis Club.

Stanley Moskowitz, a nationally known needle worker and scion of a distinguished family of Bowery skin peckers, estimates the tattooed population of New York City to be 300,000—a clientele that keeps the half dozen tattooists busy the year around on New York's side streets and waterfronts.

The typical customer of a tattoo parlor is between 18 and 25 years of age, generally muscular, and always willing to invest from $3 to $5 to get jabbed 3,000 times a minute for ten minutes by the eight tiny needles of an electric tattooer, which sounds like a dentist's drill, looks like a fountain pen, and writes under water. The colored ink is deposited about one sixty-fourth of an inch into the skin, a sensation variously dscribed as "like a mosquito bite" or "like torture." Most men prefer to be tattooed on the chest or arms, sailors running to anchors, full-rigged ships, names of their latest girl friends, and half-naked women. Soldiers prefer American flags, eagles, black panthers, serial numbers, names of their latest girl friends, and half-naked women.

Why people go in for tattooing is a matter of disagreement. Various psychologists have said it is purely ornamental, or purely sexual, or purely a fondness of some people for crude drawings. Some boys do it to appear virile, some girls do it to rebel against being girls, like the women of the Ainu tribe of northern Japan who used to wear tattooed mustaches. Some people also have practical motives for tattooing, depending on it to obscure scars and birthmarks or to imprint blood types and social security numbers. Others admit they did it on a dare, or because the gang did it, or to prove they could take the pain, or because their parents clearly said don't do it.

The current idols of New York's tattooed set are Dick Hylan, who has stars tattooed across his face, palms, and inside his lip; and Jack Dracula, who has a spread eagle on his forehead, two flapping eagles on his cheeks, and stars about his eyes, ears and nose.

Jack Dracula, who as a child wanted to grow up and become a mosaic, is tattooed 244 times, and says, "People think I'm nuts. But I'm not ashamed of being tattooed. Although when I walk down the street people scream, and everybody asks, 'Why did you do it?' I tell 'em I want to be the world's most beautifully tattooed man. People think I'm nuts."

*   *   *

Shortly after 2 A.M., a rather spooky subway train rolls slowly into the IRT station at Grand Central Terminal with its seats empty, its aisles vacant, and its lights as dim as an East Side supper club. It is a trash train, and the men who cling to its flatcars are six of the thirty men who ride after midnight through the dark tunnels cleaning up the mess of the multitudes.

Each night eight tons of litter are dumped into the city's seven trash trains, as their wheels slice through thousands of empty coffee cups and candy wrappers discarded on the tracks. The men take about five minutes at each local stop to gather the trash, although sometimes they must spend a few moments more wrestling with some drunk who is trying to push his way onto the empty train. The trash men throw him off. He staggers away and leans against a chewing-gum machine. Then the train slowly pulls away, the rattle of the cans echoing through the quiet tunnel.

"We pull gum up from the station floors all year long," one of the trash men says. "Gum holds subway floors together. In summertime we pick up lots of half oranges from the orangeade stands down here; in wintertime we pick up more coffee cups. Women leave tissues behind their seats in subways and think nobody notices. Two years ago we found a skeleton of a human near West Seventy-sixth Street. Nobody knows how it got back there."

Though many of the trash men are qualified conductors, they say they prefer the trash train that keeps them up all night. "We like garbage better than people," one of them explained.

*   *   *

At the Ethel Barrymore Theatre one morning four little white-haired cleaning ladies, bent over like workers in a rice field, were dusting off the $6.90 seats when Jo Mielziner arrived, in a hurried step, to watch the curtain go up on one of the most unpublicized productions on Broadway—the lighting rehearsal.

Mr. Mielziner, the noted scene designer and lighting expert, played the leading role in this production in the empty theater. Even the actors were absent; probably sleeping, for it was early—11 A.M. His audience, in addition to the cleaning ladies, were stagehands and electricians, among whom Mr. Mielziner plainly stood out because he was the only one wearing a necktie.

"I'm sorry, ladies," Mielziner said, as he removed his coat and took a seat in the fourteenth row. "But we're going to have to take your lights away now."

"Oh, that's all right," one of them said, and then the ladies stopped dusting and walked slowly to the rear, there to sit on the carpeted steps, chat and watch as the house lights went out, the curtain went up, and the show began.

Blue, green and sunny amber light leaped down upon the stage from many angles and bathed the scenery in subdued blue, vaguely illuminating the Mielziner-designed boardinghouse; then, slowly, a warm light brought into sharp focus one room with a chair and table, and on the table books were stacked unevenly.

Mielziner's face was made feebly visible in the dark by a 10-watt lamp, clipped into a makeshift desk in front of him. A two-way intercom, box-shaped, was also there, enabling Mielziner to talk from his seat to the chief electrician, George Gebhardt, who was controlling myriad light switches backstage, buried in a smörgåsbord of lighting equipment, ladders and intricately curled cable.

Squinting a moment as he watched the light reflect onto the boardinghouse, Mielziner finally said softly, "It doesn't look right, George. Let's try it again."

George said okay, and the curtain went down again, and Scene I in lights went through a second run . . . and a third . . . until finally Mielziner was satisfied. The rehearsal with light continued through the entire play—no acting, no music, no applause, just lights dancing around the stage—for three hours. Then it was over.

Twenty-four hours later it was opening night for the play. But it was closing night for Mielziner and most of the carpenters and stage technicians hired to erect scenery and lighting. Mielziner's detailed light interpretation, carefully blueprinted on a cue-sheet, was given to the backstage cast of the show, and each night they play it over and over—like a roll in a player piano.

*　　*　　*

Each day in New York seven detectives with silver badges and a scent for culture snoop around town trying to catch some of the city's more literate criminals—book thieves. These seven detectives are employed by the New York Public Library to help recover the thousands of books stolen each year by readers who are either forgetful, careless, light-fingered, or addicted to drugs.

Of the 13,000 people who borrow books daily from the library system, an average of 500 will not return the book on the date due, and about twenty-five will keep books out two or three months beyond the due date. Many among these twenty-five are addicts, who borrow books with forged library cards and sell them to secondhand book dealers to buy drugs.

When a book is thirty days overdue, the seven detectives, directed by a veteran sleuth named John T. Murphy, are notified. They begin to search at the borrower's last known address, and from there the hunt can (and usually does) lead the detectives through some of the quaintest and most remote reaches of New York City—and beyond. In the past few years Mr. Murphy and his men caught up with the wayward chauffeur André Porumbeanu, who, before he ran way with and married the socialite Gamble Benedict, had never returned a copy of *God's County and Mine*. The detectives also traced six missing books two years ago to the body of the late Julian A. Frank, the man suspected of having carried the bomb aboard the plane that blew up over North Carolina with seventy passengers and perhaps the six books on space travel and adventure that Mr. Frank had borrowed.

Although people who maliciously keep overdue books thirty days or more can be jailed, Murphy is content to regain the books and collect the 5-cents-per-day-overdue charge, and then ban the culprit from the libraries. Many fines have run into hundreds of dollars per person. Not long ago Murphy's men caught a little lady in Brooklyn with 1,200 overdue books. They were able to track her down, despite all her pseudonyms, by matching the handwriting on her various cards and by noting that she invariably borrowed novels of light romance. Librarians were alerted to the handwriting style and the lady's penchant for light romance, and it was only a matter of time. When the lady was caught, she was sent to a mental hospital; she was an insatiable kleptomaniac—but one of New York's most well-read crooks.

*   *   *

In a frantic desire to find out what's going to happen next, New York's 200 fortunetellers have, at one time or another, gazed into crystal balls, read tarot cards, studied the stars, dabbled with ouija boards, and surveyed the palms of hands, the mounds of feet, and the bumps on heads.

There is hardly a section of the city that is without some form of occultism nowadays. Hindu swamis thrive in mid-Manhattan. Dreambooks are a bonanza in Harlem. On the East Side people are willing to pay fancy prices to hear about their favorite people—themselves. Some of the chic restaurants offer mystics with hors d'oeuvres, and from the Bronx to Bayside there are astrologers, palmists, and mediums aiming to solve everything.

Nearly 80 per cent of the customers who patronize New York's soothsayers are women, and the problems they carry to the sayers are about love, marriage, health and wealth—in that order. Male customers are interested in money problems, then love. Since fortunetellers (for $2) generally aim to please, they usually predict improvements for everybody, within six months to a year. "Women also ask us 'Is my husband cheating on me?' and 'Is this man out for my money?' and 'Where can I find a good man?' " one fortuneteller said. "If I knew where I could find a good man, I'd go for him myself and maybe *I'd* get married."

Because human beings are inclined to remember predictions that come true and to forget the rest, an astonishingly large number of people have enormous respect for, and fear of, fortunetellers. These are the New Yorkers who, sooner or later, become victims of gypsy "con games." The gypsies still rely on one of the oldest con games of all, which begins when a fortuneteller convinces the customer that his money is "evil" and that he should bring it in to have it "blessed." When he does this, the fortuneteller wraps it up and instructs the customer that the package should not be opened for twenty-four hours, giving the thief enough time to disappear before the victim realizes his stack of bills has been exchanged for worthless paper.

Policewomen, masquerading as naïve and lovesick doxies, frequently visit fortunetellers, seek advice and wait for the con game to be pulled on them. "We can actually arrest fortunetellers as disorderly persons only if they predict the future or get caught stealing money," explained a New York policewoman, Clare Faulhaber. "If they just babble about how nice we are and how nobody appreciates us, then we can't get a thing on them. At any rate, this cat-and-mouse game with fortunetellers in New York is great sport. Gypsies clip pictures of policewomen out of New York newspapers and have copies made and send them around to all the other gypsies in their tribe. We know a lot of gypsies on a first-name basis and we're quite chummy."

Lady cops play many parts in their time as they scout various New York neighborhoods. Miss Faulhaber explains: "If we're going to tearooms in some areas, we may dress like prostitutes. When going to Houston Street, downtown, the policewomen usually wear house dresses, flat shoes. On Orchard Street, on the Lower East Side, we'll be as sloppy as we can. On Eighth Avenue in the Forties we'll carry grocery packages into tearooms, and maybe even bring along somebody's child so we'll be mistaken for neighborhood folks. On the East Side we'll dress up a bit and have on a hat and wear gloves."

At a recent séance in the West Eighties, Miss Faulhaber, still happily unmarried despite repeated gypsy predictions that a "dark, handsome man" is pursuing her, went dressed in a maternity outfit. "It was on a Sunday at 6 P.M., and about fifty people—all very nice—were in this brownstone sitting on folding chairs listening to a bad piano player lead us in hymns," Miss Faulhaber says. "It was a group séance, which are common in New York, and they're easy to get into. Just check the *Times* religious pages on Saturdays and you'll see advertised 'Spiritualist' meetings. Anyway, soon the medium came in. She was a small, elderly woman with white hair, dressed in a dinner gown. The people got into a circle around her, and soon she was saying, 'I'm getting vibrations—vibrations for a woman who is holding a new life within herself. Is there anyone present who is holding a new life within herself?'

"And there I was," says Miss Faulhaber, "wearing the maternity dress for all to see and the only thing I had bulging out under it was the belt and holder containing my 32-caliber pistol. Later the medium had a plate passed around, and people put $1 and $5 bills on it, and the lights dimmed. This is when she started to go into a deep trance and began talking. First she was somebody's 'Uncle Bill' and then later she was somebody's mother, but what really bothered me was that no matter who the spirits happened to be, they all made the same grammatical errors."

As mediums who communicate with spirits must some day join the spirit ranks themselves, there is always the need to train new talent; hence, in New York there are "development classes" for mediums all over the West Seventies and Eighties in Manhattan and also in Brooklyn. At these classes veteran mediums teach those who are up-and-coming the tricks of the trade. Mediums sometimes compete in this business with the vigor of Macy's and Gimbel's, and on rare occasions there even appear to be price wars when one medium, to best another, will offer a $10 course for only $5.

Palmists and crystal-gazers—police rarely find crystal balls in Manhattan, but have come across them in Coney Island—vie with the mediums and others for the public trade, too, so the competition can become pretty keen. New York policewomen say that some gypsies keep the law informed frequently about the non-U habits of other gypsies, this being apparently a gypsy's way of holding the competition within reasonable limits.

Despite these purely scientific days, gypsies and mediums are very much a part of New York life, and they should continue to predict their own bright futures as long as there are wives who suspect their husbands, and unmarried girls who wish to know, "Where can I find a good man?"

*   *   *

Many other New Yorkers searching for a good man, however, patronize one of Manhattan's eight duly advertised marriage brokers, a group whose files are filled with the names of rising bank clerks, poor noblemen, and rich social climbers. The fact that five of these eight New York brokers are not married themselves does not seem to reduce their popularity.

For a registration fee of usually $100, the brokers will provide clients with as many dates as they can stand. After the clients have dated, the broker waits to hear how they liked each other; if they despised each other, he provides his male clients with new telephone numbers and his female clients with new men. Should marriage result from the broker's matchmaking, each client pays an additional $100. There is no refund if the marriage fails.

"Oh, you'd be surprised at the requests marriage brokers get in New York," said Sam Pauline, who has an office opposite Macy's. "Once I had a husky Texan who wanted to meet a very fat woman. So I looked in my files and came up with this 225-pound Bronx lady who is 45 and divorced. When I called her she said, 'Sam, did you tell him I'm a little heavy?' I said yes, and arranged for her to meet him at my office the next day. Well, when they first saw each other I could tell they were attracted to one another. And, as they were leaving together for a drink, I saw him holding her under the arm. Four weeks later they got married. Next time I saw her she was wearing mink, had diamonds all over her, and drove a Cadillac. She was as fat as ever."

Mr. Pauline, who was introduced to his own wife thirty-two years ago by a marriage broker (his father), says that, while many women prefer professional men, most of his female customers just want a steady, unspectacular, sober provider. "They don't want artists or actors, or anything like that," he said. "Like once I had an actor who was understudy to Sam Levene in *Guys and Dolls*. He lived at The Lambs Club, this guy, but I couldn't get anybody to marry him. Women just don't want guys who work now and then, and get bit parts. They'd rather take a plumber or carpenter any day than an actor.

"Another thing about women," he continued, "is that age is not so important as height. A woman will marry a man 20 years older than herself before she'll marry a guy who is shorter. Most men, on the other hand, want women who are beautiful or very attractive. Some men want women who are rich. And a few men—very few—want women who are intelligent."

Should men want inhibited women, Mr. Pauline can provide them too. He keeps a separate file on 200 women who do not smoke and 400 women who do not drink. Should men wish German-born blondes, a broker on East Fifty-ninth Street, Anthony Wagner, has a stack of them, in addition to a couple of impoverished European counts, overweight princesses, and a dozen archdukes. And at Lee Morgan's Scientific Introduction Service, on East Seventy-ninth Street, are the photos, statistics and phone numbers of many smart, successful American women whose dedication to career so far has, as they might put it, permitted love to pass them by.

Some brokers claim they have as many as 10,000 names of unmarried people in their files, and one broker, Clara Lane on Forty-second Street, takes credit for 8,000 marriages in the past decade. They get their clients through advertisements in the Classified Directory, or in newspapers that will accept their ads (many won't), or by reading obituary notices and later mailing circulars to the surviving member of the couple. They say they check on all the credentials and claims of prospective clients before providing them with dates, and seem to maintain an abiding skepticism of life in general, which may be one reason why more than half of them can't seem to find a marriageable mate themselves. Although one Forty-second Street broker, Ellen Joy, says she is propositioned by one out of every six male clients she interviews. But when the right one comes along, she says she will spot him.

"Appearance-wise," she said, "I cannot generalize, but my ideal man would have to be very understanding. He'd have to be of good

background. He'd have to be well-educated. What I want is not a
man who can give me the moon—but a man who would want to."

And as she spoke she looked dreamily into space, her hands were
clasped, and in her eyes there seemed to be the same sign that hangs
in so many matchmakers' offices—the sign that reads, "It's Never Too
Late."

*   *   *

The aggressive tendencies of some New York men are released when
they smack a two-ton iron ball against a wall, bombard a boulevard, and
crumble other people's creations. Nothing is so big, thick or imperishable
as to survive these assassins; nothing is so sentimenally secure as to be
forever safe from the wallops of these experts who swing the iron ball.

There are at least forty men in the city qualified to swing the ball,
but there are scarcely a half dozen old pros among them who are keen-
sighted enough to pick off a wall, brick by brick, 100 feet away. They
can drop the ball on a dime from the same distance. They can swing the
ball around as if playing billiards, caroming it off one wall to another,
and then letting it swing back to topple a smokestack. Sometimes they
cast the ball full force against a wall; at other times they gently chip
away at the concrete. Contractors have held up demolition jobs for
weeks waiting, begging, for one of these six crackerjacks to be available
for an assignment, and sometimes pay them over $300 a week to smack
things to smithereens.

These half dozen have destroyed thousands of New York buildings
in the past thirty years. Their feats and faces are known to hundreds of
sidewalk superintendents who love to watch them. There is Benny Newberg, a lanky, almost legendary 61-year-old wrecker who destroyed the
Tombs; Jim Allitt, a thick-armed 66-year-old Englishman who dropped
the Hippodrome; Mike Catusco, 52, who ruined Ebbets Field; Matt
Sullivan, 62, who blasted down the United Nations library; Ralph
Principe, 54, who wrecked the Produce Exchange, and Gil Schultz, 39,
who knocked down whatever stood in the path of the new Time-Life
Building, and also has vanquished acres of slums. One day in Brooklyn,
Schultz sent such a jolt into a decaying five-story tenement that the
whole building came crashing down with one blow.

The slums are the easiest to destroy, while the thick-walled armories,
prisons, banks and churches are the hardest. It took Newberg over a

year to bash down the Tombs, which had held 500,000 criminals during its existence and was built like a medieval castle.

One of the more difficult private homes was the old Schwab mansion on Riverside Drive and Seventy-second Street. It had two-foot-thick walls of granite. Charles Schwab had built it to last forever. But after his wife died, he tired of its seventy-five rooms and moved to a hotel. It took Jim Allitt almost six months to topple the high towers and heavy walls.

But the iron-ball men are happier when the walls are thick and the challenge great. With them it's a kind of sadistic sport. They get as big a thrill as the sidewalk superintendents when, after a direct smash, the walls begin to crack, the floor caves in, and the whole structure comes tumbling down in an avalanche of dust.

Though they make $4.90 an hour, and though they are masters of their art, the men who are paid to destroy things are forever denied one privilege. They can never point to a fine piece of craftsmanship and say, proudly, "This is my work."

New York Is a City of the Forgotten

Eighth Avenue is a sad, sick street whose neon lights dangle over the dandruff of bartenders and focus on smoking prostitutes, sailors' hats, and beer bottles that occasionally smash against jukeboxes and attract cops who say, "All right, all right, break it up!" It is a street of hockshops and flophouses and underpaid panhandlers with bloodshot eyes. It is a blend of the Garment Center's racket, the Port Authority's bus fumes, steam from the Pennsylvania Station, and the garlic of a dozen pizzerias.

Eighth Avenue begins at a defunct public bathroom off West Twelfth Street and extends in mid-Manhattan up to the Coliseum, and between these points are rows of tenements with rusty fire escapes and people who want to move. They want to escape the uncertainty of Eighth Avenue, which is a hodgepodge of both sinners and religious fanatics, darkness and light, a nickel beer and a Mike Todd party that fills Madison Square Garden. Eighth Avenue is where a fire started in a firehouse and where, after a British marine fell 85 feet to his death in a military show last June, 10,000 spectators cheered and thought it was part of the act.

Eighth Avenue is where hoodlums attacked a longshoreman named Clifford Johnson and knocked his glass eye into a sewer. It is where a cook named Raphael Torres, infuriated because a bus passed him by, jumped into a taxi, caught up with the bus driver—and stabbed him.

In September, when Manhattan was jumping with protest over the presence of Khrushchev, Castro and Tito at the United Nations, a nine-year-old girl was killed by a stray bullet in the El Prado restaurant—on Eighth Avenue.

Each year the circus comes to Eighth Avenue, and inevitably a lion or bull breaks loose and romps through traffic, gaining abundant publicity for the management. Each month the police are called to control mobs who are either denouncing the atomic bomb, demanding higher wages, or fighting for Antonino Rocca's autograph.

You can almost tell what is going on inside the Garden by observing who is standing outside it. When Rocca is wrestling, the Eighth Avenue entrance is clotted with Puerto Ricans, and you can hear a ring announcer yelling, "Amigos! No tiren más objetos en el ring!" On fight nights, you see the short, smart-money types in dark suits and white-on-white shirts standing around the box office, cigar to cigar. Before a horse show, you see men in top hats and tails, and young, blonde *Town & Country* girls. On basketball nights, you find tall crew-cuts wearing sweaters outside the Garden, and before the circus Eighth Avenue is a scene of rushing adults with three or four children each, and among Nedick's clientele are midgets and cowboys.

All around Eighth Avenue are cut-rate drugstores, some of which have telephones that are so sticky you hate to press them to your ear. It is a street through which theater crowds move quickly to Downey's restaurant, and the commuters to Penn Station, trying not to notice the panhandlers, the homosexuals, and the preacher on Forty-second Street who, with arms flailing, is yelling, "Sinners! Sinners! The Bible teaches that without shedding blood there is no redeeming of sin . . ." And a pockmarked boy with long, greasy hair shouts, "You're full of shit, mister!" To which the preacher, his face burning, answers, "Kid, you need to be saved." And then a large Irish cop wanders over and says to the crowd, "Move in, move in from the curb." Some move in closer to the preacher, but most move on, although not with the speed of the commuters racing to the Port Authority Bus Terminal, where each week they forget dozens of umbrellas, coats and suitcases in the terminal's 1,300 lockers. The leftover luggage and umbrellas pile up so high that the Port Authority each year holds an auction in the basement of the Forty-first Street station, and this lures to Eighth Avenue more bargain hunters and platoons of Ludlow Street junkmen called the Forty Thieves, and also Harry the Gonif, Eddie from Poughkeepsie, and Cheap Charley, whose Brooklyn junkshop reportedly contains the greatest collection of single gloves in the world.

"All right," the auctioneer will say in his badgering baritone, towering above the standees in the smoky basement. "I gotta fur cape here. I ain't saying it's mink . . ."

"It's wolf," says Harry the Gonif.

"Let me feel," says a lady.

"Fourteen dollars," calls Cheap Charley.

"Sixteen dollars," cries Harry the Gonif.

"You own it," says the auctioneer.

"Let me feel," protests the lady.

The auctioneer ignores her. He has too many things to auction off on this particular day and can't waste time on a lady amateur. This pleases the junkmen, who don't like amateurs either because amateurs raise the price too high and deprive them of great bargains.

"The most expensive thing ever left in a bus terminal locker was $50,000 worth of stock dividend checks," said John M. Hanrahan, the Port Authority's baggage agent. "We didn't auction *this* off; I turned it over to the Purchase and Administrative Service Department, and it's still there, as far as I know. An eccentric millionaire from the Greenpoint section of Brooklyn forgot it, and then disappeared and nobody knows what's become of him."

As he spoke, the traffic overhead continued to rumble on Eighth Avenue, and down on Abingdon Square children played punchball against the wall of the defunct public bathroom. They paid no attention to the stevedores returning from work, the fat Italian ladies with arms full of groceries, or the tall, bony Puerto Rican standing on the corner with thin fingers, alert eyes and a face scarred by somebody else's razor. A few blocks north, the cash register rang in La Ideal Market, and the fish smell from DiMartino's almost reached the Greek neighborhood with its Port Said tavern, its clanging castanets, and its curvaceous belly dancer with lovely hair and twitching navel.

In the Thirties the Garment Center's runners pushed clothes racks between trucks and over people, and in a Forty-third Street barber school five novices clipped away at 45 cents a head, and in front of them was the sign: "Calling all men! Now you can have your hair colored to your own natural shade, including silver blonde, platinum blonde, golden blonde, or any shade of red, brown, or black. All work done in absolute privacy."

In the upper Forties and Fifties are more flophouses, more delicatessens, more people with bad complexions. In this section Eighth Avenue is a street of obscure prizefighters, and of saloons that cater to them. The ex-fighter and current ladies' masseur, Biz Mackey, drinks at Bill Dunn's. Other broken-nosed men are at Mickey Walker's across the street. And at the Neutral Corner saloon, on Fifty-fifth Street, are hundreds of photographs of prizefighters who are now fat and forgotten.

Behind the bar of the Neutral Corner is a well-built young man in his early thirties with blond curly hair and blue eyes—a man who used to be a fighter but has now gotten fat. His name is Tony Janiro. Many of the pictures on the wall show Janiro in action—ramming his fist into an opponent's ribs, knocking another man through the ropes, standing proudly in the neutral corner while the referee counts out the semiconscious carcass of the loser. They were hung around the bar by the owner, Frankie Jacobs, who once managed Janiro and believed Janiro would become welterweight champion if he could only avoid his weakness— women. But Janiro never could. He chased women and drank whiskey and at twenty-five was washed up. He retired and Jacobs bought the Neutral Corner saloon and gave Janiro a job as bartender.

At the Neutral Corner today, the ex-fighter wipes beer glasses and the ex-manager is still chiding the fighter, and saying out loud (so the customers can hear):

"Scotch and women—that's what ruined Tony Janiro. Oh, I used to watch Tony, all right; I used to push my bed in front of the door at night so he couldn't sneak out. But he got out. Didn't you, Tony, didn't you get out?"

Janiro, still wiping glasses, slowly turns to his ex-manager and says, quietly, "I don't regret anything I done, Jay. Only thing I regret are the things I haven't done."

The drinkers only half-listen because they've heard it all before—hundreds of times: the story of how, between 1945 and 1951, Janiro was on his way to becoming champ, and would have made it if he'd only trained harder, only not been such a stud.

This is what is too frequently heard in the cigar smoke around the dark-brown bar: managers and trainers lamenting, like women in a laundromat, about how their young boys are breaking training rules.

"How come after 120 fights you're not more banged up?" a customer asked Janiro.

"I got that kind of skin that don't cut," Janiro says. "Like take my brother, Freddie, who was a fighter; if you hit him in the elbow he'd wind up with a black eye. He had that kind of skin. Hit him in the elbow, he'd get a black eye."

"How'd you get so many women to chase you?"

"If you got money in New York," Janiro said, "you attract women. Right? Money attracts women."

"How much did you make?"

"Close to $500,000. I lost thirteen of 120. I had some big purses with Greco, Graziano, and Beau Jack. I was a poor kid from Youngstown and I came to New York at sixteen, and when I was nineteen I had fights in the Garden. Guys hung around me, ran up big drinking bills at my hotel. And I buy a suit, I'd buy them a suit . . ."

*　　　*　　　*

It is hard to believe, as one looks out the window of the Neutral Corner saloon onto Eighth Avenue, that this has-been street was rather elegant a century ago, and that horse-drawn carriages lined outside the Havemeyer mansion on Eighth Avenue and Fifty-eighth Street.

Many of the most famous farms were around what is now Columbus Circle, and the great homes that stood on Eighth Avenue had spacious lawns, gardens and orchards that extended westward to the Hudson River. These farms were owned by the families of Matthew Dyckman, Jacob Horn, Isaac Varian, James Stewart and Samuel Van Norden, and on Fifty-third and Eighth was the mansion of General Garrit Hooper Striker who, in the War of 1812, commanded the 5th Regiment of the 82nd Brigade in the defense of the homes on Bloomingdale Heights. One of the most fashionable spots in New York was the Grand Opera House, which Jim Fisk bought in 1869 for Josie Mansfield, a showgirl known as the Cleopatra of Twenty-third Street. Fisk adorned the place with ornate mahogany doors, crystal chandeliers and chairs with nails of gold. But after his death the place declined. And by 1938 it had movies, popcorn machines and bowling alleys with pin boys who were nickel-tipped into states of sullenness.

Eighth Avenue actually went into serious decline about the turn of the century, when the residential sections opened up on the East Side, and West Side homes became tenements. And in 1925 huge holes were dug into Eighth Avenue for a subway. On a June day in 1927 the workmen scooped up six coffins on Eighth Avenue above Forty-fourth Street— coffins with expensive wood and nails. The cemetery once was part of the Medcef-Eden farm purchased by John Jacob Astor in 1803. But the workmen quickly cleared the area of coffins and built the subway and installed chewing-gum machines. And near the old Medcef-Eden farm today, in Forty-second Street's subway station, are pinball machines and boys in narrow, cuffless pants who wiggle their hips and snap their fingers at each other.

And in the summer of 1960, when the Grand Opera House got in the way of a new housing project, demolition crews moved in.

And the last old touch of elegance left Eighth Avenue.

*　　*　　*

On sunny afternoons outside the Plaza, Freddy Phillips climbs slowly up into a victoria and prepares to begin another day in a career during which he's worn out a dozen carriages, twenty horses and at least a hundred of his own silk hats. Mr. Phillips, in his eighties, has been a horse-carriage driver in New York since 1901, and he clings to the reins as tightly as to his past.

When it isn't warm, he doesn't ride; he merely stands outside the Plaza with other members of the silk-hat set—Ben Potter, who feeds apples to his horse; Broadway Jack, a reformed taxicab driver, and a few others who, with the first gleam in a tourist's eye, quickly ask, "Carriage?"

During his career in New York, Mr. Phillips has driven the disparate likes of Enrico Caruso, John D. Rockefeller, and Arnold Rothstein. "Rothstein owes me two bucks," Mr. Phillips says, inhaling on a borrowed cigarette. "Oh, I used to drive him and his blonde all over town. Them days you had dirt roads on Park Avenue, and the Tavern-On-The-Green was a sheepfold. Tiffany's was down on Fifteenth Street. Once I drove the heavyweight champion, Bob Fitzsimmons, down to Jack's Restaurant on Broadway. When we arrived he said, 'Come on in, boy, have a drink.' "

Ben Potter moved in closer, and said, "Once I had a noisy horse named Murphy, and a cop stops me one night and starts to give me a ticket because he says my horse is disturbing the peace. He asks my horse's name, and I tell him 'Murphy.' Then this big Irish cop stops writing, and says, 'Dammit, I can't give a ticket to anybody with that name!' "

"Them were the days," Mr. Phillips said. "In those days we wore good silk hats, but now we wear cheap ones. When it rains—good night! We get these cheap hats from some guy who comes around with old hats and says, 'How much you gimme for these?' I say '$2' and never give 'im any more."

In their lifetimes, most carriage drivers have toted New York's famous and infamous through Central Park, and they prefer to think of the old days when carriages clip-clopped all over the city—not just in Central Park. "But I'll never retire from this racket," Mr. Phillips says. "Might as well die up on a victoria as any place else."

*   *   *

Sitting in dark closets all over New York City are toy dolls in unfashionable clothing, in outmoded hair styles, their paint worn off, their noses crushed because they were once hugged too much by little girls who are now grandmothers. Occasionally you see such dolls in the junk pile, or you see them leaning lopsidedly in an antique shop window near a rusty sword—truly forgotten by their owners, who now live in a whirling life of the present. But there are some owners who share the sad destiny of these once-beautiful, once-loved figurines.

It is a city of silent movie stars and old fans who rarely recognize them. Although sometimes on Broadway an elderly man will swing around, stare at a passing figure, and exclaim:

"Why, you're Nita Naldi!"

The crowds bump into the man, and somebody yells:

"Hey, mister, watch where you're walking."

"Sorry."

"Say, mista, gotta dime?" a panhandler asks.

The crowds impatiently push past the panhandler and the man who spotted Nita Naldi.

Miss Naldi moves quickly around the corner to her small hotel, where few people remember that she used to play opposite Valentino, and was once the symbol of everything exotic, passionate and evil on the silent screen.

No matter where you walk in New York, you are likely to pass people who were once the toast of the town.

There, sitting in Schrafft's, unrecognized by the noonday crowd, is Gertrude Ederle. It is possible that some diners in Schrafft's were among the 2,000,000 that cheered Miss Ederle in 1926—the year she swam the English Channel and was honored with a ticker-tape parade up Lower Broadway. President Coolidge then called her, "America's Best Girl." She received marriage proposals, and somebody wrote a song called, *"Tell Me, Trudy, Who Is Going to Be the Lucky One?"*

Miss Ederle, now in her fifties and weighing 175 pounds, rarely swims any more. She wears a hearing aid. She has never married.

"I was in love once," she recalls. "Back in 1929. I was practically engaged to the chap. He was a six-foot, athletic type. This all may sound silly, but once I said to him, 'With my poor hearing it might be hard on a man . . .' Of course, I thought he'd say, 'Darling, it doesn't really matter to me about your hearing, I'm in love with you.' But instead he said, 'I guess you're right, Trudy, it would be hard on a man.' Anyway, I never quite got over it."

Nine blocks away, in a smoky saloon, a wiry, white-haired man is doing all he can to be remembered. He is buying people drinks, and handing out cards that read: "Billy Ray—Last Surviving Bare Knuckle Fighter." Mr. Ray, in his nineties, was so tough that when boxing gloves became popular, before the turn of the century, he retired; he said the game was getting too soft. Now he was on a stool in the Neutral Corner saloon, and Tony Janiro was pouring him another drink. Billy Ray's eyes were slightly closed, and he was exercising an old New Yorker's privilege—reminiscing.

"Only cost a dime for a haircut in the eighties," he rambled. *". . . they threw Florence Burns out of Sheepshead Bay race track for smoking. . . .*

*Oh, I used to love to go down to Fourteenth Street and hear Maggie
Cline sing, 'Throw 'Em Down, McCloskey.' . . . They say Steve Brodie
didn't jump from the Brooklyn Bridge . . . they're liars . . . I saw
him . . . I was there.*

"All day I could tell you about things . . . Jersey Jimmy, the national
pickpocket, had a saloon in the Bowery . . . sometimes you'd find dead
people sitting at the bar. After a wake, they'd bring dead guys in, set
'em at the bar, and begin to drink. . . . When they finished, the bartender'd say, 'Who's paying?' They'd point to the dead guy at the bar . . .
and walk out."

*   *   *

New York is not a good city for the aged. The city passes them by;
they cannot keep up with it. It is rare when the Ninth Avenue jam-shop
lady, Mary Armstrong, wanders beyond her neighborhood, but when
she does she is invariably shocked at how the city has changed, and
sometimes she points and says, "Oh, look what they've done to *that!*"
Look what they've done to *that! That's* been that way for twenty-five
years! It was the late columnist, O. O. McIntyre, who first publicized
Miss Armstrong when, in 1937, he nominated her for "Little Old Lady
of New York," after a song then current. He described her as "steel-
bespectacled, hair coiffed in a tight 1890's knot in the back, she darts
about her shelves of yum-yums like a wren in a hedge." He went on to
say that "Katherine Cornell goes there for her loganberry jam and Mrs.
Brock Pemberton for strawberries preserved in rum." After the column,
Miss Armstrong had a sign made that read: "The Little Old Lady Jam
Shop."

But New York is a city where one splash in the papers is not enough.
She is now eighty-two. Her jam shop, still at 174 Ninth Avenue, is out of
the way nowadays and is patronized only by a few old friends from Connecticut and New Jersey who are addicted to her tomato jam and lemon
butter.

Often the aged in New York die as they lived—alone. New York
newspapers are forever running stories about the belated discovery of
the dead in dark, dusty rooms. Sometimes the police find that the deceased, reputedly impoverished, had salted away thousands of dollars in
a mattress, and this news sets the whole neighborhood to buzzing. And

so the East Bronx buzzed on April 1, 1960, about the strange, quiet lady who used to gather trash in the streets—and who, on a pile of rags in her apartment at 831 East 163rd Street, was found dead with wealth approaching $100,000.

For thirty years in the Bronx Mrs. Helen Kay, who read Spinoza, was seen picking rags, returning soda bottles, feeding stray cats. She was always poorly dressed and unkempt, although there were rumors that her apartment contained dozens of expensive hats and plumes and out-of-date dresses she never wore. The neighbors said she went to college, but they did not know where. They thought she spoke seven languages, but were not sure why. They knew she was a widow of a doctor—or was he a dentist? They saw her at the trash cans every day, and yet they knew very little about this septuagenarian they called "The Rag Lady."

The Bronx police were unable to locate relatives. But in the pile of rags in the $46-a-month apartment they did uncover eight bank books with deposits totaling more than $46,000 and 124 shares of American Telephone and Telegraph, and stock in other companies.

So, on this sunny April morning, the windows of the Rag Lady's apartment were opened—"for the first time in twenty years," said the superintendent. And three men with brooms swept out the piles of paper, old coats, and empty soda bottles.

"I kept telling her to live a little," said Lillian Richman, the hatmaker who worked in the store below. "I kept telling her to move to the Concourse Plaza."

The unclaimed body of the Rag Lady was taken to the Jacobi Hospital morgue; her money, taken by the Bronx Public Administrator, still awaits state action; her apartment, repainted and its rent raised, now is occupied by a Puerto Rican family.

This is the way it is in New York, where 250 people die each day, and where the living dash for empty apartments. This is the way it is in a big, impersonal, departmentalized city—where on page 29 of this morning's newspaper are pictures of the dead; on page 31 are pictures of the engaged; on page 1 are pictures of those who are running the world, enjoying the lush years before they land back on page 29.

"Say, mista, gotta dime?"
The old man with the outstretched hand had an intelligent face and

bright blue eyes. Who is he? How did he land down here on the Bowery?—the only spot in New York where the standard of living has not gone up.

Each afternoon you see him standing around saloons with hundreds like him: unshaved, unwashed, a bit shaken. Most of the men seem to have lost their pride and hope, although each Christmas season a number of them try to earn money by masquerading as sidewalk Santa Clauses for the Volunteers of America, an organization that houses and feeds them, pays them $4 a day, and sends them uptown in Santa uniforms to ring bells on corners and collect donations in red, chimney-shaped boxes. Millions of Christmas shoppers pass these Santas on Fifth and Madison avenues without realizing that behind those luxuriant, false whiskers are alcoholics who are trying to reform, who are trying to face life again—perhaps soon without the disguise.

Last year one of the sidewalk Santas was a former Lockheed engineer who drank himself out a job; another was an erstwhile television actor on the Captain Video show; a third was a Harvard instructor who caught his wife in bed one night with another man. He shot and killed both, and went to jail. After his release he spent four jobless, drinking years on the Bowery until, one day, he stumbled in to the Volunteers for help.

Many Bowery men seek help, but many more hit the low level and remain. They have nowhere else to go, although some say they stay on the Bowery by choice. One such case is a jolly, bearded codger who calls himself "Bozo—King of the Intellectual Hobos."

On almost any summer night you will find Bozo whooping it up at Sammy's Bowery Follies with a beer in his hand and foam on his lips. He wears four or five shirts at once, a bathing suit under his dungarees, and carries a raincoat rolled up in his shoulder bag. Most of his shirts have numbers (or team names) on them.

In the afternoons he swims and sun-bathes at Coney Island, where some old Italian and Jewish ladies give him sandwiches and fruit. He sleeps under the boardwalk at night or, if it's too cold, stays in a Bowery flophouse for 70 cents.

He is such a merry, odd-looking little man that people are forever inviting him to dinner "for laughs," and in the evening some Legionnaires invite him to all-night parties and slip him a few dollars afterwards. Since tourists like to pose next to his long, white beard at Sammy's Bowery

Follies, the management considers him an "attraction" and he drinks beer for nothing.

"After all," he says, "I'm no ordinary bum—I'm a classical, dynamic, extraordinary bum."

Bozo's real name is Frederick Aloysius Clarke, and he was born in Provincetown, Massachusetts, around 1892. He says he went to sea in his teens, and later spent several years touring with carnivals, first as a handyman, later as a target for a ball-throwing concession, and finally as a ballyhoo artist for freak tents and part-time masseur for a troupe of hoochy-koochy dancers called "The Eight Virginia Rosebuds."

Bozo admits to three marriages, all brief and unpleasant, and says with a wink that common-law marriages are best. When asked if he has any children, his standard answer is: "Every time I walk past an orphanage I throw some pennies over the wall—want my kids to get some."

He cultivates the friendship (and home address) of nearly everyone he meets, and he unexpectedly drops in around dinnertime. With his free-loading and the small pension he says he gets from participating in the Mexican border trouble in 1914, he manages to live as well as he wishes.

Bozo says New York is a good town for bums, but adds that he wouldn't want to die here and be buried with New York's unclaimed dead and paupers in Potter's Field. On these rare occasions when he speaks of death, Bozo's carefree countenance suddenly changes, and one gets the feeling that he is not entirely happy as a hobo on the Bowery. He knows a great deal about Potter's Field. He knows that it is part of Hart's Island and that prisoners are kept there. And he knows that it is the prisoners who bury the dead twice each week at Potter's Field—that they dig huge trenches large enough for 150 pine boxes, and they place one stone over each trench, and "you don't even get your own goddam stone."

Sometimes Bozo becomes so lonely and morose on the Bowery that he switches to hard liquor and goes on a drunken tear, and nobody sees him in Sammy's for a few weeks. Later he usually is found in the gutter with his face dirty and bruised, for when he goes on these binges he is obnoxious, and insults bigger Bowery men, and they slug him down. But he sobers up, and a few days later he's again the happy, beer-drinking intellectual bum in Sammy's who backslaps, and laughs, and poses for pictures with tourists, and says, "Five years ago I was a bum. Now look at me!" And later, above all the singing and slamming beer mugs, you hear him roar:

"I'm no ordinary bum—I'm a classical, dynamic . . ."

Potter's Field is a forlorn plot on Hart's Island in Long Island Sound. Sea gulls swoop around the island, and the water laps softly against its sandy, white shore. There is no grass—only weeds—on the island. There is no noise, except the occasional startings and stoppings of the warden's car, the comings and goings of the big, red ferry from City Island, and the slowgaited shuffle of prisoners and of their brooms swishing leaves from the sidewalks.

About 1,200 prisoners live on one end of Hart's Island. On the other end is Potter's Field. Potter's Field occupies 33 acres, or one third of the island. Each week about 200 bodies, and many amputated limbs from hospitals, are buried there in pine boxes which the ferry carries over the Sound in eight minutes. Twenty-five prisoners unload the pine boxes, dig the trenches, and each Tuesday and Thursday bury 150 caskets in each trench. Then they cover the 150 closely packed caskets with dirt and mark the spot with a stone—a stone that carries no names, only a number. In a filing cabinet in the warden's office are the names of the 500,000 paupers buried under the various stones since Potter's Field's first burial in 1868—that of Louisa Van Slyke, who died unbefriended at Old Charity Hospital.

The caskets remain in a trench for fifteen or twenty years. Then, since more room is needed for the new caskets that never stop coming, the trenches are dug up. The old caskets by this time have invariably deteriorated and vanished. But should some old bones still be visible, they are gathered up and put in one pine box and reburied in the trench. Now there is room for 149 new caskets in that trench.

And on and on it goes at Potter's Field. The dead get no rest. As the novelist William Styron said, these people become twice-dead, and three-times dead.

And this is the way it will probably always be in New York City: paupers die, their bodies remain unidentified for a few weeks in the City Morgue, and then they are shipped away to be buried—not within the

city of their choosing but on this remote island where the sight of them
will cause the living no further unpleasantness. They turn to dust thirteen
miles from Times Square—far from the pushing crowds and ladies' masseur; far from the pushcart maker, the court buffs, the doormen, the
midget wrestlers, the chauffeur with a chauffeur, the charwomen and
telephone operators who say,

> *"if only people would look numbers up . . ."*

and the subway announcer who says,

> *". . . watch your step getting off, please . . ."*

and the movie fan who shouts,

> *"Why, you're Nita Naldi! . . ."*

and the beer-drinking hobo who until his
dying day will convince everybody but the
gravediggers when he yells: *"I'm no ordinary bum;*
    I'm a classical
      dynamic
        extra-
             o
           r
             d
               inary
                    b
                  u
               m . . ."

About the Author

GAY TALESE, thirty-seven, was born in Ocean City, New Jersey. He graduated from the University of Alabama in 1953, worked as a staff writer on *The New York Times* for ten years, and also wrote for many national magazines, principally *Esquire*. He is married to an editor at Random House, and they reside in Manhattan with their two daughters.

For those who, like Mario Puzo, looked up from the pages of *The Kingdom and the Power* and pronounced Gay Talese the "best non-fiction writer in America," here is a connoisseur's collection of his work.

Fame and Obscurity is a gallery of portraits of people: the famous (Frank Sinatra, Joe DiMaggio, Joe Louis); the celebrity in obscurity (Floyd Patterson); the infamous (Frank Costello); the once unsung Alden Whitman, writing memorable obituaries in *The New York Times;* the wild latter-day expatriates who staffed *The Paris Review;* and the stylized patricians who breathe the scented air of *Vogueland.*

It also contains two complete books. *The Bridge* is the story of the building of the Verrazano-Narrows Bridge. It is delineated in the lives of the people displaced for the project, the dreams of the designers, the death and drama among the Irish and Indians, who with the other